Will All Be Saved?

An Assessment of Universalism in Western Theology

PATERNOSTER THEOLOGICAL MONOGRAPHS

Series Editors

Trevor A. Hart, Head of School and Principal of St Mary's College School of Divinity, University of St Andrews, Scotland, UK

Anthony N.S. Lane, Professor of Historical Theology and Director of Research, London School of Theology, UK

Anthony C. Thiselton, Emeritus Professor of Christian Theology, University of Nottingham, Research Professor in Christian Theology, University College Chester; and Canon Theologian of Leicester Cathedral and Southwell Minister, UK

Kevin J. Vanhoozer, Research Professor of Systematic Theology, Trinity Evangelical Divinity School, Deerfield, Illinois, USA

PATERNOSTER THEOLOGICAL MONOGRAPHS

Will All Be Saved?

An Assessment of Universalism in Western Theology

Laurence Malcolm Blanchard

Foreword by Colin Brown

Copyright © Laurence Malcolm Blanchard 2015

First Published 2015 by Paternoster

Paternoster is an imprint of Authentic Media
52 Presley Way, Crownhill, Milton Keynes, Bucks, MK8 0ES, UK

www.authenticmedia.co.uk
Authentic Media is a division of Koorong UK, a company limited by guarantee

09 08 07 06 05 04 03 8 7 6 5 4 3 2 1

The right of Laurence Malcolm Blanchard to be identified as the author of this Work
has been asserted by him in accordance with the Copyright, Designs
and Patents Act 1988.

*All rights reserved. No part of this publication man be reproduced, stored in a
retrieval system, or transmitted, in any form or by any means, electronic, mechanical,
photocopying, recording, or otherwise, without the prior permission of the publisher of
a license permitting restricted copying. In the UK such licenses are issued by the
Copyright Licensing Agency, 90 Tottenham Court Road, London, W1P 9HE.*

British Library Cataloguing in Publication Data
A catalogue record for this book is available from the British Library

ISBN 978-1-84227-804-8

Typeset by Laurence Malcolm Blanchard
Printed and bound in Great Britain
for Paternoster
by Lighting Source, Milton Keynes

Series Preface

In the west the churches may be declining, but theology—serious, academic (mostly doctoral level) and mainstream orthodox in evaluative commitment—shows no sign of withering on the vine. This series of *Paternoster Theological Monographs* extends the expertise of the Press especially to first-time authors whose work stands broadly with the parameters created by fidelity to Scripture and has satisfied the critical scrutiny of respected assessors in the academy. Such theology may come in several distinct intellectual disciplines—Historical, dogmatic, pastoral, apologetic, missional, aesthetic and no doubt others also. The series will be particularly hospitable to promising constructive theology within an evangelical frame, for it is of this that the church's need seems to be greatest. Quality writing will be published across the confessions—Anabaptist, Episcopalian, Reformed, Arminian, and Orthodox—across the ages—patristic, medieval, reformation, modern, and counter-modern—and across the continents. The aim of the series is theology written in the twofold conviction that the church needs theology and theology needs the church—which in reality means theology done for the glory of God.

To Melody, Justin, and Bethany,
to Faith and Phil, with love

To Colin Brown
a better friend, mentor, and Christian man one will never find

βλέπομεν γὰρ ἄρτι δι' ἐσόπτρου ἐν αἰνίγματι,
τότε δὲ πρόσωπον πρὸς πρόσωπον

מְעֹנָה֙ אֱלֹהֵי קֶ֔דֶם וּמִתַּ֖חַת זְרֹעֹ֥ת עוֹלָ֑ם

Table of Contents

Foreword

From the dawn of religion people have wrestled with the question, "Will all be saved?" With our growing awareness of the world as a global village, that question is even more pressing. Despite the plethora of answers, there is a shortage of guides that give in-depth overview combined with judicious evaluation of competing claims. *Will All Be Saved?* meets that need.

Against a background survey of the history of universalism, Dr. Blanchard focuses on Protestant and Catholic thought since 1960. He identifies approaches that center on Christology and those which stress religious pluralism. His work is a masterful summary of contemporary thought that does not shy away from critical assessment. *Will All Be Saved?* is a unique guidebook and reference tool.

Colin Brown
Pasadena, CA
February 14, 2015

Preface and Acknowledgements

The topic of this book is timeless, urgent, and one that has an impact on all human beings. No matter where one stands regarding the debate over universal salvation, the stakes are high and hanging in the balance is nothing less than eternal destiny itself. From the Christian point of view, if the universalists are right then everyone should sit back, take a deep breath, and relax—for God will see to it in the end that we will all enter into his kingdom. If the universalists are wrong then we should sound the alarm, redouble our efforts to evangelize the world, and not rest until we have assured ourselves that the Gospel is being proclaimed throughout the earth.

To disclose my particular biases at the outset of this study, I am one who thinks that the universalists are wrong. I am convinced of this not because I am a sadist who revels in the suffering of others or because I am some maladjusted individual who enjoys seeing other people fail. I say this because I am convinced that it is the position urged upon us by the Scriptures and I believe that the Scriptures should be given the final say in this matter.

This book is based on the Ph.D. dissertation that I wrote while I was attending Fuller Theological Seminary in Pasadena, CA. It was approved in March 2007 and has since gone through a substantial revision in order to bring it up to date. The book seeks to survey and to critically assess the recent debate over universal salvation in western theology within the context of the historical development of the doctrine. It aims to provide a survey of major statements of the doctrine, an evaluation and critique of the arguments involved, and a final taxonomy of the field that will highlight important trends and developments.

Focusing primarily upon the era dated from 1960 to the present, this book seeks to fill a gap in the academic literature that has been left largely unexplored from the point of view of the development of universalist doctrine. To be sure, many of the proponents who are analyzed in the study have been discussed at some length in isolation. Nevertheless, there remains a need to integrate their contributions and to allow for a clear overview of the field to emerge. By bringing the various proponents of universalism together in one place the study seeks to take on the challenges of understanding the field as a coherent whole while providing a clean system of categorization.

The book concludes by offering a four quadrant matrix that provides a new taxonomy of the field as well as a graphical representation of important recent developments.

I am indebted to many people for their encouragement and the contributions that they have made towards the writing of this book. First and foremost, I would like to thank Colin Brown, my friend and the mentor of my Ph.D., for the many insights and significant comments that he provided along the way. Dr. Brown is the consummate scholar and he labored greatly in his efforts to pass on his skills to me. Another important contributor was my secondary reader at Fuller, Veli-Matti Kärkkäinen. Dr. Kärkkäinen provided an extensive review and critique that greatly improved the quality of the finished product. The CATS Committee (Center for Advanced Theological Studies) at Fuller Theological Seminary also deserves a kind mention here because they gave me an extra year extension on my program, which enabled me to focus attention on my father who was dying of cancer at the time.

I have found that the nuts and bolts of writing such a large manuscript can very easily lead to a sort of tunnel vision that artificially erases the small errors by causing the mind to auto-correct them and then skip over them. I am indebted to my proofreader, Austin Camacho, who went through the original manuscript meticulously and winnowed out a great many of these minor flaws. If any have been re-introduced through the editing process they are my fault and not his. I would also like to thank Gary Swanson for contributing to the proofreading as well as providing for the off-site storage of my precious files.

Robin Parry, now with Wipf and Stock, was the commissioning editor of this work at Paternoster and I am thankful for his efforts at shepherding this project along as well as his insights and encouragement. Mike Parsons, my current editor at Paternoster, ably picked up the project and carried it through to the finish line. His insightful suggestions and keen attention to detail have been invaluable. I would like to thank Mike for his patience with me and his determination to see things through.

Of course families always suffer with the long hours of research and writing required to complete a task such as this one. I would like to thank my family— my wife Melody, and my children Justin and Bethany—for always encouraging me. I will never forget the day that I was very close to quitting. They came into my office and insisted that I finish what I had started. This book is the fruit of their encouragement on that day. I am so blessed to have them in my life.

I take full responsibility for any errors or inaccuracies that remain in the manuscript. My goal in this work has been accuracy and fairness. Where I fall short of that, grace will have to suffice.

Soli Deo gloria.

Laurence M. Blanchard
Easter Sunday, 2015
La Verne, CA

Abbreviations

ABD	*Anchor Bible Dictionary*
AJTP	*American Journal of Theology and Philosophy*
ANF	*Ante-Nicene Fathers*
ATR	*Anglican Theological Review*
BDAG	Walter Bauer, *A Greek English Lexicon of the New Testament and Other Early Christian Literature,* third edition, revised by F.W. Danker, W.F. Arndt, F.W. Gingrich
BibSac	*Bibliotheca Sacra*
CC	*Christian Century*
CD	Karl Barth, *Church Dogmatics,* trans. G.W. Bromiley and T.F. Torrance
ChH	*Church History*
Chm	*Churchman*
CJT	*Canadian Journal of Theology*
Com	*Communio*
CSR	*Christian Scholar's Review*
CT	*Christianity Today*
Cx	*Crux*
DEC	*Decrees of the Ecumenical Councils,* ed. G. Alberigo, N. Tanner, et al.
Dia	*Dialogue*
DTC	*Dictionnaire Théologie Catholique,* ed. A. Vacant and E. Mangenot
EAJET	*East Africa Journal of Evangelical Theology*
EDNT	*The Exegetical Dictionary of the New Testament*
EL	*Ephermerides Liturgicae*
EMQ	*Evangelical Missions Quarterly*
EQ	*Evangelical Quarterly*
ERT	*Evangelical Review of Theology*
ET	*Expository Times*
ETR	*Études Théologiques et Religieuses*
Ev	*Evangel*
EvT	*Evangelische Theologie*
FP	*Faith & Philosophy*
FT	*First Things*

GLRBP	*Greek Lexicon of the Roman and Byzantine Periods*, ed. Evangelinus A. Sophocles
Greg	*Gregorianum*
HPR	*Homiletic and Pastoral Review*
HTR	*Harvard Theological Review*
IBMR	*International Bulletin of Missionary Research*
IJPR	*International Journal for Philosophy of Religion*
JBL	*Journal of Biblical Literature*
JEH	*Journal of Ecclesiastical History*
JES	*Journal of Ecumenical Studies*
JETS	*Journal of the Evangelical Theological Society*
JHI	*Journal of the History of Ideas*
JSNT	*Journal for the Study of the New Testament*
JTS	*Journal of Theological Studies*
JTSA	*Journal of Theology for Southern Africa*
LXX	Septuagint
MC	*Modern Churchman*
MS	*The Modern Schoolman*
MT	*Modern Theology*
NASB	New American Standard Bible
NB	*New Blackfriars*
NIDNTT	*The New International Dictionary of New Testament Theology*, ed. Colin Brown
NIV	New International Version Bible
NPNF[1]	*Nicene and Post-Nicene Fathers*, Series 1
NPNF[2]	*Nicene and Post-Nicene Fathers*, Series 2
NRSA	New Revised Standard Version Bible plus Apocrypha
NTS	*New Testament Studies*
ODCC	*The Oxford Dictionary of the Christian Church*, third edition, ed. Frank L. Cross and Elizabeth A. Livingstone
PBR	*Patristic and Byzantine Review*
PG	*Patrologiae Cursus Completus: Series Graeca*, ed. Jacques Paul Migne
PGLex	*A Patristic Greek Lexicon*, ed. G.W.H. Lampe
PL	*Patrologiae Cursus Completus: Series Latina*, ed. Jacques Paul Migne
R&E	*Review and Expositor*
RelS	*Religious Studies*
RHPR	*Revue d'Historie et de Philosophie Religieuses*
RR	*Reformed Review*

RSR	*Recherches de Science Religieuse*
RSVA	Revised Standard Version Bible plus Apocrypha
RTR	*Reformed Theological Review*
SBJT	*Southern Baptist Journal of Theology*
ScC	*La Scuola Cattolica*
SJT	*Scottish Journal of Theology*
Soph	*Sophia*
STR	*Sewanee Theological Review*
TDNT	*Theological Dictionary of the New Testament*, ed. Gerhard Kittel and G. Friedrich
Th	*Themelios*
ThD	*Theology Digest*
ThS	*Theological Studies*
TMSJ	*The Master's Seminary Journal*
TZ	*Theological Zeitschrift*
ZKG	*Zeitschrift für Kirchengeschichte*
ZNW	*Zeitschrift für die neutestamentliche Wissenschaft und die Kunde der älteren Kirche*
ZRG	*Zeitschrift für Religions und Geitsegeschichte*
ZST	*Zeitschrift für systematische Theologie*

INTRODUCTION

On July 8, 1741 in the city of Enfield, Connecticut, the famous Puritan theologian, Jonathan Edwards (1703-58), delivered a sermon entitled, "Sinners in the Hands of an Angry God."[1] Based upon the text found in Deuteronomy 32:35, "their feet shall slip in due time," Edwards' sermon painted a horrific picture of sinners suspended over the pit of hell ready to tumble in at any time when death overtakes them:

> Unconverted men walk over the pit of hell on a rotten covering, and there are innumerable places in this covering so weak that they won't bear their weight, and these places are not seen ... This that you have heard is the case of every one of you that are out of Christ. That world of misery, that lake of burning brimstone is extended abroad under you. There is the dreadful pit of the glowing flames of the wrath of God; there is hell's wide gaping mouth open; and you have nothing to stand upon, nor anything to take hold of, there is nothing between you and hell but the air; 'tis only the power and mere pleasure of God that holds you up ... O sinner! Consider the fearful danger you are in: 'tis a great furnace of wrath, a wide and bottomless pit, full of the fire of wrath, that you are held over in the hand of that God, whose wrath is provoked and incensed as much against you, as against many of the damned in hell; you hang by a slender thread, with the flames of divine wrath flashing about it, and ready every moment to singe it, and burn it asunder; and you have no interest in any Mediator, and nothing to lay hold of to save yourself, nothing to keep off the flames of wrath, nothing of your own, nothing that you ever have done, nothing that you can do, to induce God to spare you one moment.[2]

A witness who heard Edwards preach on many occasions reported that he had "a natural way of delivery, without any agitation of body, or anything else in the manner to excite attention."[3] In point of fact, Edwards was not a stereotypical "fire and brimstone" preacher—he often read his sermons verbatim from a manuscript in a thin, monotone voice hardly ever looking up from the page.[4] Yet, in spite of these seeming stylistic drawbacks, the effect that the sermon had upon the congregation in Enfield was quite remarkable.

---

[1] Harry S. Stout, Nathan O. Hatch, and Kyle P. Farley, eds., *The Works of Jonathan Edwards, Volume 22: Sermons and Discourses, 1739–1742* (New Haven, Conn.: Yale University Press, 2003), 400–18.

[2] Stout, Hatch, and Farley, *The Works of Jonathan Edwards*, 22:407–12.

[3] The words are those of Thomas Prince recorded in 1744 and quoted in Iain H. Murray, *Jonathan Edwards: A New Biography* (Carlisle, Penn.: Banner of Truth Trust, 1987), 175.

[4] Kate Kinsella, et al., *Prentice Hall Literature: Timeless Voices, Timeless Themes–The American Experience* (Upper Saddle River, N.J.: Prentice Hall, 2002), 108.

The Reverend Stephen Williams, who witnessed the event, tells us that men and women throughout the assembly shrieked and moaned. Cries such as, "Oh, I am going to hell!" and "What shall I do to be saved?" were heard amongst the audience. After the message a throng of people came forward and gave their lives to Christ.[5]

Edwards' sermon, along with the emotions it evoked in its listeners—and continues to evoke in its readers today—offers a graphic illustration of the utter seriousness that attaches to matters of eternal destiny. The fact that it remains the most widely published and best known sermon ever preached in America is no mere happenstance but rather is a product of Edwards' fame, his topic, and his thunderous diction.[6] "Sinners in the Hands of an Angry God" taps into the tension, anxiety, and raw emotions that the debate over eternal destiny stirs up. There is no greater issue that a human being must face in life. There is no greater issue encountered collectively by the human race. For all parties concerned the matter of eternal destiny is at the same time both intensely personal and exceptionally momentous. All human beings have a vested interest in the final outcome.

"Sinners in the Hands of an Angry God" represents the epitome of the traditional Christian view of soteriology/eschatology with its well developed dichotomies between the saved and the unsaved, eternal life and eternal suffering, and heaven and hell. The traditional view, of course, has been the dominant view espoused by Christians down through the ages from the very inception of the faith. It is the established orthodoxy and the confessional position taken by most churches.

However, there has always been a small, and often vocal minority, who have rejected the traditional view and argued instead for universalism—the notion that in the end all human beings will be saved.[7] Typically formulated as a response to the horrors of the accepted view of eternal punishment, universalism has provided a safe haven for those who cannot countenance the thought that a loving God would allow such a state of affairs to exist forever. With roots reaching back into the patristic era, universalism has a long history of providing a refuge for the conscientious objector. This is not to imply, however, that the doctrine has engendered no controversy. Indeed, as we shall see, if the history of universalism is anything, it is a history of controversy. As a challenge to what many theologians down through the centuries considered to be one of the most important doctrines in Christianity, there could be no other outcome. Sparks had to fly and historically universalism was always on the losing side.

Nevertheless, universalism has survived and in our own day the debate over universalism has been conducted with an ever increasing openness. With the rise of the historical critical method along with source, form, and redaction criticism, contemporary theologians have felt freer to explore alternative interpretations of scripture and doctrine. Whereas earlier generations of theologians were usually constrained by church affiliation and doctrinal

---

[5] Stout, Hatch, and Farley, *The Works of Jonathan Edwards,* 22:400.
[6] Kinsella et al., *Prentice Hall Literature,* 106–112.
[7] A more detailed discussion of terminology will follow shortly.

statements, contemporary theologians abandoned such constraints en masse and instead insisted on exercising the right to scholarly independence and the right to submit any and all theological conclusions to the bar of human reason and rationalization.

Perhaps the greatest casualty in this wave of doctrinal reassessment has been the notion of eternal punishment itself—the avowed archenemy of universalism. Long seen by many as an awkward artifact from a more barbaric age, the notion of eternal punishment has been subjected to hostile attack by a contingent of Christian thinkers who would like to jettison this discomforting belief. For its detractors eternal punishment is no longer deemed to be an affirmation of God's righteousness and justice, but instead it is seen as a symbol of all that is wrong with confessional Christianity and its view of God. Fredric W. Farrar, the Archdeacon of Westminster in the late nineteenth-century, summed up the sentiments of many when he dismissed popular constructions of eternal suffering in hell as "acrid fumes from the poisoned crucible of mean and loveless conceptions."[8]

The move toward the elimination of the doctrine of eternal punishment has gained considerable traction in recent years. Piero Camporesi announced the death of the doctrine in contemporary theology with this obituary: "We can now affirm with some justification that hell is finished, that the great theatre of torments is closed for an indeterminate period, and that after almost 2,000 years of horrifying performances the play will not be repeated. The long, triumphal season has come to an end."[9] Spurred on by an increasing awareness of global realities, religious pluralism, and the plight of the majority of the human race who are born into non-Christian cultures, many contemporary theologians have written off the ideas of hell and eternal punishment altogether. This in turn has led to considerable confusion among Christian pastors who are increasingly loathe to take up the issue in the pulpit and be branded as heartless and unfeeling throwbacks to a bygone era. The net result of all this has been to sow the seeds of confusion among parishioners. As Robert Peterson notes, "The old preaching dictum is ever so true: a fog in the pulpit is a mist in the pew . . . And many people today are confused about hell."[10]

Into this eschatological breach has arisen a revitalized and robustly defended universalism. No longer automatically relegated to heresy status, universalism has made a comeback of sorts in contemporary western theology and is now being given an open minded hearing that it never received in previous eras. For those who do not want to fall into a shadow world of eschatological agnosticism, the optimistic message of universalism has become a valid alternative to the doctrine of endless punishment and thus the battle over universalism has been strenuously joined in recent years. It is with this renaissance of universalist thought in contemporary western theology and its connection to its historical antecedents that this dissertation will concern itself.

---

[8] Fredric W. Farrar, *Eternal Hope: Five Sermons* (New York: Dutton, 1885), 64.

[9] Piero Camporesi, *The Fear of Hell: Images of Damnation and Salvation in Early Modern Europe,* trans. Lucinda Byatt (University Park, Pa.: Pennsylvania State University Press, 1990; 1991), vi.

[10] Robert A. Peterson, *Hell on Trial: The Case for Eternal Punishment* (Phillipsburg, New Jersey: Presbyterian and Reformed, 1995), 17.

1. Purpose

The purpose of this dissertation is to survey and to critically assess the recent debate over universal salvation in western theology within the context of the historical development of the doctrine.

Its goal will be to provide a deeper understanding of contemporary expressions of universalism through the use of critical interaction and comparison. To achieve this goal the study will survey the broad historical landscape of Christian universalism and then use the historical survey as a lens through which the contemporary expressions will be viewed. Critical analyses will be performed on contemporary expressions with an eye toward exposing important issues as well as weaknesses and strengths. It is hoped that in the end this approach will provide a comprehensive overview of contemporary universalism that highlights its unique historical connections as well as its recent developments and challenges.

The year 1960 has been selected as the *terminus a quo* for the study of contemporary universalism. The decade of the 1960s was a watershed period in world history that greatly influenced the trajectory of modern Christian theology. Indeed, with the exception of the Reformation era, there is no other time in Christian history where so many radical challenges and changes were compressed into so short a period. The 1960s saw the materialization of entirely new schools of theological thought virtually overnight. Black theology emerged out of the civil rights movement. Feminist theology emerged out of the feminist movement. Political theologies emerged out of the theological reflection of post-reconstruction Europe. The various liberation theologies emerged out of the struggle against poverty and oppression. The documents issued by the Second Vatican Council in the mid-sixties radically altered Roman Catholic theology and practice. The movement towards religious pluralism underwent a stage of rapid development as the sixties generation began to abandon traditional Christianity and to dabble in mysticism, Eastern religions, yoga, and meditation.

In light of the important developments and considerations that make the 1960s a milestone decade that literally divides one era from another, this study will focus attention on the development contemporary universalism within that crucial period of time that extends from 1960 to the present.

2. Method

1. The principal method employed in this study will be one of summary and critical review of the primary literature. Secondary literature and critiques will be referred to when appropriate. Comparisons will be made and historical connections explored. Contemporary exegetical studies and hermeneutical developments will be engaged and applied.

2. Particular attention will be paid to the role of scripture, philosophy, tradition, worldview, socio-cultural, and global factors in the formulation of recent universalist proposals.

3. The principle of selection is the primary limitation of the study to those writers who have made universalism a central feature of their theology. To be sure there are many theologians who are sympathetic to the concept of universalism or even endorse it in an offhanded sort of manner. However, this

study will be primarily concerned with those theologians who make universalism a fundamental component of their theological schema and have done so extensively in their writings.

As with any doctrinal position, there is always the existence of moderating forms. In recognition of this reality, in this study we will engage in discussion with moderating positions only insofar as they have something important to add to the debate.

4. Major divisions between the various views presented within this study will be made along broad confessional lines demarcated by Protestant and Catholic subdivisions. It is acknowledged that this typology departs from the typologies that are currently being explored in the theology of religions and might be viewed by some as a step backward rather than forward.[11] However, the decision to divide the primary literature in this way has been made in recognition of the unique dogmatic and academic traditions out of which universalist writers function and that, to a greater or lesser degree, still affects the outcome of their work. In particular, the Roman Catholic theologians are still profoundly influenced by their church affiliation and their proposals are best understood when they are seen within the context of the dogmatic system that shaped their creation. It is believed that the advantages to be gained by following this more traditional typology outweigh other considerations and that these advantages will become apparent to the reader as the study progresses.

3. Definition of Terms

With the scope of the study clearly defined, we must now enter into a discussion of several soteriological terms that have become clouded due to the variety of meanings and loose interpretations that theologians have poured into them. At the outset it must be realized that in order for this study to succeed that a higher level of precision must be obtained than that found in the standard literature. Indeed, the definitions and usages we find in the literature are often contradictory and sometimes at total odds with one another. For this reason we shall have to choose those definitions that appear to be the most accurate and

---

[11] It should be noted that at this point in time no typology has gained universal acceptance and that there is still a great diversity of opinion expressed on the matter. For instance, Wilfred Cantwell Smith in his classic book *The Meaning and End of Religion: A Revolutionary Approach to the Great Religious Traditions* (New York: Harper & Row, 1962; 1978) uses a typology that approaches the issue from a west versus others perspective. Alan Race, on the other hand, in his book *Christians and Religious Pluralism: Patterns in the Christian Theology of Religions* (Maryknoll, N.Y.: Orbis, 1982), follows a typology that approaches the issue by theological outlook: (1) exclusivism, (2) inclusivism, and (3) pluralism. Jacques Dupuis in his book *Toward a Christian Theology of Religious Pluralism* (Maryknoll, N.Y.: Orbis, 1997) uses a typology of "centrisms": Ecclesiocentrism, Christocentrism, Theocentrism, and Realitycentrism (or as he puts it "Reality–Centeredness"). Veli–Matti Kärkkäinen loosely follows Dupuis' approach in his book *An Introduction to the Theology of Religions* (Downers Grove, Ill.: InterVarsity, 2003). Paul Knitter prefers to speak of "models" and sets up his typology accordingly: (1) The Replacement Model, (2) The Fulfillment Model, (3) The Mutuality Model, and (4) The Acceptance Model. Cf. Paul Knitter, *Introducing Theology of Religions* (Maryknoll, NY: Orbis, 2002).

use the words consistently according to those definitions throughout the rest of the study. It is hoped that the following definitions will add continuity and uniformity to the study and that in the end they will help us to avoid confusion over conflicting meanings and usages.

3.1. Universalism

The word "universalism" has been used in a variety of ways by Christian theologians.[12] It has been used to describe God's universal offer of salvation to humanity.[13] It has been used to describe an interpretation of the final outcome in the book of Revelation where some but not all people are saved from "from every nation and all tribes and peoples and tongues."[14] It has been used to describe the syncretistic assimilation of other religions by Christianity.[15] In this study we are concerned strictly with this word as it is used to describe a soteriological outcome in which it is asserted that all human beings will enter the Kingdom of God.

Soteriological universalism in Christian theology comes in a variety of forms and nuances. We shall leave off engaging in a discussion of those differences until the main body of the study at which point they will be addressed as they make their appearance in the theologies of those proponents under consideration. Our primary goal in this section of the study is to simply develop a good working definition of the word.

Several efforts have been made to define the word "universalism" in the literature and some of these are instructive as we seek to put forward an adequate definition. Timothy Beougher has cast his definition of universalism in terms of the avoidance of hell: "Universalism may be defined as the teaching that though hell may exist it will eventually empty as God's will to save all persons individually will finally triumph."[16] Despite Beougher's conclusion that all people will eventually be saved, there is a problem with his definition in that his focus on hell creates an unnecessary limitation and distraction from the main point of universalism, which is focused on the outcome and not necessarily the means. In his article "Universalism and the Logic of Revelation" Nigel M. de S. Cameron prefers to define universalism in terms of what it denies, namely, Christian particularism and a final separation between

---

[12] Universalism in the broader context has been used to describe a specific position taken within the confines of a myriad of scholarly disciplines including theology, sociology, economics, and ethics. In this study we are concerned only with universalism of the theological variety.

[13] Cf. Isa. 55:1; Matt. 11:28–30; John 3:16–17; Acts 17:30–31; 1 Tim. 2:3–4; 2 Pet. 3:9; Rev. 3:20.

[14] Cf. Revelation 5:9 & 7:9. Robin Parry and Christopher Partridge refer to this as "multiracial universalism." See Robin Parry and Christopher H. Partridge, eds., *Universal Salvation: The Current Debate* (Carlisle, U.K.: Paternoster, 2003), xix. Unless otherwise noted all English Bible quotations will be taken from *The New American Standard Bible* (La Habra, Calif.: The Lockman Foundation, 1977).

[15] Harry H. Hoehler, "Syncretistic Universalism: A Critique," *AJTP* 6/2–3 (May–September, 1985): 159–171.

[16] Timothy K. Beougher, "Are All Doomed to be Saved? The Rise of Modern Universalism," *SBJT* 2/2 (Summer 1998): 6.

the saved and the lost.[17] While this definition serves to buoy Cameron's thesis that universalism is a "threat to the faith as an integrated whole," it has the drawback of not allowing the universalists a positive statement of their own position.[18] In another definition, Paul Jensen makes a distinction between what he calls "hard universalism"—"the view that no person *can be* finally lost" and "soft universalism"—"the view that no person *will be* finally lost."[19] The problem here is that Jensen's definitions focus on a minor distinction that makes no material difference to the end result and thus seems to add unnecessary confusion to the issue.

A more outcome oriented definition may be found in *The Oxford English Dictionary* that defines a universalist as: "One who believes or maintains the doctrine that redemption or election is extended to the whole of mankind and not confined to a part of it."[20] A simplification of this definition would be *the belief that in the end all human beings will be saved.*[21] The word "saved" here denotes a final state that avoids eternal punishment and places one in the presence of God and his blessings for eternity. This simple definition of universalism is the one that will be employed in this study. Note that it is intentionally vague. It does not say how or through what means this salvation will be accomplished. It does not set a definitive timeline or eschatological schema. It does not speak of the final state of the universe or other creatures. The focus is simply upon the final outcome for humanity—"in the end all human beings will be saved." If one believes this statement to be true, then by this definition one is a universalist.

As with any doctrinal position there are always moderating forms. Robin Parry and Christopher Partridge make a distinction between "strong universalisms" and "hopeful universalism."[22] The former expressing a certainty about universal salvation in the final state of affairs while the latter expresses a hope that things will be so while allowing for the regrettable possibility that some may remain alienated from the Kingdom.[23] As we shall see, this

---

[17] Nigel M de S. Cameron, "Universalism and the Logic of Revelation," *ERT* 11 (October 1987): 322.

[18] Cameron, "Universalism and the Logic of Revelation," 322.

[19] Paul T. Jensen, "Intolerable but Moral? Thinking about Hell," *FP* 10/2 (1993): 236.

[20] John Simpson, ed., *The Oxford English Dictionary Online* (Oxford: Oxford University Press, 2015), http://www.oed.com/, s.v. "Universalist." (Accessed on March 16, 2014.)

[21] Similarly Marcus Braybrooke defines universalism as "the belief that ultimately all people will be saved." See Alan Richardson and John Stephen Bowden, eds., *The Westminster Dictionary of Christian Theology* (Philadelphia: Westminster Press, 1983), s.v. "Universalism."

[22] Parry and Partridge, *Universal Salvation*, xx–xxii.

[23] The views of Charles S. Duthie are representative those who embrace universalism as a sincere hope but in the end draw back from expressing it with dogmatic certainty: "Thus the hope which Christians cannot but cherish that God in His great love will find His way ultimately to the throne of every human heart, cannot become the subject of preaching in the form of a dogma . . . The tension between Christian hope and the possibility of continuing repudiation of God cannot be resolved in this life." Charles S. Duthie, "Ultimate Triumph," *SJT* 14/2 (June 1961), 170. I. Howard Marshall sees Duthie's form of "crypto–universalism" as a slippery slope that could potentially lead one down the path to hard universalism. See I. Howard Marshall, "Does the New

distinction will prove to be helpful to our study particularly when it comes to our discussion of Roman Catholic theologians such as Karl Rahner and Hans Urs von Balthasar. While hopeful universalism is a fairly non-controversial position for a Protestant theologian to take, in the minds of many Catholics it still represents a significant departure from orthodoxy.

3.2. *Apokatastasis* ('Ἀποκάτασταςις, ἀποκάτασταςις πάντων)

The English word *apokatastasis* is a transliteration of the Greek noun ἀποκάτασταςις, which is, in turn, a contracted form of the Greek phrase *apo kathistanai* (ἀπὸ κάθίσταναι).[24] The phrase means literally "to set up again." Originally the contracted word carried the idea of restoring to a previous state or reestablishment, but it also came to be used more generally of restoration.[25] The verb form, *apokathistami* (ἀποκαθίσταμι), occurs eight times in the New Testament (Matt. 12:13, 17:11; Mk. 3:5, 8:25, 9:12; Lk. 6:10; Acts 1:6; Heb. 13:19) and the noun form, *apokatastasis* (ἀποκάτασταςις), occurs just once in the New Testament in Acts 3:21 in the oft quoted phrase *apokatastaseōs panton* (ἀποκαταστάσεως πάντων)— "restoration of all things."[26]

The bulk of the occurrences of the verb speak of the healing or restoration of the sick (cf. Matt. 12:13; Mk. 3:5, 8:25; Lk. 6:10). In Hebrews 13:18–19 the

---

Testament Teach Universal Salvation?" in Trevor A. Hart and Daniel P. Thimell, *Christ in our Place: The Humanity of God in Christ of the Reconciliation of the World: Essays Presented to Professor James Torrance* (Exeter, U.K.: Paternoster; Allison Park, Pa.: Pickwick Publications, 1989), 326.

[24] See the etymology in Simpson, *The Oxford English Dictionary Online* (http://www.oed.com/, s.v. "Apocatastasis." (Accessed on March 16, 2014.)

[25] Walter Bauer, *A Greek English Lexicon of the New Testament and Other Early Christian Literature*, 3rd edition, revised by F. W. Danker W. F. Arndt, and F. W. Gingrich (Chicago: University of Chicago Press, 2000), 91–92—hereafter referred to as BDAG; G.W.H. Lampe, *A Patristic Greek Lexicon* (Oxford: Clarendon Press, 1961), 195–hereafter referred to as *PGLex*; Hans–Georg Link, ἀποκάτασταςις, in Colin Brown, ed., *The New International Dictionary of New Testament Theology*, Vol. 3 (Grand Rapids, Mich.: Zondervan, 1978; 1986), 146–48—hereafter referred to as *NIDNTT*; Albrecht Oepke, ἀποκάτασταςις, in Gerhard Kittel, ed., *Theological Dictionary of the New Testament*, trans. and ed. Gerhard Friedrich and Geoffrey W. Bromiley (Grand Rapids, Mich.: Eerdmans, 1964–1976), 1:387—hereafter referred to as *TDNT*; John Parkhurst, *A Greek and English Lexicon to the New Testament* (London: William Baynes & Son, 1822), 57; Edward Robinson, *Greek and English Lexicon of the New Testament* (New York: Harper & Brothers, 1872), 80–81; Evangelinus A. Sophocles, *Greek Lexicon of the Roman and Byzantine Periods (From B.C. 146 to A.D. 1100)*, vol. I (New York: Fredrick Unger, 1870; 1957), 219—hereafter referred to as *GLRBP*. Erwin Preuschen in his classic German lexicon gives the primary meaning as "Wiederherstellung" (re–establishment). See Erwin Preuschen, *Vollstäandiges Griechisch–Deutsches Handwöterbuch Schriften des Neuen Testaments und der übrigen urchristlichen Lituratur* (Gießen: Alfred Töpelmann, 1910), 142. See also Morwenna Ludlow's highly nuanced discussion of the word as used in the theology of Gregory of Nyssa in *Universal Salvation: Eschatology in the Thought of Gregory of Nyssa and Karl Rahner* (Oxford: Oxford University Press, 2000), 38–44.

[26] Unless otherwise noted, all quotations of the Greek New Testament will be take from Kurt Aland and Eberhard Nestle et al., eds., *Novum Testamentum Graece*, 27th edition (Stuttgart: Deutsche Bibelgesellschaft, 2001).

writer requests for prayer that ". . . I may be *restored* [ἀποκατασταθῶ] to you the sooner." This usage was a common way of speaking of returning from a trip.[27] In Mark 9:12 and its parallel in Matthew 17:11 Jesus speaks of the promised return of the prophet Elijah as it is embodied in the ministry of his forerunner John the Baptist. In these verses Jesus affirms the prophesy found in Malachi 3:23: "Elijah is coming first and *restores* [ἀποκαθιστάνει] all things."[28] (cf. Mk. 9:12) Donald Hagner argues forcefully that this reference to Elijah coming as a restorer "must here refer not to the eschatological renewal of the present order itself (which would make Elijah the Messiah himself, rather than the forerunner of the Messiah) . . . but to a preparatory work of repentance and renewal."[29] In Acts 1:6 the disciples ask Jesus if he will "at this time *restore* [ἀποκαθιστάνεις] the kingdom to Israel?" Here we have restoration conceived of in broadly political terms.

This list of verb usage as outlined above is helpful in that it gives us an idea of the context and the range of meaning that was commonly poured into the word. However, none of these examples really model for us the truly universal tone that the word was capable of taking. Link and Oepke as well as several other lexicographers note that this word group had a special connection to cosmological speculation in the Hellenistic age and became identified with "the restitution of the cosmic cycle" of the constellations.[30] Morwenna Ludlow notes that the word was associated with

> the Stoic idea of the restoration of the cosmos to its original state. The Stoics believed that when the planets reached the place in the heavens which they occupied when they were first created there would be a conflagration (*ekpurōsis*), followed by the recreation or restoration of the world—the *apokatastasis* (literally, a setting back to the beginning). From this specific astronomical meaning, the term came to refer simply to the end of the world.[31]

When one couples this cosmological connection with the idea of restoration to a previous state then it is easy to see how an overarching concept of a universal restoration of the cosmos linked to eschatology could develop within the context of Christian theology around the idea of ἀποκάτασστασις.

The only example of this kind of usage within the New Testament is found in Peter's sermon delivered at Solomon's portico within the Temple precincts in Acts 3:11–26. The pertinent verses are Acts 3:19–21 where Peter spoke of

---

[27] Link, ἀποκάτασστασις, *NIDNTT* 147.

[28] In the Matthew parallel the tense is changed from the present ἀποκαθιστάνει to the future ἀποκαταστήσει, which follows more closely the translation of the LXX.

[29] Donald A. Hagner, *Matthew 14–28*, Word Biblical Commentary, vol. 33b (Dallas: Word, 1995), 499.

[30] Link, ἀποκάτασστασις, *NIDNTT* 146. Oepke, ἀποκάτασστασις, *TDNT* 390. See also BDAG 92; *PGLex* 195; *GLRBP* 219. See also the discussion of Ilaria L. E. Ramelli, *The Christian Doctrine of Apokatastasis: A Critical Assessment from the New Testament to Eriugena* (Leiden/Boston: Brill, 2013), 4–5.

[31] Morwenna Ludlow, "Universalism in the History of Christianity," in Parry and Partridge, *Universal Salvation? The Current Debate*, 192.

the necessity of the ascension of Christ and is quoted as saying: [19] "Repent therefore and be converted, that your sins may be blotted out, so that times of refreshing [καιροὶ ἀναψύξεως] may come from the presence of the Lord, [20] and that He may send Jesus Christ, who was preached to you before,[21] whom heaven must receive until the times of restoration of all things [χρόνων ἀποκαταστάσεως πάντων], which God has spoken by the mouth of all His holy prophets since the world began." Here then we have the word ἀποκάτασσις clearly being used in the context of a universal restoration "of all things." The fact that the restoration is focused upon the fulfillment of the wide-ranging promises made through the Old Testament prophets further enhances the comprehensive scope in which the word was used and its attraction for those who want to include the salvation of all human beings (and often all living creatures) in such a restoration.[32]

No doubt, it was these very features that caused Origen to gravitate toward ἀποκάτασσις as a descriptor for his eschatological outlook. For Origen it was inconceivable that the end could come without all created things ultimately returning to the loving creator who created them—this return included even Satan himself. Origen wrote: "We believe however that the goodness of God through Christ will restore his entire creation to one end, even his enemies being conquered and subdued."[33] For Origen the effects of sin, which brought disorder into the creation, had to be reversed and harmony restored. In an interesting twist on the Hellenistic concept of a cyclical cosmic restitution Origen reasoned that the creation had to return to the pure and pristine state in which it was created. Commenting on Genesis 1:1 he explained: "For if we rightly understand the matter, this is the statement of Moses found in the beginning of his book, when he says, 'In the beginning God created the heavens and the earth.' For this is the beginning of the entire creation: To this beginning the end and consummation of all things must be returned."[34] Thus Origen's doctrine of ἀποκάτασσις has been rightly called "the doctrine of the restoration of all created things"[35] and it fits loosely within the context of Hellenistic cosmic speculation and its conceptual framework of ἀποκάτασσις.[36]

---

[32] Nevertheless, there are serious problems associated with trying to use this verse as a proof text for the universal salvation of individuals and as a result it has not been a favorite of universalists down through the centuries. The primary difficulty relates to the fact that the verse occurs in the context of an affirmation of the utter destruction (ἐξολεθρευθήσεται) of those who refuse to hear the words of Jesus Christ. (cf. vv. 22–23) Oepke notes that ὧν in v. 21 can only be grammatically related to πάντων and not χρόνων, and based upon this he argues that the restoration "cannot denote the conversion of persons but only the reconstitution or establishment of things." See Oepke, ἀποκάτασσις, *TDNT* 391.

[33] Origen, *De principiis*, 1.6.1 (my translation).

[34] Origen, *De principiis*, 3.6.8 (my translation).

[35] Link, ἀποκάτασσις, *NIDNTT* 148.

[36] Ramelli argues that there are two main differences between Origen's conception of ἀποκάτασσις and that of the Stoics: (1) Origen argues for a singular restoration event as opposed to the Stoics' infinite series of events; and (2) Origen conceived of the

For Origen then the idea of soteriological universalism was just a component part of the bigger picture of ἀποκάταστασις. Therefore, in Origen's theological system universalism and ἀποκάταστασις are not synonyms and from a strictly technical point of view using the word ἀποκάταστασις to refer to universalism is a misappropriation. However, the fact remains that historically ἀποκάταστασις came to be used in theological circles to simply refer to the concept of universalism apart from the idea of a restoration of all created things and thus the two definitions are at odds with one another.

Due to the fact that there is a need to differentiate Origen's original concept of total restoration through ἀποκάταστασις from soteriological universalism, this study will maintain the distinction between the two words. The reader should bear in mind that some writers in the field use the words synonymously. We will note this lack of distinction when we encounter it.

3.3 *Aïdios and Aiōn/Aiōnios* (Ἀΐδιος and Αἰών/Αἰώνιος)
Much of the debate surrounding universal salvation in the New Testament has to do with the meaning that one accepts for the Greek words that serve as duration of time indicators. Indeed, at the very heart of the discussion concerning hell and the nature of judgment is the issue of time. Is hell eternal? Does punishment last forever? Are people eternally separated from God? These are the sorts of questions that stand at the center of the debate and whose answers are greatly affected by the lexicography of the Bible.

Crucial to the issue at hand are three very important Greek words that are used in the New Testament and patristic writings to connote long periods of time—*aïdios* (ἀΐδιος), *aiōn* (αἰών), and *aiōnios* (αἰώνιος). The adjective ἀΐδιος seems to have developed from the adverb ἀεί (aei—"always").[37] It is used only two times in the New Testament. In Romans 1:20 it is used to speak of God's "eternal power and divine nature" (ἥ τε ἀΐδιος αὐτοῦ δύναμις καὶ θειότης). In Jude 6 it is used to speak of fallen angels whom God has "bound with everlasting chains for judgment on the great day" (εἰς κρίσιν μεγάλης ἡμέρας δεσμοῖς ἀϊδίοις ὑπὸ ζόφον τετήρηκεν). In their book, *Terms for Eternity: Aiōnios and Aïdios in Classical and Christian Texts*, Ilaria Ramelli and David Konstan argue that "the term *aïdios* has its roots in the earliest Greek philosophical vocabulary, and more or less consistently refers to a strict eternal stretch of time, without beginning or end, or at least endless. This use obtains in later pagan as well as Christian writers."[38] The problem with this conclusion is

---

aeons as being very different from each other whereas the Stoics assumed that they would be repetitively the same. Cf. Ramelli, *The Christian Doctrine of Apokatastasis*, 9.

[37] BDAG, s.v. ἀεί.

[38] Ilaria L. E. Ramelli and David Konstan, *Terms for Eternity: Aiōnios and Aïdios in Classical and Christian Texts* (Piscataway, NJ: Gorgias Press, 2007; 2013) 237. I have chosen to use Ramelli & Konstan as dialogue partners in this section because their book is so recent and ideally focused on the issue at hand. Ramelli has contributed another extended discussion of the definition these words in her book, *The Christian Doctrine of Apokatastasis*, which essentially follows the same trajectory as that found in *Terms for Eternity*. Cf. Ramelli, *The Christian Doctrine of Apokatastasis*, 25–34.

that it seems to be directly contradicted by how the word is used in Jude 6.[39] There can be no doubt that in Romans 1:20 ἀΐδιος is used to speak of God's eternality and unending nature. However, in Jude 6 we have an entirely different use of the adjective as a modifier of a temporal object—in this case, the chains used to bind fallen angels (*desmois aïdios*—δεσμοῖς ἀϊδίοις). This usage presents a difficult problem for the thesis of Ramelli and Konstan, which asserts that the word invariably refers to eternity. Certainly chains (or "fetters") are not eternal sorts of things in the sense of being "without beginning or end," but rather are created items that have a starting place in time. Given the very physical nature of the crimes committed by these angels—"sexual immorality and perversion" (cf. v. 7)—it would appear that v. 6 underscores the fact that they require a very physical form of restraint until their day of judgment arrives and so we have the use of the word *desmois* (chains) to describe their bonds. This being the case, it would be problematic to argue that the chains that bind such offenders are just metaphoric or symbolic in some way. This reasoning, in turn, would lead one to admit that the chains being discussed in the passage are indeed physical and had a beginning. As to the notion that the chains could be imbued with eternal properties from the point of their creation, this point seems to be negated by the idea that they will last only until the day of the angel's judgment—and thus they have a fixed life-span. The impermanent nature of these bonds is also confirmed through a comment that Jesus made in Matt. 24:41 where he tells us that the ultimate destiny of fallen angels is not chains, but rather to be cast into the Lake of Fire, which he says was prepared "for the devil and his angels."

Obviously the use of ἀϊδίοις in Jude 6 does not fit into the hypothesis advanced by Ramelli and Konstan and therefore a translation of the word that is not so solidly wedded to eternity seems to be in order.[40] Perhaps ἀϊδίοις was very rarely used synonymously with αἰώνιος in the first century to carry the more limited sense of "age" rather than eternity. Certainly if the notion of a strict eternity were so tightly wedded to this word, then we would have expected to see the author use αἰώνιος in the sense of "age" rather than ἀϊδίοις in the sense of "eternal" when referring the chains. The fact that ἀϊδίοις appears to be used in this passage in the former sense is an indicator that there is something here we do not yet understand about its proper translation.

---

[39] It also appears that this conclusion is directly contradicted by their own explanation of Jude 6: "We may suppose that the chains of the fallen angels are called ἀΐδια rather than αἰώνια because they continue from the moment of their incarceration, at the beginning of the world, or even before it, until the judgment that signals the entry into the new αἰών: thus, the term indicates the uninterrupted continuity throughout all time in this world and the next (that is, prior to the end of times)" (Ramelli and Konstan, *Terms for Eternity*, 68). Obviously, if the chains have a limited life span that is cut short by the angels' day of the judgment, then they are not eternal and this use of ἀΐδιος cannot refer to, as Ramelli and Konstan aver that it must, "a strictly eternal stretch of time" (Ramelli and Konstan, *Terms for Eternity*, 237).

[40] The usages of the adverb ἀεί, from which this word developed, might be helpful. BDAG notes two ranges of meaning: (1) a continuous duration of time in the sense of "always," and (2) an episodic duration of time as a frequently recurring action that might be translated as "constantly" or "continuously." Cf. BDAG, s.v. ἀεί.

Perhaps the most contentious debate in the lexicography of the New Testament and universal salvation is over the meaning of the Greek noun *aiōn* (αἰών) and its corresponding adjective *aiōnios* (αἰώνιος). These words stand at the center of the storm regarding the doctrine of eternal punishment and are to be found in some of the most disputed passages in the Bible such as Matt. 25:46, 2 Thes. 1:9, Jude 13, Rev. 14:11, and 20:10. *Aiōn* (αἰών) is used some 122 times in the Greek New Testament and the modifier *aiōnios* (αἰώνιος) appears some 71 times.[41] The standard lexical reference works gravitate towards advancing two essential meanings for *aiōn* (αἰών): (1) A long period of time, without reference to beginning or end. Of time past—"earliest days" "time immemorial," "ancient days," "of old." Of time future—"eternity," "eternally," "in perpetuity." These meanings are often expressed through the use of three significant Greek formulae or idioms: *ap aiōnos* (ἀπ᾽ αἰῶνος)[42] and *ek tou aiōnos* (ἐκ τοῦ αἰῶνος),[43] which both signify "from age or eternity past," and *eis ton aiōna* (εἰς τὸν αἰῶνα), which signifies "forever" or "to all eternity" and is sometimes rendered "never" based upon the context.[44] The second meaning for *aiōn* (αἰών) is typically held to be: (2) A segment of time as a particular unit of history—an age, an era, or an aeon—as in "the age past," "this present age," "the age to come."[45] *Aiōnios* (αἰώνιος), as the adjective of *aiōn* (αἰών), would presumably carry through these concepts in modifier form and thus offer several translational options. We find this to be the general conclusion that is drawn in the most important academic Greek lexicons.

A significant portion of the debate over these words centers around adjectival activity of αἰώνιος and whether it brings to bear the standard translations available through its root αἰών or if it has actually taken on a

---

[41] In my opinion the most balanced and useful extended discussion of the meaning and application of these words in the Bible remains the contribution that Hermann Sasse made to the *TDNT*, cf. *TDNT*, 1:197–209. See also Ramelli and Konstan, *Terms for Eternity*, 57–70; *NIDNTT*, 3:826–33; Heleen M. Keizer, *Life Time Entirety: A Study of ΑΙΩΝ in Greek Literature and Philosophy, the Septuagint and Philo* (The Hague: n.p., 1999; 2010); *EDNT*, 1:44–48;

[42] ἀπ᾽ αἰῶνος is used three times in the New Testament. Cf. Luke 1:70, Acts 3:21, and Acts 15:18.

[43] ἐκ τοῦ αἰῶνος is used two times in the New Testament. Cf. John 9:32 and Gal. 1:4.

[44] εἰς τὸν αἰῶνα is used twenty–eight times in the New Testament—twelve of these are found in the Gospel of John. Cf. Matt. 21:19; Mark 3:29, 11:14; Luke 1:55; John 4:14, 6:51, 6:58, 8:35 (twice), 8:51, 8:52, 10:28, 11:26, 12:34, 13:8, 14:6; 1 Cor. 8:13; 2 Cor. 9:9; Heb. 1:8, 5:6, 6:20, 7:17, 7:21, 7:24, 7:28; 1 Pet. 1:25; 1 John 2:17; 2 John 2. For a few interesting examples of the use of the formula to connote "never" cf. Mark 3:29, John 4:14, 8:51–52, 10:28, 11:26, 13:8; and 1 Cor. 8:13.

[45] A third, much more limited meaning has been advanced for αἰών and that is the use of the word to connote the creation/world/universe as a spatial concept encapsulated in time. Along these lines, a few possible uses occur in the Book of Hebrews. Cf. Heb. 1:4, 9:26, and 11:3. In 1 Tim. 1:17 it is said that Christ is the "king of the ages" (βασιλεῖ τῶν αἰώνων). The use of "ages" here seems to encapsulate all of the space–time creation in to the word *aiōnōn* (αἰώνων) as the ode to Christ put forward by Paul seems to be put in absolute terms: 17 "Now to the King eternal, immortal, invisible, the only God, be honor and glory forever and ever. Amen." (Τῷ δὲ βασιλεῖ τῶν αἰώνων, ἀφθάρτῳ ἀοράτῳ μόνῳ θεῷ, τιμὴ καὶ δόξα εἰς τοὺς αἰῶνας τῶν αἰώνων, ἀμήν.)

special meaning and usage all its own in the New Testament. Ramelli and Konstan note that extremes in the debate range from those who would say that αἰώνιος should be rendered "eternal/everlasting" in every occurrence to those who would always render it "age/aeon" with the exception of when it is modifying God, in which case eternality is clearly indicated.[46] Ramelli and Konstan endorse the latter position in the conclusion of their study:

> What emerges from the present analysis is that, apart from the Platonic philosophical vocabulary, which is specific to few authors, *aiōnios* does *not* mean "eternal"; it acquires this meaning only when it refers to God, and only because the notion of eternity was included in the conception of God: for the rest, it has a wide range of meanings and its possible renderings are multiple, but it does not mean "eternal." In particular, when it is associated with life or punishment, in the Bible and in Christian authors who keep themselves close to the Biblical usage, it denotes their belonging to the world to come.[47]

While studies based on the historical usage and development of words are helpful, they can sometimes work against our goal of *delineating precisely how these words are used in the New Testament* by offering us no clear way to choose between rival translations. Simply examining the broad historical occurrences of words like αἰών/αἰώνιος can become frustratingly unenlightening because in a great many of the occurrences that one encounters the case can be made for a translation of either "age" or "eternity" and thus the translation that is advanced tends to hinge upon the biases of the translator. In this regard a work like that produced by Ramelli and Konstan, which focuses on the history of occurrences, can be profoundly unhelpful in actually shedding light on how we are to translate these words within a specific context and then build a doctrinal system upon them.

What is needed here is a way to break out of this miasma of indeterminate argumentation. Ideally, the best way to prove the real meaning of a word would be to let the writers do it for us; if this could be done, then we could be confident in both our translation and doctrinal stance. With the synoptic gospels we have a unique opportunity to find out the true meaning that the writers had in mind by examining parallel passages. By employing such an examination we occasionally find that there are significant variations in the words used and these variations give us great insight into the author's actual intent. In the case of whether or not αἰώνιος was ever used unambiguously to refer to eternal punishment the New Testament, we encounter a pair of parallel passages in the synoptic gospels that appear to definitively establish the case in the affirmative. The passages contain a significant variation in word choice, which, when taken together, appears to establish that Jesus Christ did in fact believe in and teach the doctrine of eternal punishment. The parallel passages may be found in Mark 9:43–48 and Matthew 18:7–9 in which Jesus discusses sin and Gehenna fire.

---

[46] Ramelli and Konstan, *Terms for Eternity*, 59.
[47] Ramelli and Konstan, *Terms for Eternity*, 238.

Let's begin by examining Mark 9:43–48. In several places Jesus warned his listeners about the danger of being cast into γέεννα (Gehenna),[48] which he twice qualified as being τὴν γέενναν τοῦ πυρός ("Gehenna fire")—typically translated as "hell fire" by the English versions.[49] In Mark 9:43–48, Jesus makes a particularly revealing statement regarding γέεννα fire where he emphasizes the extreme consequences that sin brings upon the offender:

> [43] "And if your hand causes you to stumble, cut it off; it is better for you to enter life crippled, than having your two hands, to go into hell, into the unquenchable fire [εἰς τὸ πῦρ τὸ ἄσβεστον]. [45] And if your foot causes you to stumble, cut it off; it is better for you to enter life lame, than having your two feet, to be cast into hell, 47 And if your eye causes you to stumble, cast it out; it is better for you to enter the kingdom of God with one eye, than having two eyes, to be cast into hell, [48] where THEIR WORM DOES NOT DIE, AND THE FIRE IS NOT QUENCHED." [ὁ σκώληξ αὐτῶν οὐ τελευτᾷ καὶ τὸ πῦρ οὐ σβέννυται.][50]

The very severity of Jesus' comments here emphasizes how horrifying he understood the threat of Gehenna fire to be: Better to cut off a hand, better to cut off a foot, better to pluck out an eye, than to experience the consequences of judgment in Gehenna. The fact that Jesus understood the suffering of Gehenna to be both final and eternal is stressed in the opening and closing sentences of the declaration, which serve as bookends to the whole. In both cases the idea of unending fire refers back to Isaiah 66:24 in which the LORD (יהוה) announced judgment upon the bodies of those who have transgressed (הַפֹּשְׁעִים) against him. Verse 48 expands on the concept and follows fairly closely the wording found in the LXX with a few minor variations. It must be noted that Jesus modifies the scene a bit here in that rather than speaking of dead bodies being eternally consumed, as occurs in Isaiah 66:24, he envisions live people being cast into eternal fire on the Day of Judgment. Although the phrase "Day of Judgment" does not occur in the passage, it is surely lurking in the background through the imagery of people entering into the eternal life of the Kingdom or being cast into the eternal suffering of the fire. The important thing is that Jesus

---

[48] Cf. Matt. 5:22, 5:29–30, 10:28, 18:9, 23:33; Mark 9:43–48; Luke 12:5. The word "Gehenna" is a loose transliteration of the Hebrew word that means "Valley of Hinnom." The valley was originally the location of the idolatrous worship of the Canaanite gods of Molech and Baal in which children were frequently sacrificed by fire. In the intertestamental period the valley became a refuse dump with continuously smoldering flames that added to its sinister reputation. By the time of the New Testament Gehenna was viewed metaphorically as a place of fiery, eternal judgment. See Hans Bietenhard, γέεννα (Gehenna), Gehenna, hell, *NIDNTT* 2:208–209; Chaim Milikowsky, "Which Gehenna? Retribution and Eschatology in the Synoptic Gospels and in Early Jewish Texts," *NTS* 34/2 (1988): 238–49; and Duane F. Watson, "Gehenna," in *ABD* 2:926–928.

[49] Cf. Matt. 5:22 and 18:9.

[50] Verses 44 and 46 are understood to be secondary in nature by the compilers of the NA27 text and so they are not included here. As they are repetitive and superfluous to our task at hand, we will not spend any time reviewing that debate.

envisions Gehenna fire to be every bit as severe as the unending fire (וְאִשָּׁם לֹא תִכְבֶּה) discussed in Isaiah 66:24.[51] In v. 43 Jesus qualifies his understanding of Gehenna by saying that to be thrown into Gehenna is to be thrown into τὸ πῦρ τὸ ἄσβεστον—the phrase meaning literally an inextinguishable fire—a fire that has no end.[52]

The fact that Jesus intended us to understand the fire to be unending in nature is further confirmed by the illustration he draws in v. 48 where he declares that Gehenna is a place where ὁ σκώληξ αὐτῶν οὐ τελευτᾷ ("THEIR WORM DOES NOT DIE . . ."). Again, the imagery is taken from Isaiah 66:24 with the grotesque notion of worms feeding endlessly upon the damned reinforcing the severity of the eternal torment that will be inflicted. An interesting choice of words is made in this verse in that the Greek verb *teleutaō* (τελευτάω— following the reading of the LXX) is used rather than one of the more typical words for death—e.g. *apothneiskō* (ἀποθνήσκω) or *thanatos* (θάνατος). *Teleutaō* means to literally "complete or bring to an end." [53] It became a euphemism for death—as life is seen to be brought to an end by death—with the emphasis being upon the ending aspect of the word. By negating the verb, the text is emphasizing not just the fact that the worms do not die, but rather is focused on the incomplete and unending nature of the punishment that they inflict. It is not just that the worms do not die, but the horror is that their task of consuming the damned never ends.

Corresponding directly to this vivid illustration is the final phrase of verse 48 in which Jesus declares: καὶ τὸ πῦρ οὐ σβέννυται ("AND THE FIRE IS NOT QUENCHED"). It is interesting to note here that Jesus exchanges the phrase *ou sbennutai* (*ou* in the Greek language carries the meaning of "not") for the word *asbeston* (ἄσβεστον), which is used in verse 43. As Jesus uses them, both words speak to the inextinguishable nature of the fire they describe and they are in that sense the inverse sides of the same coin. However, this precise inverse nature of the two words extends even more deeply into the root meanings from which they eventually became related to the quechability/unquechability of fire. In the case of *sbennutai* (σβέννυται) we have a word that carries the meaning of "to cause an action, state, or faculty to cease to function or exist" and thus when related to fire it came to mean "to quench or to put out."[54] Interestingly enough, *asbeston* (ἄσβεστον) developed from an opposite root meaning "something whose state of being cannot be nullified or stopped" and thus when related to fire it came to mean "unquenchable." [55] Therefore, *asbeston* (ἄσβεστον) represents a true polar opposite of *sbennutai* (σβέννυται). The key point for our study here is the fact that when applied to fire both the word *asbeston* (ἄσβεστον) and the negated phrase *ou sbennutai* (οὐ σβέννυται) speak of an absolute state of being that cannot be stopped. In other words, they

---

[51] The fact that the Hebrew word for "age/eternity"—olam (עוֹלָם)—is not used here, removes us from the need to enter into that contentious debate.

[52] BDAG, s.v. ἄσβεστος, notes that ἄσβεστος speaks of a fire "whose state of being cannot be nullified or stopped."

[53] BDAG, s.v. τελευτάω; *NIDNTT*, 1:430, 2:59–66.

[54] BDAG, s.v. σβέννυμι.

[55] BDAG, s.v. ἄσβεστος.

speak to the unending nature of the fire Jesus is discussing and they tell us that the punishment inflicted by that fire will be eternal.

Moving over to the parallel passage in Mathew's Gospel we find that Matthew's translation of Jesus' words (assuming Jesus spoke mainly in Aramaic) has some significant differences from that of Mark's:

> [8] "And if your hand or your foot causes you to stumble, cut it off and throw it from you; it is better for you to enter life crippled or lame, than having two hands or two feet, to be cast into the eternal fire [τὸ πῦρ τὸ αἰώνιον]. [9] And if your eye causes you to stumble, pluck it out, and throw it from you. It is better for you to enter life with one eye, than having two eyes, to be cast into the fiery hell [τὴν γέενναν τοῦ πυρός]."

It seems safe to assume here that verse 8 in Matthew's account corresponds to verses 43 and 45 in Mark's account since all three verses deal with the cutting off of the hands and the feet. In Matthew's account the two actions are combined into one verse. Critical for our analysis is Matthew's choice of words at the end of verse 8. Matthew uses the phrase *to pur to aiōnion* (τὸ πῦρ τὸ αἰώνιον) to refer to the same eternal fire that Mark calls *to pur to asbeston* (τὸ πῦρ τὸ ἄσβεστον) in verse 9:43. This leads to the crucial insight that Matthew felt free to substitute the adjective *aiōnion* (αἰώνιον) for the adjective *asbeston* (ἄσβεστον).[56] Because *asbeston* (ἄσβεστον) carries the meaning of "unending" then we are on firm exegetical footing to assert that in this context *aiōnion* (αἰώνιον) must also carry the meaning of "unending" or "eternal." Therefore, we conclude that in Matthew 18:8–9 we have a clear and unambiguous use of the adjective *aiōnion* (αἰώνιον) to indicate eternal punishment. This conclusion is not based on mere conjecture or theological bias, but rather upon a powerful linkage between two parallel texts found in the Gospels. For us, the one interprets the other, and therefore we have a clean case here of the New Testament writers interpreting themselves, which is the very best proof of usage we could hope for.

Pressing our case further let us now take up the correct translation of perhaps the most fiercely contested verses regarding eternal punishment to be found in the pages of the New Testament: Matthew 25:41 and 46. The context of the overall passage is a prophesy given by Jesus in which he predicts an eschatological separation of the sheep from the goats—the sheep and the goats being metaphors for the saved and the lost. In verses 41 and 46 Jesus elaborates on the ultimate outcome of the judgment:

---

[56] This would be true if, as most modern scholars accept, Mark wrote first with Matthew using him as a source. If the order of writing is reversed then there is still no problem in that we would have Matthew writing first and Mark interpreting him later—in which case we would still have a parallel passage based interpretation of the meaning of αἰώνιος. If we think in terms of some sort of independence between Matthew and Mark regarding this incident, we still understand that they would have been trying to translate Jesus' teaching into Greek and the independent translations would still then present a powerful witness to the original meaning of Jesus' words.

[41] "Then He will also say to those on the left hand, 'Depart from Me, you cursed, into the eternal fire [τὸ πῦρ τὸ αἰώνιον] prepared for the devil and his angels."

[46] "And these will go away into eternal punishment [κόλασιν αἰώνιον], but the righteous into eternal life [ζωὴν αἰώνιον]."

As we examine verse 41 we note that the punishment meted out is identical to that which is brought to bear in Matthew 18:8, namely, *to pur to aiōnion* (τὸ πῦρ τὸ αἰώνιον). If Matthew is consistent in his usage of *aiōnios* (αἰώνιος) in the context of eschatological judgment—and we have no reason to believe that he is not—then the best translation of *to pur to aiōnion* (τὸ πῦρ τὸ αἰώνιον) in Matt. 25:41 would be "eternal fire" as we have rendered it in Matt. 18:8.

Moving on to verse 46 we can apply our exegetical insight in a similar fashion and conclude that, given the context of eschatological judgment, Matthew's use of *kolasin aiōnion* (κόλασιν αἰώνιον) is best translated as "eternal punishment" and that his use of *zōēn aiōnion* (ζωὴν αἰώνιον) is best translated as "eternal life." This remains true to Matthew's rendering of v. 18:8 in light the parallel found in Mark 19:43. It also matches the declaration of the judgment that Jesus makes in Matthew 25:41. Finally, it makes the best sense of the elegant parallel structure we find in verse 46, which is clearly intended to show an absolute contrast between the two outcomes and the simple coextensive nature of the two when it comes to duration of time.

There are those who have tried to argue that *kolasis* (κόλασις) is never used of "punishment" but rather is always used of "correction."[57] However, against this idiosyncratic interpretation stands a large body of data that points to the essential meaning of *kolasis* (κόλασις) as being "punishment."[58] One need only to look at the use of the noun in 1 John 4:18 to see that a translation of "correction" would not be sufficient to elicit the kind of abject fear that the Apostle John is talking about:

[17] Love has been perfected among us in this: that we may have boldness on the Day of Judgment, because as he is, so are we in this world. [18] There is no fear in love, but perfect love casts out fear; for fear has to do with punishment [ὅτι ὁ φόβος κόλασιν ἔχει], and whoever fears has not reached perfection in love. (NRSA)

The fear John is discussing here is the sort of paralyzing fear of punishment that will come upon people as they are confronted with their sin and wrong doing on the Day of Judgment by the eternal Judge. Fear of the Day of Judgment is an essential theme in the Bible[59] and in Revelation 20:11 we are

---

[57] Cf. Thomas Talbott, "Three pictures of God in Western Theology," *Faith and Philosophy* 12 (1995): 91–92. Ramelli, *The Christian Doctrine of Apokatastasis*, 32.

[58] BDAG, s.v. κόλασις; *NIDNTT*, 3:98–100; *EDNT*, 2:306. In the *TDNT* Schneider discusses the root meaning to "mutilate, maim, cut off" developing into the idea of punishment and even retribution. He notes that the word was often used of the punishment meted out to slaves. Cf. *TDNT* 3:814–16.

[59] And in John's writings if you accept that he wrote the book of Revelation.

given a vivid picture of the sort of fear that judgment at the Great White Throne will provoke: "And I saw a great white throne and Him who sat upon it, from whose presence earth and heaven fled away, and no place was found for them." In 1 John 4:18, John is essentially saying that the Christian may have boldness on the fearful Day of Judgment because he or she has been loved perfectly by Christ and his sacrifice on the cross (cf. 1 John 4:14–16). When the believer realizes how perfect the love of Christ is because of the salvation from God's punishment that has been provided by it, then he/she will be set free to face the Day of Judgment with boldness and without fear. Therefore, we see that the idea of a mere "correction" being made by the Great Judge on that Day does not do justice to the somber and terrifying description of the kind of fear that we find in these verses. That sort of overwhelming fear fits best into the context of eternal punishment.

Ramelli, citing the definition of Aristotle with the support of Plato, argues that *kolasis* (κόλασις) "is inflicted in the interest of the sufferer." This, she argues, is in contrast to the use of the word *timōria* (τιμωρία)— "punishment/penalty"), which is inflicted "in the interest of him who inflicts it, that he may obtain satisfaction" (*Rhet.* 1369b13).[60] Based on this observation she concludes: "In the NT the punishment of sinners in the world to come is therefore understood to be inflicted in their interest, which implies that it is purifying rather than retributive. If this is the case, it should be supposed that it will come to an end once it has achieved its function."[61] The problem here is that by the time of the first century such a distinction in usage (if it ever really existed) between the two words had essentially become blurred and *kolasis* (κόλασις) and *timōria* (τιμωρία) had largely become synonymous with one another. This is why we encounter passages such as 4 Mac. 8:9 where *kolasis* is certainly used of inflicting retributive punishment. It is interesting to note that in this passage the tyrant uses *kolasis* and not *timōria* as a warning of severe retribution: [9] "But if by disobedience you rouse my anger, you will compel me to destroy each and every one of you with dreadful punishments (δειναῖς κολάσεσιν) through tortures (τῶν βασάνων)." (NRSA)

With this analysis behind us, we can conclude that the thesis of Ramelli and Konstan regarding the use of *aiōnios* (αἰώνιος) in New Testament is incorrect. Their assertion was that, apart from reference to the divine, "*aiōnios* does *not* mean 'eternal.'"[62] If this were true, the occurrences of the word found in Matthew 25:41 & 46 would have to be translated as "age-long" as opposed to "eternal." However, our analysis of parallel passages has revealed that a translation of "eternal" is required in certain instances and is especially warranted in the context of eschatological judgment in order to maintain consistency with the teaching of Jesus Christ. Certainly Jesus' disciples would have noted his outlook on this crucial area of theology and as his disciples they would have sought to carefully follow it in their own writings.

With this in mind, we are well within our exegetical rights to assert that when it comes to the use of αἰών/αἰώνιος in an eschatological context within

---

[60] Ramelli, *The Christian Doctrine of Apokatastasis*, 32.
[61] Ramelli, *The Christian Doctrine of Apokatastasis*, 32.
[62] Ramelli and Konstan, *Terms for Eternity*, 238.

the New Testament that the preferred primary translation should default to "eternity/eternal." In such a context, the translation of these words as "age/age-long" should only be considered if there is some other mitigating circumstance in the text to warrant it.

3.4. Exclusivism/Particularism/Restrictivism

Christian exclusivism, sometimes called particularism or restrictivism, is simply defined as the idea "that salvation is attainable only within the embrace of explicit Christian faith."[63] Ronald Nash, in his defense of Christian exclusivism, offers the following working definition:

> Christian exclusivism can be defined as the belief that (1) Jesus Christ is the *only* Savior, and (2) explicit faith in Jesus Christ is necessary for salvation. The first claim denies that there are or can be other saviors, a fact that distinguishes it from pluralism. The second claim denies that people may be saved without conscious and explicit faith in Jesus Christ, which sets it apart from inclusivism. Christian exclusivists begin by believing that the tenets of one religion—in this case Christianity—are true and that any religious beliefs that are logically incompatible with those tenets are false.[64]

Thus, Christian exclusivism—as we define it here—restricts access to salvation to only those who have heard the gospel message and responded to it.[65]

In this view then, all who have not heard the gospel message are outside of the purview of salvation and therefore face certain damnation. All who have heard the message and have not responded to it are also understood to be lost.[66]

---

[63] Joseph A. DiNoia, "Varieties of Religious Aims: Beyond Exclusivism, Inclusivism, and Pluralism," in Bruce D. Marshall, ed., *Theology and dialogue: Essays in Conversation with George Lindbeck* (Notre Dame, Ind.: University of Notre Dame Press, 1990), 250.

[64] Ronald H. Nash, *Is Jesus the Only Savior?* (Grand Rapids, Mich.: Zondervan, 1994), 11–12.

[65] For a concise discussion of exclusivism including the historical background, leading advocates, and arguments for and against, see the second chapter of John Sanders' book *No Other Name: An Investigation into the Destiny of the Unevangelized*, 37–79. See also Alan Race's extended discussion in *Christians and Religious Pluralism: Patterns in the Christian Theology of Religions,* 10–37.

[66] Based upon population statistics and estimates of Christian missionary penetration into the world, John Sanders concludes that holding to exclusivism requires one to affirm that the vast majority of human beings who ever lived will have to be consigned to hell. See Sanders, *No Other Name,* 15–16. Exclusivists have been severely criticized on this point. John Hick, for instance, finds it "morally and religiously revolting" that "the large majority of the human race would be condemned by God to eternal perdition." John Hick, "Response to R. Douglas Geivett and W. Gary Phillips," in Dennis L. Okholm and Timothy R. Phillips, eds., *Four Views on Salvation in a Pluralistic World* (Grand Rapids, Mich.: Zondervan, 1995), 246.

Historian Arnold Toynbee railed against the seeming intolerance of exclusivism calling it "a sinful state of mind" and made an appeal for its elimination. See Arnold Toynbee, *Christianity among the Religions of the World* (New York: Charles Scribner's

John Calvin in his *Institutes of the Christian Religion* offers a classic statement of this perspective:

> It is certain after the fall of our first parent, no knowledge of God without a Mediator was effectual to salvation. Christ speaks not of his own age merely, but embraces all ages, when he says, "This is eternal life, that they might know thee the only true God, and Jesus Christ, whom thou hast sent" (John 17:3). The more shameful, therefore is the presumption of those who throw heaven open to the unbelieving and profane, in the absence of that grace which Scripture uniformly describes as the only door by which we enter into life.[67]

In taking in the discussion found in the literature, it appears that some might not agree with the definition as delineated above in that they might not understand exclusivism and particularism to be synonymous or that they may find the definition to be a bit too restrictive. Paul Knitter, as an example, seems to define particularism a bit differently when he clarifies his definition to be the idea that "God would offer one way to find truth."[68] Similarly, Gavin D'Costa defines exclusivism as "Christianity's claim that it is the only path."[69] Perry Schmidt-Leukel also appears to have a looser understanding of exclusivism when he defines it as the conviction that "Salvific knowledge of a transcendent reality is mediated by only one religion (which naturally will be one's own.)"[70] These definitions, and definitions like them, appear to leave the door open to certain forms of Christian universalism or inclusivism in that they focus on the idea of "one way" as opposed to the requirement of an explicit faith in Christ that is exercised in this life. For the purposes of this study we shall maintain a

---

Sons, 1957), 95–96. Wilfred Cantwell Smith commented: "Exclusivism strikes more and more Christians as immoral. If the head proves it true, while the heart sees it as wicked, un–Christian, then should Christians not follow the heart? Maybe this is the crux of our dilemma." Wilfred Cantwell Smith, "An Attempt at Summation," in G.H. Stransky and T.F. Stransky, eds., *Christ's Lordship and Religious Pluralism* (Maryknoll, N.Y.: Orbis, 1981), 202. For an extended defense of exclusivism against these charges and others see the following: Millard J. Erickson, *How Shall They Be Saved? The Destiny of Those Who Do Not Hear of Jesus* (Grand Rapids, Mich.: Baker, 1996); Ronald H. Nash, *Is Jesus the Only Savior?*; R.C. Sproul, *Reason to Believe* (Grand Rapids, Mich.: Zondervan, 1978); and Brad Stetson's *Pluralism and Particularity in Religious Belief* (Westport, Conn.: Praeger Publishers, 1994), which is essentially a book–length defense of the doctrine. Philosopher William Lane Craig offers a unique defense of exclusivism using the concept of middle knowledge as put forward by Catholic theologian Louis Molina. See his article "No Other Name: A Middle Knowledge Perspective on the Exclusivity of Salvation Through Christ," *FP* 6/2 (April 1989): 172–88.

[67] John Calvin, *Institutes of the Christian Religion*, trans. Henry Beveridge (1845; repr., Grand Rapids, Mich.: Eerdmans, 1995), 2:6:1.

[68] Knitter, *Introducing Theologies of Religions*, 30.

[69] Gavin D'Costa, *Theology of Religious Pluralism: The Challenge of Other Religions* (Oxford: Basil Blackwell, 1986), 22.

[70] Perry Schmidt–Leukel, "Exclusivism, Inclusivism, Pluralism: The Tripolar Typology Clarified and Reaffirmed," in Paul F. Knitter, ed., *The Myth of Religious Superiority: Multifaith Explorations of Religious Pluralism* (Maryknoll, N.Y.: Orbis, 2005), 19.

more restrictive definition of exclusivism that focuses on specific salvific limitations as opposed to other more generalized Christocentric ideas. In this study exclusivism, particularism, and restrictivism will be used synonymously to speak of the idea that salvation can only be obtained through an explicit faith that is placed in Jesus Christ.

Exclusivism has been the hallmark theme of Christian theology down through the centuries and has been the driving force behind local evangelism and world missions. The dominance of the exclusivist viewpoint is certainly understandable given the fact that its roots are firmly planted in the kerygma of the New Testament and the confession of the early church. Indeed, the writings of the Apostles are rife with declarations of exclusivism and the uniqueness of salvation through Jesus Christ.[71]

3.5. Inclusivism

Christian inclusivism is a moderating position that challenges exclusivist claims. Inclusivism affirms that, although salvation is ontologically based upon the person and work of Jesus Christ, it does not necessarily mean that a person must hear the gospel and express an explicit faith in Christ in order to be saved. Clark Pinnock, a leading evangelical exponent of inclusivism, puts forward his definition in this way: "By 'inclusivism' I refer to the view upholding Christ as the Savior of humanity but also affirming God's saving presence in the wider world and in other religions."[72]

The essential argument of the inclusivist is that if a person seeks by faith for whatever "light" that God has given them, then they will be received by God on the basis of that faith and the blood of Christ will be applied to them regardless of the fact that they did not cognitively know who Jesus Christ was. The "faith principle" is central to the inclusivist thesis. Pinnock elaborates:

---

[71] Copious allusions to exclusivity, both direct and indirect, are found throughout the text of the New Testament. What follows is a brief sampling that is by no means all inclusive but sufficient to show just how pervasive statements of exclusivism are in the New Testament: Matt. 1:21, 7:21–27, 16:13–20, 16:24–28, 24:27–31, 25:31–46, 26:26–29, 26:36–44, 26:62–64, 28:18–20; Mark 1:14–15, 2:8–12, 2:17, 3:22–30,4:1–20, 8:34–38, 9:36–37, 10:45, 13:24–27, 14:22–25, 14:32–39, 14:60–64, 16:15–16; Luke 2:8–14, 2:29–32, 2:38, 3:6, 3:15–17, 4:16–28, 4:42–44, 5:17–26, 5:31, 6:46–49, 7:40–50, 8:4–15, 8:18, 9:23–26, 10:22, 11:15–23, 12:8, 13:22–30, 19:11–27, 20:9–18, 21:34–36, 22:19–20, 22:66–71, 23:39–43, 24:46–48; John 1:1–4, 1:10–13, 1:29–34, 3:14–21; 3:35–36, 4:14, 5:22–30, 6:26–27, 6:29, 6:32–33, 6:35–40, 6:43–58, 6:68, 8:12, 8:24, 8:34–36, 8:51, 10:7–10, 10:15, 10:27–30, 11:25–26, 12:32, 12:44–50, 14:6, 15:1–11, 17:1–3, 18:37, 20:29, 20:30–31; Acts 3:25–26, 4:12, 5:29–32; 10:42–43, 13:38–39, 16:30–33, 19:4; Rom. 1:16–17, 3:21–26, 4:23–35, 5:1, 5:6–11, 5:18–21, 6:23, 8:1 8:28–30, 10:9–13, 10:14–17, 11:25–27, 14:9–13, 15:7–12; 1 Cor. 1:18–31, 3:1, 11:13, 15:1–8, 15:12–19, 15:50–58, 16:22; 2 Cor. 4:3–7, 5:12–21, 10:4–6, Gal. 1:6–10, 3:8–9, 3:13–14, 3:22–25, ; Eph. 1:7–13, 1:15–23, 2:1–22, 3:1–13, 5:5–7; Phil. 2:5–11; Col. 1:9–23, 2:8–9, 3:11; 1 Thes. 1:9–10, 5:1–11; 1 Tim. 1:15–16, 2:5–6; Tit. 2:11–15; Heb. 1:1–4, 2:1–4, 7:25, 12:25; 1 Pet. 1:20–21, 2:9–10, 3:18; 2 Peter 1:16–21, 3:8–9; 1 John 2:1–2, 2:22–23, 3:4–6, 5:9–13; 2 John 9–11; Rev. 1:5–6, 5:9–10, 6:14–17, 7:9–10, 20:11–15, 21:6–8.
[72] Pinnock, *A Wideness in God's Mercy: The Finality of Jesus Christ in a World of Religions*, 15.

In my judgment, the faith principle is the basis of universal accessibility. According to the Bible, people are saved by faith, not by the content of their theology. Since God has not left anyone without witness, people are judged on the basis of the light they have received and how they have responded to that light. Faith in God is what saves, not possessing certain minimum information.[73]

The inclusivist position opens up a broad range of possibilities for salvation while at the same time affirming the centrality of Christ in the final outcome. In Pinnock's case, that range of possibilities can include participation in other religions as well as the simple desire of an individual to know God.[74] In all cases, seeking the divine by faith is the active ingredient that results in salvation.

Inclusivism is currently the official position of the Catholic Church and has been codified into the Vatican II documents.[75] The Dogmatic Constitution of the Church, *Lumen gentium*, promulgated on November 21, 1964, offers this affirmation of inclusivism:

> There are others who search for the unknown God in shadows and images; God is not far from people of this kind since he gives to all life and breath and everything (See Ac 17, 25–28), and the Saviour wishes all to be saved (See 1 Tm 2, 4). There are those who without any fault do not know anything about Christ or his church, yet who search for God with a sincere heart and, under the influence of grace, try to put into effect the will of God as known to them through the dictate of conscience: these too can obtain eternal salvation. Nor does divine Providence deny the helps that are necessary for salvation to those who, through no fault of their own, have not yet attained to the express recognition of God yet who strive, not without divine grace, to lead an upright life.[76]

In keeping with other definitions of inclusivism, the Catholic Church affirms that the key to salvation is faith—those "who search for God with a sincere heart."

In the Declaration of the Church to Non-Christian Religions, *Nostra aetate*, promulgated on October 28, 1965, the church added further support for inclusivism by affirming its respect for non-Christian religions as sources of truth: "The Catholic Church rejects nothing of those things which are true and

---

[73] Pinnock, *A Wideness in God's Mercy*, 157. So also Sanders, *No Other Name*, 62–68. For a critique of this view see Erickson, *How Shall They Be Saved?*, 82–89; Ramesh P. Richard, *The Population of Heaven: A Biblical Response to the Inclusivist Position on Who Will Be Saved* (Chicago: Moody, 1994), 64–65; and Daniel Strange, *The Possibility of Salvation Among the Unevangelized: An Analysis of Inclusivism in Recent Evangelical Theology* (Carlisle, U.K.: Paternoster, 2001), 108–36; 139–98.

[74] Pinnock, *A Wideness in God's Mercy*, 92–113.

[75] The Vatican II documents are available online on the Vatican website. They may be accessed by pointing your web browser to: http://www.vatican.va/archive/hist_councils/ ii_vatican_council/index.htm. (Accessed on October 2, 2014.)

[76] *DEC Lumen gentium*, §16

holy in these religions. It regards with respect those ways of acting and living and those precepts and teachings which, though often at variance with what it holds and expounds, frequently reflect a ray of that truth which enlightens everyone."[77] The Declaration goes on to encourage all Catholics to dialogue and collaborate with the followers of other religions in an effort to "recognize, preserve and promote those spiritual and moral good things as well as the socio-cultural values which are to be found among them."[78] It should be noted that there are some significant differences between the inclusivism advocated by the Catholic Church and that of evangelicals such as Pinnock. In particular, the former is merely open to the possibility of the salvation of other people in other religions whereas the latter makes the salvation of other people in other religions a doctrinal tenet.

3.6. Pluralism
In an essay entitled "Religious Pluralism" Ian Hamnett noted the difficulty of defining the phrase as well as the ambiguity that has resulted from its irregular usage. He observed:

> There are indeed two senses in which the term "religious pluralism" is imprecise. One kind of imprecision arises from the uncertain definition of the empirical situation to which it refers . . . . A subtler kind of imprecision (or perhaps "ambiguity" would be a better word) in the notion of religious pluralism arises from the fact that the term can refer either to a state of affairs as we have just seen (namely the coexistence of two or more religious systems within one society or culture), or to an ideological posture, commonly associated with a "liberal", syncretistic, and relativist approach to religious belief as such. In the first sense, only a society or culture or state can be described as "plural". In the ideological sense, however, it is possible to describe an individual, or a school, or a theology, or a tradition of thought and practice, as manifesting "religious pluralism". This is usually intended to mean a posture or perspective where differences of religious belief and practice are treated as legitimate, and where as a rule "exclusivist" (cf. D'Costa) claims are not advanced on the behalf of one particular system at the expense of the others.[79]

In this study, our definition of religious pluralism will focus on the ideological aspect of the phrase as noted by Hamnett. While the phrase "religious pluralism" has been used in many ways by many people, we will attempt to define it in such a way as it clearly delineates an ideological perspective that stands in stark contrast to that of exclusivism.

Contemporary religious pluralism is the direct descendent of several significant historical developments. Perez Zagorin in his book *How the Idea of Religious Toleration Came to the West* traces the foundation of modern

---

[77] *DEC Nostra aetate*, §2.
[78] *DEC Nostra aetate*, §2.
[79] Ian Hamnett, "Religious Pluralism," in Ian Hamnett, ed., *Religious Pluralism & Unbelief: Studies Critical and Comparative* (London: Routledge, 1990), 6–7.

religious pluralism to the humanist movement that developed during the Renaissance.[80] Renaissance humanism was in large part engaged with the rediscovery of classical writers and thinkers as well as the recovery of the more humane aspects of New Testament theology and the teachings of Christ. This focus led naturally into a bias away from the more strident forms of Christian religious intolerance that had characterized church teaching for many centuries. In its place emerged a new appreciation and toleration for ideas and philosophies that were located outside the Christian sphere. With the advent of the Protestant Reformation and the movement of the intellectual world into the Age of Reason, the egalitarian elements found within Renaissance humanism flowered into an Enlightenment pluralism that called for an equal and fair treatment of all religious points of view.[81] This Enlightenment pluralism became the foundational element that still lies at the heart of most forms of contemporary religious pluralism.

Although contemporary pluralism is the direct descendent of Enlightenment egalitarian thought, recent proponents have given it a decidedly postmodern twist that combines Enlightenment egalitarianism with a postmodernist view of the world that denies transcendent categories such as absolute truth, absolute morality, and absolute ethics.[82] In explaining postmodernism Anthony Thiselton in his book *Interpreting God and the Postmodern Self* notes: "The postmodern self follows Nietzsche and Freud in viewing claims to truth largely as devices which serve to legitimate power-interests. *Disguise covers everything. Hence a culture of distrust and suspicion emerges.*"[83] For the postmodernist truth is something that is produced by a culture rather than discovered by it. Thus truth is viewed as context sensitive and relative: "In the perceptions of the postmodern self, everything addresses issues only within the localized context, and may seem to count as meaningful or truthful *only in relation to the goals and projects already established within this pre-given social context.*"[84]

---

[80] Perez Zagorin, *How the Idea of Religious Toleration Came to the West* (Princeton, N.J.: Princeton University Press, 2003), 47–49.

[81] The First Amendment to the Constitution of the United States enshrined the Enlightenment concept of religious pluralism into law: "Congress shall make no laws respecting an establishment of religion, or prohibiting the free exercise thereof . . ." A discussion of Enlightenment thought and its impact upon theology may be found in Colin Brown, *Christianity and Western Thought: A History of Philosophers, Ideas, and Movements, From the Ancient World to the Age of the Enlightenment*, vol. 1 (Downers Grove, Ill.: InterVarsity, 1990), 173–330.

[82] The connection between religious pluralism and postmodernism is not often made but one that I believe is critical to gaining a deeper understanding of the far reaching issues at hand. Without understanding the connection one is reduced to describing the phenomenon of pluralism without understanding its true source. A scholar who has made such a connection and thoughtfully explored it is Brad Stetson in his book *Pluralism and Particularity*, cf. 87–114.

[83] Anthony C. Thiselton, *Interpreting God and the Postmodern Self: On Meaning, Manipulation, and Promise* (Grand Rapids, Mich.: Eerdmans, 1995), 12 (italics in the original).

[84] Thiselton, *Interpreting God and the Postmodern Self*, 33 (italics in the original). An alternate way of understanding this phenomenon is offered by Jean–François Lyotard

The relativism that the postmodern position engenders has become an essential element of the movement toward pluralism in general and, along with Enlightenment egalitarianism, has become a vital principle upon which most contemporary religious pluralism is based.[85] Robert Wilken observed: "[B]ehind the term "religious pluralism" lurks not so much a question as an answer, the view that particular traditions cannot be the source of ultimate truth."[86] Dennis Okholm and Timothy Phillips offer a good working definition of contemporary religious pluralism that captures well the relativism that is central to it:

> Pluralism, or more accurately, normative religious pluralism, maintains that the major world religions provide independent salvific access to the divine Reality. The contemporary case for pluralism is argued on several grounds: (1) ethically, as the only way to promote justice in our intolerant and oppressive world; (2) in terms of the ineffability of religious experience, so that no religion can claim an absolute stance; and (3) through the historicist thesis that varying cultural and historical contexts preclude absolutist religious claims.[87]

According to this definition, the essential contention made by contemporary religious pluralism is that independent access to salvation is provided through many different religions or spiritual paths.[88] Given the context sensitive nature of truth within pluralist thought, it makes perfect sense that the soteriological equality of religions must be affirmed. Thus religious pluralism is also a powerful endorsement of theological egalitarianism as well as theological relativism. In this view, all religions are placed on more or less equal footing and no religion has access to absolute, objective truth. Along these lines it must be noted that many religious pluralists reject any effort made toward syncretism or the creation of a one world religion as well as any movement made in the

---

who argues that a key feature of postmodernism is "incredulity towards metanarratives." See Jean–François Lyotard, *The Postmodern Condition: A Report on Knowledge*, trans. Geoff Bennington and Brian Massumi (Minneapolis, Minn.: University of Minnesota Press, 1984), xxiv.

[85] In his book, *No Other Name? A Critical Survey of Christian Attitudes Toward the World Religions*, Paul Knitter has contributed an interesting and valuable discussion of religious pluralism and relativism from the perspective of a confirmed pluralist. See Paul Knitter, *No Other Name? A Critical Survey of Christian Attitudes Toward the World Religions* (Maryknoll, N.Y.: Orbis, 1985), 23–36.

[86] Robert Wilken, *Remembering the Christian Past* (Grand Rapids, Mich.: Eerdmans, 1995), 26.

[87] Dennis L. Okholm and Timothy R. Phillips, eds., *Four Views on Salvation in a Pluralistic World* (Grand Rapids, Mich.: Zondervan, 1995), 17.

[88] John Hick explains his own pluralism along similar lines: "There is not merely one way but a plurality of ways of salvation or liberation . . . taking place within the contexts of all the great religious traditions" (John Hick, *Problems of Religious Pluralism* [New York: St. Martin's Press, 1985], 34). A comprehensive review of the biblical data relating to religious pluralism may be found in Donald A. Carson, *The Gagging of God: Christianity Confronts Pluralism* (Grand Rapids, Mich.: Zondervan, 1996), chapters 5–7.

direction of a single religion that "imperialistically" dominates the others.[89] Instead, the religious pluralist argues that religions stand on their own, within their own socio-cultural contexts, as equally valid attempts to commune with the divine and should be appreciated and celebrated as such.

Two important theological inferences flow out of the pluralist perspective: (1) salvation/deliverance is diversely mediated, and (2) salvation/deliverance is universally accessible. In this view then, Christianity is just one way among many; it is just one option among several. Joseph DiNoia goes so far as to argue that, "In the pluralist perspective, therefore, each religious founder must be regarded as in some sense a savior. Exclusive or unique status, with respect to the knowledge of, provision for, or access to, salvation can no more be claimed for Jesus of Nazareth than it can be claimed for Gautama the Buddha or for Muhammad."[90]

It is important to note for the purpose of our study that embracing religious pluralism does not necessarily make one into a universalist. There are plenty of religious pluralists who do not hold to a doctrine of universal salvation. For them salvation is still something to be strived for and attained no matter what religion one adopts and there is the very real chance of failure. On the other hand, there are those theologians who, like John Hick, argue for universalism from within a specifically pluralistic perspective.[91] It is important that as we discuss recent expressions of universalist thought that we do not make the mistake of automatically equating universalism with religious pluralism. It is quite possible to embrace the one without endorsing the other.

4. Current State of Scholarship
Sustained scholarly treatments of recent theological trends in Christian universalism are rare. Most of the work done in describing this field of study has been limited to unpublished dissertations or to fairly brief and narrowly focused journal articles. Scholarly works that attempt to provide an overview and analysis of the field are noticeably lacking and therefore there is considerable need for contributions to be made in the areas of categorization and systemization.

---

[89] On this point see Knitter's comments regarding "unitive pluralism" in *No Other Name? A Critical Survey of Christian Attitudes Toward the World Religions*, 9. Yale theologian Kathryn Tanner has argued that religious pluralism as commonly conceived has nevertheless succumbed to "colonialist discourse" due to the pluralist quest of searching for "commonalities" among religions (e.g. Smith, Hick, and Knitter) and a penchant for overgeneralization. See Kathryn Taylor, "Respect for other Religions: A Christian Antidote to Colonialist Discourse," *MT* 9 (1993): 1–18.

[90] Joseph A. DiNoia, "Christian Universalism: The Nonexclusive Particularity of Salvation in Christ," in Carl E. Baaten and Robert W. Jensen, eds., *Either/or: The Gospel or Neopaganism* (Grand Rapids, Mich.: Eerdmans, 1995), 38.

[91] "In my view, the cosmic optimism of the great traditions—their proclamation that a limitlessly better existence is available to all because it is rooted in the ultimate structure of reality—strongly suggests that all will in the end, perhaps after many lives in many worlds, attain to it." John Hick, "A Pluralist View," in Dennis L. Okholm and Timothy R. Phillips, eds., *Four Views on Salvation in a Pluralistic World* (Grand Rapids, Mich.: Zondervan, 1995), 45.

The three most significant books to emerge in the last twenty-five years that are dedicated to more broadly examining some recent developments in the field have taken on the form of symposia and thus are amalgams of collected analyses done by multiple authors on a fairly wide band of issues.[92] The first book dates from 1991 and the Fourth Edinburgh Conference in Christian Dogmatics that focused its attention on "Universalism and the Doctrine of Hell." The papers presented at the conference were compiled and edited by Nigel M. de S. Cameron and published under the title *Universalism and the Doctrine of Hell: Papers Presented at the Fourth Edinburgh Conference in Christian Dogmatics, 1991*.[93] This book is fairly general in its approach to the issue of universalism and contains articles that cover a wide range of associated topics. The second book on the subject is a symposium that was edited by Robin A. Parry and Christopher H. Partridge and published in the year 2003 under the title *Universal Salvation? The Current Debate*. This book uses the universalism of Thomas Talbott as a point of departure and disputation. Talbott begins the discussion by systematically setting out his scheme of universal salvation and a sustained defense of it. He is then joined by several scholars who take sides in the debate and use Talbott's universalism as a starting point for their discussion. In the end Talbott is permitted to offer a final rebuttal of his critics. The third and most recent book that attempts to take a broader view of developments in the field is another symposium edited by Robin Parry (under the pseudonym Gregory MacDonald) and given the title *"All Shall Be Well": Explorations in Universal Salvation and Christian Theology from Origen to Moltmann*.[94] This book divides the field into three basic eras: (1) Third to fifteenth centuries; (2) Seventeenth to nineteenth centuries; and (3) Twentieth to twenty-first century. Within each of these divisions essays are contributed that focus on the key proponents of universal salvation from that time frame. While the book leaves out a good number of important advocates of universalism from each era, it is notable for its wide-ranging approach in describing historical developments within universalist thought.

Doctoral work done in an effort to categorize and describe this field of study is also fairly limited. In 1959 Robert A. Byerly submitted a dissertation to Temple University entitled "A Biblical Critique of Universalism in Contemporary Theology." Byerly's operating hypothesis was that within the Bible there are teachings that both support and deny universal salvation. Because of this antithesis in biblical theology Byerly concluded that one cannot formulate a supportable theory of universalism based upon Scripture. His analysis of the subject is fairly complete including both discussions and

---

[92] Many books have been written that focus on soteriology in general, but mention universalism only in passing. A good example of this would be William V. Crockett and James G. Sigountos, eds., *Through No Fault of Their Own? The Fate of Those Who Have Never Heard* (Grand Rapids, Mich.: Baker, 1991).

[93] Nigel M. de S. Cameron, ed., *Universalism and the Doctrine of Hell: Papers Presented at the Fourth Edinburgh Conference in Christian Dogmatics, 1991* (Carlisle, U.K.: Paternoster, 1992).

[94] Gregory MacDonald, ed., *"All Shall Be Well": Explorations in Universal Salvation and Christian Theology from Origen to Moltmann* (Eugene, Ore.: Cascade Books, 2012).

critiques of historical and contemporary universalists. The primary problem with Byerly's study at this point in time is that it has become dated and it does not include significant developments that have occurred over the last fifty years.[95] A dissertation coming from the same era as Byerly's is the one written by Joseph D. Bettis in 1964 entitled, "The Good News and the Salvation of All Men: A Critique of the Doctrine of Universal Salvation."[96] In this dissertation Bettis critiques what he perceives to be an "inadequate description of the goodness of God's love" on the part of the universalists.[97] There are two main problems that standout regarding Bettis' dissertation at this time: (1) It is too narrowly focused, and (2) as with Byerly's, it is dated.

In 1968 Harry Friesen submitted a dissertation to Dallas Theological Seminary entitled "A Critical Analysis of Universalism."[98] Friesen investigates "new universalism" and compares it to various forms of universalism in the past, using the universalism of Origen as a central baseline. He concludes that the "new universalism" is essentially unchanged from the ancient versions. The weakness of Friesen's work is that it is more dogmatic than analytic in nature. The homogenizing temperament of his thesis forces him to shoehorn all universalists into one theological mold. Friesen's work at this point is also dated.

The most current and up to date dissertation that attempts to survey the landscape of contemporary universalism is that of S. Edward Baxter, Jr. who submitted a dissertation entitled "A Historical Study of the Doctrine of Apokatastasis" to Mid-America Baptist Theological Seminary in 1988. In this wide-ranging dissertation, Baxter examines the doctrine of apokatastasis from a historical perspective. He investigates influential persons and groups with two goals in mind: (1) providing a historical overview of the field, and (2) identifying "some of the various motivations which appear among the advocates of universalism."[99] Beginning with the "pre-Origen" period, Baxter moves historically through three clearly delineated eras of development: post-apostolic, Reformation, and twentieth century. The dissertation is notable for its encyclopedic approach to the issue. Problems arise, however, from the brevity with which significant figures are dealt with as well as a lack of critical engagement with the methods and justifications used. There is a disproportionate reliance on secondary sources. The dissertation falls into a "who said what" sort of rhythm with a conclusion that merely summarizes a few of the main theological motivations used. Overall, critical engagement with the advocates of universalism and the issue at hand seems to be lacking. Baxter also fails to link recent universalist proposals to the tremendous social/cultural

---

[95] Robert Allen Byerly, "A Biblical Critique of Universalism in Contemporary Theology" (S.T.D. dissertation, Temple University, 1959).

[96] Joseph D. Bettis, "The Good News and the Salvation of All Men: A Critique of the Doctrine of Universal Salvation" (Ph.D. dissertation, Princeton University, 1964). See also F.R. Bourke, "Universalism" (Ph.D. dissertation, Trinity College, Dublin, 1961).

[97] Bettis, "The Good News and the Salvation of All Men: A Critique of the Doctrine of Universal Salvation," iv.

[98] Harry Friesen, "A Critical Analysis of Universalism" (Th.D. dissertation, Dallas Theological Seminary, 1968).

[99] Baxter, "Apokatastasis," 8.

upheavals that have occurred in the world since the 1960s and to address those linkages.

There are other dissertations that approach the issue of universalism from a more narrow perspective.[100] Notable among these is the Oxford University dissertation of Kendall S. Harmon entitled "Finally Excluded by God? Some Twentieth-Century Theological Explorations of the Problems of Hell and Universalism with Reference to the Historical Development of These Doctrines." In this dissertation Harmon discusses the collision between the traditional doctrine of Hell and "Enlightenment humanitarianism." He argues that it was this collision that renewed interest in the development of universalist doctrines and culminated in modern expressions of the same. However, rather than surveying the recent universalist landscape, Harmon chooses to engage representatives selected from what he believes to be the three key soteriological options available today. These are: (1) universalism, (2) conditionalism, and (3) traditional teaching. Harmon's dissertation is illustrative of much of the scholarship that has been done in this area of study. Although it is excellent in its own right, it is still relatively narrow in its focus. Similarly Morwenna Ludlow has produced another first-rate dissertation entitled "Restoration and Consummation: The Interpretation of Universalistic Eschatology by Gregory of Nyssa and Karl Rahner."[101] Although this dissertation is an exceptional piece of work, it is still quite limited in its scope and focus.

5. The Need and Academic Contribution

The mere passage of time or the lack of on-going scholarship in a particular area is not sufficient to establish the case for proceeding with an extended academic study of a particular issue or problem. In certain instances time affects the subject matter little. In other situations, where a definitive study has already been done, there may not be much of value to add to it. However, this is not the case regarding the subject at hand.

---

[100] For instance see William V. Crockett, "Universalism and the Theology of Paul" (Ph.D. dissertation, University of Glasgow, 1986); Esteban Deák, "Apokatastasis: The Problem of Universal Salvation in Twentieth Century Theology" (Ph.D. dissertation, University of St. Michael's College, Canada, 1977); Ward J. Fellows, "The Dilemma of Universalism and Particularism in Four Christian Theological Views of the Relation of Christianity to Other Religions (Tillich, Rahner, Smith, Hick)" (Ph.D. dissertation, Union Theological Seminary, New York, 1988); Steven R. Harmon, "Apokatastasis and Exegesis: A Comparative Analysis of the Use of Scripture in the Eschatological Universalism of Clement of Alexandria, Origen, and Gregory of Nyssa" (Ph.D. dissertation, Southwestern Baptist Theological Seminary, 1997); Sven Hillert, "Limited and Universal Salvation: A Text Oriented and Hermeneutical Study of Two Perspectives in Paul" (Ph.D. dissertation, Uppsala University, 1999); and Stephen T. Pegler, "The Nature of Paul's Universal Language of Salvation in Romans" (Ph.D. dissertation, Trinity Evangelical Divinity School, 2002).

[101] Morwenna Ludlow, "Restoration and Consummation: The Interpretation of Universalistic Eschatology by Gregory of Nyssa and Karl Rahner" (D.Phil. dissertation, Oxford University, 1996). Published under the title: *Universal Salvation: Eschatology in the Thought of Gregory of Nyssa and Karl Rahner* (Oxford: Oxford University Press, 2000).

As has already been discussed, the passage of time has been a crucial factor in the direction that recent universalist proposals have taken. Recent developments in the world at large have greatly influenced the shape of universalist theology over the last fifty-five years. In addition to this, there have been few extended academic treatments of the subject that attempt to gain an overview of the field and then draw valuable insights about the trajectory of scholarship in this area of study from that unique perspective.

Finally, it is important to keep in mind the abiding significance of the subject matter at hand. The issue of the eternal destiny of humankind is worthy of vigorous ongoing study, research, and debate. In my view, the definitive study in this area is yet to be written. For all of these reasons I believe that the time is ripe for this study to move forward.

6. Organization

The study will be divided into three principal parts. Part 1 will focus on the historical development of the doctrine of universalism. This section will be subdivided into three chapters and it will concentrate primarily on providing a descriptive backdrop against which the contemporary expressions will be compared and contrasted. As the purpose of this section is to be primarily explanatory in nature, detailed critiques of the positions taken historically will be dispensed with. In making this decision, it is assumed that the critiques offered later for the various contemporary proposals will have a retroactive application to similar varieties of universalism found historically. Therefore, it is believed that the contemporary critiques should serve to provide a sufficient basis for the assessment of historical expressions to those who would desire to apply them in that way.

Part 2 of the dissertation will focus on the Protestant contribution to contemporary universalism since 1960. This section will be subdivided into two chapters. Chapter four will concentrate on Christocentric expressions, while chapter five will focus on Plurocentric expressions. The proponents of the various positions will be examined individually and a historical comparison as well as a critical analysis will be offered for each one.

Part 3 of the dissertation will focus on the Catholic contribution to contemporary universalism since 1960. This section will be organized in a similar fashion to Part Two with chapters six and seven dealing with the Christocentric and Plurocentric contributions respectively. In these chapters particular attention will be paid to the impact that the Second Vatican Council has had upon contemporary expressions of universalism within Catholic theology. We shall also take note of recent developments in Catholic doctrine as well as the conflicts that the Catholic discussion has engendered.

Due to constraints on length, it was also decided to leave out a discussion of contemporary universalism within groups that are widely outside the mainstream of Christian thought such as the Unitarian Universalist Church and The Church of Jesus Christ of Latter Day Saints (commonly known as the Mormons). Although groups like these do espouse various forms of universalist eschatology, their current doctrinal positions essentially remove them from the playing field of orthodox Christian theology altogether.

Finally, a brief comment should be made about references. In this dissertation I have chosen to give the fullest references possible in order to aid the research of others. Special attention has been paid to foreign language works that have been translated into English. In these cases an effort has been made to provide the original title and publisher along with the information regarding the English edition. This approach was applied with particular rigor to the primary sources used in the dissertation. It is hoped that this extra information will prove to be helpful to those who follow.

We now move on to an examination of the historical development of the doctrine of universalism. It is a history that is bound up with the efforts of the church to develop an authoritative doctrinal system. It is a history that is bound up with the efforts of the church to provide a practical apologetic to all challengers.

PART 1

HISTORICAL DEVELOPMENT

CHAPTER 1

The Development of the Patristic Apologetic

The long history of the development of universalist thought in Christian theology is both fascinating and instructive.[1] Far from being a monolithic doctrinal system that developed along a single theological trajectory, universalism instead arose in a variety of theological contexts as an answer to a whole host of doctrinal concerns. Issues as diverse as scriptural authority, eternal destiny, predestination and free will, the nature of God's love and justice, and the need to provide answers to non-Christian critics have all elicited universalist responses. Thus it is important to understand that universalism in general cannot be oversimplified or forced into a single theological straightjacket. While it is true that universal salvation is the common theme among universalists, it is also true that there is often a world of difference in how that conclusion is arrived at. In this section we shall seek to gain an in-depth understanding of the historical development of universalist thought within Christianity and the theological methodology and pressures that guided its formation. This analysis will serve to lay the ground floor for what will

---

[1] Several scholars have taken in hand the task of writing a history of Christian universalism. Pride of place must go to Ilaria L. E. Ramelli's work, *The Christian Doctrine of Apokatastasis: A Critical Assessment from the New Testament to Eriugena*, which we have already encountered in the Introduction. Ramelli spent 15 years researching this book and at this point it offers the most detailed analysis of the patristic development of the doctrine. Perhaps the most cited work in the post 60's era has been the brief, yet fact laden article of Richard J. Bauckham entitled "Universalism: A Historical Survey," *Themelios* 4/2 (January, 1979): 48–53. Other surveys include the dissertations of Baxter, Byerly, and Friesen as well the following: Beougher, "Are All Doomed to be Saved? The Rise of Modern Universalism," 6–24; Deák "Apokatastasis: The Problem of Universal Salvation in Twentieth Century Theology", 1–19; Alan M. Fairhurst, "Death and Destiny," *Chm* 95/4 (1981): 313–325; Ajith Fernando, *A Universal Homecoming? An Examination of the Case for Universalism* (Madras, India: Evangelical Literature Service, 1983), 9–17; David Hilborn and Don Horrocks, "Universalistic Trends in the Evangelical Tradition: An Historical Perspective," in Parry and Partridge, *Universal Salvation? The Current Debate*, 219–244; Ludlow, "Universalism in the History of Christianity," 191–218; Thomas Talbott, *The Inescapable Love of God* (U.S.A.: Universal Publishers/uPUBLISH.com, 1999), 1–39.

Of some limited value are the more dated and subjective works of universalist apologists who sought to prove the historical credibility of universalism as well as the orthodoxy of its post-Reformation resurgence. See Hosea Ballou, *The Ancient History of Universalism from the Time of the Apostles to its Condemnation in the Fifth General Council, A.D. 553 with an Appendix Tracing the Doctrine Down to The Reformation* (Providence, R.I.: Z. Baker, 1842); J.W. Hanson, *Universalism: The Prevailing Doctrine of the Christian Church During Its First Five-Hundred Years* (Boston: Universalist Publishing House, 1899); Thomas Whittemore, *The History of Modern Universalism from the Era of The Reformation to the Present Time* (Boston: Power Press, 1830).

follow in the study and help us to place more recent universalist proposals into the overall context of the historical development of the doctrine.

What stands out in this survey is the marked degree to which external pressures influenced universalist conclusions from the very beginning. Far from being a forgone theological conclusion based solely upon scriptural evidence, universalism developed in the crucible of both theological and religious conflict. The birth of Christianity and its expansion into the Greco-Roman empire put two incongruent worlds on a collision course. The resulting impact had a larger influence upon the development of universalism than has been commonly recognized.

The post-Apostolic history of universalism is difficult to reconstruct due to the paucity of verifiable firsthand references. Decay and the long march of time have conspired to winnow our sources and to obscure the ones that have come down to us. Where later sources are used to reconstruct earlier ones, such as the gnostic writings for instance, there are always questions to be raised concerning the accuracy of the estimated date and the precision of the redaction. Therefore drawing an accurate picture of the development of early post-Apostolic universalism is a difficult task and should proceed with the caveat that all conclusions are necessarily tentative and can be subject to rapid change as better quality sources become available.

Without question Origen was the most prominent proponent of universalism in this era and his unique theological system continues to define the debate and influence theologians to this day. In recognition of Origen's exceptional contribution to the field we shall divide this chapter into three parts: Pre-Origen, Origen, and Post-Origen.

1. The Pre-Origen Era
The pre-Origen era in the evolution of universalist thought can be best categorized as a time of undisciplined speculation. By undisciplined it is meant that theology in this era lacked the formal development and argumentation that would come later as various theological and catechetical schools gradually found their way into existence. By speculation it is meant that the presentation of universalist themes in this era are typically disjointed and not based upon a fully developed theology or exegesis of scripture. In most cases universalist ideas in this period are presented without any reference to the Bible and are frequently associated with ecstatic visions and dreams. In some cases these visions expand upon the canonical text or use the canonical text as a point of departure. Often the visions or dialogues are presented as being of equal value to any other New Testament witness or revelation.

1.1. Posthumous Deliverance of the Dead
Jeffery Trumbower, in an important monograph entitled *Rescue for the Dead: The Posthumous Salvation of Non-Christians in Early Christianity*, puts forward a compelling argument for the idea that early Christian concern for the posthumous deliverance of the unsaved "grew out of ancient concern for the welfare of the dead" that was manifested in Greek, Roman, and Jewish

antiquity.[2] Trumbower presents several pieces of evidence in support of his thesis. The first has to do with Hellenistic/Roman burial practices during the first through third centuries C.E. At this time providing food and succor for the dead was a common practice that reinforced the idea that the lot of the dead could be changed or improved.[3] Often graves were equipped with pipes that connected to the burial chamber for this purpose (so-called "pipe burials"). Some gravestone epitaphs from the era also reflected the belief that actions of the living could affect the dead either negatively or positively. A second century epitaph from Egypt expresses a typical prayer for the dead: "You underworld divinities who dwell by the plain of Lethe, welcome Epichares and be kind to him."[4] The provision of grave goods such as coins that were supposed to be used by the dead to pay the ferryman Charon for the journey across the river Styx into Hades also testify of a desire on the part of the living to help the dead reach a level of eternal bliss.[5]

In addition to these details there is strong evidence that during the inter-testamental period certain Jewish thinkers embraced the idea of postmortem deliverance. For instance, 2 Maccabees 12:43b–45 discusses the provision of a postmortem atonement and salvation.[6] Moreover, the idea of the righteous interceding for the less righteous is a common theme found in the rabbinic literature, which eventually developed into the theory that Gehinnom was a place of temporary punishment for a maximum period of twelve months.[7] Based upon a comparison of this evidence with Christian writings and practice regarding posthumous salvation, Trumbower concludes that early Christian thought regarding the posthumous deliverance of the dead was greatly influenced by the special religious context of the first-century Roman Empire.

---

[2] Jeffrey A. Trumbower, *Rescue for the Dead: The Posthumous Salvation of Non-Christians in Early Christianity* (Oxford: Oxford University Press, 2001), 10.

[3] Joycelyn C. M. Toynbee and John Ward Perkins, *Death and Burial in the Roman World* (Baltimore, Md.: Johns Hopkins University Press, 1996), 62; Trumbower, *Rescue for the Dead*, 12–14; 16–19

[4] *Supplementum Epigraphicum Graecum* (Amsterdam: J.C. Gieben, 1923), 8:799; Trumbower, *Rescue for the Dead*, 15.

[5] Ian Morris, *Death-Ritual and Social Structure in Classical Antiquity* (Cambridge: Cambridge University Press, 1992), 106; Trumbower, *Rescue for the Dead*, 13.

[6] The actions of Judas Maccabeus on behalf of slain Jews caught in the sin of idolatry are described in this way: "He also took up a collection, man by man, to the amount of two thousand drachmas of silver, and sent it to Jerusalem to provide for a sin offering. In doing this he acted very well and honorably, taking account of the resurrection. For if he were not expecting that those who had fallen would rise again, it would have been superfluous and foolish to pray for the dead. But if he was looking to the splendid reward that is laid up for those who fall asleep in godliness, it was a holy and pious thought. Therefore he made atonement for the dead, that they might be delivered from their sin." (RSVA)

[7] The comments made in *Pesikta Rabbati* 53:2 are particularly striking: "After going down to Gehenna and receiving the punishment due him, the sinner is forgiven all his iniquities, and like an arrow from the bow he is flung forth from Gehenna." Trumbower, *Rescue for the Dead*, 31.

1.2. Four Ancient Texts

With this background in mind we turn our attention to four important Christian texts from the pre-Origen era: (1) the *Apocalypse of Peter* 14:1–4, (2) *Sibylline Oracles* 2:194–338, (3) *The Acts of Paul and Thecla*, and (4) the *Passion of Perpetua and Felicitas*. These texts give us a unique glimpse into the early development of the notion of postmortem deliverance in early Christian thought. This concept would later become a central element in several varieties of universalism. While it is acknowledged that this idea is not yet a fully developed doctrine of universalism, theologically speaking it represents a sort of halfway house or bridge between universalism and orthodoxy.

The Apocalypse of Peter. The *Apocalypse of Peter* is essentially a detailed description of the punishments that will be inflicted upon the lost as they reside in hell. The document uses the Olivet Discourse of Christ (cf. Matthew 24 and 25; Mark 13; Luke 21) as a point of departure and has Jesus delivering to his disciples lengthy descriptions of the special sufferings that will be used to punish those who engaged in various kinds of sin in their lives on earth. For each category of sin there is a unique form of punishment.

The verses in question, *Apoc. Pet.* 14:1–4, exist in Ethiopic and a number of Greek fragments, the most important of which resides in the Rainer collection in Vienna.[8] It is important that this version of the *Apocalypse of Peter* not be confused with the Nag Hammadi text that carries the same name.[9] The context in which the passage in question occurs is at the end of the description of punishments. At this point in the Greek text[10] the righteous are granted the power to save some of the lost from the horrors of eternal damnation. The verses read:

> I will give to my called and my elect whoever they request of me from out of punishment. And I will give them a beautiful baptism in salvation from

---

[8] The definitive study on this version of the *Apocalypse of Peter* may be found in the 1984 Ph.D. dissertation of Dennis D. Buchholz, which was supervised by James M. Robinson at the Claremont Graduate School. See Dennis D. Buchholz, *Your Eyes Will Be Opened: A Study of the Greek (Ethiopic) Apocalypse of Peter* (Atlanta, Ga.: Scholar's Press, 1988). See also Richard J. Bauckham's discussion of the provenance of the *Apocalypse of Peter* in "Jews and Jewish Christians in the Land of Israel at the Time of the Bar Kochba War, with Special Reference to the *Apocalypse of Peter*," in Graham N. Stanton and G.G. Stroumsa, eds., *Tolerance and Intolerance in Early Judaism and Christianity* (Cambridge: Cambridge University Press, 1998), 228–38. Trumbower also provides a brief discussion of the text. See *Rescue for the Dead*, 49–52.

[9] Cf. James M. Robinson, ed., *The Nag Hammadi Library in English*, 3rd revised edition (San Francisco: HarperSanFrancisco, 1978; 1988), 372–78.

[10] The Ethiopic version has been sanitized in order to expunge any indication that the wicked might be posthumously saved. Both Buchholz and James agree that the Greek text is the more accurate version. See Buchholz, *Your Eyes*, 344–51; M.R. James, "The Rainer Fragment of the Apocalypse of Peter," *JTS* 32 (1931): 270–79.

the Acherousian Lake which is said to be in the Elysian Field,[11] a share in righteousness with my saints.[12]

Buchholz argues that the doctrine found in this passage represents universal salvation based upon the idea that "no saved person could be happy as long as any are being punished."[13] However, Trumbower effectively counters this premise by citing statements made to the contrary elsewhere in the *Apocalypse of Peter*.[14] In light of the fact that no overt endorsement of universalism is made in the text, the most that can be said about the passage is that it opens up the possibility of a universalist outcome. Certainly no limit is placed upon those who can be chosen by the elect so that a universalist outcome is at least conceivable. The important point to bear in mind regarding the passage is that it expresses a concept of postmortem salvation that will become an essential element found in many universalist proposals down through history.

The Sibylline Oracles. A companion passage to *Apoc. Pet.* 14:1–4 is found in the *Sibylline Oracles* 2:194–338. Trumbower classifies it as a poetic paraphrase of the *Apocalypse of Peter* and given this connection identifies it as a Christian text.[15] *Sib. Or.* 2:330–38 reads:

To these pious ones imperishable God, the universal ruler, will also give another thing. Whenever they ask the imperishable God to save men from the raging fire and deathless gnashing he will grant it, and he will do this. For he will pick them out again from the undying fire and set them elsewhere and send them on account of his own people to another eternal life with the immortals in the Elysian plain where he has the long waves of the deep perennial Acherusian lake.[16]

The parallels with *Apoc. Pet.* 14:1–4 are particularly striking: (1) the request is made by the righteous to God for the deliverance of certain lost souls, (2) the salvation granted is to those who are experiencing postmortem punishment, (3) the Elysian plain along with the Acherusian Lake are mentioned as the final destination of the saved. In light of these points of contact there can be little doubt that the two texts are closely related. As the product of a Christian

---

[11] The Elysian fields are also known as the "Isles of Blest." The allusion comes out of Greek mythology and is particularly important in Homer's works. See Homer's *Odyssey*, 4:561–69.

[12] Buchholz, *Your Eyes*, 228.

[13] Buchholz, *Your Eyes*, 348.

[14] Trumbower, *Rescue for the Dead*, 51.

[15] Trumbower, *Rescue for the Dead*, 51–52. See also the comments of M.R. James in "New Text of the Apocalypse," *JTS* 12 (1910): 53.

[16] The translation is that of John J. Colins in James H. Charlesworth, ed., *The Old Testament Pseudepigrapha*, vol. 1, *Apocalyptic Literature and Testaments* (Garden City, N.Y.: Doubleday, 1983–1985), 353. An alternate translation may be found in Milton S. Terry, *The Sibylline Oracles Translated from the Greek into English Blank Verse* (New York: Hunt & Eaton, 1890), 66–67. It should be noted that Terry's verse numbers do not correspond to those of Colins. Terry numbers these verses as 2:397–403.

community cross-pollinated with Jewish and Greco/Roman thought these two texts give us a window into the development of early universalist streams of reflection in ancient Christianity. Although a fully developed universalism is not on display here, there is at least a strong affinity exhibited.

The Acts of Paul and Thecla and the ***Passion of Perpetua and Felicitas.*** Two other early Christian texts that are important to our study on this point may be classified as prayers for the posthumous deliverance of the dead. The first prayer is found in *The Acts of Paul and Thecla.*[17] The second prayer is found in the *Passion of Perpetua and Felicitas.*[18]

Trumbower dates *The Acts of Paul and Thecla* at mid-second century C.E. although A. Hilhorst has argued that an earlier date is possible.[19] *The Acts of Paul and Thecla* is a fictional work in which the heroine Thecla is condemned to a martyr's death in a beast filled arena. Before she is taken to the arena Thecla prays for the posthumous salvation of Falconilla who is the deceased daughter of a woman named Tryphaena. Tryphaena is a pagan whom Thecla recently befriended. Tryphaena had a dream in which her daughter Falconilla came to her from the grave and made this request: "Mother, thou shalt have in my place the stranger, the desolate Thecla, that she may pray for me and I be translated to the place of the just."[20] At Tryphaena's request Thecla offers up this prayer: "Thou God of heaven, Son of the Most High, grant to her according to her wish, that her daughter Falconilla may live forever!"[21] The confirmation of the effectiveness of Thecla's prayer comes after Tryphaena witnesses Thecla's miraculous delivery from the lions in the arena. She and her family convert to Christianity and she declares: "Now I believe that the dead are raised

---

[17] The Greek text may be found in Richard A. Lipsius and Maximilian Bonnet, eds., *Acta Apostolorum Apocrypha* (Leipzig: Hermann Mendelssohn, 1891–1903; repr., Darmstadt: Wissenschaftliche Buchgesellschaft, 1959), 235–72. A complete English translation may be found in the following: Wilhelm Schneemelcher, ed., *New Testament Apocrypha*, 2 vols. (Philadelphia: Westminster, 1964), 2:322–90; James Orr, ed., *New Testament Apocryphal Writings* (London: J. M. Dent & Co., 1903), 78–98.

[18] The Latin and Greek texts may be found in J. Armitage Robinson, *Texts and Studies: Contributions to Biblical and Patristic Literature*, vol. 1 (Cambridge: Cambridge University Press, 1891), 59–103. A recent English translation may be found in Herbert Musurillo, trans., *The Acts of the Christian Martyrs* (Oxford: Clarendon Press, 1972), 115–17. See also Walter Shewring, *The Passion of SS. Perpetua and Felicity, MM: A New Edition and Translation of the Latin Text, Together with the Sermons of St. Augustine upon These Saints, Now First Translated into English* (London: Sheed & Ward, 1931).

[19] Trumbower, *Rescue for the Dead*, 58; A. Hilhorst, "Tertullian on the Acts of Paul," in Jan M. Bemmer, ed., *The Apocryphal Acts of Paul and Thecla* (Kampen: Kok Pharos, 1996), 158–61.

[20] Schneemelcher, *New Testament Apocrypha*, 2:361; Orr, *New Testament Apocryphal Writings*, 89.

[21] Schneemelcher, *New Testament Apocrypha*, 2:361; Orr, *New Testament Apocryphal Writings*, 89.

up! Now I believe that my child lives!"[22] Through these events the idea that the posthumous fate of the unsaved might be changed is affirmed.

The prayer found in the *Passion of Perpetua and Felicitas* is similar in nature to that found in *The Acts of Paul and Thecla* in that it is aimed at improving the lot of the non-Christian dead although explicit salvation is not in view in the text. Dated to the third century C.E. the text purports to contain, among other things, the firsthand diary of a woman named Perpetua in which she recorded her thoughts and experiences while she was in prison.[23] We are told that Perpetua's younger brother, Dinocrates, had died from a facial tumor two years earlier at the age of seven. Perpetua had a vision of the boy in a dark place. He was alive but he was also dirty, thirsty, and still in torment from the wound left by the deadly tumor on his face. She relates: "Then I woke realizing that my brother was suffering. But I was confident I could help him in his trouble; and I prayed for him every day until we were transferred to the military prison."[24] After praying night and day for her brother for an extended period of time, Perpetua received another vision in which his healing and well-being were confirmed. She concludes: "I awoke and realized that he had been delivered from his suffering [poena]."[25]

Trumbower argues that Perpetua understood the "poena" from which Dinocrates suffered as being the penalty for not being a Christian and that she believed her prayers to actually have a salvific effect.[26] This inference seems to be a reasonable one to draw from the text. After all, Perpetua's final vision was one of bliss in which Dinocrates was delivered from the dark world of the first vision and placed into a world of healing and plenty: His clothes were clean; there was plenty of water to drink from a golden bowl; the deadly wound had become just a scar. In the ultimate sign of childhood happiness and well being Perpetua even saw Dinocrates begin to play "as children do" [ludere more infantium gaudens].[27]

The prayer passages found in *The Acts of Paul and Thecla* and the *Passion of Perpetua and Felicitas* are a reflection of a larger phenomenon that occurred in the ancient Christian church. Along with *Apocalypse of Peter* and the *Sibylline Oracles* these writings reveal that there was indeed a belief on the part of some in the ancient church that at least a limited number of the dead could be posthumously delivered from suffering and even eternal condemnation. This is significant in that it mirrors beliefs that were commonly held in the Greco-Roman world at the time. The degree to which these beliefs influenced these ecstatic visions cannot be ascertained, but that there must have been some cross-pollination, even at a subconscious level, there can be no doubt. These

---

[22] Schneemelcher, *New Testament Apocrypha* , 2:363; Orr, *New Testament Apocryphal Writings*, 93.

[23] Trumbower, *Rescue for the Dead*, 6; 80–81.

[24] Musurillo, *The Acts of the Christian Martyrs*, 16; Robinson, *Texts and Studies*, 72.

[25] Musurillo, *The Acts of the Christian Martyrs*, 17; Robinson, *Texts and Studies*, 74.

[26] Trumbower, *Rescue for the Dead*, 84.

[27] Robinson, *Texts and Studies*, 74. See the discussion of Joyce Salisbury relating the vision of Dinocrates to "pagan dream wisdom" in Joyce E. Salisbury, *Perpetua's Passion: The Death and Memory of a Young Roman Woman* (New York: Routledge, 1997), 104–106.

writings also confirm that from the very outset of Christian theological development that there were those who attempted to soften the rigid line between heaven and hell and the saved and the unsaved—from the very beginning of Christianity there were those who tended to think along universalist rather than exclusivist lines.

1.3. An Expanding Offer of Salvation

The idea of postmortem salvation has been promoted down through the centuries based upon a few controversial New Testament texts that seem to speak to the subject. These texts are controversial in that they appear to contradict the traditional eschatological schema and instead offer evidence for the existence of an expanding offer of salvation during the apostolic age.

One such text is I Corinthians 15:29. It reads: [29] "Otherwise, what will they do who are baptized for the dead, if the dead do not rise at all? Why then are they baptized for the dead?"(Επεὶ τί ποιήσουσιν οἱ βαπτιζόμενοι ὑπὲρ τῶν νεκρῶν; εἰ ὅλως νεκροὶ οὐκ ἐγείρονται, τί καὶ βαπτίζονται ὑπὲρ αὐτῶν;). On the face of it, this verse would seem to prove that a belief in postmortem salvation through proxy baptism existed within the first-century church.[28] At least it appears that the practice was prevalent enough that the Apostle Paul appropriated it in order to argue in favor of the reality of the resurrection. Hans Conzelmann is one of several contemporary exegetes who interpret the verse in this way. He concludes: "The wording is in favor of the 'normal' exposition in terms of 'vicarious baptism': in Corinth living people having themselves vicariously baptized for dead people."[29]

In contrast to this interpretation is the perspective of Anthony C. Thiselton who argues that the use of the future tense in the word *poiēsousin* (ποιήσουσιν) should be taken as a logical present with a subjective or self-involving aspect. Therefore he translates the first part of the verse in this way: "What do those people think they are doing who . . . ?"[30] Furthermore, Thiselton argues that the word *huper* (ὑπέρ) should be translated "for the sake of " as opposed to "for" or "on behalf of."[31] Thus the phrase ὑπὲρ τῶν νεκρῶν would be read "for the sake of the dead." This translation would imply a baptism that was received by the living with the motivation of eventually being united with the dearly departed Christian dead—perhaps friends or relatives. Thiselton quotes the conclusion of G.G. Findlay in support of this thesis: "Paul is referring rather to a much commoner, indeed normal experience, that the

---

[28] Based primarily on this verse, the Church of Jesus Christ of Latter Day Saints (i.e. the Mormons) includes proxy baptism of dead relatives as an important rite in its secret Temple ministry. This also explains why the Mormon Church is the leading authority in the world when it comes to genealogical research.

[29] Hans Conzelmann, *1 Corinthians: A Commentary on the First Epistle to the Corinthians*, ed. George W. MacRae, trans. James W. Leitch (Philadelphia: Fortress, 1975), 275.

[30] Anthony C. Thiselton, *The First Epistle to the Corinthians: A Commentary on the Greek Text*, The New International Greek Testament Commentary (Grand Rapids, Mich.: Eerdmans, 2000), 1241.

[31] Thiselton, *The First Epistle to the Corinthians*, 1248.

death of Christians leads to the conversion of survivors . . ."[32] Thus, on this view, baptism for the sake of the dead would simply mean the living being converted and baptized with the goal of being reunited in eternity with their dead Christian relatives.

Given the fact that Thiselton notes that prior to the year 1950 there existed more than forty different explanations for this verse in the scholarly literature, it does not seem likely that a consensus view will emerge in our own day. Indeed, as the views of Conzelmann and Thiselton illustrate, contemporary scholars appear to be just as sharply divided on the issue as their historical predecessors. In light of this reality, I Corinthians 15:29 does not commend itself as a likely candidate to prove that a substantial number of first-century Christians embraced the notion of postmortem salvation and has not been a popular proof text used for this purpose.

Several other controversial New Testament texts refer to Jesus' soul descending into the spirit world and the realm of the dead sometime during the period after he died upon the cross and before his resurrection on the third day. Texts such as Luke 23:43, Rom. 10:7, Acts 2:24–31, Eph. 4:7–10 speak in vague generalities of this phenomenon. Two texts in particular, 1 Pet. 3:18–20 and 4:6, have been interpreted by many—both ancient and modern—to specifically describe the activity of Christ upon his descent as that of proclaiming or preaching the gospel to the souls of the dead in Hades.[33] In 1 Pet. 3:19–20 we are told that Christ "made proclamation [ἐκήρυξεν] to the spirits now in prison, who once were disobedient, when the patience of God kept waiting in the days of Noah."[34] In 1 Peter 4:6 we are told: "For the gospel has for this purpose been preached [εὐηγγελίσθη] even to those who are dead, that though they are judged in the flesh as men, they may live in the spirit according to the will of God."[35] While there has always been great

---

[32] Thiselton, *The First Epistle to the Corinthians*, 1248.

[33] Richard Bauckham's article "Descent to the Underworld" describes the phenomenon as it occurs in the tradition of several ancient cultures. See "Descent to the Underworld" in *ABD* 2:159. Several speculative works have been written that attempt to trace the historical development of the doctrine of Christ's descent. See Markwart Herzog, *Descensus ad Inferos* (Frankfurt: Josef Knecht, 1997); Joseph Kroll, *Gott und Hölle: Der Mythos vom Descensuskampfe* (Darmstadt: Wissenshaftliche Buchgesellshaft, 1963); J.A. MacCulloch, *The Harrowing of Hell* (Edinburgh: T. & T. Clark, 1930); Heinz-Juergen Vogels, *Christi Abstieg ins Totenreich und das Laeuterungsgericht an den Toten* (Frieburg: Herder, 1976).

[34] J. Ramsay Michaels argues that the allusion to "spirits now in prison" is best understood as an allusion to demonic forces of evil. See J. Ramsay Michaels in *1 Peter*, Word Biblical Commentary, vol. 49 (Waco, Tex.: Word, 1988), 205–13. The fact that the word "spirits" should be taken as a reference to imprisoned demons or evil spirits rather than human beings is strongly supported by the overall context of the passage and how Peter concludes the passage by speaking of Jesus' ascent into heaven with this affirmation in v. 22, ". . . who is at the right hand of God, having gone into heaven, after angels and authorities and powers had been subjected to Him."

[35] William J. Dalton makes the case that this verse speaks of the gospel being preached to Christians who have since died. See William J. Dalton, *Christ's Proclamation to the Spirits: A Study of 1 Peter 3:18–4:6*, 2nd rev. ed. (Rome: Editrice Pontificio Instituto Biblico, 1989), 59–60. See also Michaels, *1 Peter*, 235–42.

disagreement as to whether or not these verses present evidence of a postmortem second chance for the lost, what really matters for our study is that this interpretation has been commonly made down through the ages and from the very earliest time served as a point of departure for speculation regarding the idea of postmortem salvation and universalism.

Several ancient works dated to the second century C.E. use the notion of Christ's descent and preaching to the dead as a means of expanding the offer of salvation beyond the boundaries of strict Christian confession. The writings of both Irenaeus and Justin Martyr contain quotations from an otherwise un-recovered work that is known as the *Jeremiah Apocryphon*.[36] Irenaeus uses the *Apocryphon* to justify the belief that Old Testament saints and prophets were offered salvation at the descent of Christ to the underworld. Justin also uses the *Apocryphon* to endorse such a view. Trumbower notes, however, that the quotations of the *Apocryphon* itself found in both Irenaeus and Justin do not limit the offer of salvation to Israel's ancient "worthies" alone as Irenaeus and Justin do in their exposition. The quotations allow that the author of the *Apocryphon* could have conceivably envisioned a preaching of the gospel to *all* the Israelite dead—both worthy and unworthy—regardless of the limits placed upon it by Irenaeus and Justin.[37] In his *First Apology* Justin expands the concept of salvation even further as he allows for the salvation of righteous persons among the ancient pagans. He declares in *1 Apol.* 46 that men such as Socrates and Heraclitus who "lived reasonably (μετὰ λόγου) are Christians."[38]

The *Gospel of Peter*, which has been dated to at least the late second century C.E., also enunciates an expanded offer of salvation to the dead.[39] Verses 39–42 describe an animated cross, which follows three men out of Christ's empty tomb. In answer to the question, "Have you preached to those who have fallen asleep?" The cross responds, "Yes."[40]

---

[36] What survives of the work must be reconstructed entirely from the quotations found in Irenaeus and Justin. See Justin, *Dial.* 72.4; Irenaeus, *Adv. Haer.* 3.20.4, 4.22.1, 4.33.1, 4.33.12, 5.31.1; *Dem.* 78. Bauckham argues that the apocryphon is of Christian origin. See "Descent to the Underworld," 156.

[37] The relevant passage in Justin's *Dialogue with Trypho* reads: "The Lord God remembered his dead from Israel who had fallen asleep in an earthly tomb, and he went down to them, to proclaim to them the good news of his salvation." Justin, *Dial.*, 72.4, trans. Trumbower, *Rescue for the Dead*, 97.

[38] Justin, *I Apol.*, 1:178.

[39] Schneemelcher, *New Testament Apocrypha*, 1:183–87. John Dominic Crossan believes the gospel preserved an early source that was used to construct the passion narratives of the canonical gospels. See John Dominic Crossan, *The Cross that Spoke* (San Francisco: Harper and Row, 1988). See also his triple stratification of the gospel from which he extracts his "Cross Gospel" in *The Historical Jesus: The Life of a Mediterranean Jewish Peasant* (San Francisco: HarperSanFrancisco, 1991), 429, 462–66. Crossan's thesis has been ably challenged by several scholars. See Gregory A. Boyd, *Cynic, Sage, or Son of God: Recovering the Real Jesus in an Age of Revisionist Replies* (Wheaton, Ill.: BridgePoint/Victor Books, 1995), 113–63; Raymond E. Brown, *Death of the Messiah*, 2 vols. (New York: Doubleday, 1994), 2:1317-49; J.B. Green, "The Gospel of Peter: Source for a Pre-Canonical Passion Narrative?" *ZNW* (1987): 293–301; and J.W. McCant, "The Gospel of Peter: Docetism Reconsidered," *NTS* 40 (1994): 572–95.

[40] Schneemelcher, *New Testament Apocrypha*, 1:186.

In the final hymn found in the *Odes of Solomon* there is a first person description of the descent of Christ into the underworld. Some of the dead held in chains of darkness see Jesus Christ coming to them and cry out, "Son of God have pity on us and deal with us according to your mercy and bring us out from the chains of darkness." To which Christ responds, "Then I heard their voice, and placed their faith in my heart. And I placed my name upon their head, because they are free and they are mine."[41] Although not all of the dead are rescued in this hymn, the horizon of salvation has certainly been greatly enlarged.

Along these lines one final text, the *Gospel of Nicodemus*, is worth mentioning. It is a combination document that actually consists of the *Acts of Pilate* and a text commonly known as "Christ's Descent into Hell."[42] After reviewing the sparse evidence regarding the provenance of the documents Clayton Jefford concludes, "A firm date for the original composition of the Acts cannot be established with certainty." Trumbower notes that estimates of as early as 200 C.E. have been placed upon the *descensus* narrative.[43] With this in mind we must be careful concerning the significance we accord to this text realizing that its value may be more in the realm of the anecdotal. [44]

The Greek version of the *descensus* text envisions Hades being completely emptied by Christ when he descends. A personified Hades complains to Satan, "Turn and see that not one dead man is left in me, but that all which you gained through the tree of knowledge you have lost through the tree of the cross . . . How were you bent on bringing down such a man into this darkness, through whom you have been deprived of all who have died since the beginning?" (*Gosp. Nicod.* 23).[45] After saving Adam first, Jesus then calls out to the whole host of the dead: "Come with me, all you who have suffered death through the tree which this man has touched. For behold, I raise you all up again through the tree of the cross." The narrator then concludes, "With that he put them all out." (*Gosp. Nicod.* 24)

The *Gospel of Nicodemus* and the other texts we have examined illustrate how the notion of Christ's descent and preaching to the dead could be expanded into a broad offer of salvation and even into universalism itself. As we shall see later in the study, the descent of Christ into the underworld has been a favorite theme of universalists and has been used down through the centuries to provide theological justification for their perspective. In the first and second centuries the New Testament *descensus* narrative offered an opportunity for the developing notion of postmortem salvation to be expanded upon and given

---

[41] James H. Charlesworth, ed., *The Old Testament Pseudepigrapha, vol. 2, Expansions of the "Old Testament" and Legends, Wisdom and Philosophical Literature, Prayers, Psalms, and Odes, Fragments of Lost Judeo-Hellenistic Works* (Garden City, N.Y.: Doubleday, 1985), 771.

[42] The *Ante-Nicene Fathers* series contains translations of several complete Greek and Latin versions of the text. See *ANF* 8:416–58. For a brief discussion of the issues at hand consult Clayton N. Jefford, "Pilate, Acts of," in *ABD* 5:371–72. Cf. Trumbower, *Rescue for the Dead*, 105–108.

[43] Trumbower, *Rescue of the Dead*, 106.

[44] Jefford, "Pilate, Acts of," 371.

[45] Scheenmelcher, *New Testament Apocrypha*, 2:522.

scriptural legitimacy. It provided a point of departure through which other speculations regarding the deliverance of the dead might be introduced.

1.4. The Gnostics

Before we examine more closely the contribution that the gnostic movement made to post-Apostolic universalism it is important to understand that the essential relationship between Gnosticism and Christianity has been hotly debated.[46] Since the late nineteenth century the German Religionsgeschichtliche Schule (or "History of Religions School") advocated a pre-Christian origin to advanced forms of Gnosticism and posited the theory that Christianity was actually a modified expression of gnostic themes and doctrines.[47] Up to that point in history the broadly accepted view had been that well developed gnostic systems were a post-Christian heresy that were the result of Christianity being contaminated by Hellenistic speculation and philosophy.[48] The History of Religions School proposal turned this traditional model on its head and posited that Christianity actually grew out of Gnosticism. Richard Reitzenstein in his book *Poimandres: Studien zur griechisch-ägyptischen und früh-christlichen Literatur* went so far as to assert that the New Testament teaching regarding the redeeming Son of Man in the Gospels was a later expression of a Persian/gnostic redeemer legend.[49] The famed twentieth-century theologian Rudolf Bultmann, building on the work of the History of Religions School scholars, incorporated this theory of the gnostic Redeemer Myth into his own writings asserting that the myth served as a model

---

[46] For a comprehensive discussion regarding the definition of the term "Gnosticism" see Edwin M. Yamauchi, *Pre-Christian Gnosticism: A Survey of Proposed Evidences*, 2nd ed. (Grand Rapids, Mich.: Eerdmans; Baker, 1973; 1983), 13–19. See also the more recent discussions of Bentley Layton, *The Gnostic Scriptures* (Garden City, N.J.: Doubleday, 1987), 5–12, and Michael Allen Williams, *Rethinking "Gnosticism": An Argument for Dismantling a Dubious Category* (Princeton, N.J.: Princeton University Press, 1996), 265. Layton prefers to narrow the use of the word to a specific second century group while referring to the various allied sects by their specific names. Williams champions the use of a more precise term—"biblical demiurgical"—as opposed to the more generalized "gnostic." His definition includes "all sources that made a distinction between the creator(s) and controllers of the material world and the most transcendent divine being, and that in so doing made use of the Jewish or Christian scriptural traditions" (Williams, *Rethinking "Gnosticism,"* 265).

[47] One of the first to advocate a pre-Christian origin to Gnosticism was Wilhelm Anz in *Zur Frage nach dem Ursprung des Gnostizismus: ein religionsgeschichtlicher Versuch* (Leipzig: J.C. Hinrichs, 1897). Anz was no doubt influenced by F.C. Baur's book *Die Christliche Gnosis oder die christliche Religions-Philosophie in ihrer geschichtlichen Entwicklung* (Tübingen: C. F. Osiander, 1835). The two leading proponents of a pre-Christian Gnosticism from the History of Religions School were Wilhelm Bousset (1865–1920) and Richard Reitzenstein (1861–1931). See Wilhelm Bousset, *Hauptprobleme der Gnosis* (Göttingen: Vandenhoeck und Ruprecht, 1907); and Richard Reitzenstein, *Poimandres: Studien zur griechisch-ägyptischen und früh-christlichen Literatur* (Leipzig: Teubner, 1904).

[48] Robert Mcl. Wilson, *Gnosis and the New Testament* (Oxford: Blackwell, 1968), 5; Yamauchi, *Pre-Christian Gnosticism*, 20–21.

[49] Reitzenstein, *Poimandres*, 81.

for the presentation of Christ as redeemer in the New Testament.[50] According to Bultmann, Gnosticism provided a "stock of concepts" that "served to clarify *the history of salvation*" (italics in the original) for the New Testament writers.[51]

With the discovery of the library of Coptic gnostic texts near Nag Hammadi in upper Egypt in 1945, the debate over the existence of a highly developed pre-Christian Gnosticism and its influence on Christianity has intensified.[52] The find has given tremendous impetus to the study of the relationship between Gnosticism and the New Testament with several contemporary scholars arguing for the existence of a pre-Christian Gnosticism that profoundly influenced Christianity and the formation of the New Testament.[53] This theory has not gone unchallenged with several scholars calling into question the fundamental conclusions drawn by the History of Religions scholars as well as casting doubt on the basic methodology employed.[54] Despite the amount of effort put into the matter, the fact remains that to this date there has been no *tangible evidence* of a full-blown pre-Christian Gnosticism uncovered in any form (e.g. papyri, manuscripts, inscriptions, etc . . .). The extraction of evidence in support of the theory typically involves the use of sources from the second century C.E. and

---

[50] Bultmann laid out twenty-eight characteristics that formed the framework of his version of the myth in his article, "Die Bedeutung der neuerschlossenen mandäischen und manichäischen Quellen für das Verständinis des Johannesevangeliums," *ZNW* 24 (1925): 100–146. In his two volume work, *Theology of the New Testament*, Bultmann refined the myth and applied it to the New Testament. See Rudolf Bultmann, *Theology of the New Testament*, 2 vols., trans. Kendrick Grobel (New York: Charles Scribner's Sons, 1951; 1955), 1:164–65; 1:172–83.

[51] Bultmann, *Theology of the New Testament*, 1:175.

[52] For the complete text of the find in English see James M. Robinson, ed., *The Nag Hammadi Library in English*, 3rd edition (San Francisco: HarperSanFrancisco, 1978; 1990). Robinson dates the find to November or December of 1945. See James M. Robinson, "Nag Hammadi: The First Fifty Years," in John D. Turner and Anne McGuire, *The Nag Hammadi Library After Fifty Years: Proceedings of the 1995 Society of Biblical Literature Commemoration* (Leiden: Brill, 1997), 3–33.

[53] The standard bibliography on Gnosticism and the Nag Hammadi library may be found in the following two volumes compiled by David M. Scholer: *Nag Hammadi Bibliography: 1948–1969* (Leiden: Brill, 1971) and *Nag Hammadi Bibliography: 1970–1994* (Leiden: Brill, 1997). The pro side includes scholars such as John Dominic Crossan, John Dart, Robert Funk, Charles Hedrick, Helmut Koester, Gerd Lüdemann, Hyam Maccoby, Jean Magne, Elaine Pagels, Pheme Perkins, Kurt Rudolf, and Karl Tröger.

[54] See Carsten Colpe's critique of the History of Religions School in *Die Religionsgeschichtliche Schule; Darstellung and Kritik ihres Bildes vom gnostischen Erlösermythus* (Göttingen: Vandenhoeck & Ruprecht, 1961). For a challenge to the methodology used see Yamauchi, *Pre-Christian Gnosticism*, 187–249. For a discussion of problems related to the dating of the text see Robert McL. Wilson, "Gnosis at Corinth," in Morna D. Hooker and S.G. Wilson, *Paul and Paulinism: Essays in Honor of C.K. Barrett* (London: SPCK, 1982), 111; Martin Hengel, *The Son of God: The Origin of Christology and the History of Jewish-Hellenistic Religion* (Philadelphia: Fortress, 1976), 33–34; Barbara Aland, "Gnosis und Christentum," in Bentley Layton, ed., *The Rediscovery Gnosticism, vol. 1, The School of Valentius* (Leiden: Brill, 1980), 340.

beyond. These sources are then redacted through the use of various subjective criteria and retrojected backward in time. Both the methodology and the conclusions drawn are highly controversial and, according to the critics, far from proven.

Due to the extremely tenuous nature of the evidence presented in favor of a highly developed pre-Christian Gnosticism, this study will hold to the more traditional view that advanced gnostic systems are a post-Christian development and represent an amalgam in which Christianity has been cross-pollinated with other various speculative Hellenistic philosophies. There can be no doubt that Gnosticism did exert an increasingly significant influence upon early Christian theological thought. However, this influence is felt most keenly from the second century C.E. forward.

It should be noted that much of our information regarding early gnostic systems comes from the writings of the church fathers. Early church apologists such as Irenaeus wrote their accounts against the gnostics with a definite bias that always sought to portray them in the worst light possible. Therefore we must use these sources with caution and realize that the picture that emerges from them has been colored by theological partiality. This bias might well explain the reason why the picture given by the church fathers does not seem to be typical of the Nag Hammadi texts. On the other hand, Williams argues that the use of the word "Gnosticism" as a category is "a laborsaving device conducive to anachronism, caricature, and eisegesis."[55] In Williams view, what is typically called "Gnosticism" is actually a constellation of ideas that often defies attempts at neat categorization.[56] When confronting such a diversity of thought we should not be surprised to find a great deal of differentiation among the resultant systems. With this said, let us take a look at some early gnostic contributions to early universalist thought in the post-Apostolic era.

It is well known that certain ancient gnostic sects held to a form of universalism that involved the migration of all human souls to heaven through a successive series of cosmic or spiritual levels. While universal salvation was not a feature of all gnostic systems, it appears that certain sects with roots in Alexandria, Egypt embraced this view. In particular the doctrinal systems of the Basilidians, the Carpocatians, and the Valentinians seem to have embraced this form of universal salvation in various ways.[57]

The Basilidians were the followers of Basilides who was a gnostic Christian philosopher who died in Alexandria between the years 130 and 140 C.E.[58] According to Irenaeus, the Basilidians taught that there were three hundred and sixty-five levels or Æons controlled by evil powers through which a soul must travel to attain eternal bliss in the genuine heaven where God dwells.[59] In the Basilidian system the souls of the true partakers in the secret knowledge of

---

[55] Williams, *Rethinking "Gnosticism,"* 51.

[56] Williams, *Rethinking "Gnosticism,"* 80–212.

[57] Baxter, "Apokatastasis," 41–44; Friessen, "A Critical Analysis of Universalism," 36–39; Layton, *The Gnostic Scriptures*, xxii, 5–12, 217–22, 267–75, 413–19; Trumbower, *Rescue for the Dead*, 110–11.

[58] Paul Allan Mirecki, "Basilides," in *ABD* 1:624–25. Ballou, *The Ancient History of Universalism*, 26.

[59] Irenaeus, *Adv. Haer.*, 1.24.3–4.

Christ were rendered invisible to the evil powers and therefore could ascend directly into heaven.[60] Those who ignored or rejected the Savior and his teaching would be subject to successive reincarnation until they were prepared to transcend the world.[61] Ballou describes the cycle of reincarnation in this way, "[O]n the contrary, such as neglect and disobey, will be condemned to pass into other bodies, either of men or of brutes, until by their purification they shall be fitted to share in the joys of the incorporeal blest; and so all will finally be saved."[62]

The Carpocratians taught a similar form of reincarnation and transmigration of the soul.[63] Carpocrates was another gnostic Christian philosopher who lived and taught in Alexandria, Egypt, in the first half of the second century C.E.[64] According to Carpocratian teaching there were two avenues a soul may take in order to migrate into the sphere of the unbegotten God. A soul that, like Christ, retained a perfect memory of heavenly things could pass straight through to God and avoid confrontation with the evil creators of this world.[65] The soul that did not attain this level of perfection must travel through every form of life until restitution was made and freedom attained. Once this transmigration was accomplished the soul could ascend into the presence of God and into a state of eternal rest.[66] Either way, all would be saved.

Valentinus (approx. 100 C.E.–175 C.E.) was born in the Egyptian delta and was educated in Alexandria.[67] Layton believes that he was very likely influenced by the teaching of Basilides and Philo Judaeus.[68] Paul Mirecki notes that Valentinus was "a speculative theological reformer" who sought to "revise the classic gnostic myth according to the terms and conceptual categories of emerging orthodoxy."[69] Valentinian universalism focused primarily upon the composition of man. According to Valentinus, man was composed of four parts: (1) the outer visible body, (2) the inner body composed of fluid matter, (3) the animated or animal soul, which was the seat of life and sensation only, and (4) the rational, intelligent soul. Valintinus taught that both the outer and inner bodies would perish at death—in keeping with typical gnostic dualism there could be no saving these. However it was possible for the animated soul to be saved through obedience; otherwise it too would perish at death. Finally, the rational soul would always be admitted to heaven without exception.[70]

---

[60] Irenaeus, *Adv. Haer.*, 1.24.6.
[61] See fragment E of Clement's *Stromata*, 4.165.3, in Layton's, *The Gnostic Scriptures*, 436–37.
[62] Ballou, *The Ancient History of Universalism*, 25.
[63] Ballou, *The Ancient History of Universalism*, 25.
[64] Baxter, "Apokatastasis," 43.
[65] Irenaeus, *Adv. Haer.*, 1.25.1–2.
[66] Irenaeus, *Adv. Haer.*, 1.25.4; Baxter, "Apokatastasis," 43.
[67] Paul Allan Mirecki, "Valentinus," *ABD* 6:783–84; Baxter, "Apokatastasis," 43–44.
[68] Layton, *The Gnostic Scriptures*, 217–19, 417–44.
[69] Mirecki, "Valentinus," 783.
[70] Irenaeus, *Adv. Haer.*, 1.6.1–4, 1.7.5 (it appears that Irenaeus' description of Valentinus' anthropology is a bit confused); Baxter, "Apokatastasis," 43–44; Ballou, *The Ancient History of Universalism*, 29–30.

Given that Egypt appears to be the birthplace of gnostic universalism, it is not surprising then that we find hints of universalist thought in the Nag Hammadi corpus. In particular the *Apocryphon of John* comes extremely close to endorsing universal salvation.[71] The text presents to us a dialogue that occurs between the risen Savior and the Apostle John. At one point John asks the Savior, "Lord, will all souls be brought safely into the pure light?" The Savior explains that the souls from "the immovable race" upon whom "the Spirit of life" has descended will receive immediate salvation and eternal life.[72] Other souls who did not do the works of the first group must contend with "the counterfeit spirit" until they become strong enough to resist it and be taken up to the rest.[73] The souls of a third group "who have not known to whom they belong" are handed over to authorities and each soul is imprisoned until "it is liberated from the forgetfulness and acquires knowledge."[74] In the treatment of this group there is an implied progression of reincarnation. In the end we are told that only apostates are in danger of being damned—"apostates" being defined as those who have "turned away" from the revealed gnostic truth. In the economy of the *Apocryphon of John* it is only the apostates who will be "punished with eternal punishment." [75] Thus the *Apocryphon of John* comes very close to endorsing universal salvation. The singular exception was made for those who chose to abandon the elect group. The threat of damnation appears to have been used primarily as a control mechanism and was not a central feature of the group's overarching eschatological schema regarding the salvation of humanity. The menace of damnation was simply utilized by the group as a means through which the unity, solidarity, and regulation of the cult was insured. Apart from this exception universalism was affirmed.

It is fascinating to note that the one consistent connection that bound these gnostic groups together was geography—a close proximity that allowed for interaction and refinement. Basilides, Carpocrates, and Valentinus were all contemporaries who were raised and educated in Alexandria.[76] While we have no explicit evidence that they knew one another personally, there can be little doubt that at a minimum the groups they founded interacted robustly and that there was an exchange of ideas occurring. The fact that this amalgamation of ideas took place in Alexandria also fits in well with what we know of the history of the city at this time. Alexandria in the first century with its huge library, scholarly community, and cosmopolitan character was the crossroads at which Hellenism collided with Judaism, fledgling Christianity, and virtually every other theological and philosophical system found in the ancient Roman world. Thus Alexandria was uniquely endowed to provide the fertile soil in which the seed of speculative Christian universalism could be planted and then later flourish in Christian theology. It is no accident that Alexandria became the

---

[71] The complete text may be found in Robinson, *The Nag Hammadi Library*, 104–23.

[72] *Apocryphon of John*, Robinson, *The Nag Hammadi Library*, 119.

[73] *Apocryphon of John*, Robinson, *The Nag Hammadi Library*, 120.

[74] *Apocryphon of John*, Robinson, *The Nag Hammadi Library*, 120.

[75] *Apocryphon of John*, Robinson, *The Nag Hammadi Library*, 120.

[76] Although Valentinus traveled to Rome and later died on the island of Cyprus, it is well known that the eastern branch of his school resided in Alexandria. Cf. Mirecki, "Valentinus," 784.

birth place of a more formalized, academic universalism, which, as we shall see, was expressed first tentatively in the writings of Clement and then more powerfully in the writings of Origen and those who followed him.

In Alexandria the Christian church encountered universalist speculation on several fronts. As we have seen, popular Roman/Hellenistic religious culture embraced the notion of deliverance of the dead, inter-testamental Judaism experimented with the idea, and certain first-century Christians sought to expand the offer of salvation beyond the prevailing limits. Added to these factors were the Alexandrian gnostics who sought to marry universalism to a nominally Christian theological schema. The response of the church in Alexandria to the challenge of universalism was to essentially embrace it and to make it a significant part of its theology and cultural apologetic. To be sure, there were those who opposed such a move, but as we shall see the clarion call of apokatastasis won out in the early formative years.

1.5. Clement of Alexandria

Titus Flavius Clemens (150–approx. 215 C.E.), known more commonly as Clement of Alexandria, dedicated his life to the reconciliation of the Christian faith with secular philosophy. As a young man Clement traveled far and wide in search of higher instruction attaching himself sequentially to different teachers in Greece, Italy, Palestine, and finally in Egypt.[77] In Alexandria he met Pantaenus, the leader of a Christian catechetical school, who became his most influential mentor. After Pantaenus' death sometime before the year 200 C.E. Clement succeeded him as the leader of the school. Under the persecution of Septimius, Clement left Alexandria in 202 or 203 C.E. and emigrated to Asia Minor where he died in approximately 215 C.E.

In his efforts to reconcile Christianity with Hellenistic philosophical thought Clement created a body of work that presents us with an interesting and eclectic mixture of the two. At his core Clement was always an ardent defender of the faith and sought to show the superiority of Christ and Christian revelation to all other forms of knowledge.[78] However, Clement was also ready to acknowledge the accomplishments of philosophy and was more than willing to recognize the positive contributions of such men as Socrates, Plato, and Heraclitus.[79] Clement believed that a limited form of the truth could be found in Greek philosophy, however, he also believed that much of Greek philosophy was in error. He asserted that the truth found in Hellenistic thought could be traced back to the

---

[77] Clement, *Stromata*, 1.1.11.1–12.1. Critical editions of Clement's writings may be found in the series "Die griechischen Schriftsteller der ersten drei Jahrhunderte" and "Source Chrétiennes." This study consulted the Greek text of the *Stromata* found in Otto Stählin, Ludwig Früchtel, and Ursula Treu, eds., *Clemens Alexandrinus*, vol. 2, *Stromata Buch I–VI*, 4th ed., Die griechischen Schriftsteller der ersten drei Jahrhunderte, vol. 52 (15) (Berlin: Akademie-Verlag, 1985) and Otto Stählin, ed., *Clemens Alexandrinus*, vol. 3, *Stromata Buch VII und VIII, Excerpta ex Theodoto, Eclogae propheticae, Quis dives salvetur, Fragmente*, Die griechischen Schriftsteller der ersten drei Jahrhunderte, vol. 17, pt. 2 (Leipzig: J.C. Hinrichs, 1909).
[78] See, for instance, his sustained attack on pagan religion and philosophy and defense of Christianity as contained in his *Protrepticus*.
[79] Clement, *Stromata*, 1.19.92.3–93.6.

teaching of the Old Testament. In an interesting twist he argued that such truth was stolen and given to the Greeks by "some power or angel that had learned something of the truth, but abode not in it."[80] He viewed such philosophy as preparatory for the preaching of the gospel and went so far as to declare that, "philosophy was necessary to the Greeks for righteousness . . . philosophy was given to the Greeks directly and primarily, till the Lord should call the Greeks . . . . Philosophy, therefore, was a preparation, paving the way for him who is perfected in Christ."[81] Given such a positive view of philosophy, it is not remarkable that we find Clement frequently using certain forms of philosophical argumentation in support of Christian doctrine and beliefs. His understanding that the truths of philosophy originated with God and his word allowed him to claim these truths as his own and to use them in his writings.

Clement was never much of a systematician. Much of his writing is filled with quotations from a myriad of sources and proceeds forward along several parallel tracks at the same time. It is instructive to note that he once likened the truths he had found through his studies to being flowers gathered from "the prophetic and apostolic meadow."[82] The random picking represented by that picture is a good metaphor for Clement's writing style. As a result of not producing a systematic and discernable body of doctrine Clement is often misinterpreted and misunderstood. With this in mind we must be cautious before hanging an endorsement of any particular doctrine around Clement's neck. We must be cognizant of the fact that he was capable of generating both soaring discourse and contradictory statements at the same time.

In terms of universalist thought, we find scattered throughout Clement's writings a somewhat limited exploration of the idea that God would eventually save all intelligent creatures.[83] This proposal seems to be linked to a robust belief in God's omnipotence and benevolence along with the idea that ultimately all punishment would be both remedial and reformatory. A good example of this linkage is found in *Stromata* 7.2:

> But the nature of the Son, which is nearest to Him who is alone the Almighty One, is the most perfect, and most holy, and most potent, and most princely, and most kingly, and most beneficent. . . .
>
> For from His own point of view the Son of God is never displaced; not being divided, not severed, not passing from place to place; being always everywhere, and being contained nowhere; complete in mind, the complete paternal light; all eyes, seeing all things, hearing all things, knowing all things, by His power scrutinizing the powers. To Him is placed in subjection all the host of angels and gods; He, the paternal Word, exhibiting the holy administration for Him who put [all] in subjection to Him.

---

[80] Clement, *Stromata*, 1.17.81.5.

[81] Clement, *Stromata*, 1.5.28.3–4.

[82] Clement, *Stromata*, 1.1.11.3.

[83] Brian Daley characterizes Clement's approach toward universal salvation as one of "great caution," but I think that it was not so much cautious as it was partial and incomplete. See Brian Daley's discussion in *The Hope of the Early Church: A Handbook of Patristic Eschatology* (Cambridge: Cambridge University Press, 1991), 47.

> Therefore all men are His; some through knowledge, and others not yet so; and some as friends, some as faithful servants, some as servants merely. This is the Teacher, who trains the gnostic by mysteries, and the believer by good hopes, and the hard of heart by corrective discipline through sensible operation. Thus His divine providence is in private, in public, and everywhere.[84]

In this passage we have a strong affirmation of Christ's divine attributes, which, in turn, leads to the conclusion that "all men are His." The conclusion is itself followed by an affirmation that he will use any means necessary to ensure that in the end all will *remain* his. Of particular importance is Clement's startling assertion that the Lord Jesus Christ "is the Teacher, who trains the gnostic by mysteries, and the believer by good hopes, and the hard of heart by corrective discipline." Here then we have a clear connection being made between Gnosticism and Christianity in such a way that both are said to participate in the same universalist outcome. Notice that Clement's list of participants is drawn up in such a way that each group's unique mode of participation in universal salvation is noted. The gnostic is trained through "mysteries." The believer is trained through "good hopes." The hard of heart will be changed through "corrective discipline." The net result will be salvation so that "all men are His." While we do not want to push the evidence found in this passage too far, it is interesting that Clement seems to be aware of the speculations that the Alexandrian gnostics had regarding universal salvation and places them as a separate entry on his list.[85] This would imply that Clement had some understanding of gnostic universalism and could very well have been influenced, at least in part, by it.

A connection to Hellenist speculation regarding universal restoration may well be found in Clement's comment that the Teacher will "train/educate (παιδεύων) the hard of heart by corrective (ἐπανορθωτικῇ) discipline." *Epanorthōsis* (Επανορθωσις) typically carries the meaning of correction with a goal of restoration or improvement.[86] Often the word was used simply to indicate restoration. In light of the association of the Alexandrian School with the Hellenistic idea of apokatastasis conceived of in terms of a universal restoration, it is hard to dismiss the synonymous relationship between the two words. There can be little doubt that Clement was thinking of "restorative discipline" when he penned the phrase and it could very well be that what we have here is apokatastasis in germ form. Certainly the idea of posthumous restoration is present and moving from the restoration of people to the restoration of the universe would be a matter of degree and not kind.

This analysis is confirmed further on in *Stromata* 7.2 where Clement elaborates his perspective on the relationship of the structure of the universe to ultimate salvation:

---

[84] Clement, *Stromata*, 7.2.5.3–6.2
[85] We are not saying here that Clement endorsed all gnostic teaching, and we must be equally careful regarding Clement's usage of the word "gnostic."
[86] BDAG, s.v. ἐπανορθωσις.

For all things are arranged with a view to the salvation of the universe by the Lord of the universe, both generally and specifically. It is then the function of the righteousness of salvation to improve everything as far as practicable. For even minor matters are arranged with a view to the salvation of that which is better, and for an abode suitable for people's character. Now everything that is virtuous changes for the better; having as the proper cause of change the free choice of knowledge, which the soul has in its own power. But necessary corrections, through the goodness of the great overseeing Judge, both by the attendant angels, and by various acts of anticipative judgment, and by the perfect [παντελοῦς = full or complete] judgment, compel egregious sinners to repent."[87]

Thus Clement affirms that "the salvation of the universe" is an inherent part of God's goal and design for the universe. Here then is a full-blown declaration of apokatastasis. The deliverance of the entire universe is an essential element in God's eschatological plan. God's quest to provide salvation for his creation was not an afterthought and will not be defeated even by the free choice of man. If a person will not respond to the goodness and discipline of God in the present life then in the end they will experience the "full" or "complete" judgment of God by which they will eventually be constrained to posthumously repent.[88]

Perhaps the most explicit statement that Clement made regarding universal salvation is found in a passage from a lost commentary that he wrote on the Epistle of 1 John. Cassiodorus (485–580 C.E.) preserved the passage in a Latin text. In commenting on 1 John 2:2 ("and He Himself is the propitiation for our sins; and not for ours only, but also for those of the whole world") Clement affirmed:

"And not only for our sins,"—that is for those of the faithful—is the Lord the propitiator, does he say, "but also for the whole world." He, indeed, saves all; but some [He saves], converting them by punishments; others, however, who follow voluntarily [He saves] with dignity of honour; so "that every knee should bow to Him, of things in heaven, and things on earth, and things under the earth;" that is, angels, men, and souls that before His advent have departed from this temporal life.[89]

Here then Clement is playing a sort of forerunner to Origen in that he affirms the universal salvation of both angels and human beings. In Clement's view the souls of those who died before Christ appeared will be saved as well as those who must be converted posthumously "by punishments." All creatures will eventually submit to salvation through Christ. We are also given here a limited

---

[87] Clement, *Stromata*, 7.2.12.2–5.

[88] I take παντελοῦς to mean "full" or "complete" in the sense that God will not let up until the sinner is ultimately ushered into the kingdom of God and no one remains in hell.

[89] Clement, *Hypotyposes*, in Otto Stählin, *Clemens Alexandrinus*, vol. 3, *Stromata Buch VII und VIII, Excerpta ex Theodoto, Eclogae propheticae, Quis dives salvetur, Fragmente*, 211. Cf. Phil. 2:10.

glimpse into Clement's exegetical method regarding those New Testament passages that seem to imply universal salvation: he comes down forcefully here on the side of reading those verses through the lens of universalism. The passage closes with an allusion to Philippians 2:10, and although it is questionable whether Paul really envisaged universalism here, Clement nevertheless interprets it that way.

There has been a great deal of debate over whether or not Clement was a true universalist. The argument against the idea has been built around the fact that he spoke often about hell and eternal punishment (cf. *Quis dives salvetur* 33.3; *Stromata* 5.14.90–91.2, 4.24.154) and stated that some evil might be "incurable" and punishable by death (cf. *Stromata*, 1.27.171.4–5; 1.27.173.1– 3). The key to unraveling this issue is to be found in gaining a better understanding of Clement's concept of time. Steven Ray Harmon has effectively argued that Clement thought of punishment linked to αἰώνιος as a Greek philosophical concept that focused primarily on corrective discipline rather than on unending time.[90] Given that Clement used numerous biblical texts to prove that God's punishment is not retributive,[91] it makes sense to view Clement's use of αἰώνιος as simply an expression of whatever time was necessary to accomplish correction. In this sense time was open ended for Clement. Eternal punishment was only eternal in that it provided enough time for God to correct and restore all things to himself in eternity.[92]

Clement's writings signal the beginning of a formalized and theologically reasoned doctrine of universalism within Christianity. By the time of Clement we see that a solid orthodoxy was beginning to emerge that was based upon the Old Testament and the essential apostolic writings that were already solidifying into the New Testament. This emerging orthodoxy had a proportionally diminishing need for undisciplined speculations and/or ecstatic visions that occurred apart from its revealed writings. As a theologian and the leader of a Christian catechetical school Clement felt obligated to support his theology more concretely within the framework of writings that the church had always revered. On the other hand, Clement also developed his apologetic in light of Greek philosophy and the Hellenistic religious thought of his age.[93] As we have seen, he believed that all truth, whether pagan or Christian, came from God and thus he had no problem with marrying Christian theology to Greek philosophy. Clearly Clement's universalism was influenced by his engagement with

---

[90] Harmon, "Apokatastasis and Exegesis: A Comparative Analysis of the Use of Scripture in the Eschatological Universalism of Clement of Alexandria, Origen, and Gregory of Nyssa," 19–23.

[91] Cf. Clement, *Stromata*, 7.2.12.5; 7.16.102.5; 7.6.34.4; Clement, *Paedagogus* 1.1.3.1; 1.1.1.4; 1.8.64.4; 1.8.72.1.

[92] Clement, *Stromata*, 7.2.12.2.

[93] Evert Proctor has carefully documented citations from the writings of Basilides and Valentinus within Clement's work as well as Clement's response to them. In so doing Proctor confirms for us the great awareness that Clement had of the other theological systems that swirled around him in Alexandria. See Evert Proctor, *Christian Controversy in Alexandria: Clement's Polemic Against the Basilideans and the Valentinians* (New York: Peter Lang, 1995).

Gnosticism and Greek philosophy as well as Christian theological thought. What we have within Clement's proposal is a mixture of the three.

2. Origen

Origen is a towering figure both in the history of Christian theology and Christian universalism. He was the first Christian theologian to devote a large part of his work to the exploration and systemization of Christian doctrine. He was the first Christian theologian to make universalism a central feature of his eschatological system. He was the first Christian theologian to formulate and defend a coherent doctrine of ἀποκάταστασις. Because of the influence that his writings have exerted upon succeeding generations of universalist thinkers Origen has been rightly called the "Father of Universalism." Origen's tremendous influence over the field to this very day demands that we gain a thorough understanding of the intricacies of his thought.

Origen was born in Alexandria, Egypt, into a Christian family of some means in the year 185 C.E. When he was a teenager his father was martyred for his faith during the reign of Septimius Severus (193–211 C.E.). At that time the family's property was confiscated and they were left destitute. Throughout his life several key patrons sponsored Origen's education and work enabling him to become one of the most prolific authors in antiquity. Eusebius reported that a wealthy patron named Ambrose paid for several stenographers and copyists who assisted Origen in the production of his books.[94] Jerome commented that a list of Origen's writings extant in his day included no less than two thousand titles. At the age of eighteen Origen became the leader of the catechetical school in Alexandria replacing Clement.[95] He held the position for almost thirty years and then moved to Caesarea where he established another school and presided over it for approximately twenty more years. At some point in his adult life (the precise timing is the subject of debate) Origen underwent a radical change of heart, abandoning an interest in pagan literature and adopting a lifestyle of rigorous asceticism and self-mortification, which—by most accounts—included self-castration. As a result of the imprisonment and torture inflicted upon him during the Decian persecution (251 C.E.) Origen's health was broken and he died in Tyre in the year 253 C.E.

Before we explore Origen's formulation of ἀποκάταστασις, a few cautionary notes must be made. The first concerns the current state of the Origen corpus. As a result of the later condemnation of Origen's writings by the church in 553 C.E. many of Origen's original Greek works were destroyed. Most of his remaining works survive only in Latin translations of the original Greek.[96] The situation is further complicated by the fact that key treatises such as *De principiis* have come down to us only through the rather questionable translation of Rufinus of Aqueleia (345–410 C.E.) who is known to have taken

---

[94] Eusebius, *Ecclesiastical History*, 6.23.

[95] Crouzel thinks that Origen's school was different from Clement's. Cf. Henri Crouzel, *Origen: The Life and Thought of the First Great Theologian* (San Francisco: Harper and Row, 1989), 7.

[96] A discussion of the problem along with some appropriate methodological warnings and strategies may be found in John Clark Smith, *The Ancient Wisdom of Origen* (Cranbury, N.J.: Associated University Presses, 1992), 260–69.

liberties with the text in an effort to make Origen's ideas more easily understood and generally less offensive.[97] Because of this we cannot be certain of the accuracy of much of the text we now possess. On the upside, it would seem that Origen's ideas have been softened and made more orthodox in our text as opposed to being made more harsh and heretical. If this is true then we can be fairly confident that Origen held to at least what is there, if not significantly more.

A second issue to be kept in mind concerns the nature of Origen's writings. Origen was an incredibly adaptable scholar who wrote his works with several different audiences in mind. Treatises such as *De principiis* and *Contra Celsum* were written from a decidedly intellectual/philosophical point of view and aimed at a more secular audience than his Bible commentaries and homilies. John Clark Smith notes that although Origen enjoyed engaging in high philosophical debate, "Scripture, however, was the product of Origen's life-long contemplation."[98] Thus taking works like *De principiis* and *Contra Celsum* in isolation from what Origen said elsewhere, especially in his commentaries on scripture, will result in a view of Origen that will be decidedly skewed toward his philosophical/speculative side. Indeed, Steven Harmon notes that *De principiis* and *Contra Celsum* are "his two most uncharacteristic works."[99] The difficulty for our study lies in the fact that much of what Origen has to say about ἀποκάτασσις is found in these two works. Nevertheless, comments regarding the idea are to be found scattered throughout Origen's writings. In this study we shall attempt to survey Origen's thought regarding ἀποκάτασσις from the full spectrum of his work.

Origen's most explicit formulations of universalism may be found in books 1 and 3 of *De principiis*. Book 1.6 discusses the "finis vel consummatio" in great detail.[100] In the opening paragraph Origen wanted to make it clear that what followed was put forward tentatively and with caution rather than as dogma: "However, these things are said by us with great fear and caution, [with] greater discussing and investigating than settling things certainly and definitely."[101] Thus Origen himself warns his readers that his discussion of

---

[97] Rufinus himself admitted to paraphrasing, shortening, lengthening, and inserting his own explanations into the text as a means of avoiding confusion for his Latin readers. He also claimed that "heretics" had altered Origen's original text and that his changes corrected these corruptions. See Rufinus, *Ad Heraclium* (PG 14:1292–1294); *De principiis*, Preface. For a detailed discussion see Elizabeth A. Clark, *The Origenist Controversy: The Cultural Construction of an Early Christian Debate* (Princeton, N.J.: Princeton University Press, 1992), 163–65.

[98] Smith, *The Ancient Wisdom of Origen*, 267.

[99] Harmon, "Apokatastasis and Exegesis," 64.

[100] Origen, *De principiis*, 1.6.1. Two critical editions of Origen's writings may be found in the series "Die griechischen Schriftsteller der ersten drei Jahrhunderte" and "Source Chrétiennes." This study consulted the Latin text of *De principiis* found in Henri Crouzel and Manlio Simonetti, eds., *Origène: Traité des Principes*, 5 vols., Sources Chrétiennes, edition (Paris: Éditions du Cerf, 1978–1984). The English translation is mine.

[101] Origen, *De principiis*, 1.6.1. "Quae quidem etiam a nobis cum magno metu et cautela dicuntur, discutientibus magis et pertractantibus quam pro certo ac definito statuentibus."

eschatological matters is more of an experimental dialogue as opposed to a dogmatic certainty. As we review his comments we will do well to keep this caveat in mind and remember Henri Crouzel's admonition that for Origen speculative theology was just that: It was speculative.[102]

Origen's theology of ἀποκάτασσις flowed from two primary observations that he made based upon scriptural reflection: (1) In the end all things must return to the original state that God had intended for them from the beginning, and (2) that in the eschaton all things must be brought under subjection to Christ. Thus for Origen ἀποκάτασσις represented the ultimate victory of God that came through a cycle of creation, disintegration, and restoration. As we noted earlier in defining ἀποκάτασσις[103] Origen's concept fits loosely within the context of Hellenistic cosmic speculation that came to be associated with the word and that posited a cyclical cosmic restitution of the universe.

The idea that in the end all things must return to the original state was expressed by Origen in several ways. In *De principiis* 1.6.1 Origen affirmed:

We believe however that the goodness of God through Christ will restore[104] his entire creation to one end, even his enemies being conquered and subdued.

Continuing on in *De principiis* 1.6.2 Origen explained:

For the end is always like the beginning; and therefore as there is one end of all things, so we should understand that there is one beginning of all things, and as there is one end of many things, so from one beginning springs many differences and varieties, which in their turn are restored, through God's goodness, through their subjection to Christ and their unity with the Holy Spirit, to one end, which is like the beginning.

In his *Commentarii in Romanos* the restoration is visualized in terms of a restoration of all things to "health" or "soundness" [sanitatem]:

But we maintain that the cross of Christ and his death is so great that it brings to health and remedy not only the things of the present and future but also of previous ages, and it is sufficient not only for our human order, but also for the heavenly powers and orders.[105]

In *De principiis* 3.6.8 Origen used Genesis 1:1 as the ultimate expression and goal of ἀποκάτασσις:

For if we rightly understand the matter, this is the statement of Moses found in the beginning of his book, when he says, "In the beginning God

---

[102] Crouzel, *Origen*, 163–79.

[103] Cf. the Introduction, section 3.2 in this study.

[104] It makes sense that Rufinus' use of "revoco" here is likely his translation of Origen's ἀποκαθίσταμι.

[105] Origen, *Commentarii in Romanos*, s.v. Romans 5:11, PG 14:1053.

created the heavens and the earth." For this is the beginning of the entire creation: To this beginning the end and consummation of all things must be returned.

Thus Origen drew his justification for ἀποκάτασταϲιϲ from the famous opening sentence of the Bible.[106] For Origen, ἀποκάτασταϲιϲ rightly began with the beginning. Implied in this phrase is not only the way God intended things to be, but also a promise on God's part to see to it that his intent would ultimately be accomplished. Neither man, nor creature, nor creation itself would thwart God's will. Ultimately, God would be vindicated and emerge victorious in spite of the disintegration brought upon the world through humanity's sin. In the end all things would be restored and the beginning would be recapitulated. For Origen, any outcome less than total and complete ἀποκάτασταϲιϲ was unthinkable in light of God's power and ability. It is no coincidence that the passage most cited by Origen in support of ἀποκάτασταϲιϲ is 1 Cor. 15:22–28, which ends with the famous declaration of triumph, "that God may be all in all" (ἵνα η ὁ θεὸϲ [τὰ] πάντα ἐν πᾶϲιν).

The chosen instrument through which ἀποκάτασταϲιϲ would be achieved was, of course, Jesus Christ. The method through which ἀποκάτασταϲιϲ would be achieved was "subjection" to Christ and his will. In the end all creatures and things would be brought into subjection to Christ and nothing would escape him. In *De principiis* 1.6.1 Origen quotes several Bible passages in support of this thesis: Ps. 110:1: "The LORD said to my Lord, Sit at My right hand, till I make Your enemies Your footstool"; 1 Cor. 15:25: "For He must reign till He has put all enemies under His feet"; and 1 Cor. 15:27: "For all things must be made subject to Him."

Having established that it was through subjection to Christ that ἀποκάτασταϲιϲ would come, Origen then argued that this subjection meant nothing less than salvation itself:

> What then is the "subjection," by which "all things must be made subject" to Christ? I think that it is the same subjection by which we too desire to be subjected to him, and by which the apostles and all saints who have followed Christ were subject to him. For the word "subjection," when used of our subjection to Christ, indicates the salvation which is from Christ of those who are subject; as David also said, "Shall not my soul be subject to God? For through him comes my salvation."[107]

So strong was Origen's belief in restoration through subjection to Christ that he declared that "even his enemies" (i.e. Christ's) would be "conquered and

---

[106] This connection is also made in his *Commentarii in evangelium Joannis* where he explains that the goal of "the beginning" used in the opening verse of the Gospel of John is ἀποκάτασταϲιϲ. See Origen, *Commentarii in evangelium Joannis*, 1.16.91 (PG 14:49).

[107] Origen, *De principiis*, 1.6.1. See also *De principiis*, 1.6.2; 2.1.3, 3.6.3; *Contra Celsum*, 8.72; *Commentarii in Romanos*, 9.41 (PG 14:1243–44); *Commentarii in evangelium Joannis*, 32.3.26–33. Cf. 1 Cor. 15:28; Ps. 62:1.

subdued."[108] In *De principiis* 3.6.5 Origen discussed the destruction of "the last enemy" who is personified as death (cf. 1 Cor. 15:26): "For the destruction of the last enemy must be understood in this way, not that its substance which was made by God shall perish, but that the hostile purpose and will which proceed not from God but from itself will come to an end. Therefore, it will be destroyed, not in the sense of ceasing to exist, but of being no longer an enemy and no longer death. For to the Almighty nothing is impossible, nor is anything beyond the reach of cure by its maker."[109] Most take this reference and others like it to mean that even Satan himself would be included in the restoration.[110] Certainly Origen's sweeping language of ἀποκάτασταςις does not allow for the destruction of any rational creature. In Origen's eschatology there could be no enclave of evil that was not brought into compliance with Christ's will.[111]

Origen did, however, recognize the role of human freedom in the process of ἀποκάτασταςις. Because of his strong belief in the sovereignty of the human will Origen posited a system of postmortem deliverance similar to that of Clement's where all punishment is remedial and reformatory. In *De principiis* 3.6.6, he describes the restoration of "those who are making progress and becoming reconciled to God from their state of hostility." The process happens, "gradually and by degrees, during the lapse of infinite and immeasurable ages, seeing the improvement and correction will be realized slowly and separately in each individual person."[112] So then for Origen postmortem punishment was envisioned as a process that in the end resulted in universal salvation. In his *Commentarii in evangelium Matthaei* Origen maintained that the word αἰώνιος described only long rather than everlasting durations of time and thus he argued that it could not justify the notion of eternal punishment.[113] Sooner or later all rational beings would see the light of God's goodness and through the gradual application of corrective punishment they would eventually decide to return to him.

Origen's conception of ἀποκάτασταςις represents the first formal exposition and defense of universalism in the history of Christian theology. It is significant for both its audacity and its immense eschatological scope. In terms of theological method, Origen's construction is an interesting mixture of philosophical speculation made subservient to several biblical texts that imply a universal outcome. In particular it appears that Origen was influenced by the

---

[108] Origen, *De principiis*, 1.6.1.

[109] See also his comments in *De principiis*, 3.6.6 where he talks about the "last enemy, who is called death" being reconciled to God through "correction."

[110] Rufinus attempted to defend Origen against the charge that he had championed the possibility of the devil's salvation by producing a "translation" of one of Origen's letters in which he supposedly denied ever asserting this. Jerome exposed this attempt on Rufinus' part to be a gross distortion of what Origen actually wrote. Both the explicit statements made by Origen in *De principiis* and the logic of Origen's eschatology inevitably lead to the conclusion that he did indeed believe that Satan would be restored into a relationship with God. See also Butterworth's comments in Origen, *On First Principles*, trans. G.W. Butterworth (New York: Harper & Row, 1966), xxxix–xl.

[111] Cf. *Contra Celsum*, 8.72.

[112] See also *Commentarii in evangelium Joannis*, 13.23.138; *Commentarii in evangelium Matthaei*, 13.7; and *In Ezechielem homiliae*, 1.3.

[113] Origen, *Commentarii in evangelium Matthaei*, 15.31.

Hellenistic conception of ἀποκάτασταστς as a cyclical process of restoration. For Origen this cycle begins and ends with Genesis 1:1 as he noted in *De principiis*, 3.6.8: "To this beginning the end and consummation of all things must be returned."[114] Thus, as with Clement before him, we have in Origen a formulation of ἀποκάτασταστς that shows clear signs of being the product of interaction with the theological and philosophical thought of his day. To be certain, Origen's concept of ἀποκάτασταστς exhibits a far greater reliance on scripture than Clement's did. Nevertheless, outside influences still played a significant role in his formulation of the doctrine.

From a structural point of view, Origen's universalism is thoroughly Christocentric in its orientation and theoretical in its justification. Origen is not concerned with exploring extra-biblical real world factors in his conception of ἀποκάτασταστς. This then represents the starting point of a theology of Christian universalism: (1) universal salvation comes through Christ and Christ alone; (2) justification for that assertion is found primarily in the Bible and philosophical reasoning as opposed to other more tangible factors.

Initially Origen's formulation of ἀποκάτασταστς did not receive much attention from the arbiters of orthodoxy within the church. However, this is not to say that it would have been viewed as benign.[115] We know that later in Origen's life his theology was attacked by the bishop of the Alexandrian church, Demetrius, who held two synods in order to remove Origen from his teaching office and priesthood as well as to excommunicate him.[116] However, Origen also had his supporters, notably Theoctistus of Caesarea who ordained him and encouraged him to teach and preach within his jurisdiction until his death in 253 C.E.

It was not until after Origen's death, when the real machinery of Christian theology developed in a post-Constantine world, that theologians focused serious attention on the issue of heresy in Origen's writings and concomitantly on the issue of universalism and ἀποκάτασταστς. G.W. Butterworth recounts the gradual turn of the orthodox tide against Origen's theology.[117] In the early

---

[114] Origen, *De principiis*, 3.6.8.

[115] It has often been suggested by later proponents of universalism that the doctrine was accepted as orthodox and commonplace in the Patristic era. They argue that it was only through the process of a gradual assertion of rigid orthodoxy that the doctrine fell into disrepute and eventual repudiation in the sixth century. A classic presentation of this thesis may be found in Hansen, *Universalism: The Prevailing Doctrine of the Christian Church During its First Five Hundred Years with Authorities and Extracts*. In point of fact there had always been a strong affirmation of a dualistic belief in eternal salvation and eternal damnation within the church from the earliest time. Early writings such as the *Didache* and *The Epistle of Barnabas* reveal ancient evidence of this belief (see *Didache* 1:1 and 16:5; see also *The Epistle of Barnabas*, chapter 20). Early church fathers such as Irenaeus, Tertullian, and Justin Martyr also affirmed a strong belief in the dichotomy (See Irenaeus, *Adv. Haer.*, 2.28.7; Tertullian, *De resurrectione carnis*, ch. 35; Justin Martyr, *Dial.*, ch. 5).

[116] Berthold Altaner, *Patrology*, Hilda C. Graef, trans. (Freiburg: Herder, 1960), 224; Joseph W. Trigg, "Origen," in *ABD* 5:43.

[117] Origen, *On First Principles*, trans. Butterworth, xxxii–xlvi. See also Daley, *The Hope of the Early Church*, 89–91; Ludlow, "Universalism in the History of Christianity," 194–95; and Joseph Cullen Ayer, *A Source Book for Ancient Church History: From the*

years of the fourth century Methodius the bishop of Patara in Lycia (d. 311 C.E.) attacked Origen's views on creation and eternity, the pre-existence of souls, and the resurrection body. This attack was followed by condemnations issued by Epiphanius the bishop of Salamis (315–403 C.E.), Jerome (345–420 C.E.), and Theophilus the bishop of Alexandria (d. 412 C.E.). In 400 C.E. Theophilus convened a council at Alexandria and issued a formal condemnation of "Origenism"—a blanket and fluid term used to speak of Origen's departures from orthodoxy. In a famous turn of phrase Theophilus called Origen, the "hydra of heresies."[118] In 494 C.E. a Roman council condemned Origen and his writings. In his epic work, *The City of God*, Augustine of Hippo (354–430 C.E.) added considerable fuel to the fire when he denounced Origen and his theology.[119]

By the sixth century C.E. the works of Origen were under full scale attack. In 543 C.E. Emperor Justinian I condemned the theology of Origen by issuing ten anathemas against it. The ninth that censured ἀποκατάστασις read: "If anyone says or thinks that the punishment of demons and impious men is only temporary and will have an end, and that a restoration [ἀποκατάστασις] will take place, let him be anathema."[120] In 553 C.E. the final nail was driven into Origen's theological casket. At the Fifth Ecumenical Council of Constantinople (Constantinople II) the church formally condemned Origen and his work.[121] Appended to the acts of the Council were 15 anathemas condemning specific aspects of "Origenism" including ἀποκατάστασις. Although several scholars have argued that the original reference to Origen and the appended anathemas were a later addition to the text, the important point for our study is that down through the centuries the church commonly accepted the condemnation of Origen and ἀποκατάστασις to be valid. Therefore the church at large believed that the doctrine of universal salvation had been officially proscribed from this point forward.[122]

Apostolic Age to the Close of the Conciliar Period (New York: Charles Scribner's Sons, 1952), 483–93.

[118] Geddes McGregor, *Reincarnation in Christianity* (Wheaton, Ill.: Theosophical Publishing House, 1978), 58.

[119] Cf. Augustine, *The City of God*, 21.17. Ramelli notes that there was a considerable development in Augustine's theology regarding Origen and the doctrines of ἀποκατάστασις and eternal punishment. She argues that Augustine actually embraced Origen's eschatology early on in his career, especially during his anti-Manichaean phase. It was only later in life, through the crucible of the Pelagian controversy, that Augustine's theology solidified into his well known embrace of eternal punishment and a strict dichotomy in outcome between the elect and the non-elect. Regardless of his earlier position (Augustine recanted of it in his *Retractationes* 1.7.6) the fact remains that Augustine's mature eschatology became a bellwether for the church orthodoxy down through the centuries. See Ramelli, *The Christian Doctrine of Apokatastasis*, 659–76.

[120] Ayer, *A Source Book for Ancient Church History*, 543.

[121] See Capitula XI in *DEC* 1:119.

[122] For a detailed, albeit dated, introduction to the issue along with the relevant text, see the discussion contained in *NPNF*[2] 14:316-17. The text of the *DEC* does not include the anathemas against Origen due to the questionable nature of them. See *DEC* 1:105–106. The anathemas may be found in *NPNF*[2] 14:318–20.

This condemnation of ἀποκάτασταις marked a significant turning point in Christian theology. Infancy and puberty were over. A more rigid orthodoxy had asserted control and moved to excise what it saw to be the dangerous indiscretions of youth. This formal denunciation insured that the doctrine of universalism would remain largely unexplored and undeveloped for centuries to come. The enemies list was being defined and universalism was near the top. It would remain there until the challenge of the Reformation began to loosen the grip of the Catholic Church over the definition of orthodoxy.

3. The Post-Origen Era

Before the official condemnation of ἀποκάτασταις in 553 C.E. a few prominent theologians picked up Origen's thesis and expanded on it. It must be noted at the outset of this discussion that most of the Greek Fathers fell under the long shadow that Origen cast upon the theology that followed him. Between Origen and Constantinople II came a period of theological grayness as the wheels of orthodoxy began to gather momentum in its battle against Origenism. Therefore, it is not surprising to find that several theologians of this era incorporated ἀποκάτασταις into their theological thought. Due to constraints on length we will focus only on the more prominent advocates from this period.

3.1. Other Authorities

The greatest problem one faces when researching Christian universalism in the post-Origen era has to do once again with the scarcity of sources. The writings that survive from this time are extremely fragmentary and incomplete. This scarcity, in turn, must of necessity give our research an unbalanced perspective. Certainly there must have been much more written on the topic than survives. The fragments that do survive should not be construed as being normative or representative of what might have been. As Baxter notes, "[I]t is often difficult to determine exactly where some of the Fathers stood on apokatastasis." Therefore, we must proceed with caution.[123]

Didymus the Blind. Didymus (313–398 C.E.) was an Alexandrian theologian who was blind from infancy. He led the Catechetical School in Alexandria counting Rufinus and Jerome among his pupils. Because of the strong influence of Origen on his eschatology he was condemned by the Councils of 553 C.E. (Constantinople), 680 C.E. (Constantinople), 787 C.E. (Nicea), and 869 C.E. (Constantinople) and was anathematized by them as an Origenist.[124] In particular, Didymus seems to have argued for the ἀποκάτασταις of souls. He believed that souls were originally created in a purely immaterial state and asserted that through a cyclical process, which included a period of embodiment on the earth, all souls must be eventually restored to the purely immaterial state or bodiless existence in which they were created.[125] In Didymus' view, the resurrection of the dead should be understood in purely

---

[123] Baxter, "Apokatastasis," 60.
[124] *DEC* 1:125, 1:135, 1:161; Baxter, "Apokatastasis," 64–65.
[125] Daley, *The Hope of the Early Church,* 90; Ludlow, "Universalism in the History of Christianity," 194.

spiritual terms. Following Origen's lead on 1 Cor. 15:28 ("God will be all in all") Didymus held to the prospect that all enmity to God would eventually cease and that all "rational substances" would return to him, thus opening the possibility of salvation for Satan and his demons.[126]

Titus of Bostra (d. approx. 371 C.E.). Little is known about Titus other than that he was the bishop of Bostra in Arabia who was driven from his see through the trickery of Julian the Apostate.[127] Later on he returned to his position under the rule of Valens. Jerome lists Titus as being among those who were equally erudite in both scriptural and secular knowledge.[128] Titus' most influential work was his *Contra Manichaeos*, which is noted for being the only surviving work from the early Greek church that presents a thoroughgoing theodicy.[129] Titus' support for universalism seems to be based in his acceptance of Origen's view that the torments of hell were remedial and corrective in nature. He commented in book 1, chapter 32 of *Contra Manichaeos*:

> The abyss of hell is, indeed, the place of torment; but it is not eternal, nor did it exist in the original constitution of nature. It was made afterwards, as remedy for sinners, that it might cure them. And the punishments are holy, as they are remedial and salutary in their effect upon transgressors; for they are inflicted, not to preserve them in their wickedness. The anguish of their suffering compels them to break off their vices.[130]

Evagrius of Pontus (346–399 C.E.). Evagrius was a spiritual writer and ascetic monk who spent most of his life in the Nitrian desert. His works promoting spiritual progress through deep contemplation greatly influenced his generation.[131] As an admirer of Origen, Evagrius developed an Origenistic metaphysic in his writings. Although no explicit statements regarding universalism exist in the surviving corpus of Evagrius' works, certain aspects of his writings strongly hint at it. For instance, he predicted that, "the whole nature of rational beings will bow before the name of the Lord, who reveals the Father who is in him."[132] Evagrius also embraced Origen's views on the ultimate destruction of evil. He reasoned: "There was a time when evil was not, and there will be a time when it will not be; but there was no time when virtue

---

[126] Daley, *The Hope of the Early Church*, 90.

[127] For a narrative of the incident see Sozomen's *Ecclesiastical History*, 3:14.

[128] Jerome, *Epistulae*, 70:4: "All these writers so frequently interweave in their books the doctrines and maxims of the philosophers that you might easily be at a loss which to admire most, their secular erudition or their knowledge of the scriptures."

[129] For a comprehensive discussion of this work see Nils Arne Pedersen, *Demonstrative Proof in Defense of God: A Study of Titus of Bostra's Contra Manichaeos—The Work's Sources, Aims and Relation to its Contemporary Theology* (Leiden, U.K.: Brill, 2004).

[130] As cited and translated by Ballou, *Ancient History of Universalism*, 152–53.

[131] A measure of this influence can be seen in the intensity with which Jerome condemned his writings. Jerome dismissed Evagrius as an "Origentist" and a progenitor to Pelagius in his *Epistulae*, 133:3.

[132] Cited in Daley, *The Hope of the Early Church*, 91.

was not, nor will there be a time when it will not be."[133] Such a bold declaration does not seem to allow for an eternally existent hell that continues on without remedy for evil or evil doers. Certainly Evagrius' critics understood this to be the case and he was condemned as an Origentist by the Councils of 553 C.E. (Constantinople), 680 C.E. (Constantinople), 787 C.E. (Nicea), and 869 C.E. (Constantinople).[134]

Diodorus of Tarsus (d. approx. 394 C.E.). Diodorus headed a monastic school in Antioch and counted the famous John Chrysostom among his students.[135] He became the bishop of Tarsus in 378 C.E. and was a leading defender of Nicene orthodoxy in opposition to several heresies including Apollinarianism, Arianism, and Sebelianism.[136] In the late fourth century Cyril of Alexandria attacked Diodorus' writings for Nestorian tendencies and they were officially condemned by the church in 399 C.E. Although Diodorus voiced his disagreement with much of what Origen taught, it appears that he accepted Origen's argument that the torment of hell was temporary. However, in contrast to Origen who argued that the torment of hell was remedial and corrective, Diodorus argued that torment of hell was punitive and mediated in proportion to the amount of sin a person committed in life. In his work *De aecon.* Diodorus put forward a punitive conception of hell that nevertheless held out the promise of universal salvation:

> For the wicked also there are punishments, not perpetual however, lest the immortality prepared for them should become a disadvantage; but they are to be tormented for certain brief period, proportioned to the desert and measure of their faults and impiety, according to the amount of malice in their works. They shall, therefore, suffer punishment a brief space, but immortal blessedness, having no end awaits them.[137]

Marcellus of Ancyra (d. approx. 374 C.E.). Marcellus was a bishop at Ancyra who was deposed for his heterodox views primarily regarding the Trinity. He was a strong opponent of Arianism but in his opposition he adopted an extreme form of Sabellian modalism, which quite literally encompassed the sweep of world history.[138] In his affirmation of the radical unity of God, Marcellus

---

[133] Cited in Daley, *The Hope of the Early Church*, 91. Daley attributes this view to the influence of Gregory of Nyssa upon Evagrius' thought, however it seems to make more sense to tie this aspect in with Origen's influence especially since Origen was the primary influence on his eschatology.
[134] *DEC* 1:125, 1:135, 1:161.
[135] Baxter, "Apokatastasis," 65.
[136] Charles G. Herbermann, et al, *The Catholic Encyclopedia: An International Work of Reference on the Constitution, Doctrine, Discipline, and History of the Catholic Church*, online ed., transcribed by K. Knight (New York: Robert Appleton, 1907–1912), s.v. "Diodorus of Tarsus" by John Chapman, http://www.newadvent.org/cathen/05008a.htm. (Accessed March 20, 2014.)
[137] As cited and translated by Ballou, *Ancient History of Universalism*, 185.
[138] Herbermann, et al, *The Catholic Encyclopedia*, online ed., s.v. "Marcellus of Ancyra" by J.P. Arendzen, http://www.newadvent.org/cathen/09642a.htm. (Accessed October 27, 2014.)

proposed that God himself participated in human history in three unique stages or economies, each of which was accompanied by three unique forms or expressions of God.[139] The first economy was that of the Father, which spanned the creation of the world to the incarnation. The second economy was that of the Christ, which spanned Jesus' time on the earth. The third economy was that of the Holy Spirit, which spanned the age of the church. Marcellus argued that at the end the church as the body of Christ would take over the fleshly body of the Logos and be drawn into the immeasurable vastness of the divine.[140] In discussing Acts 3:21 and its reference to ἀποκάταστασις he explained: "This passage defines a certain limit or fixed period, in which the text says it is right that the human economy is thus united to the Word. For what else does 'until the restoration' mean, except to indicate the coming age, in which all things will share in perfect restoration (ἀποκάταστασις)?"[141] Thus Marcellus formulated a unique variation of ἀποκάταστασις that incorporated the Trinity into world history and humanity into the Trinity.

Gregory of Nazianzus (329–390 C.E.). Gregory of Nazianzus is known as one of the three great Cappodocian theologians in company with Basil of Caesarea and his brother Gregory of Nyssa. He spent most of his life as the bishop of Constantinople and was embroiled in the defense of Nicene orthodoxy against Arianism. By all accounts he was a man of reserved character who preferred to focus on spirituality and devotion as opposed to rigorous theory and analysis. Gregory appreciated Origen's work and he cautiously incorporated certain elements of Origen's theology into his own. Gregory's eschatology agreed with Origen in two key areas: (1) the temporary nature of eternal punishment, and (2) ἀποκάταστασις. Ever a careful lecturer, Gregory delicately broached the issue of eternal punishment in several of his orations. In *Oration* 39.19 Gregory obliquely endorsed the idea that the fire of hell is purgative and "consumes the stubble of every evil."[142] In *Oration* 40.36 Gregory analogized Christ to a "cleansing fire" that "takes away whatsoever is material and of evil habit."[143] Regarding ἀποκάταστασις Gregory linked it to his notion of deification in which he asserted that humanity will ultimately participate in the Godhead. In a famous passage in *Oration* 38.12 he affirmed, "And He who gives riches becomes poor, for He assumes the poverty of my flesh that I may assume the richness of his Godhead."[144] In *Oration* 30.6 Gregory defines ἀποκάταστασις in terms of the unification with God: "But God will be all in all in the time of the restoration (ἀποκάταστασις); not [just] the Father. . . but God as a whole, when we are no longer many, as we are now in our movements

[139] Martin Tetz, "Die Theologie des Markell von Ankyra III: Die pseudo-athanasianische *Epistula ad Liberium*, ein Markellisches Bekenntnis," *ZKG* 83 (1972): 188. Daley, *The Hope of the Early Church*, 78.

[140] Daley, *The Hope of the Early Church*, 78.

[141] Marcellus, "Fragment 117," in Erich Klostermann, *Gegen Marcell: Uber die kirchliche Theologie. Die Fragmente Marcells* (Berlin: Akademie-Verlag, 1972), as cited in Daley, *The Hope of the Early Church*, 79.

[142] PG 36:357.

[143] PG 36:409–12.

[144] PG 36:324.

and passions, bearing in ourselves nothing at all of God, or only a little; but the entire Godhead, receptive of God as a whole and of [him] alone. This is the perfection towards which we strive."[145] Therefore we see that Gregory's doctrine of ἀποκάταστασις is inextricably bound up with his notion of deification. Gregory believed that Christ guaranteed the participation of a unified humanity in the Godhead.

Ambrose (334–397 C.E.). Ambrose was the bishop of Milan in the late forth century. Along with Augustine and Jerome he was one of the most influential voices in the Latin Church in this era. As an admirer of Origen's theology and theological method, Ambrose was able to enlarge the Western church's esteem for Origen's style of exegesis.[146] Although Ambrose seems ambiguous at times regarding the issue of everlasting punishment, nevertheless there are clear indications in his theology that he was sympathetic to Origen's perspective and that he actually embraced the idea of universal salvation. In his exposition on Psalm 39 Ambrose took up a discussion of the thief on the cross. He saw Jesus' promise of deliverance to this man as an illustration of God's ability to save even the most hardened of sinners. Ambrose concluded: "No one can be excluded when the thief is recovered through your help."[147] In his exposition on Psalm 118 we find one of the most straightforward statements that Ambrose made regarding universal salvation: "Though salvation is far from sinners, nevertheless let no one despair, for the mercies of the Lord are many. What has been joined to sin disappears; the mercy of the Lord liberates . . . . The mercy of a man is toward his own neighbor: the mercy of the Lord is on all flesh; that all flesh may ascend to the Lord, that is the way the mercy of the Lord has been given."[148] The word "mercy" is used five times by Ambrose in this short passage, which underscores the fact that he saw universal salvation as a logical conclusion that was to be drawn based upon the fundamental compassion found in God's character.

3.2. Gregory of Nyssa
One of the three great Cappadocians, Gregory of Nyssa (335–395 C.E.) was raised in a Christian family that was particularly devoted to theology and service within the church. The two great influences in his life were his sister, Macrina, and his brother, the famous Basil of Caesarea.[149] Gregory was ordained the bishop of Nyssa in 371 C.E. and went through a period of

---

[145] PG 36:112.

[146] For a discussion of Ambrose's Origenism see Henri Crouzel, "Fonte prenicene della dottrina di Ambrogio sulla risurrezione dei morti," *ScC* 102/4 (1974): 374–88.

[147] Ambrose, *Enarrationes in XII. Psalmos Davidicos*, 39.19 in PL 14:1064a: "Nemo est qui possit excludi, quando receptus est latro, minister tuus."

[148] Ambrose, *Expositio Psalmi CXVII* in PL 15:1492d–93a. "Etsi longe est a peccatoribus salus; tamen nemo desperet, quia multae sunt misericordiae Domini. Qui enim suo peccato pereunt, misericordia Domini liberantur . . . . Misericordia enim hominis in proximum suum: misericordia Domini in omnem carnem; ut omnis caro ad Dominum ascenderet, illa Domini miseratione donata."

[149] Ludlow, *Universal Salvation: Eschatology in the Thought of Gregory of Nyssa and Karl Rahner*, 21–22.

persecution over his support for the Nicene Trinitarian formula. After being deposed from his office in 375 C.E., he was restored in 378 C.E. and contributed greatly to the pronouncements made by the Second Ecumenical Council of Constantinople. Although he was a church administrator, Gregory was known primarily for his powerful theological writing and soaring oratory.

In terms of his eschatological outlook, there can be no doubt that Gregory was heavily influenced by Origen and his theology of ἀποκάταστασις.[150] While his brother Basil of Caesarea rejected the teachings of Origen regarding universal salvation and eternal punishment, Gregory embraced them and repeatedly reaffirmed them in his writings often modifying and expanding on Origen's formulation.[151] Following in Origen's footsteps, Gregory made ἀποκάταστασις a central feature of his theology and eschatological system.

Although Gregory used the word ἀποκάταστασις in a relatively flexible way, from an eschatological point of view it did take on for him the primary meaning that we find in Origen, namely, that of referring to the restoration of the cosmos back to its perfect original state.[152] We find this perspective in an important passage that he penned in his *De hominis opificio* where he discussed the resurrection and its implications for restoration:

> The grace of the resurrection promises to us nothing other than the restoration of the fallen to their original state. For the grace we look for is a restitution to the first life restoring again to Paradise him who was cast out of it.[153]

Similarly, in his *Dialogus de anima et resurrectione Macrina* he defines the resurrection as the "restoration of our nature to the original state."[154] In his discussion of 1 Cor. 15:22–28 in *In illud: Tunc et ipse filius* Gregory describes the obliteration of evil "with nothing made by God failing to obtain the kingdom of God."[155] Thus Gregory's concept of ἀποκάταστασις was built around the basic idea of the restoration and re-establishment of all things back to God's perfect plan and order.

In a fashion much akin to Origen, Gregory noted that the primary means through which ἀποκάταστασις would be achieved was Jesus Christ and that the method through which ἀποκάταστασις would be achieved was

---

[150] For a detailed discussion of Gregory's understanding of ἀποκάταστασις including comparisons to Origen see Harmon, *"Apokatastasis* and Exegesis," 112–72; and Ludlow, *Universal Salvation: Eschatology in the Thought of Gregory of Nyssa and Karl Rahner*, 21–114.

[151] For a brief discussion of Basil's position see Daley, *The Hope of the Early Church*, 81–83.

[152] For other uses by Gregory see Ludlow, *Universal Salvation: Eschatology in the Thought of Gregory of Nyssa and Karl Rahner*, 38–44.

[153] Gregory of Nyssa, *De hom. opif.*, PG 44:188c–d. Unless otherwise noted the translations are mine.

[154] Gregory of Nyssa, *anim. et res.*, PG 46:148.

[155] Gregory of Nyssa, *In illud.* in Kenneth Downing, Jacob A. McDonough, and Hadwiga Höner, eds., *Gregorii Nysseni: Opera Dogmatica Minora*, vol. 3, pt. 2 (Leiden, U.K.: Brill, 1987), 3,2: 13–14.

"submission" to Christ and his will. In addition to 1 Cor. 15:28 ("God will be all in all"), which he referred to sixty-five times, a favorite passage of Gregory's was Philippians 2:10–11 with its reference to every knee bending to Christ, which he referred to some forty-five times.[156] He explained in *Refutatio confessionis Eunomii* that, "subjection is a protection against destruction. Just as medicine is zealously pursed by the sick, so also is subjection by those in need of salvation."[157]

This subjection was to be achieved in perfect concert with human freedom and this in turn was to be achieved in part through a process of post mortem purification and correction. Gregory understood this process to be variable and adjusted to the individual in such a way that eventually all people would be reformed, no matter how difficult or obstinate: "He had one goal after all the fullness of our nature has been perfected in each one. Some immediately who have been purified from evil in this life, others who have been healed after these things through fire for the appropriate periods of time, and still others who are unaware of the experience of both good and evil equally . . ."[158] Therefore, Gregory, in agreement with Origen, viewed the suffering inflicted in hell as a temporary experience that was both remedial and reformatory.

An important aspect of Gregory's formulation of ἀποκάτασταϲιϲ was the complete elimination of all evil from the universe. In Gregory's theology evil was necessarily temporary and would be completely eradicated in the end. This elimination was linked tightly in his thought to the necessity of the eventual subjection of the will of all rational creatures to God:

> For it is necessary that at some time evil be wholly and completely removed out of existence, and as was previous said, what does not exist should not exist at all. For since it does not belong to its nature that evil have existence outside of the will, when every will rests in God evil will depart into utter destruction since there is no container remaining for it.[159]

The phrase "every will" included the salvation of Satan and his demons. In his *Oratio catechetica magna* Gregory affirmed that Christ had accomplished his purposes by "freeing both humanity from evil and healing even the originator of evil himself."[160] Gregory, as Origen before him, could not countenance the idea that evil could survive in some corner of a restored universe. Therefore all wills, including Satan's, must be brought under subjection to Christ.

Gregory's conception of ἀποκάτασταϲιϲ represents the second most important exposition and defense of universalism in Patristic theology—the first being the work of Origen himself. Although Gregory's eschatology has much in common with Origen's thought, it is still a carefully nuanced presentation of Gregory's viewpoint and it is equally significant for both its

---

[156] Harmon, "*Apokatastasis* and Exegesis," 150; 154.
[157] Gregory of Nyssa, *Refutatio confessionis Eunomii* in Werner Jaeger, ed. *Gregorii Nysseni Opera: Contra Eunomium Libri*, 2 vols. (Leiden, U.K.: Brill, 1960), 2:396–97.
[158] Gregory of Nyssa, *anim. et res.*, PG 46:149–52.
[159] Gregory of Nyssa, *anim. et res.*, PG 46:100–101.
[160] Gregory of Nyssa, *or. catech.* in Ekkehard Mülenberg, ed., *Gregorii Nysseni Oratio Catechetica: Opera Dogmatica Minora*, vol. 3, pt. 4 (Leiden, U.K.: Brill, 1996), 3,4: 67.

independence as well as its dependence upon Origen. Gregory was certainly no mere parrot and his exposition of the subject reflects this. In terms of theological method, Gregory's formulation stands alongside Origen's as being thoroughly Christocentric in its orientation and theoretical in its justification. For Gregory the Bible was everything and he sought to justify his embrace of universalism through the Scriptures. His argument for universalism was centered completely in his exposition of the Bible.

3.3. The End of the Era

Several other prominent theologians from the post-Origen era have been labeled as universalists down through the centuries, in particular Theodore of Mopsuestia and his successor Theodoret of Cyrus.[161] Despite the fact that a few statements made by them appear to endorse universal salvation, there is abundant evidence in their writings that they both embraced a more traditional view of hell and eternal punishment.[162] This misunderstanding once again underscores for us the caution that must be exercised when examining the evidence from this period of time.

In the sixth century Origenism, with its attendant doctrine of ἀποκάταστασις, remained active in Palestine up to and even after its condemnation at the Council of Constantinople in 553 C.E. A Syrian monk named Stephen Bar Sudaili (480–543 C.E.), who lived in the Judean desert, advocated a radicalized form of Evagrian eschatology, which included an aggressive affirmation of universal salvation that envisioned the union of all things with God: "Hells shall pass, and torments shall be done away; prisoners shall be released; for even reprobates are absolved and outcasts return . . . and chastisements cease . . . for demons receive grace and humans receive mercy . . . and everything becomes one thing."[163] Along with Sudaili several other monks in Palestine affirmed this radical eschatology and even added to it positing nothing less than "the abolition of material reality in the world to come, and the ultimate absorption of all created spirits into an undifferentiated unity with the divine Logos."[164] Such mystical speculations did not gather a great audience. After 553 C.E. Origen's doctrine of ἀποκάταστασις and universalism in general rapidly became untenable in both the Eastern and the Western churches.

4. Conclusion

This section has sought to trace the birth and the development of universalism in ancient Christian thought. When viewed as a whole the data provides us with an interesting picture of how ἀποκάταστασις along with its core component of universalism made an entrance into the early church and eventually moved to the center stage of early theological debate.

The journey began with the idea of posthumous salvation that had a ubiquitous presence in the spirituality of the Greco-Roman world. Can a single

---

[161] Cf. Baxter, "Apokatastasis," 66–68.

[162] See the detailed discussion of Brian Daley in *The Hope of the Early Church*, 111–17.

[163] Stephen Bar Sudaili, "The Book of Holy Hierotheos," as cited in Daley, *The Hope of the Early Church*, 178.

[164] Daley, *The Hope of the Early Church*, 190.

source for this belief be isolated? It is doubtful. Sufficient for our study is the fact that many members of first-century Roman society steadfastly believed in it. This concept of posthumous salvation was in turn brought into the church through new converts who had absorbed it from the culture around them. Through speculative writings and ecstatic visions the idea of posthumous salvation was introduced into the primitive eschatological discussion of the early church. The passages we looked at in the *Apocalypse of Peter* and the *Sibylline Oracles* as well as the prayer passages found in *The Acts of Paul and Thecla* and the *Passion of Perpetua and Felicitas* underscore the fact there was indeed a belief on the part of some that at least a limited number of the dead could be posthumously delivered from suffering and even eternal condemnation. Other writings such as the *Gospel of Peter,* the *Odes of Solomon*, and the *Gospel of Nicodemus* bear testimony to the fact that some early Christian thinkers were attempting to expand the horizon of salvation and even vaguely dabbled with the notion of universalism itself.

These diverse strains of speculative thought collided in the city of Alexandria, which was long known for being the crossroads of all things philosophical and theological in the ancient Hellenistic world. Various forms of gnostic universalism emerged from Alexandria. The Nag Hammadi corpus contains within itself evidence of a form of gnostic universalism that had spread throughout the ranks of the gnostics in Egypt. It is no surprise that we find that the first intimations of ἀποκάτασοις and Christian universalism came out of the Catechetical School in Alexandria. Clement and Origen, with their reputations for vast cosmopolitan scholarship, would have been well aware of the myriad of eschatological opinions orbiting around them both within the church and outside of it. It would be naïve to think that these men could have remained uninfluenced by such contact. In examining the biblical evidence they naturally gravitated toward those passages in the New Testament that seemed to be pregnant with universalist meaning: 1 Cor. 15:28—"God will be all in all"; Phil. 2:8—"at the name of Jesus every knee should bow"; 1 John 2:2—"and He Himself is the propitiation for our sins; and not for ours only, but also for those of the whole world." The synthesis that emerged from the collision of the Bible and Hellenistic speculation at the Catechetical School in Alexandria was Origen's carefully crafted theory of ἀποκάτασοις, which included universalism as a foundational element.

Origen's influence extended into almost every corner of the ancient Christian world and captured the fascination of many theologians and church leaders. It is interesting to note that virtually every other expression of Christian universalism that comes after Origen takes note of him in some way, which begs the question of what would have happened without him. Certainly without his sweeping view of eschatology and scholarly presentation things would have been much different. If this brief survey of ancient Christian universalism has revealed anything to us, it is just how pervasive and influential the thought of Origen was. As the true father of Christian universalism he has indeed cast a long shadow over the field. His advocacy set off a debate within the Christian church that has continued down through the long march of centuries and up to this very day.

CHAPTER 2

Suppression and Rebirth:
The Middle Ages through the Reformation

With the condemnation of universalism by the Fifth Ecumenical Council of Constantinople in 553 C.E. the die was cast—from that point forward universalism would be regarded as a deadly heresy. With the power of the state at its disposal, the medieval church was able to enforce its theological conclusions upon all dissenters. Although there was some initial hesitation, the suppression of heretics became the standard operating procedure employed by the church for a thousand years and beyond. It took nothing less than the sea change called the Reformation to once again pry open the lid to the debate regarding universalism.

Nevertheless, despite the church's efforts to destroy it, universalism did survive during the Middle Ages and, as we shall see, there were large numbers of people who embraced it regardless of the dangers. In this chapter we will examine the phenomenon of universalism in the Middle Ages and the doctrinal revolution called the Reformation that re-ignited the controversy.

1. The Middle Ages[1]
In the battle over the doctrine of hell the basic position of Augustine (354–430) became the official position of the church in the Middle Ages. Augustine's perspective included an affirmation of eternal separation, eternal punishment, and eternal damnation.[2] Augustine's view was solidified and given a fuller expression by Gregory the Great (540–604).[3] After this, as Pierre Richard commented, "commence l'époque des compilateurs encyclopédistes, simples

---

[1] Classically the Middle Ages were dated from the fall of the Western Roman Empire in 476 C.E. through the beginning of the Renaissance in the fourteenth century. Recent writers have set the starting point in the tenth century and extended the terminus of the era down to the sixteenth century. In this study we shall use a chronology that roughly combines the two positions and encompasses the time period after the Fifth Ecumenical Council of Constantinople in 553 C.E. and extends down to the time of the Reformation in the sixteenth century.

[2] Augustine's views regarding the doctrine of hell are most clearly enunciated in chapters 21 and 22 of his book *The City of God*. As we have already noted, Ramelli argues that there was a considerable development in Augustine's theology regarding the doctrines of ἀποκάτασταϛιϛ and eternal punishment. Early in his career Augustine embraced a version of ἀποκάτασταϛιϛ that was very close to the position that Origen took. Later on he abandoned this position for the basic eschatological outline that formed the foundation for doctrine of the church in this area. See Ramelli, *The Christian Doctrine of Apokatastasis*, 659–76.

[3] The fullest statement of Gregory's eschatology may be found in his *Dialogues*.

transmetteurs. Sur l'enfer, on répéte saint Augustin et saint Grégoire."[4] Thus, from an eschatological point of view, the essential doctrine of the church regarding hell and eternal punishment was fairly well set in stone by the time the Middle Ages began.

With Constantine's conversion in 312 C.E. the Christian church moved from being an outlawed religion to being the official religion of the Roman Empire. The transfer of such enormous power to the church brought with it the temptation to use it in the service of promoting orthodoxy. Augustine himself was among those who first advocated using the coercive force of the state as a means of bringing heretics into alignment with church teaching. We do well to remember Augustine's famous justification for using force against the heretical Donatists, which sets the tone for the church's response to heresy from that point forward:

> Why, therefore, should not the Church use force in compelling her lost sons to return, if the lost sons compelled others to their destruction? . . . Wherefore, if the power which the Church has received by divine appointment in its due season, through the religious character and the faith of kings, be the instrument by which those which are found in the highways and hedges—that is, in heresies and schisms—are compelled to come in, then let them not find fault with being compelled, but consider whether they be so compelled.[5]

In discussing the appropriate response to heresy, Thomas Aquinas commented that the sin of heretics

> deserves banishment, not only from the Church by excommunication, but also from this world by death. To corrupt the faith, whereby the soul lives, is much graver than to counterfeit money, which supports temporal life. Since forgers and other malefactors are summarily condemned to death by the civil authorities, with much more reason may heretics as soon as they are convicted of heresy be not only excommunicated, but also justly be put to death [sed et juste occidi].[6]

This view still prevailed up to and even after the time of the Reformation. Reformation theologian Theodore Beza commented: "The contention that heretics should not be punished is as monstrous as the contention that patricides and matricides should not be put to death; for heretics are a thousandfold worse criminals than these."[7] In the declaration of the 11th Session of the Council of Florence (Feb. 4, 1442) the church affirmed its traditional position based upon the strict interpretation of Augustine's disciple, Flugentius of Ruspe (468–533), found in his *De fide*:

---

[4] Pierre Richard, "Enfer," in A. Vacant and E. Mangenot, eds., *Dictionnaire de Théologie Catholique* (Paris: Letouzey et Ané, 1924), 5:82. (Hereafter known as *DTC*).
[5] Augustine, *The Correction of the Donatists, 23–24, NPNF*[1] 4:642.
[6] Thomas Aquinas, *Summa Theologiae, vol. 32, Consequences of Faith*, ed. Thomas Gilby (London: Blackfriars, Eyre & Spottiswoode, 1975), 2a2ae. 11, 3, p. 89.
[7] Quoted in Thomas Talbott, *The Inescapable Love of God*, 29.

> [The Holy Roman Catholic Church] . . . believes, professes and preaches that all those who are outside the catholic church, not only pagans but also Jews and heretics and schismatics cannot share in eternal life and go *into everlasting fire which was prepared for the devil and his angels*, unless they are joined to the catholic church before the end of their lives.[8]

Therefore, in its escalating battle against heresy the church ruthlessly pursued a policy of the suppression of all other doctrinal viewpoints.[9] Indeed, medieval society became increasingly associated with and delineated by church orthodoxy. As Gordon Leff observed:

> Now it was precisely the existence of such a prevailing orthodoxy, defined by the church and enforced with the lay power, that distinguished medieval society. In this sense it was a closed society. Every member belonged to the church, and his or her salvation depended upon living and dying within it. To be outside it, for whatever reason, was to be anathema, whether as an infidel—pagan, Jew, or Moslem—or as a heretic. But whereas the first category was a matter for lamentation, opprobrium or crusade, according to the circumstances, a heretic was the church's immediate concern: either to be restored or punished. There could be no intermediate position. The church was God's communion; to reject it, or be rejected by it, was to reject God.[10]

The strong condemnation of universalism by the church at Constantinople in 553 C.E. coupled to the ascendancy of Augustinian eschatology and the rancorous suppression of heretics resulted in an environment in which few theologians were willing to discuss universalism, much less affirm it as a valid theological option. Nevertheless, there are still a few traces of universalism to be found in the theology of the Middle Ages. Although the church succeeded in large part to restrain an open embrace of the doctrine there were still some who persisted in their defiance of church orthodoxy.

1.1. Maximus the Confessor
Maximus (580–662) was a Constantinopolitan monk who is considered by many to be the last great theologian of Greek Patristic literature. Due to his

---

[8] *DEC* 1:578 (italics in the original).

[9] Malcolm Lambert commented, "After Constantine's conversion, Christians in effect held the power of the State and, despite some hesitations, they used it to impose a uniformity of belief. In both the Eastern and Western portions of the Empire it became the law that pertinacious heretics were subject to the punishments of exile, branding, confiscation of goods, and death. These regulations survived the fall of the Empire, as so did the assumption that it was the right of the Church to call on the State to put down heresy." Malcolm D. Lambert, *Medieval Heresy: Popular Movements from Bogomil to Hus* (London: Edward Arnold, 1977), 3.

[10] Gordon Leff, *Heresy in the Later Middle Ages: The Relation of Heterodoxy to Dissent c. 1250–1450* (Manchester: Manchester University Press; New York: Barnes and Noble, 1967), 1.

focus on the hope of universal salvation and the union of all creation with God, many have argued that Maximus held to a doctrine of apokatastasis that included universalism.[11] At the center of Maximus' eschatology was the concept of divinization in which he affirmed that, "God is joined with those who have become gods."[12] In his *Quæstiones ad thalassium de scriptura sacra* Maximus declared: "Even in the heart of the earth, where we were swallowed through death, having been overcome by evil, voluntarily descending, also through the raising up of the resurrection the entire continuing nature will be lifted up to heaven."[13]

Despite a superficial appearance of universalism, Maximus' eschatology makes it clear that the gift of divinization will be limited to those who freely choose to follow Christ.[14] For Maximus there was a very real chance that someone could reject God's offer of salvation and be eternally lost.[15] In his *Epistola prima* he refers to those who will go into "everlasting fire" (εἰς τὸ αἰώνιος πῦρ).[16] In the same letter he speaks of people receiving darkness instead of light, distress instead of grace, and torment and anguish instead of rest.[17] Thus Maximus embraced the conceptual framework of a more traditional eschatology that included eternal punishment. Although he clung to the hope of universal salvation and deification, he tempered these longings with a belief in the reality of an eternally existing hell and place of torment.

1.2. Johannes Scotus Eriugena
Johannes Scotus Eriugena[18] (c. 810–c. 877) was an Irish philosopher who gained the patronage of Charles the Bald of France and became the leader of the palace school in Laon. Few facts are known about his life other than those limited details that survive in his work. He was deeply influenced by the writings of Pseudo-Dionysius, Gregory of Nyssa, and Maximus the Confessor. His interest in these men was such that he spent a considerable amount of time personally translating their more important works into Latin. His theology has been rightly described as "an attempted reconciliation of the neoplatonist idea of emanation with the Christian idea of creation."[19] The resultant cosmology has a strongly pantheistic flavor. In his *Periphyseon* or *De divisione naturae* Eriugena posited that Nature be divided into four categories based upon distinctions he made regarding the character and relationship of created and non

---

[11] Cf. Baxter, "Apokatastasis," 70–71.

[12] Maximus, *Ambigua ad Joannem* 7 in PG 91:1088, C13–15. The Greek phrase reads: ὁ θεὸς θεοῖς γεγομένοις ἐνούμενος.

[13] Maximus, *Quæstiones ad thalassium de scriptura sacra* in PG 90:700, A14–B3 (my translation). See also *Capita theologiæ et œconomiæ* 47 in PG 90:1100; *Ambigua ad Joannem* 10 in PG 91:1165.

[14] Maximus, *Quæstiones ad thalassium de scriptura sacra*, 63 in PG 90:668, C6–9.

[15] Cf. *Ambigua ad Joannem*, 7 in PG 91:1076, C10–14; *Quaest ad thal.* 63 in PG 90:668, C6–9.

[16] Maximus, *Epistolai*, 1, in PG 91:381, B13.

[17] Maximus, *Epistolai*, 1, in PG 91:384, A6–8.

[18] Commonly called "Erigena," although Eriugena is more accurate.

[19] Baxter, "Apokatastasis," 71–72.

created being.[20] His final category envisions God as that "which neither creates nor is created" and to whom the entire creation must return.[21] It is in such tight associations of God with his creation that Eriugena's pantheism and universalism is most clearly seen. Eriugena argued that the creation was a "theophania" or showing forth of the very essence of God in the world. He believed that God makes the world out of his essence and that history is a progressive process of the revelation of the divine nature.

His pantheistic outlook led Eriugena to embrace the idea of universal restoration. In keeping with the earlier Greek construction of apokatastasis, Eriugena's theory of restoration included a cycling of the universe from unity in the original state to division and back to the original unity again. This restoration included, (1) the return of "causes" (Platonic forms?) to God, (2) "the general return of all human nature saved in Christ to the pristine state of its creation and to . . . the dignity of the divine image," and (3) the return of the elect who "will cross the boundaries of nature into God himself, and will be one in him and with him."[22] In defining the distinction between the general restoration of all human nature and the special elevation of the elect, Eriugena analogized it to the Garden of Eden in which all humans return to Paradise but only a few are allowed to partake of the Tree of Life.[23] Ludlow is careful to note that Eriugena's theology of universal restoration does not necessarily equate to a theology of universal salvation.[24] However, when Eriugena speaks of all human beings returning to Paradise it is hard to see how it could be interpreted in any other way. The distinction that Eriugena draws between the general return of all to God and the special elevation of the elect appears to be one of degree and not of kind and if this analysis is true then it would place Eriugena firmly within the universalist camp.

In Eriugena's eschatology we find a universalism that was profoundly influenced by philosophical thought that was external to Christian theology. In particular, his pantheism and emanationism were drawn from the neoplatonic thought of Pseudo-Dionysius. His effort to reconcile this neoplatonic mysticism with Christian creationism resulted in an interesting amalgam of the two, which, in turn, led him to draw universalist conclusions. Thus, what we have in Eriugena is not a universalism that is driven by Christian revelation and theology, but rather a universalism that is thoroughly grounded in peripheral contemplation.

1.3. The Heresy of the Free Spirit

The heresy of the Brothers and Sisters of the Free Spirit is an enigmatic phenomenon in Medieval theology. Although some have held that it was "an artificial heresy heavily 'developed' by persecutors,"[25] there is overwhelming

---

[20] John Scotus Eriugena, *De divisione naturae*, in PL 122:439–1022.

[21] *ODCC*, 558.

[22] Eriugena, *De divisione Naturae*, V:39 as quoted in Ludlow, "Universalism in the History of Christianity," 195.

[23] Ludlow, "Universalism in the History of Christianity," 196.

[24] Ludlow, "Universalism in the History of Christianity," 196.

[25] Lambert, *Medieval Heresy*, 48; 177–81. Lambert supports his thesis by noting two important factors: (1) We have very little primary source literature from the actual

evidence to suggest that it was in fact much more than this. The problem in defining the movement lies in the fact that it was so doctrinally diverse and spread out over a large portion of Europe. Most historians trace the beginnings of the Free Spirit movement to Amaury of Bène (d. c. 1207—also known as Amalric of Bena) who was a lecturer in theology and logic at the University of Paris.[26] Amaury espoused a doctrine of mystical pantheism that took its primary cues from the neoplatonism of Johannes Scotus Eriugena. In 1206 Amaury was required to make a public recantation by the Pope. Not long after this several of his unrepentant followers were burnt for heresy. Because of its use by Amaury, the Council of Sens condemned Eriugena's *De divisione naturae* as heretical in 1225. After Amaury's death, Amaurian thought was spread primarily through two groups: The Beghards and the Beguins. The Beghards were a fraternity of "holy beggars" who were patterned after itinerant monks. In time they came to receive the message of the Free Spirit and became a powerful missionary arm for the movement. The Beguins were a movement of women who accepted Free Spirit ideas and often formed communal homes from which they proselytized.

Amaurian doctrine has interesting parallels to that of Marcellus of Ancyra (d. 374) and Joachim of Fiore (c. 1135–1202) in that it divides world history into three ages that correspond to the persons of the Trinity.[27] According to the

---

people who supposedly promoted the heresy, and (2) most of what we know about the heresy comes to us from the writings of the inquisitors who used extreme threats and torture to obtain confessions. In Lambert's view the persecution of the heresy is more a study in Medieval hysteria as opposed to the research of an actual phenomenon. A major problem with Lambert's thesis rests in the fact we do know that the Catholic Church zealously sought to commit every form of heretical literature to the flames. The fact that little survives does not necessarily mean that the literature never existed, but rather can be seen as mute testimony to the effectiveness of the persecution. Norman Cohn argues that a few seminal documents have survived and that these documents do largely validate accusations of the inquisitors. See Norman Cohn, *The Pursuit of the Millennium* (London: Secker & Warburg, 1957), 150–55. The fact that the church put so much effort into the elimination of this heresy is another indication of just how profoundly disturbed the keepers of orthodoxy became over the situation.

[26] Cohn, *The Pursuit of the Millennium*, 156–57; Walter L. Wakefield and Austin P. Evans, *Heresies of the High Middle Ages: Selected Sources Translated and Annotated* (New York: Columbia University Press, 1969), 39–40. For a dissenting opinion see Robert Learner's discussion in *The Heresy of the Free Spirit in the Later Middle Ages* (Berkeley, Calif.: University of California Press, 1972), 13–14.

[27] It is worth noting that Joachim was condemned by the Fourth Lateran Council in 1215 for apparently blurring the distinction between the Creator and the creature. Amalric was declared to be mad. Cf. *DEC* 1:232–33. More recently Jürgen Moltmann has taken up Joachim's view of the kingdoms, but adds a fourth, the Kingdom of Glory: "Finally, the kingdom of glory must be understood as the consummation of the Father's creation, as the universal establishment of the Son's liberation, and as the fulfillment of the Spirit's indwelling . . . The kingdom of glory is the goal—enduring and uninterrupted—for all of God's works and ways in history" (Jürgen Moltmann, *Trinität und Reich Gottes: Zur Gotteslehre* [Munich: Christian Kaiser, 1980] English edition trans. Margaret Kohl, *The Trinity and the Kingdom: The Doctrine of God* [San Francisco: Harper & Row, 1981], 212).

Amaurians each of the ages had its appropriate incarnation—Father, Son, and Holy Spirit. In the age of the Father the incarnation had taken place in Abraham. In the age of the Son the incarnation had taken place in Christ. The final age, the age of the Holy Spirit, would witness the greatest incarnation of all—the incarnation of the Holy Spirit into humanity. The Amaurians believed that this incarnation of the Spirit had begun with them and would proceed universally into all people. Eventually each person would realize that they are divine.[28] Amaurian thought was essentially a theology of realized pantheism. God was "all in all" in the here and now. Cohn notes that this belief in divinization resulted in an attitude of faultlessness on the part of the adept: "[H]e believed that he had attained a perfection so absolute that he was incapable of sin."[29] In this view the individual person became so identified with God that everything he or she did was considered to be equivalent to the divine will. Furthermore, these human actions could not be considered to be sinful in any way because nothing that God does can be sinful. Regarding this belief Jeffery Russell quotes the incredibly profane Free Spirit mantra that it produced: "In every evil is the glory of God made manifest."[30]

The consequences of such beliefs were twofold. First, it resulted in an antinomianism which, in the case of the Free Spirit heresy, became particularly related to promiscuity and aberrant sexuality.[31] Secondly, it resulted in, as Morwenna Ludlow put it, "a radically realized universalist eschatology: not the belief that all people *will* be saved, but that they *already* are."[32] In reality, through their pantheism, adherents to the doctrines of the Free Spirit had eliminated the need for salvation altogether. This, in turn, effectively eliminated the need for Christ and eradicated any logical justification offered by the church for maintaining the doctrines of hell and eternal punishment. In a move that anticipated the trajectory taken by twentieth-century redaction critics by some seven hundred years, the proponents of Free Spirit doctrines argued that the drama of salvation was a mere invention of the church created for the purposes of institutional self-promotion and control.[33] At its root the heresy of the Free Spirit was an attack on the authority of Scripture. By asserting a realized pantheism the adherents to Free Spirit doctrine in effect made every human being into a unique revelation of God. Free Spirit universalism was simply the logical outworking of this concept. Where there is no possibility of sin there can be no possibility of damnation, and thus universalism becomes the defacto eschatology du jour.

The heresy of the Free Spirit represented a frontal assault on medieval orthodoxy by the advocates of a pure, unadulterated form of neoplatonism. By challenging the authority of Scripture and the essential doctrines of the Christian faith, Free Spirit adherents were not engaging in theological dialogue, but instead were mounting a theological insurgency. The goal was not the

---

[28] Cohn, *The Pursuit of the Millennium*, 160.

[29] Cohn, *The Pursuit of the Millennium*, 152.

[30] Jeffrey B. Russell, "The Brethren of the Free Spirit," in Jefferey B. Russell, ed., *Religious Dissent in the Middle Ages* (New York: John Wiley & Sons, 1971), 89.

[31] Learner, *The Heresy of the Free Spirit in the Later Middle Ages*, 10–34.

[32] Ludlow, "Universalism in the History of Christianity," 197.

[33] Learner, *The Heresy of the Free Spirit in the Later Middle Ages*, 86–87.

reformation of Christian thinking and practice, but rather its essential destruction. Therefore the universalism of the Free Spirit heresy can be seen primarily as a weapon in the hands of those who sought to break the bonds of orthodox domination.

1.4. The Cathars

Perhaps the most serious and widespread challenge made to Catholic orthodoxy in the Middle Ages was Catharism.[34] Catharism was a radically dualistic system of belief in which it was posited that two antagonistic deities, one good and one evil, ruled over the universe. Early Catharists tended to be "mitigated dualists" in that they believed that the evil deity was inferior to the good.[35] Later Catharists believed that both deities were equally powerful and coeternal. In a fashion similar to many ancient gnostic sects, the Catharists believed that God of the Old Testament was an evil being (typically Satan) who created the physical world and therefore was to be rejected.[36] Man was seen in dualistic terms with the physical body being evil and the spiritual soul being good. The goal of Catharism was to purge adherents of the evil flesh so that the soul could be liberated at death and ascend to the good god. If the soul did not escape the grip of the evil flesh then the soul would be reincarnated until such time as it did.[37] Some Catharists believed that after a limited number of reincarnations that a soul could be eternally lost, although this view was most certainly not accepted by all.[38] Because of the inherent evil of the human body, sex and marriage were viewed with particular revulsion since the result of such activity would be procreation and the imprisonment of more souls within the injurious flesh.[39] In another parallel to Gnosticism we find that the Cathars viewed Christ as a unique messenger sent from God with a message that would help release trapped souls from the evils of the flesh and the cycles of reincarnation.

Hints of universalism are to be found in the views of the mitigated dualists, many of whom believed that the evil deity Satan originated from God, fell from his angelic status, and would eventually return to God.[40] This conviction seems to have grown out of a basic assumption made by the mitigated dualists that in

---

[34] For a discussion of Catharism including its origins and beliefs see Michael Costen, *The Cathars and the Albigensian Crusade* (Manchester: Manchester University Press, 1997), 52–76; Lambert, *Medieval Heresy*, 108–150; Jeffery B. Russell, "Radical Revolution: The Catharists," in Russell, *Religious Dissent in the Middle Ages*, 55–59. English translations of important Catharist literature may be found in Wakefield and Evans, *Heresies of the High Middle Ages: Selected Sources Translated and Annotated*, 447–630.

[35] Russell, "Radical Revolution: The Catharists," 55.

[36] For a discussion of gnostic parallels see Renè Nelli, *Spiritualitè De L'Hèrèsie: Le Catharisme* (Paris: Presses Universitaires de France, 1953), 167–204.

[37] Russell, "Radical Revolution: The Catharists," 57.

[38] Costen, *The Cathars and the Albigensian Crusade*, 63.

[39] We note here the comment made by Rainier Sacconi, a thirteenth-century inquisitor of Catharism: "Also, it is a common opinion of all the Cathari that carnal marriage is always a mortal sin" (Edward Peters, *Heresy and Authority in Medieval Europe: Documents in Translation*, [Philadelphia, Penn.: University of Pennsylvania Press], 125). See also Costen, *The Cathars and the Albigensian Crusade*, 64.

[40] Ludlow, "Universalism in the History of Christianity," 198.

the end all evil would be done away with and that all sentient beings would return to the good god.[41] Some mitigated dualists went so far as to posit a cyclical return to a pristine beginning and thus recapitulated Origen's doctrine of apokatastasis including its concept of restoration.[42] Universalism was a natural corollary to a belief system that affirmed the elimination of all evil and the restoration of all things to God. For the mitigated dualists universalism was an unavoidable outcome rooted in the fundamentals of their faith.

As with the heresy of the Free Spirit, Catharism represented another attempt to definitively break the bondage of orthodoxy by decisively doing away with it. Here again we have a group that did not seek a nuanced dialogue within the traditional Christian faith. Instead they attacked its veracity and offered their own solutions to the plight of humanity. The affinity of Catharism with early gnostic thought cannot be dismissed as a mere coincidence of history. The embrace of universalism by certain Cathars is much more likely to be the result of contact with early gnostic literature than not.

1.5. Other Medieval Pantheists
Several well-known Medieval theologians have been accused of holding pantheistic beliefs similar to those of the Free Spirit heretics that would imply a possible embrace of universalism. Prominent among those mentioned along these lines are Meister Eckart (c. 1260–1328) and three others who were profoundly influenced by him: Jan van Ruysbroeck (c. 1293–1381), Johann Tauler (c. 1300–1361), and Heinrick Suso (c. 1295–1366).[43] Although the validity of labeling Eckart a pantheist has been hotly debated over the years,[44] there can be no doubt that at a minimum he came dangerously close to it in his view of the inseparable union of God with the soul, which he argued came about as a result of the birth of the word in the soul.[45] Similarly Ruysbroeck, Tauler, and Suso all had pantheistic tendencies.

The contention that this borderline pantheism resulted in full-blown universalism can be decisively rejected. In Eckhart's case there is abundant evidence to show that he believed in the existence of hell and eternal punishment. In his sermon, "The Attractive Power of God," Eckhart affirmed the following affects of unrepented sin: "Therefore deadly sin is a breach of nature, a death of the soul, a disquiet of the heart, a weakening of power, a blindness of the sense, a sorrow of the spirit, a death of grace, a death of virtue,

---

[41] Sacconi notes that the Cathari sect of the Albanenses affirmed that "no creature of the good god will perish." Peters, *Heresy and Authority in Medieval Europe: Documents in Translation*, 125.

[42] Ludlow, "Universalism in the History of Christianity," 198.

[43] Baxter, "A Historical Study of the Doctrine of Apokatastasis," 78–84.

[44] For instance, Gordon Leff defends Eckhart's orthodoxy arguing that he was primarily "mystical" as opposed to being heretical: "That Eckhart had heretical leanings can be rejected out of hand. As I hope to show, the whole tendency of his beliefs was to a profound spirituality; any errors, if such they were, came from the way he expressed his frequently difficult notions as opposed to the almost calculated profanities of the Free Spirit" (Leff, *Heresy in the Later Middle Ages*, 261).

[45] Cf. the comments made by Eckhart in his, *Commentary on the Book of Wisdom* in *Archives* III, 1928, 415–16 as quoted in Leff, *Heresy in the Later Middle Ages*, 280.

a death of good works, an aberration of the spirit, a fellowship with the devil, an expulsion of Christianity, a dungeon of hell, a banquet of hell, an eternity of hell. Therefore, if thou committest a deadly sin thou art guilty of all these and incurrest their consequences."[46] In discussing the need for the incarnation of Christ in the same sermon Eckhart notes: "Now, we should know that before our Lord Jesus Christ was born, the Heavenly Father drew men with all His might for five thousand, two hundred years; and yet, as far as we know, brought not one into the heavenly kingdom."[47] A view that no person was saved prior to the incarnation of Christ can hardly be labeled as universalism.

The same is true also for Ruysbroeck, Tauler, and Suso. In his book, *The Adornment of Christian Marriage*, Jan van Ruysbroeck speaks of the judgment of God and Christ consigning people to hell: "And with due justice He will give eternal woe and eternal sorrow to the damned; for these despised and rejected the Eternal Good for a good that cannot endure."[48] In a sermon for Lent, Johann Tauler affirmed: "For know ye that this is the worst torment which the souls in hell have to endure, that they know themselves to be afar off, and utterly parted from God and all His elect, and know that it will last for ever, and that they shall never see God."[49] In his book *A Little Book of Wisdom* Heinrich Soso wrote an entire chapter entitled "On the Everlasting Pains of Hell" in which he warns sinners to repent and be reformed so as to avoid "the lamentation of eternal misery."[50] Whatever deviations from orthodoxy these men were guilty of, universalism was not one of them.

1.6. Conclusion
The Middle Ages were a time in which church-defined orthodoxy reigned supreme over Christian theology for almost a millennium. To be sure there were challenges made to the doctrinal hegemony of the church, but these challenges were effectively suppressed through both societal and ecclesiastical pressure. Ultimately the will and the means to enforce orthodoxy proved to be far greater than the forces that opposed it. It is interesting to note that the main proponents of universal salvation during this era were those who rejected the authority of the church and Scripture altogether, primarily the Free Spirit heretics and the Cathars. During the Middle Ages we have virtually no voices

---

[46] Meister Johannes Eckhart, "The Attractive Power of God," in Meister Johannes Eckhart, *Meister Eckhart's Sermons: First Time Translated into English*, trans. Claud Field (London: H.R. Allenson, 1900–1910), 12.

[47] Eckhart, "The Attractive Power of God," 14–15.

[48] Jan van Ruysbroeck, *The Adornment of Christian Marriage* in John of Ruysbroeck, Evelyn Underhill, ed., *The Adornment of Christian Marriage; The Sparkling Stone; The Book of Supreme Truth*, trans. C.A. Wynschenk (Grand Rapids, Mich.: Christian Classic Ethereal Library, 2002), I:IX.

[49] Johann Tauler, "Sermon for the Second Sunday in Lent—Matt. 15:21–28," in Susannah Winkworth, ed., *The History and Life of The Reverend Doctor John Tauler with Twenty-Five of His Sermons Translated from The German, with Additional Notices of Tauler's Life and Times* (London: Allenson & Co., Ltd., 1905), 291.

[50] Blessed Henry Suso and Walter Hilton, *A Little Book of Eternal Wisdom to Which is Added the Parable of the Pilgrim by Walter Hilton* (London: Burns, Oates, & Washbourne, Ltd., 1910), chapter XI.

within the church arguing for universalism. This is not to say that there were no theologians who found the idea attractive, but rather it is a reflection of the church's ability to effectively muzzle opposition and clamp down on dissent.

All this would change rapidly with an earthshaking event we call the Reformation. Coupled to the Renaissance on the front end and the Enlightenment on the back end, the Reformation was the key that ultimately unlocked the door of orthodoxy and allowed for Christian theologians to once again openly discuss the merits and shortcomings of universal salvation without fear.

2. The Reformation and Post-Reformation Eras

The official start of the Reformation Era is typically traced to the day that Martin Luther nailed his famous ninety-five theses to the door of the Wittenberg Church in 1517. However, there were many events that precipitated the general challenge that was made to the authority and doctrinal supremacy of the Catholic Church. Of course there was the huge contribution made by the Renaissance with its focus on intellectual rigor and a renewed appreciation for the classical past. There were the attacks of the Lollards and the Hussites upon the hierarchical structure of the Church. There were the moves made by the monarchies in England and France to expand their control over their respective national churches. There was the general mood of the people who were open to the arguments made by the Reformers that the doctrine of the Church had gotten seriously off track and needed to be returned to an earlier state of apostolic purity. There was also the invention of the printing press, which turned out to be the mechanical engine that propelled the Reformation forward and made its ideas available to the common man. Developed by Johann Gutenberg in the 1450s, the printing press radically revolutionized the channels of communication and made the Reformation logistically possible. Although the original Gutenberg Bible was printed in Latin, it was still a harbinger of things to come. The monopoly held by the Church over the Bible and theological discourse was decisively broken.

As a movement of historical renewal the Reformation produced a backlash of religious opinion in opposition to developed church orthodoxy and a re-evaluation of essential church doctrine. The ignition point for the Reformation was the sale of indulgences and Papal abuses centered on the doctrine of purgatory. When this spark was fanned into a flame, once again Christian theologians were critically assessing the eternal destiny of human beings. A byproduct of this debate was the initiation of a gradual resurgence in universalist thought, which has continued to accelerate into our own times.

Be this as it may, it must be acknowledged that the essential issue addressed by the Reformation had to do primarily with soteriology and the doctrine of justification. The Reformers had a minimal interest in eschatology and accepted with little or no modification the Church's doctrines regarding hell and eternal punishment. George Williams has noted that the Reformers' lack of interest may well be linked to their revulsion at the excesses engendered by the advocates of the Radical Reformation.[51] Whatever the case, the works of the three major Reformers, Luther, Zwingli, and Calvin, all testify to the fact that they staunchly supported the accepted dichotomy between heaven and hell and that they affirmed, in no uncertain terms, the doctrine of eternal punishment.

However, there are indications that the controversy over universalism did resurface early on during the Reformation. In a letter written in 1522 to Hans von Rechenberg, Martin Luther discussed at some length people who held to the universalist position:

> For the opinion that God could not have created man to be rejected and cast away into eternal torment is held among us also, as it was at all times by some of the most renowned people, such as Origen and his kind. They regarded it as to harsh and cruel and inconsistent with God's goodness. They based their opinion on Psalm 77 [:7 ff.], where the Psalmist says, "Will God cast off forever, and never again be gracious? Has his steadfast love forever ceased? And his promises at an end for all time? Has God forgotten to be gracious? Has he in anger shut up his compassion?" [They also cite] Paul, 1 Timothy 2[:4], "God desires all men to be saved and to come to the knowledge of the truth." Proceeding from this premise they argued that in the end even the devils will be saved and will not be eternally damned, etc., etc., one step following from the other."[52]

Although we do not know precisely of whom Luther was speaking, the contours of his description are sufficient to reveal that the doctrine of universalism was once again surfacing after a long millennium of banishment.

2.1. The Anabaptists
The name "Anabaptist" has been used down through the centuries as a label for many disparate and incongruous groups that emerged during the time of the Reformation. From the very beginning the term was used in a pejorative sense by both Roman Catholics and Protestants alike who severely persecuted Anabaptists and put them to death by the thousands.[53] Anabaptist theology was typically defined by a rejection of infant baptism and an endorsement of believers' baptism. Anabaptism or "re-baptism" was recommended to those who were baptized as infants and not as believing adults, hence the name "Anabaptist." Other doctrinal positions varied greatly from group to group.

---

[51] George H. Williams, *The Radical Reformation*, 3rd edition (Kirksville, Mo.: Sixteenth Century Journal Publishers, Inc., 1962; 1992), 857 ff. See also Gordon Rupp, *Patterns of Reformation* (Philadelphia: Fortress, 1969), 182–83.

[52] Martin Luther, "Letter to Hans von Rechenberg," in Helmut T. Lehmann and Gustav K. Wiencke, eds., *Luther's Works, vol. 43, Devotional Writings II* (Philadelphia: Fortress, 1968), 51.

[53] For more on the persecution of the Anabaptists see the various comments made by George H. Williams in his book *The Radical Reformation*. In particular see pp. 247–313; 316; 614–16; 1178; 1200–1209.

Although several scholars have argued that universalism found a notable following within Anabaptist circles,[54] this is an assertion that needs to be re-evaluated. To be sure Anabaptist universalism was denounced in the seventeenth article of the Augsburg Confession of 1530[55] and in the forty-second article of the 1553 English Articles. Based upon these condemnations it would only be natural to assume that where there was smoke there must have been fire. However, it should be noted that the charge of universalism seems to be founded more upon a misunderstanding of Anabaptist writings and theology rather than upon reality.

Hans Denck (c. 1495–1527) for instance is often cited as being the leading universalist among the Anabaptists. Apart from the fact that Denck might not have been an Anabaptist at all,[56] it appears that his perspective on salvation has been misunderstood from the very beginning. Read through Calvinist eyes, Denck's assertions that God willed for all to be saved and that Christ died for all people might appear to be an endorsement of the idea of a universal election of all to salvation. However, Anabaptists were known for their embrace of free will and Denck's theology must be understood within the context of the radical assertion of human freedom.[57] Denck saw no contradiction between the idea that while God willed for all to be saved that some might be able to resist his will.[58] Similarly several other Anabaptist theologians and radical Reformers have been accused of embracing universalism down through the centuries, however it remains an open question as to whether any of these unambiguously endorsed the idea of universal salvation.[59] Certainly the evidence cited seems to be scanty and often contradictory.[60] Although several of these theologians might have opened the door to the *possibility* that in the end all might be saved, this does not mean that they took the next step and declared that possibility to be an absolute reality.

2.2. The European Mystics, Pietists, and Intellectuals
On the European continent mysticism and pietism had long been deeply rooted in the universities and among the intellectual elites, albeit secretly for fear of

---

[54] Cf. Bauckham, "Universalism," 50; Baxter, "Apokatastasis," 88–91; Fairhurst, "Death and Destiny," 314; Williams, *The Radical Reformation*, 1269–76.

[55] Article XVII reads: "They condemn the Anabaptists who think that to condemned men and the devils shall be an end of torments."

[56] Re-baptism was not an essential element of Denck's theology. See Baxter, "Apokatastasis," 89–90, and Ludlow, "Universalism in the History of Christianity," 199.

[57] Cf. Williams, *The Radical Reformation*, 1199; 1269.

[58] Ludlow, "Universalism in the History of Christianity," 200.

[59] Williams mentions Denck, Ziegler, Bader, and Pocquet. See Williams, *The Radical Reformation*, 1275–76.

[60] For instance it is often noted that the fifth of seven theses that Jacob Kautz (c. 1500–1533) nailed to the door of the Predigerkirche in Worms in 1527 seems to endorse universalism. It reads: "All that was lost in Christ shall all be quickened and blessed forever." Cf. Byerly, "A Biblical Critique of Universalism," 40. However, it is not at all plain what Kautz meant by this thesis. It could just as easily be a statement regarding soteriology as opposed to eschatology. Also there is evidence that by the end of his life Kautz recanted all of his unorthodox views. See Baxter's discussion in "Apokatastasis," 90–91.

persecution.[61] The Reformation provided the intellectual freedom necessary for more radical and unorthodox expressions of spirituality to come to the surface and take hold. In several cases universalism was openly endorsed and advocated by prominent European intellectuals and university professors in the Reformation/post-Reformation era. In addition to this, expressions of universalism are to be found among some of the less educated laity who claimed to have had mystical experiences and revelations from God.

The Reformation created a vast rupture in the theological dam of Christian orthodoxy and out of that breach flowed a stream of long suppressed spirituality. A particular tributary of thought can be traced to Renaissance humanism and its new found appreciation for religious tolerance. A prototype for the movement would be the German ecclesiastic and philosopher Cardinal Nicholas of Cusa (1401–1464). In his book *De pace fidei* Cusa posited a meeting of representatives from the world's religions.[62] In the ensuing colloquy the leaders realize their kinship vis-à-vis their common belief in one God and resolve to unite on that basis. Although Christianity retained its foremost position among the religions in Cusa's work, a limited form of pluralism was affirmed. This Renaissance-inspired pluralism would be developed into a full-blown system of universal salvation through the work of a French mystic named Guillaume Postel (1510–1581).[63]

Postel was a professor, linguist, astronomer, Cabbalist, diplomat, Jesuit, and eccentric visionary who may well have been the founder of modern religious pluralism. At least his attempt at identifying certain core beliefs and values amongst major religions and his advocacy of world and religious unity anticipates the major contours of twentieth-century religious pluralism by some four centuries. A major turning point came in Postel's life when he encountered an illiterate Venetian virgin named Johanna who was about fifty years old at the time. Johanna had founded a hospital and given her life to the service of the sick and the poor. Postel believed her to be the messianic "Feminine Angelic Pope." He called her "mater mundi" and the "new Eve" and thought her to be a woman "in whom dwells the fullness of the substance of Christ, just as in Him dwells corporeally the fullness of divinity."[64] After her death, Postel claimed that Johanna took possession of him and he asserted that "it is now she and not I who lives in me."[65] Postel believed that Johanna conveyed to him a doctrine of universal restitution, universal pardon, and universal baptism.[66] He also

---

[61] Remember that the Medieval heresy of the Free Spirit, which had many mystical aspects, began with Amaury of Bène and his followers at the University of Paris.

[62] Nicholas of Cusa, *On Interreligious Harmony: Text, Concordance, and Translation of De pace fidei*, ed. James E. Biechler and H. Lawrence Bond (Lewiston: E. Mellen Press, 1991).

[63] An introduction into Postel's life and theology may be found in the following: William J. Bouwsma, *The Career and Thought of Guillaume Postel (1510–1581)* (Cambridge, Mass.: Harvard University Press, 1957); Marion L. Kuntz, *Guillaume Postel: Prophet of the Restitution of All Things—His Life and Thought* (The Hague: Martinus Nijhoff, 1981).

[64] Bouwsma, *The Career and Thought of Guillaume Postel (1510–1581)*, 15.

[65] Bouwsma, *The Career and Thought of Guillaume Postel (1510–1581)*, 17.

[66] Kuntz, *Guillaume Postel*, 80–81.

believed that she had conferred upon him the offices of prophet and priest in which he was to move forward toward the goal of the unification of the world and the eventual restoration of all things into the state in which they had existed before the Fall. A central feature of his priestly function was the dispensing of the benefice of Pardon or Absolution of all men.[67] Thus Postel believed that ultimately all people would be forgiven and restored to God and that he himself would play a key part in this restoration.

In a manner that runs amazingly parallel to recent Catholic doctrine as conveyed in the Vatican II documents, Postel argued for the existence of an *ecclesia generalis* that included "external members" who were not explicitly Christian.[68] This group consisted of several categories of people who would be received by God regardless of the circumstances they found themselves in. Some of Postel's categories included those who were of good will, those who failed to understand Christ, those who followed their conscience, those who were forgotten through the neglect of pastors, and so on. In Postel's view, no circumstance a person faced in life could keep him/her from ultimate deliverance. The reason for this confidence lies in the fact that Postel believed that the key factor that insured the salvation of all was the latent presence of Jesus in every person. This latent presence created within them a natural desire to do good that impelled them toward salvation and eventually resulted in true deliverance. The essential difference between the modern Catholic perspective and that of Postel can be found in the fact that Postel believed that in the end all human beings would become members of the *ecclesia generalis*, whereas current Catholic inclusivist doctrine is not willing to go that far.

Although Postel's system was highly idiosyncratic and filled with fantastic mystical declarations and revelations, Postel still regarded himself as a Christian and his universalism must be understood as being broadly Christocentric. In his book *De orbis terrae concordia* Postel argued that Christianity best expressed features found in common between the religions of the world and that eventually all people should be brought into the Christian fold.[69] As a part of his vision of universal restoration Postel developed a grand scheme for world unity that included the creation of a universal world monarchy and a universal world religion based upon the teachings of Christianity informed by Catholic orthodoxy. His central thesis was that "all things are in all" and that "God is the All Who is One."[70] Postel's vision focused on the unity of all nature with God. He believed that humanity would glorify God best when it became a seamless expression of this unity. Postel's reduction of Christianity to a set of general moral propositions as opposed to specific theological claims and practices was the key innovation that drove him towards universalism. His attempt to find common ground among disparate religions resulted in his universalist conclusions, albeit from a Christocentric point of view. Thus Postel's universalism was not an expression of pure Christian theology, but rather was a combination of theological contemplation

---

[67] Kuntz, *Guillaume Postel*, 87.
[68] Bouwsma, *The Career and Thought of Guillaume Postel (1510–1581)*, 191–202.
[69] Guillaume Postel, *De orbis terrae concordia* (Basel: Oporinus, 1544).
[70] Kuntz, *Guillaume Postel*, 171.

coupled to an exercise in comparative religions. Postel sought to create a broad tent under which adherents of several religious systems could dwell in relative peace and harmony. He concluded: "I have tried to promote that end for which the world was created, universal peace."[71]

As can be anticipated, Postel was not well received by many within the Catholic Church. In 1555 all of his writings were placed in an index of forbidden books.[72] In the same year a group of judges in Venice bypassed a pronouncement of heresy against him and instead declared him to be mad.[73] In Postel's view, this was a blow that was much worse than being branded a heretic. After all, who would want to listen to the ranting of a lunatic? He spent the final eighteen years of his life confined to the monastery of Saint Martin, attempting to regain his academic reputation while at the same time continuing to promote his unique vision of religious unity. He died in 1581.

Several other European intellectuals advocated universalism during the post-Reformation era. Chief among these were the German mystics Johann Wilhelm Petersen (1649–1727) and Johann Heinrich Haug (1680–1753). In a fashion similar to Postel, Petersen's universalism was fueled by a radical form of mysticism that included spiritual visions and revelations. In 1680 Petersen married a fellow universalist and mystic named Johanna Eleanor von Merlau and the two dedicated themselves to the promotion of "Philadephianism"—a movement based in mysticism and founded by the English universalist Jane Lead. As a means of promoting and defending his universalist views Petersen wrote a three volume set entitled *Mysterion apokatastaseos panton, das ist, Das Geheimniss der Wiederbringung aller Dinge durch Jesum Christum,* which presented both a history and defense of universalism.[74] The essential thrust of Petersen's argument was that there was no limit to the work of Christ and that in the end all would be saved. In addition to Petersen, Johann Heinrich Haug also published an extensive written defense of universalism. Haug was a professor at Strasbourg who also became involved with the Philadelphians. Because of his association with the group he was expelled from his professorship and the city. In 1742 Haug finished a new German translation of the Bible that included a commentary that defended the universalist position from a mystical perspective. Created with the assistance of several other mystics the eight volume work became known as the "Berleburger Bibel."[75] Both Petersen and Haug presented a universalism that was thoroughly Christocentric.

Besides the mystics who can be traced to the universities and intellectual elites of Europe, the post-Reformation era also produced a few less credentialed

---

[71] Guillaume Postel, *De originibus*, as quoted by Bouwsma in *The Career and Thought of Guillaume Postel (1510–1581)*, 214.

[72] Franz Heinrich Reusch, ed., *Die Indices liborum prohibitorum des sechzehnten Jahrhunderts* (Tübingen: Litterarischer Verein in Stuttgart, 1886), 158–59.

[73] Bouwsma, *The Career and Thought of Guillaume Postel (1510–1581)*, 22.

[74] Johann Wilhelm Petersen, *Mysterion apokatastaseos panton, das ist, Das Geheimniss der Wiederbringung aller Dinge durch Jesum Christum*, 3 vols. (n.p.), 1700; 1703; 1710)

[75] A thorough discussion of the work may be found in Martin Hoffmann, *Theologie und Exegese der Berleburger Bibel (1726–42)* (Gütersloh: C. Bertelsmann, 1937).

mystics from among the laity in Europe who picked up the banner of universalism. Perhaps the most influential of these was a German shoemaker named Jakob Boehme (1575–1624). Boehme had several mystical experiences in his life, which he recorded along with his theological speculations into several popular books.[76] At the center of Boehme's universalism was the belief that heaven and hell were contained within the soul and that one chooses to dwell in either as an existing reality through an act of the will. In essence Boehme argued that heaven and hell are an ongoing present state of mind.[77] Boehme's universalism was similarly linked to self-knowledge and introspection. He wrote:

> All Christian Religion wholly consisteth in this, to learn *to know ourselves*; whence we are come, and what we are; how we are gone forth from the Unity into Dissension, Wickedness, and Unrighteousness; how we have awakened and stirred up these Evils in us; and how we may be delivered from them again, and recover our original Blessedness.[78]

Thus Boehme posited a remedial cycle of unity, rebellion, and restoration. His work was particularly focused on Jesus Christ and a mystical exegesis of Christ's teaching. The central theme of his universalism was a restoration of humanity from the effects of the fall. As he put it, to "enter again into that one Tree, Christ in us, out of which we all sprung in *Adam*."[79] Boehme's writings would later have a profound influence upon both German and English intellectuals. He was esteemed highly by such German luminaries as Friedrick von Hardenberg, Jung Stilling, Friedrick Schlegel, Ludwig Tieck, and Georg W.F. Hegel. On the other side of the Channel Boehme influenced the likes of Samuel T. Coleridge, Thomas Erskine, George Fox, William Law, Jane Lead, F.D. Maurice, Isaac Newton, and Peter Sterry.[80]

Of lesser influence than Boehme, but nonetheless still significant, was the Flemish mystic Antoinette Bourignon de la Porte (1616–1680). Abandoning all semblance of orthodoxy, Bourignon claimed to be "the woman clothed with the sun" found in Revelation 12 as well as the second revelation of the Son of Man

---

[76] A collection of Boehme's essential works may be found in Jakob Boehme, *Saemtliche Schriften*, 11 vols., ed. August Faust and Will E. Peuckert (1730; repr., Stuttgart, Frommanns, 1955–1960).

[77] "The Soul hath Heaven and Hell within itself before, according as it is written, 'The Kingdom of God cometh not with Observation, neither shall they say, Lo here! or Lo there! For behold the Kingdom of God is within you.' And whichsoever of the two, that is, either Heaven or Hell is manifested in it, in that the Soul standeth" (Jakob Boehme, *Of Heaven and Hell: A Dialogue between a Student with his Master*, http://www.passtheword.org/DIALOGS-FROM-THE-PAST/heaven.htm. (Accessed on October 31, 2014.)

[78] Jakob Boehme, *Of Regeneration and the New Birth*, chapter 8, line 180, http://www.passtheword.org/DIALOGS-FROM-THE-PAST/jb-regen.htm. (Accessed on October 31, 2014.)

[79] Jakob Boehme, *Of Regeneration and the New Birth*, chapter 8, line 182.

[80] F. Ernest Stoeffler, *Mysticism in the German Devotional Literature of Colonial Pennsylvania* (Allentown, Penn.: Pennsylvania Folklore Society, 1950), 27.

on the earth.[81] Building a system based upon her fantastic visions, Bourignon believed her mission was to gather her spiritual children into a communist type fellowship. Her universalism flowed out of a belief that in the end God would be united with the world in perfect harmony and thus the promise of a perfect paradise would be achieved.[82] Bourignon was particularly influential in Scotland where her ideas were specifically denounced by the General Assembly of the Church of Scotland that required its candidates for ordination to explicitly disavow Bourignonism.[83]

2.3. The British Advocates

Political and religious developments in England during the Reformation/post-Reformation eras would have a profound effect upon the future of universalism in the history of Christian theology. With the split between Henry VIII and the Roman Catholic Church over his marriage to Anne Boleyn an entirely new and independent Church of England was created. In the wake of the general upheaval that followed that event, numerous challenges to orthodoxy were made throughout England. To answer those challenges the new church published forty-two articles of religion under the authority of King Edward VI in 1552. The forty-second article condemned "the pernicious opinion that all men, (though they never so ungodly) shall at last be saved."[84] In 1562 the articles were examined by a Convocation of the clergy and reduced to thirty-nine with the forty-second article condemning universalism being one of the three that were omitted.[85] Eventually in 1571 the Thirty-Nine Articles were adopted by Parliament and made the general rule of faith for the Church of England. With the removal of the forty-second article from thirty-nine, the Church's stance against universalism was considerably softened and from that point forward universalism was not officially considered to be heretical by the Church. Thomas Whittemore, a nineteenth-century American universalist, declared in 1860 that "from the time of the revision of the Articles, it has not been considered an offense, in the Church of England, to avow the doctrine of universalism."[86] There can be no doubt that Whittemore's conclusion was a bit triumphalistic, as history shows that the Anglican Church has gone through its own epic battles over the doctrine of universalism. Nevertheless, it must be conceded that there is a bit of truth lurking in Whittemore's observation. At least the Anglican Church has produced more universalist divines than any other while at the same time providing a home for a great many eschatological traditionalists. This willingness to discuss and accept universalism can be

---

[81] J.J. Herzog, Philip Schaff, et al., eds., *The New Schaff-Herzog Encyclopedia of Religious Knowledge* (New York: Funk and Wagnalls Co., 1908–1914), 2:240–41. A discussion Bourignon de la Porte's life and work may be found in Marthe van der Does, *Antoinette Bourignon: sa vie (1616–1680), son oeuvre* (Groningen: Druk, Verenigde Reproduktie Bedrijven, 1974).

[82] Baxter, "Apokatastasis," 96.

[83] *ODCC*, 229; Baxter, "Apokatastasis," 97.

[84] Whittemore, *The Modern History of Universalism*, 85–86.

[85] *ODCC*, 1611.

[86] Whittemore, *The Modern History of Universalism*, 90.

traced directly to the doctrinal history of the Thirty-Nine Articles. Certainly George Rust (d. 1670) made this connection in 1661:

> I would fain know why fhe [i.e. the Church of England] who in her *39 Articles* does fo punctually follow the Articles agreed upon in *K. Edward's* daies, or with little variation, fhould wholly omit that *Article* which condemns the reftorers of this Opinion, if fhe had thought it ought to have been condemn'd.[87]

Without a clear denunciation and prohibition of universalism within the dogmatic tenets of the church it was inevitable that those who felt passionately about the issue would put the dogmatic limits to the test. As a result the Anglican Church, perhaps more than any other, has carried out an ongoing dialogue regarding the doctrine of universalism. Space limits this study from fully engaging the history of universalism in England during the reformation and post-reformation eras. What is presented here amounts to some of the significant high points in that history.

An early universalist work that attracted much attention in England was a little book that became known as *Divine Light*. Written anonymously the book advocated the idea of the universal election of all people to salvation in Christ and the ultimate deliverance of even Satan and his demons. On February 4, 1646 the Parliament set aside a day of public humiliation and repentance to atone for the rise of heresy in the land. Among the errors specifically singled out in the legislative order were the kinds of universalist ideas enumerated in *Divine Light*. The emergence and success of *Divine Light* in the public domain and the steps taken against it offers a window into the tension that already existed in England over the issue at this time. The dogmatic consensus on eternal punishment was breaking down. As more voices were raised in favor of universalism, accommodation would eventually replace condemnation as the preferred method of treatment.

The proliferation of printed materials in the Reformation/post-Reformation eras spurred a renaissance in the study of patristic literature as the works of many ancient Christian writers became more commonly available. One such writer was Origen whose works were widely circulated and began to once again exert influence over the eschatological debate. In England some associates of a group of seventeenth-century college professors known as the Cambridge Platonists took quite an interest in Origen's ideas and began to construct neo-Origen theologies that focused on the pre-existence of the soul and the impact that the fall into sin had upon the soul.[88] Tied into a central doctrine of Platonic

---

[87] George Rust, *A Letter Concerning Origen and the Chief of His Opinions* (1661; repr., New York: Facsimile Text Society / Columbia University Press, 1933), 133. Because the book was published anonymously, there has been some controversy over who the author was, however, at this point the consensus seems to be that the work is rightly attributed to Rust.

[88] David W. Dockrill, "The Heritage of Patristic Platonism in Seventeenth-Century English Philosophical Theology," in Graham A. J. Rogers, Jean M. Vienne, and Yves C. Zarka, eds., *The Cambridge Platonists in Philosophical Context: Politics, Metaphysics and Religion* (Dordrecht, Netherlands: Kluwer Academic Pub., 1997), 55–77.

theism—the idea that God cannot will that which is other than what is best—was a reassertion of universal salvation conceived of in terms of God's love and his desire to eventually actualize ultimate eschatological goodness. Assuming that this goodness was incompatible with the notion that some would be doomed to suffer endlessly in hell, universalism was advanced as a solution.

A Letter Concerning Origen and the Chief of His Opinions was published anonymously in 1661 and it put in a vigorous defense of universalism from the perspective of the Cambridge Platonists. Generally considered to be the work of George Rust, the letter embraced Origen's view that God's punishment was remedial and corrective as opposed to retributive. Rust stressed that pain was necessary for conversion and that postmortem punishment would eventually result in salvation.[89] Within Rust's circle of friends was Anne Conway (1631–1679), the wife of Lord Conway. Anne Conway, an outstanding scholar in her own right, was in agreement with Rust's basic premises. She elaborated her universalism in a book written in Latin that was published posthumously in 1690 and entitled *Principia philosophiae antiquissimae et recentissimae.*[90] Conway's book represents more than just a treatise on Platonic metaphysics—it is in fact a theodicy in its own right. Conway suffered from chronic migraine headaches and came to believe that she was being punished in order to purify herself from sin committed in a previous life.[91] As a result she argued that pain and suffering was purgative with the ultimate goal being the destruction of evil and the restoration of all souls to God:

> But as all the Punifments, God inflicts on his Creatures, have fome portion with their Sins; fo all thefe Punifments (the worft not excepted) do tend to their Good and Reftoration, and fo are Medicinal, that by them thefe difeated Creatures may be cured and reftored to a better condition than before they enjoyed.[92]

Two other prominent universalists associated with the Cambridge Platonists were the chaplains to Oliver Cromwell, Peter Sterry (1613–1672) and his student Jeremiah White (1629–1707).[93] As has been noted, Sterry was greatly influenced by the work of Jakob Boehme. In addition to Boehme, White was also influenced by the work of several patristic universalists including Clement of Alexandria, Origen, and Gregory of Nazianzus. Both men based their universalism upon the belief that love was the supreme attribute of God and that the supremacy of this love would compel God to save all people. Interestingly enough, and perhaps not surprisingly, there was also a mystical

---

[89] Ludlow, "Universalism in the History of Christianity," 202.

[90] The book was translated into English and printed in 1692 under the title, *The Principles of the Moft Ancient and Modern Philosophy* (Amsterdam; London: M. Brown, 1692).

[91] Ludlow, "Universalism in the History of Christianity," 202.

[92] Conway, *The Principles of the Moft Ancient and Modern Philosophy*, 76.

[93] A succinct discussion of theology of Sterry and White along with its historical background may be found in D.P. Walker's book *The Decline of Hell: Seventeenth-Century Discussions of Eternal Torment* (Chicago: University of Chicago Press, 1964), 104–21.

aspect that contributed to the universalism of the two. In his writings Sterry often appealed to the experiential side of things. Richard Roach, one of White's editors, reported that White once told him of a profound incident that he had while he was at Cambridge. Frustrated over finding no theological system that "presented God as love," White believed that his perplexity caused him to become dangerously ill. Through means of the illness White told Roach that God had given him "a new set of thoughts" concerning his love and eternal punishment. Before he died, White recorded these thoughts in a book entitled *The Restoration of All Things*, which was published posthumously in 1712.[94] The book offers extensive biblical exegesis in support of universalism and in it White puts forward a unique combination of a predestinarian soteriology with a universalist eschatology. White argued that the separation between the elect and the reprobate was a temporary circumstance that God used to illustrate his divine grace.[95] In the end the distinction would be removed and all people would be delivered through Christ.

At this time in British history there also developed a group of pure mystics who were sympathetic to universalism. Chief among these would be Jane Lead (1623–1704) whose book *The Enochian Walks with God* puts forward an account of mystical revelations that Lead received regarding universal salvation and the nature of eternal punishment.[96] In the book, Lead's primary focus is upon the "universal love of the God of love" and how this love will eventually save the "whole Adamical Fallen Race" in Christ.[97] The net result of this salvation would be the creation of a new "God-like similitude" in each soul.[98] Lead argues that "God's Love is ſo great and large, as All Fall'n-Angels and Spirits ſhall be Redeemed."[99] She also contends that all postmortem punishment is reformatory and will eventually purge the "Poyſon of Sin that hath infected All of *Adam's* Poſterity."[100] Lead preached her universalism openly in London and a small congregation known as the "Philadelphians" rallied to her. An interesting display of cross-pollination between European and British universalism can be seen in the fact that Lead herself had been influenced by the writings of the German mystic Jakob Boehme and in turn her writings influenced a substantial number of European universalists including the

---

[94] Jeremiah White, *The Restoration of All Things, or, A Vindication of the Goodness and Grace of God to be Manifested at Last in the Recovery of His Whole Creation out of Their Fall* (London: N. Cliff & D. Jackson, 1712).

[95] White argued "universal Grace doth no longer thrust out his Special and Peculiar Favour. Reprobation here will be found in combining with Election, yea Damnation it self with Salvation, here all those knots which other systems of Divinity have hitherto tied faster, are in a great Measure loosened" (White, *The Restoration of All* Things, 8). On this point see also Ludlow, "Universalism in the History of Christianity," 203.

[96] Jane Lead, *The Enochian Walks With God: Found Out by a Spiritual-Traveller whoſe Face Towards Mount-Sion Above Was Set* (London: D. Edwards, 1694).

[97] Lead, *The Enochian Walks With God*, i.

[98] Lead, *The Enochian Walks With God*, i.

[99] Lead, *The Enochian Walks With God*, 37.

[100] Lead, *The Enochian Walks With God*, 36.

German mystics Johann Peterson and Johann Haug.[101] As has already been noted, both Peterson and Haug promoted Lead's Philadelphian movement in Germany.

William Law (1686–1761) was another English mystic who was profoundly influenced by the writings of Jakob Boehme.[102] A hugely popular devotional writer, Law embraced the traditional doctrine of hell in his early works but later abandoned it in favor of full-blown restorationism. In describing his view of apokatastasis, Law included the redemption of the fallen angels:

> All was Heaven, and they all were so many created Gods, eternally sinking down, and rising up, into new Heights and Depths of the Riches of the Divine Nature. With this Degree of Glory and Happiness was the whole Extent of the Place of this World filled, before the Angels fell: and to this Degree of Happiness, and heavenly Glory, will the whole Place of this World be again raised, when the Love of God shall have finished the great Work of the Redemption of Mankind.[103]

In a manner reminiscent of Origen, Law argued that universalism was the logical conclusion based upon Christ's power and ultimate triumph: "[H]e has a Power of redeeming us, which nothing can hinder; but sooner or later, he must see all his and our Enemies under his Feet, and all that is fallen in *Adam* into Death must rise and return to a Unity of an Eternal Life in God."[104]

Law is representative of several who ultimately embraced restorationism. The Welch preacher James Relly (1720–1778) came to universalism later in life in a similar manner to that of Law. Starting off as a Calvinistic Methodist minister, Relly gradually came to question the doctrines of double predestination and eternal punishment. Eventually, Relly became a universalist and wrote several books defending universalism. Chief among these was *Union: Or a Treatise of Consanguinity and Affinity Between Christ and His Church*. In this book Relly argued that if all human beings were born into sin under the corporate headship of Adam, then all human beings would be purged of that sin under the corporate headship of Christ.[105] Relly's books and preaching spurred the creation of a few Rellyan Universalist societies in

---

[101] See Thune, *The Behmenists and The Philadelphians*, 18–67, for an analysis of the connections between Boehme and the Philadelphians.

[102] A biography of William Law's life as well as a chronology and critical introduction to his work may be found in the following: Erwin Paul Rudolph, *William Law* (Boston: Twayne Pub., 1980); and A. Keith Walker, *William Law: His Life and His Thought* (London: SPCK, 1973).

[103] William Law, *The Spirit of Prayer or The Soul Rising out of the Vanity of Time into the Riches of Eternity*, vol. 2, 3rd edition (London: J. Richardson, 1750), http://www.passtheword.org/DIALOGS-FROM-THE-PAST/prayer3.htm, 2.1–44. (Accessed on October 31, 2014.)

[104] William Law, *The Spirit of Love*, vol. 2 (London: M. Richardson, 1754), 2.3–152, http://www.passtheword.org/DIALOGS-FROM-THE-PAST/love2.htm. (Accessed on October 31, 2014.)

[105] James Relly, *Union: Or a Treatise of Consanguinity and Affinity Between Christ and his Church* (London: n.p., 1759).

England. His greatest convert was John Murray who went to America and founded an organization that eventually became the Universalist Church of America. This church in turn merged in 1961 with the American Unitarian Association to form the Unitarian Universalist Association.

2.4. Conclusion

In the Reformation/post-Reformation period we have the rebirth and resurgence of a robust advocacy of Christian universalism. The freedom from rigid church doctrine coupled to a renaissance in Patristic studies provided the soil in which universalism could once again begin to take serious root.

While the universalism developed in this era was still broadly Christocentric and biblically oriented, what stands out about it was the influence that extra-biblical factors had upon it. In particular, mysticism emerges as a primary contributor and motivator in Reformation/post-Reformation universalism. Postel, Peterson, Haug, Boehme, Bourignon de la Porte, and several others all claimed to have received mystical revelations regarding universal salvation. Even the more intellectual and scripturally predisposed Sterry and White acknowledged that their universalism was profoundly influenced by their personal, mystical experiences. The hugely successful popularizers of British universalism, Jane Lead and William Law, were also mystics at heart who included a strong dose of mysticism in their writings supporting the universalist cause. All of this reveals that the rebirth of universalism during the Reformation era was not merely a dry exercise in ivory tower theological reasoning and debate. It was, above all things, an intensely personal expression of deeply held beliefs and private experiences.

Coupling together the universalism articulated in both the Middle Ages and the Reformation Era, we find that once again external factors played a significant role in its development and promulgation. This was not a universalism that was the product of strictly traditional Christian theological debate—instead it was the enunciation of an altogether different way of thinking and looking at divine revelation.

CHAPTER 3

Enlightenment Humanitarianism and the Development of Modern Universalism

Along with the Reformation, the Enlightenment stands out as a watershed event in the history of universalism. As we shall see, Enlightenment thinking has profoundly shaped the trajectory and profile of universalist proposals and continues to influence universalism even into our own times. In this chapter we shall examine the profound impact that the Enlightenment had upon the historical development of universalist thought. We begin with a discussion of the Enlightenment era itself and then move on to trace its influence upon twentieth-century universalist thought.

1. The Enlightenment and Its Impact on the Eighteenth and Nineteenth Centuries

Out of the womb of the Renaissance came the Age of Reason and its successor, the Age of Enlightenment. Although not necessarily a strict inevitability of history, it is hard to imagine Western thought taking another path. In many ways the Enlightenment was the climax of the age old struggle for intellectual autonomy, which became coupled to a robust infusion of Reformation freedom. As primarily a movement of intellectuals, it was only natural that the intellect would become the focus of attention. In throwing off the shackles of rigid Church orthodoxy Enlightenment thinkers believed that they were creating an entirely new paradigm for the discovery of the truth—the paradigm of reason. In his famous discussion of the meaning of Enlightenment, Immanuel Kant (1724–1804) offered this definition:

> Enlightenment is man's release from his self-incurred tutelage. Tutelage is man's inability to make use of his understanding without direction from another. Self-incurred is the tutelage when its cause lies not in lack of reason but in lack of resolution and courage to use it without direction from another. *Sapere aude!* "Have courage to use your own reason!"— that is the motto of enlightenment.[1]

As a means of breaking free from the tutelage imposed by the past, Enlightenment thinkers in general discarded the instruction of the Church and Christian tradition in long-established areas of intellectual inquiry in favor of reason, observation, and experimentation. In his famous tract *The Age of Reason* (1795) Thomas Paine dismissed Christian theology as being "the study

---

[1] Immanuel Kant, "What is Enlightenment?" in *Foundations of Metaphysics and What is Enlightenment?* trans. Lewis White Beck (Indianapolis, Ind.: Bobbs-Merrill, 1959), 85.

of nothing" because, in his view, it was not founded upon hard scientific data.[2] In its place Paine advocated a natural religion built upon "the Bible of Creation."[3] Thus, with the elevation of reason as the sole arbiter of truth, came also an emphasis on natural religion often expressed in deism, and natural law often expressed in egalitarian concepts.[4]

Enlightenment egalitarianism was a manifestation of a general commitment within the movement to humanitarian ideals. The advocacy of equality, tolerance, justice, material welfare, and religious pluralism established Enlightenment humanitarianism as a revolutionary force that sought to bring fundamental changes to the structures of Western society. In his dissertation entitled "Finally Excluded by God? Some Twentieth-Century Theological Explorations of the Problems of Hell and Universalism with Reference to the Historical Development of these Doctrines," Kendall S. Harmon has effectively argued that it was the collision between the traditional doctrine of hell and Enlightenment humanitarianism that greatly renewed an interest in the development of universalist doctrines in the theologies of the eighteenth and nineteenth centuries and culminated in modern expressions of the same.[5] In short, Harmon argues that the notion of eternal punishment was not consonant with Enlightenment humanitarianism and its social program and thus became subject to increasingly hostile attack by the theologians of the Enlightenment era, which ultimately resulted in a paradigm shift away from it.[6] In his book, *The Decline of Hell*, D.P. Walker traces overt attacks on the doctrine of hell to the mid-seventeenth century, which ramp up significantly as the eighteenth century progressed. Walker's chronology corresponds well with Harmon's thesis and confirms the influence that Enlightenment thought progressively exerted over the debate.[7]

---

[2] Thomas Paine, "The Age of Reason," in Thomas Paine, *The Complete Writings of Thomas Paine*, 2 vols., ed. Philip S. Foner (New York: Citadel Press, 1947), 1:601.

[3] Thomas Paine, "The Age of Reason," 1:601.

[4] The American Declaration of Independence, authored primarily by Thomas Jefferson, is perhaps the most concise and the best known expression of these enlightenment concepts. It begins by declaring: "When in the Course of human events, it becomes necessary for one people to dissolve the political bands which have connected them with another, and to assume among the powers of the earth, the separate and equal station to which the Laws of Nature and of Nature's God entitle them, a decent respect to the opinions of mankind requires that they should declare the causes which impel them to the separation. We hold these truths to be self-evident, that all men are created equal, that they are endowed by their Creator with certain unalienable Rights, that among these are Life, Liberty and the pursuit of Happiness." "The Declaration of Independence: A Transcription," *National Achieves*, http://www.archives.gov/exhibits/charters/charters.html. (Accessed on October 31, 2014.)

[5] Harmon, "Finally Excluded by God?" 105–31.

[6] Harmon concluded: "For our purposes the development may be described by saying that whereas in the sixteenth century the doctrine of hell was rarely challenged, in the seventeenth century the doctrine of hell began to be questioned more publicly and more often, in the eighteenth century this questioning intensified, and in the nineteenth century hell underwent a sustained moral assault, after which the old Augustinian consensus was abolished" (Harmon, "Finally Excluded From God," 105–06).

[7] Walker, *The Decline of Hell*, 3–4.

Chief among the criticisms leveled against Christian theology by Enlightenment thinkers was its dogged attachment to eternal punishment.[8] Eternal punishment became increasingly viewed as a barbaric and cruel fabrication developed in a less sophisticated time. In his article "Irresistible Compassion: An Aspect of Eighteenth-Century Sympathy and Humanitarianism" Norman Fiering defines modern humanitarianism as the "inclination to protest against obvious and pointless physical suffering."[9] Application of this definition retroactively to more ancient Enlightenment expressions reveals a common connection between both the early and modern forms of humanitarian philosophy. Indeed, much of what Enlightenment thinkers had to say regarding eternal punishment was an objection and a protest against what they believed to be senseless suffering. For instance, Voltaire's anonymous poem *Epître à Uranie* (1722) was a denunciation of the Christian belief in a jealous, tyrannical Old Testament deity and what he saw to be the inhumane condemnation by this deity of all pagans to eternal punishment. William Wollaston (1659–1724) in his *Religion of Nature Delineated* (1722) declared that it is "according to *nature* to be affected with the fufferings of other people and the contrary is *inhuman* and *unnatural*."[10] Based upon observations like these it was argued that God's character and action could be determined by simply asking, "What would a good and just man do in like circumstances?"[11] The Enlightenment answer increasingly focused on God's love and compassion to the exclusion of his justice and judgment.

It is no surprise then to find that universalism was often advanced by Enlightenment and post-Enlightenment thinkers as a solution to the problem of eternal punishment. It would be wrong to think that the bulk of Enlightenment intellectuals were devoid of religious commitment. Indeed a great many of them sought to reconcile their intellectual inquiry with their religious beliefs. Their advocacy of religious pluralism and toleration reveal not an effort to eliminate religion but rather an effort to bring about its proliferation and perfection. It was the passionate advocates of the Enlightenment such as Voltaire, Jefferson, and Paine who denounced revealed religion and sought to develop a natural religion as a replacement for what they saw to be a greatly flawed orthodoxy. For those who did not want to entirely abandon a more conventional belief system and yet were troubled by the seeming inhumanity of eternal punishment, universalism became an attractive alternative in both the Enlightenment and post-Enlightenment eras.

---

[8] In this brief introduction we are focusing our attention on those Enlightenment thinkers who placed a high level of importance on theological engagement. Of course there was also that other stream of Enlightenment thought that denied the existence of God and the immortality of the soul altogether. Many of the founders of the French revolution would serve as an outstanding example of those who desired to dispense with theology altogether.

[9] Norman Fiering, "Irresistible Compassion: An Aspect of Eighteenth-Century Sympathy and Humanitarianism," *JHI* 37/2 (April–June, 1976), 195.

[10] William Wollaston, *Religion of Nature Delineated*, 6th edition (London: John and Paul Knapton, 1722; 1738), 140 (italics in the original). Cf. Harmon, "Finally Excluded by God?" 117–18.

[11] Harmon, "Finally Excluded From God," 118.

Often characterized as "the larger hope," universalism eventually came to be embraced by the advocates of Romanticism. Although Romanticism is often characterized as an emotional reaction against Enlightenment rationalism, it still retained certain Enlightenment values including a focus on a common humanity and a commitment to egalitarianism. Among the Romantics universalism was popularized by such poets as Tennyson, the Brownings, Wordsworth, and Coleridge.[12] Tennyson's *In Memoriam* (1849) was instrumental in spreading the universalist message and was probably more influential at that time than any other written work on the subject. It ends with these familiar words that anticipate the final restoration:

> That God, which ever lives and loves,
> One God, one law, one element,
> And one far-off divine event,
> To which the whole creation moves.[13]

For those who were not willing to embrace universalism dogmatically, the larger hope offered an optimistic outlook in an age of awakening. If universalism was not a certainty, at least one could hope for it to be so. In this way the horrors of eternal punishment could be mitigated and the demands that Enlightenment humanitarianism placed upon the mind could be comfortably met.

1.1. The German/European Contribution

The Enlightenment was rooted in Dutch and German rationalism, particularly that of Benedict Spinoza (1632–1677), Christian Wolff (1679–1754), and Immanuel Kant (1724–1804). From a theological point of view the Enlightenment presented a considerable challenge to the necessity of divine revelation and in particular the revelation of God as communicated through Jesus Christ and the New Testament. After all, if it were possible to ascertain a clear understanding of the nature and purposes of God through reason alone then the necessity of the Christ being a revelational vehicle was superfluous. Believing that the possibility of miracles was precluded by observational history, many Enlightenment thinkers rejected supernaturalism in general and specifically the idea that Jesus Christ was the supernatural, resurrected redeemer of humanity. Instead they argued that Christ's significance lies in his moral teaching and example.[14] This point of view in turn led to the

---

[12] Baxter, "Apokatastasis," 115.

[13] Alfred Lord Tennyson, "In Memoriam A.H.H." http://www.online-literature.com/tennyson/718/. (Accessed on September 13, 2014.)

[14] Thomas Jefferson, for instance, was one of the first who took scissors to the Bible and created his own gospel account. Jefferson's gospel was entirely devoid of the miraculous and focused instead on the moral teaching of Jesus. His account eliminates the resurrection and concludes with these momentous words: "Now in the place where he was crucified, there was a garden: and in the garden a new sepulcher, wherein was never a man yet laid. There laid they Jesus, and rolled a great stone to the door of the sepulcher, and departed." Thomas Jefferson, *The Life and Morals of Jesus of Nazareth* (1803; repr., Boston: Beacon Press, 1989), 132.

development of modern Bible criticism and also to the "quest of the historical Jesus" in its various forms.

Friedrich D. E. Schleiermacher (1768–1834) challenged the rational and ethical reduction of Christianity offered by Enlightenment thinkers such as Kant[15] and instead offered a re-conception of religion based in human experience. Considered by many to be the most influential theologian of the nineteenth century, Schleiermacher located the foundation of religion in the self and in the conscious feeling of absolute dependence that a person has toward God. For Schleiermacher the origin of faith was both pre-cognitive and pre-moral. Therefore, he argued that religious consciousness was common to all people and in this sense there were no true atheists. Schleiermacher saw atheism as "merely a disease of the understanding" that was brought on by either "a wicked fear of the sternness of the God-consciousness" or by "inadequate representations of the religious consciousness."[16]

Significant for this study are Schleiermacher's views regarding the universality of religion and religious feeling. He argued that all religions are an expression of dependence upon God, although some are more developed than others, with the three monotheistic religions—Judaism, Christianity, and Islam—being the most highly developed of all.[17] Schleiermacher expressed this view in the following proposition:

> *Those forms of piety in which all religious affections express the dependence of everything finite upon one Supreme and Infinite Being, i.e. the monotheistic forms, occupy the highest level; and all others are related to them as subordinate forms, from which men are destined to pass to those higher ones.*[18]

Regarding the three monotheistic religions, Schleiermacher argued that Judaism was too narrowly focused on the race of Abraham and thus was inferior to Christianity. He also noted that Islam had affinities that were too close to polytheism and as a result was also inferior to Christianity. Therefore, he concluded that Christianity "takes its place as the purest form of Monotheism which has appeared in history."[19] Thus Schleiermacher advocated a system of religious pluralism in which all religions were given credit for the various levels of truth that they contained, with Christianity being accorded the highest standing. Not surprisingly, Schleiermacher eschewed the notion that any religion should be dismissed out of hand as being "false." He commented, "Our proposition excludes only the idea, which indeed is often met with, that the Christian religion (piety) should adopt towards at least most other forms of

---

[15] Cf. Immanuel Kant, *Religion within the Boundaries of Mere Reason: And Other Writings*, ed. Allen W. Wood and George Di Giovani (1793; Cambridge: Cambridge University Press, 1998).

[16] Friedrich Schleiermacher, *Der christliche Glaube* (Berlin: G. Reimer, 1821–22); English edition trans. and ed. H.R. Mackintosh and J. S. Stewart, *The Christian Faith*, 2nd German edition (Edinburgh: T. & T. Clark, 1928; 1989), 135–36.

[17] Schleiermacher, *The Christian Faith*, 31–39.

[18] Schleiermacher, *The Christian Faith*, 34 (emphasis in the original).

[19] Schleiermacher, *The Christian Faith*, 38.

piety the attitude of true towards false. . . . The whole delineation which we are here introducing is based rather on the maxim that error never exists in and for itself, but always along with some truth, and that we have never fully understood it until we have discovered its connection with truth, and the true thing to which it is attached."[20]

Accordingly, Schleiermacher's theology took a broad view of salvation. When one considers that he believed that all human beings experience a form of God consciousness and that all religions have value as expressions of that consciousness, then it comes as no surprise to find that Schleiermacher's eschatological schema included universalism. Concerning eternal punishment as presented in the New Testament he asserted that the sayings of Christ on the subject were "figurative" in nature and were "insufficient to support any such conclusion,"[21] while on the other hand he affirmed that certain scriptures "forbid us to think of the definitive victory of evil over part of the human race."[22] Schleiermacher found a guarantee of the total deliverance of the human race in his concept of foreordination and election. He believed that all human beings were foreordained to salvation and fellowship with Christ, the only difference between them being the timing of their deliverance.[23] In his view of election Schleiermacher allowed for a postmortem salvation commenting that there is a "possibility of death intervening in some individual case before fore-ordination had fulfilled itself."[24] Thus Schleiermacher believed that salvation was a certainty for all human beings whether it was obtained in this life or the next.

Schleiermacher also argued in favor of universalism based upon an abstract discussion regarding the sympathy that those who experience eternal bliss would have toward those who experience eternal punishment. In his view, a high degree of bliss would not be possible for people in heaven because an awareness of the existence of eternal misery would create a sort of cognitive dissonance that "must of necessity be a disturbing element in bliss."[25] Based on this observation Schleiermacher reasoned that the notion of eternal punishment posed a far greater difficulty than that of universalism. He concluded:

> Hence we ought at least to admit the equal rights of the milder view, of which likewise there are traces in Scripture; the view, namely, that through the power of redemption there will one day be a universal restoration of all souls.[26]

Given Schleiermacher's affirmation of the foreordination of all human beings to salvation we must understand this comment to refer to the relative strength of the arguments for each side. In other words, apart from his theory of foreordination, Schleiermacher felt that the arguments in favor of universalism

---

[20] Schleiermacher, *The Christian Faith*, 33.

[21] Schleiermacher, *The Christian Faith*, 720. Cf. Matt. 25:46; Mark 9:44; John 5:29.

[22] Schleiermacher, *The Christian Faith*, 720. Cf. 1 Cor. 15:25–26.

[23] Schleiermacher, *The Christian Faith*, 547–50.

[24] Schleiermacher, *The Christian Faith*, 549.

[25] Schleiermacher, *The Christian Faith*, 721.

[26] Schleiermacher, *The Christian Faith*, 722.

were compelling and could stand on their own merit when confronting the doctrine of eternal punishment.

Schleiermacher's universalism marks a significant mile-post in the development of modern forms of the doctrine. Although he was ultimately Christocentric in his view of salvation, he did embrace a religious pluralism that acknowledged other religions as having some salvific effect in the lives of their adherents. Schleiermacher's pluralism represents a significant break with the exclusivist perspective that had prevailed in Christian theology for almost two millennia. Along with Guillaume Postel he stands out as a principal contributor to plurocentric universalism, which would be given a more thorough and refined presentation in the late twentieth century by men such as John Hick and Paul Knitter.[27] In Schleiermacher's pluralism and universalism we see an effort to satisfy the demands of Christian doctrine as well as an attempt to deal with the global reality of the existence of large numbers of people in the world who are committed to other religious systems. The fact that Schleiermacher made an effort to stratify the relative value of non-Christian religions stands as a testimony to the fact that he had a keen awareness of what existed beyond the borders of the Christian faith and that he desired to reconcile the two together. His solution was not to dismiss non-Christian religions, but rather to incorporate them within God's larger plan for salvation and to grant to them a certain limited level of validity.

Albrecht Benjamin Ritschl (1822–1889) was another leading German Protestant theologian of the nineteenth century who had universalist leanings. Educated in the finest theological schools in Germany (Bonn, Halle, Heidelburg, and Tübingen), Ritschl was a disciple of F.C. Baur but later came to reject Baur's theological perspective. The primary focus of his career was upon the exposition of systematic theology. Regarding spirituality, Ritschl agreed with Schleiermacher's view that faith was not to be apprehended by reason, but rather was to be understood in the context of religious experience.[28] As with Schleiermacher, what we have with Ritschl is a reaction to the rational and ethical reduction of Christianity offered by many Enlightenment thinkers. For Ritschl, the life of faith was not so much to be explained, but rather used to offer an explanation of everything else.

In terms of his soteriology and eschatology, Ritschl focused much of his attention upon presenting God as love. A central thesis in his theology was that God's activity towards man was based entirely upon his attribute of love. This perspective in turn led Ritschl to draw certain conclusions regarding salvation and eternal damnation that appear to embrace universalism. For instance, Ritschl argued that it was the "consciousness of guilt" that makes conversion possible and, it would seem, inevitable. He defined the consciousness of guilt "as the *removal of the separation* which, in consequence of sin, has entered

---

[27] A discussion of Postel may be found on pp. 98–100 of this study.
[28] Albrecht B. Ritschl, *Die christliche Lehre von der Rechtfertigung und Versöhnung*, 3 vols. (Bonn: A. Markus, 1870–74); English trans. H.R. Mackintosh and A.B. Macaulay, *The Christian Doctrine of Justification and Reconciliation*, 3 vols. (Edinburgh: T. & T. Clark, 1902), 3:100–108.

between man and God."[29] Thus, for Ritschl, the presence of the consciousness of guilt within a person ultimately resulted in the removal of a person's separation from God, which implied the restoration of union with him. When this view is coupled with Ritschl's contention that the consciousness of guilt could not be removed from the hardest sinner, it would seem that a universalist outcome is unavoidable. In light of this perspective, Ritschl argued that the idea of the double retribution of God—visited upon sinners in the form of spiritual and eternal death—is a questionable proposition at best.[30]

Ritschl also asserted that, "The Kingdom of God is the *summum bonum* which God realizes in men."[31] He elaborated on this point by explaining that the Kingdom of God is "the final end of the world and therefore the world itself."[32] The combination of these assertions once again implies a universalist outcome, for how can anyone escape the realization of the Kingdom of God within him/herself if such a realization embraces everything as we know it? Surely such a sweeping eschatological vision allows for no escape in the end. On the contrary, it seems to make full participation in the Kingdom unavoidable.

In speaking of sinners in general, Ritschl declared, "The authority of the Holy Scriptures gives us no right to relate the wrath of God to sinners as such, for *ex hypothesi* we conceive sinners to be known and chosen by God, as partakers in His Kingdom and the objects of His redemption from sin."[33] This statement also seems to imply a universalist outcome. The basis through which such an outcome would be achieved was the universal election of all sinners by God. Particularly striking here is the fact that Ritschl does not qualify the word "sinners" in any way. His language indicates that he understands the word "sinner" to be dispositive of the entire group who are the object of God's choice for redemption.

Although Ritschl never explicitly endorsed universalism in his writing, it is hard to see how his view of soteriology/eschatology can be interpreted otherwise. He certainly was not, as Baxter put it, "an agnostic concerning the matter of man's final destiny."[34] On the contrary, Ritschl positively advocated an eschatology in which the world would be transformed into the Kingdom of God. This eschatology included the redemption of all sinners from sin and the extension of the Kingdom of God into the life of every human being.

In the wake of the Enlightenment, other Europeans also questioned the validity of the doctrine of eternal punishment. Of particular note was Søren Kierkegaard (1813–1855) who, despite his characteristic negativism, appears to have embraced the concept of universal salvation on the basis of Christ's overwhelming ability to save.[35] In a response to a critic he once said:

---

[29] Ritschl, *The Christian Doctrine of Justification and Reconciliation*, 3:53 (emphasis in the original).

[30] Ritschl, *The Christian Doctrine of Justification and Reconciliation*, 3:52–53.

[31] Ritschl, *The Christian Doctrine of Justification and Reconciliation*, 3:30 (emphasis in the original).

[32] Ritschl, *The Christian Doctrine of Justification and Reconciliation*, 3:319.

[33] Ritschl, *The Christian Doctrine of Justification and Reconciliation*, 3:323.

[34] Baxter, "Apokatastasis," 124.

[35] Ludlow, "Universalism in the History of Christianity," 208.

I do not make myself better than others. And it is therefore not true what the old bishop once said to me that I spoke as though others go to hell, no, if I may say differently regarding the goes-to-hell discussion, I speak thus: If others go to hell, I will go also. However, I do not believe that, I believe the opposite, that all will be saved, myself also, which is something that arouses my deepest surprise.[36]

Kierkegaard was one among several European Protestants who embraced "the larger hope" of universalism in the nineteenth century. The intellectual freedom spawned by the Reformation allowed for such views to be expressed with little or no recrimination. However, the same was not true of countries that remained under largely Catholic control. In these countries universalism was still viewed as a heresy and a profound error. In particular France and Italy remained broadly hostile to the doctrine of universalism although, as Gotthold Müller notes, there was some sympathy shown it among the ranks of the poets and the philosophers.[37]

1.2. British Controversies
Enlightenment humanitarianism had a profound impact upon England and much of the opposition to the doctrine of eternal punishment came from British sources who were greatly influenced by Enlightenment thinking.[38] As the eighteenth and nineteenth centuries progressed the controversy over the doctrine of eternal punishment was formally taken up within both the university system of England and by the Church of England itself.

At the university level the issue came to a head with the controversy generated by the writings of Frederick Denison Maurice (1805–1872). Maurice was the son of a Unitarian minister who made a progressive spiritual journey from Unitarianism into Anglicanism. Initially Maurice was unwilling to subscribe to the Thirty-Nine Articles at Trinity Hall, Cambridge and this refusal deprived him of a degree and fellowship.[39] Eventually he accepted the Anglican faith and in 1840 was elected Professor of English Literature and History at King's College in London, which was an independent Anglican institution at this time. In 1846 Maurice was moved to the chair of theology in the newly created Theology School. However, Maurice's tenure at King's was cut short as a result of the controversy generated over the publishing of his controversial

---

[36] Eduard Geismar, "Das ethische Stadium bei Søren Kierkegaard," *ZST* 1 (1923): 260 (my translation).

[37] Regarding the debate in France, Müller commented: "Auch in dem überwiegend katholischen *Frankreich* hat es im 19. Jahrhundert zahlreiche Vertreter der Apokatastasis-Lehre gegeben, meistens in den Kreisen der Dichter und Philosophen." He noted the same thing regarding Italy: "Auch hier sind es vornehmlich die Philosophen und Ditcher, die das Gespräch weiterführen." Gotthold Müller, "Die Idee einer Apokatastasis ton panton in der europäischen Theologie von Schleiermacher bis Barth," *ZRG*, 16:1 (1964), 12; 15.

[38] Geoffrey Rowell, *Hell and the Victorians* (Oxford: Clarendon Press, 1973), 1–17, 62–89; Walker, *The Decline of Hell*, 104–263.

[39] *ODCC*, 1059.

Theological Essays in 1853. In an essay entitled "On Eternal Life and Eternal Death" Maurice challenged the view that eternal punishment meant endless punishment and instead asserted that "eternal" referred to a quality as opposed to a duration.[40] In the ensuing uproar, the college council dismissed Maurice from his professorship at King's.[41] A measure of the publicity brought on by Maurice's case may be seen in the fact that Tennyson wrote a special poem for him in order to buoy his spirits after his dismissal.[42] While some have accused Maurice of being a universalist, he most certainly was not; he was instead a firm believer in the efficacy of God's love and a non-dogmatic advocate for the hope that in the end all would be saved.[43] Although Maurice's dismissal might have been viewed as a setback for the advocates of intellectual freedom in England at the time, in the end it brought about a revolution of change. By 1866 Maurice was effectively absolved of all wrong doing and was installed as the Knightsbridge Professor of Moral Philosophy at Cambridge.

In 1860 the controversy over eternal punishment was taken up publicly in the Anglican Church with the case of the Rev. H.B. Wilson. Wilson was an Oxford tutor, Bampton Lecturer, and country vicar. A lawsuit was brought against Wilson in the church courts for a passage he wrote that advocated universalism within the pages of the controversial book *Essays and Reviews*.[44] *Essays and Reviews* was a joint effort made by seven Broad Church scholars to convince the church to embrace modern thought. As an academic exercise the book left much to be desired.[45] As an issue of church politics, the book proved to be a bombshell.

In an essay entitled "Séances historiques de Genève—the National Church" Wilson expressed his concern for the destiny of humanity and his dissatisfaction with those who were undisturbed by not knowing the final outcome. He declared: "We cannot be content to wrap this question up and leave it for a mystery, as to what shall become of those myriads upon myriads

---

[40] F.D. Maurice, "On Eternal Life and Eternal Death," in *Theological Essays*, New edition with Introduction by Edward F. Carpenter (London: James Clark, 1957), 302–32.
[41] Rowell, *Hell and the Victorians*, 80–86.
[42] Alfred Lord Tennyson, "To the Rev. F.D. Maurice" (1854), http://www.online-literature.com/tennyson/731. (Accessed on November 11, 2014.)
[43] Maurice's comments regarding the priority of God's love are particularly revealing: "I ask no one to pronounce, for I dare not pronounce myself, what are the possibilities of resistance in a human will to the loving will of God. There are times when they seem to me—thinking of myself more than others—almost infinite. I am obliged to believe in the abyss of love which is deeper than the abyss of death: I dare not lose faith in that love. I sink into death, eternal death, if I do" (Maurice, *Theological Essays*, 323).
[44] The best text of the book may be found in Victor Shea and William Whitla, eds., *Essays and Reviews: The 1860 Text and Its Reading* (Charlottesville and London: University of Virginia Press, 2000). This edition contains extended documentation regarding the disputes, trials, appeals, and public comment. For a comprehensive discussion of the historical context and long term consequences of the controversy see Ieuan Ellis, *Seven Against Christ: A Study of 'Essays and Reviews'* (Leiden: Brill, 1980).
[45] Ellis, *Seven Against Christ*, x.

of non-Christian races."[46] At the end of the essay Wilson proposed his own solution to the problem. He rejected the Calvinist response to the issue, not because it clung to the biblical admonition that "many are called but few chosen," but rather because it drew the wrong conclusion that all of the non-elect were relegated to "one mass of perdition." To Wilson's way of thinking, the pagan multitudes were largely "neutral" in character and it would be "inappropriate to apply to them, either the promises, or the denunciations of revelation."[47] Noting that he considered many *within* the Church to not be ready at death "for entering a higher career . . . but are rudimentary spirits—germinal souls," Wilson concluded:

> [W]e must rather entertain a hope that there shall be found, after great adjudication, receptacles suitable for those who shall be infants, not as to years of terrestrial life, but as to spiritual development—nurseries as it were and seed-grounds, where the undeveloped may grow up under new conditions—the stunted may become strong, and the perverted be restored. And when the Christian Church, in all its branches, shall have fulfilled its sublunary office, and its Founder shall have surrendered His kingdom to the Great Father—all, both small and great, shall find refuge in the bosom of the Universal Parent, to repose, or be quickened into higher life, in the ages to come, according to his Will.[48]

Wilson's solution is notable in that it presents us with a universalism in which non-believers are dealt with largely apart from biblical revelation. To be sure, it is vaguely Christocentric, but there is a substantial drift away from key elements of the Christian faith such as the centrality of the cross and the necessity of the atonement. It is more of an exercise in an outcome-driven narrative theology than an attempt to square the plight of the spiritually lost with the intricacies of biblical revelation. This approach fits well with the position that Wilson took elsewhere in the essay against the inspiration of scripture and what he saw as a rigid "Scripturalism."[49] Given his lenient view of scriptural authority, Wilson's conclusions are not surprising.

Of course the bishops of a High Church persuasion found Wilson's declarations to be quite disturbing and pressed their case forward. Eventually, even E. B. Pusey at Oxford organized a petition against the book at the urging of the Bishop of Oxford. In a reflection of the schisms that existed within the Church at the time, the Court of Arches sentenced Wilson to a one year deprivation of his position, but this was reversed by the Judicial Committee of the Privy Council (February 8, 1864).[50] Lord Chancellor Baron Westbury rendered the considered judgment of the Committee:

---

[46] H.B. Wilson, "Séances historiques de Genève—the National Church," in Shea and Whitla, *Essays and Reviews*, 280.

[47] Wilson, *Essays and Reviews*, 309.

[48] Wilson, *Essays and Reviews*, 309.

[49] Wilson, *Essays and Reviews*, 291–93, 308.

[50] Shea and Whitla, *Essays and Reviews*, 732–65. The Committee consisted of seven members: The Lord Chancellor presiding, three Law Lords, the Archbishops of Canterbury and York, and the Bishop of London. All agreed that Wilson's hopes for

We are not required or at liberty to express any opinion upon the mysterious question of final punishment, further than to say that we do not find in the Formularies to which this article [i.e. accusation] refers any such distinct declaration of our Church upon the subject as to require us to condemn as penal the expression of hope by a clergyman that even the ultimate pardon of the wicked who are condemned in the day of Judgment may be consistent with the will of Almighty God.[51]

With these words a posture of inscrutability regarding the doctrine of eternal punishment became the official stance of the Church of England.[52] To mark the occasion a joker composed a mock epitaph for Lord Chancellor Westbury, which ended with this verse:

> Towards the close of his earthly career
> In the Judicial Committee of the Privy Council
> He dismissed Hell with costs,
> And took away from orthodox members of the Church of England
> Their last hope of everlasting damnation.[53]

With the imprecise resolution of the *Essays and Reviews* controversy, it became clear to all involved that an official condemnation or approbation of eternal punishment would not be in the offing. As a result the debate moved out of the church courts and into the courts of public opinion. Several popular books advocating universalism were written in England at this time, chief among these would be Andrew Jukes' *The Second Death and the Restitution of All Things* (1867) and Samuel Cox's *Salvator Mundi* (1877).[54] F.W. Farrar and E.B. Pusey also entered into their famous debate over eternal punishment at this time with Farrar attempting to repudiate the doctrine while Pusey sought to defend it.[55]

---

universal pardon did not necessarily contradict the teaching of the Church of England. However, the two Archbishops dissented publicly over the question of denying the inspiration of Scripture.

[51] *Fendall v. Wilson*, as cited in Geoffrey Faber, *Jowett: Portrait with a Background* (Cambridge, Mass.: Harvard University Press, 1957), 275. See also Rowell, *Hell and the Victorians*, 119.

[52] It appears that this stance has been consistently maintained since Baron Westbury's declaration. See The Doctrinal Commission of the Church of England, *The Mystery of Salvation: The Story of God's Gift* (London: Church House Publishing, 1995), 180–81, 197, 199, 204–205.

[53] Faber, *Jowett: Portrait with a Background*, 276.

[54] Andrew J. Jukes, *The Second Death and the Restitution of All Things: With Some Preliminary Remarks on the Nature and Inspiration of Holy Scripture; A Letter to a Friend* (London: Longmans, Green, 1867, 1873); Samuel Cox, *Salvator Mundi or Is Christ the Savior of All Men?* (London: Henry S. King & Co., 1877).

[55] Farrar's first exposition was based upon series of sermons given by him at Westminster Abbey and was entitled *Eternal Hope: Five Sermons Preached in Westminster Abbey, November and December 1877*. Pusey's response may be found in his book *What is of Faith as to Everlasting Punishment? In Reply to Dr. Farrar's*

The net result of all this was that the influence of the doctrine of hell and eternal punishment was greatly diminished within the various denominations of England and in British society at large, while at the same time the notion of universalism was being promoted more than ever before. Geoffrey Rowell concluded:

> Mr. Gladstone's comment, at the end of the nineteenth century, that the doctrine of hell had been "relegated . . . to the far-off corners of the Christian mind . . . there to sleep in deep shadow as a thing needless in our enlightened and progressive age," is a reminder of the change that had taken place in Christian eschatology during the century. It is true that the doctrine of hell had not been removed from the official confession of any denomination, but men were no longer deprived of office for teaching a tentative universalism or regarded with suspicion for espousing the doctrine of conditional immortality.[56]

1.3. The Universalist Societies and Churches in Britain and America

Tracing the development of the universalist societies and churches in Britain and America during the eighteenth and nineteenth centuries is no easy task.[57] Important factors as diverse as post-Reformation religious freedom and Enlightenment ideals played a role as well as popular opinion and the broad dissemination of universalist literature.[58] In many ways the increased acceptance and expansion of universalism during this time was a direct reaction against the deterministic straightjacket of Calvinist theology, which had become so prevalent.[59] There was also the establishment of America itself, which was founded in large part as a result of the quest for religious freedom. This quest became enshrined in the First Amendment to the Constitution of the United States, which declared: "Congress shall make no law respecting an

---

Challenge in His 'Eternal hope,' 1879 (Oxford: James Parker, 1880). The final rejoinder in the exchange came from Farrar in his book *Mercy and Judgment: Last Words on Christian Eschatology with Reference to Dr. Pusey's 'What is of faith?'* (London: Macmillan, 1887).

[56] Rowell, *Hell and the Victorians*, 212.

[57] The following sources provide some guidance in untangling the history: Ann Lee Bressler, *The Universalist Movement in America* (Oxford: Oxford University Press, 2001); Richard Eddy, *Universalism in America: A History*, 2 vols. (Boston: Universalist Publishing House, 1884); Russell E. Miller, *The Larger Hope: The First Century of the Universalist Church in America 1770–1870* (Boston: Unitarian Universalist Association, 1979); Kenneth R. Morris, "Puritan Roots of American Universalism," *SJT* 44/4 (1991): 457–487; Geoffrey Rowell, "The Origins and History of Universalist Societies in Britain, 1750–1850," *JEH* 22/1 (January 1971): 35–56; Alan Seaburg, "Recent Scholarship in American Universalism: A Bibliographical Essay," *ChH* 41 (December 1972): 513–523.

[58] By 1886 Richard Eddy, the preeminent nineteenth-century historian of universalism, had amassed a bibliography of no less than 2,096 books and pamphlets published in America alone on the subject of universalism. See Eddy, *Universalism in America*, 2:485–599.

[59] Morris, "The Puritan Roots of American Universalism," 457–80; Bressler, *The Universalist Movement in America*, 9–30.

establishment of religion, or prohibiting the free exercise thereof . . ."[60] Consequently America has always taken pride in its rich tradition of religious independence and diversity. When taken as a whole, all of these factors made a significant contribution toward developing an environment that was conducive to the expansion of universalist thought and doctrine in both England and the United States.

Alan Seaburg traces the establishment of American universalism to two primary sources: (1) German sectarian universalism, and (2) British universalism.[61] If Seaburg's thesis is correct then American universalism must be seen initially as being a derivative development, although unique expressions would soon follow. German sectarian universalism in America seems to have been centered around Germantown, Pennsylvania, where pietistic émigrés from Wittgenstein, Germany, settled. George de Benneville (1703–1793) and the German Dunkers (German Baptist Brethren) were early advocates of universalism in colonial America as well as certain Moravians such as Peter Bohler.[62] Not surprisingly, British universalism made its preliminary appearance in America through the Episcopal and Congregational churches, which still maintained strong connections with England.[63] In an interesting process of cross-pollination John Murray (1741–1815) traveled from England to America in order to spread the doctrine of universal salvation, while Elhanan Winchester (1751–1797) traveled from America to England in order to do the same thing. Largely through the efforts of these two men several universalist churches and societies were established in both countries.[64] Winchester came to embrace universalism primarily through the influence of a book entitled *The Everlasting Gospel* that attempted to prove that universalism was not contrary to the Augsburg Confession.[65] Murray was himself a convert of the Welch preacher, James Relly, who had already established a few Rellyan Universalist societies in England.

In terms of theology, the universalism of Winchester focused on restorationism and a purgatorial future punishment before entrance into the kingdom. The universalism of Murray, on the other hand, derived from the antinomian Calvinism of Relly and advocated a position of no future punishment at all.[66] Representatives of both groups co-existed in the United

---

[60] "The Bill of Rights: A Transcription," *The National Archives and Records Administration,* Washington D.C. http://www.archives.gov/national-archives-experience/charters/bill_of_rights_transcript.html. (Accessed on Sept. 26, 2006.)
[61] Alan Seaburg, "Recent Scholarship in American Universalism: A Bibliographical Essay," 514.
[62] Rowell, "The Origins and History of Universalist Societies in Britain, 1750–1850," 37–38; Baxter, "Apokatastasis," 133–35.
[63] Baxter, "Apokatastasis," 134–35.
[64] Baxter, "Apokatastasis," 132–44.
[65] Rowell, "The Origins and History of Universalist Societies in Britain, 1750–1850," 38. Rowell notes that George de Benneville was responsible for the book's translation into English and that Winchester went to Germantown to meet with him in 1781.
[66] Morris observes that Murray's theology was "orthodox in every respect except for its optimistic view of the atonement." Morris, "Puritan Roots of American Universalism," 483.

States. For most of their early existence in America the two groups were united together in common cause, but in 1831 the two split apart for a period of about ten years before once again reuniting.[67] Hosea Ballou (1771–1852), considered by many to be the greatest theologian of American universalism, eventually led the denomination decisively away from its early Calvinistic associations. In his book *A Treatise on Atonement* (1805) Ballou advocated a moral influence theory of the atonement. He argued that the essential work of the atonement was not to be found in God being changed (i.e. satisfied) by the cross of Christ, but rather that the essential work of the atonement was focused on presenting a moral example to human beings who would be changed by viewing Christ's example on the cross. In conjunction with this perspective came an affirmation of Christ's subordination to the Father that brought American universalism much closer to the position of the Unitarians. In the book Ballou also denied virtually every cardinal doctrine of the Christian faith including the deity of Christ, the Trinity, vicarious atonement, human sin and depravity, as well as several others.[68] Ballou's position regarding salvation was pejoratively termed by his opponents as a "death and glory" soteriology. In Ballou's view, death automatically brought an unregenerate soul to repentance and thus salvation was instantaneous and assured without the need for any postmortem remediation.[69] Eventually the Universalist Church of America merged with the American Unitarian Association and in 1961 they formed the Unitarian Universalist Association.

On balance, the universalism of this era, as it was espoused by the universalist churches and societies founded in England and America, was largely Bible focused and Christocentric. To be sure, with Ballou we get a deliberate shift away from orthodoxy, yet it must be noted that his universalism is presented solidly within a Christian framework and that he still reserves a place for Jesus Christ within his theology. As a practical matter the most likely convert to universalist doctrine at this time would be an orthodox Christian who was most comfortable with biblical language and concepts. It was to these Christians that the universalism of this period was chiefly aimed.

2. The Twentieth Century Leading up to 1960

The first half of the twentieth century turned out to be a period of extreme upheaval and change that had a profound effect upon modern formulations of universalism. Victorian idealism and optimism in the progress of humanity was crushed under the weight of the many millions injured and killed in two world wars. The disclosure of the horrors of the Holocaust illustrated graphically the seemingly endless potential of "man's inhumanity to man." The ascendancy of stridently atheistic communist regimes in Eastern Europe plunged entire populations into the darkness of official non-belief. The proliferation of nuclear weapons threatened to annihilate vast portions of the human population. A huge movement toward secularism and the abandonment of religion decimated the

---

[67] Rowell, "The Origins and History of Universalist Societies in Britain, 1750–1850," 47.

[68] Ballou, *A Treatise on Atonement*, 71; 93–104; 116–22; 123–27; 132–36; 141; 223.

[69] Ballou, *A Treatise on Atonement*, 127–28; 140–41.

ranks of Christians in Europe and Britain. All of these factors brought with them an ever increasing awareness concerning the fate of the human race and raised anew the age old questions regarding hell, salvation, and eternal destiny.

In addition to these things, improvements in communications, modes of travel, and information dissemination made the world a much smaller place in the twentieth century. The shrinking globe brought with it an unprecedented recognition of other cultures, religions, and the enormous populations that lived outside of the orbit of Christianity. This global consciousness had the effect of throwing fuel on the fire when it came to the subjects of soteriology and eschatology and once again the question of eternal destiny loomed large in the minds of many theologians.

2.1. Universalism and Higher Criticism
While world events and socio-political realities were impacting the growth and shape of universalism in the early twentieth century, so were developments within the world of theology itself. With the invention and application of various types of higher criticism to the Bible, theologians were taking a fresh look at biblical eschatology and arriving at myriad of disparate conclusions. For instance, the German New Testament scholar William Wrede (1859–1906) took the view that Jesus was essentially a teacher of timeless truths into whose mouth his followers had placed an eschatology that he never actually articulated or embraced.[70] On the other hand Albert Schweitzer (1875–1965) argued that the Gospels' portrait of Jesus as an eschatological prophet was essentially correct, although Schweitzer himself believed that Jesus was seriously mistaken regarding the issue.[71] Obviously, eschatological concerns would matter little to a theologian who, like Wrede, rejected New Testament eschatology as being a secondary redactional accretion. However, many found Schweitzer's case for the centrality of eschatology to be compelling and were eager to apply recently developed higher critical methods to the problem of eternal destiny.

From the days of Origen much of the exegetical debate over universalism centered upon the usage and meaning of key words in the New Testament such as αἰώνιος. As we have already seen, even the more recent nineteenth-century debates in England were focused to a large degree upon the meaning and nuanced use of words. From the perspective of twentieth-century universalism the problem with the debate over lexicology was that it appeared that the case for the traditional understanding of hell and eternal punishment within the text of the New Testament had grown much stronger.[72] In summarizing the

---

[70] William Wrede, *Das Messiasgeheimnis in den Evangelien: Zugleich ein Beitrag zum Verständnis des Markusevangeliums* (Göttingen: Vandenhoeck & Ruprecht, 1901), English edition trans. J.C.G. Greig, *The Messianic Secret* (Cambridge: J. Clark, 1971).
[71] Albert Schweitzer, *Von Reimarus zu Wrede: eine Geschichte der Leben-Jesu-Forschung* (Tübingen: J.C.B. Mohr [Paul Siebeck], 1906); English edition trans. W. Montgomery, with a new introduction by James M. Robinson, *The Quest of the Historical Jesus: A Critical Study of Its Progress from Reimarus to Wrede* (New York: Macmillan, 1968), 370–71.
[72] See the Introduction to the present work and our discussion of the meaning of Ἀΐδιος and Αἰών/Αἰώνιος in section 3.3. Although there have been some recent efforts made

exegetical developments made in the twentieth century concerning the New Testament and the doctrine of eternal punishment, Richard Bauckham declared:

> In this century, however, exegesis has turned decisively against the universalist case. Few would now doubt that many NT texts clearly teach a *final* division of mankind into saved and lost, and the most that universalists now commonly claim is that alongside these texts there are others which hold out a universal hope (e.g. Eph. 1:10; Col. 1:20).[73]

Along these lines Bauckham notes that C.W. Emmet's essay "The Bible and Hell" (1917) was something of a landmark work.[74] After conducting an extensive survey of New Testament teaching Emmet concluded that the case for a final separation and judgment was so strong in the New Testament that, "it only leads to insincerity if we try to satisfy ourselves by artificial explanations of its language."[75] As a result Emmet suggested that any "tolerable" eschatological doctrine regarding the eternal destiny of unbelievers must be built upon "the moral principles of the New Testament" and not its explicit teaching.[76] Similarly, C.F.D. Moule, in his little booklet *The Meaning of Hope: A Biblical Exposition with Concordance*, acknowledged the force of what is found in the New Testament text: "Regarding the details of 'the beyond,' the New Testament is notoriously reticent. What it does emphasize is the terrible urgency and seriousness of a man's choice in this life—so much so that it does (let us face it) speak of eternal destruction, eternal fire, a second death for those who are obdurate."[77] However, despite this observation, Moule goes on to advocate a hopeful universalism based upon what he sees as the overriding New Testament principle of love: "I find it well-nigh impossible to believe that the overwhelming, infinitely patient love as God shows us in Christ can, in the last resort, be defeated."[78]

With both Emmet and Moule we have a move away from the letter of the New Testament text toward what is perceived to be the spirit of the text. While Moule acknowledged the possibility of eternal separation from God, he argued that the overriding principles found in the Bible spoke against this ever

---

by universalists to cast doubt on the conclusions made by the foremost Greek lexicographers, those arguments have been largely defeated in the scholarly literature and the lexicography of the New Testament up to this point remains decidedly in favor the traditionalist perspective. Perhaps the recent work of Ramelli and Konstan, *Terms for Eternity*, will re-ignite some discussion. Nevertheless, the weakness of their arguments remain a serious impediment to convincing the bulk of New Testament scholarship.

[73] Bauckham, "Universalism," 52.

[74] C.W. Emmet, "The Bible and Hell," in Burnett H. Streeter, A. Clutton-Brock, C.W. Emmet, and J.A. Hadfield, eds., *Immortality: An Essay in Discovery Co-ordinating Scientific, Psychical, and Biblical Research* (London: Macmillan, 1917), 167–217.

[75] Emmet, "The Bible and Hell," 212.

[76] Emmet, "The Bible and Hell," 212.

[77] C.F.D. Moule, *The Meaning of Hope: A Biblical Exposition with Concordance* (Philadelphia: Fortress, 1953), 46.

[78] Moule, *The Meaning of Hope*, 46.

becoming a reality. This distinction between possibility and reality becomes a central feature of the apologetic employed by several twentieth-century theologians who wanted to remain faithful to the difficult passages found in the text while at the same time embracing universalism.

With the support of traditional exegesis turning against a novel interpretation of the words and phrases at hand, another group of twentieth-century universalists turned to the use of higher critical methods as a means of providing support for their conclusions. The Anglican Bishop John A.T. Robinson was one such scholar. As one who appreciated Schweitzer's reemphasis on eschatology as a central theme in the New Testament, Robinson's formulation of universalism is an important milestone in the development of the doctrine because of its thoroughgoing application of modern techniques of higher criticism to the issue at hand.[79]

In a manner that has much in common with the methodology and existential thought of Rudolf Bultmann, Robinson argued that New Testament eschatology was built upon two myths that represent "the two sides of the truth that is in Jesus."[80] According to Robinson, what is most important about how these myths are presented in the Bible is not whether they are presented with historical accuracy, but rather whether or not the essential truth they seek to illustrate is valid.[81] The first myth, seen from the perspective of man, requires an insistence on the reality of the decision between heaven and hell. "To the man in decision—and that means to all men, always, right up to the last hour—hell is in every way as real a destination as heaven." The second myth, seen from the perspective of God, requires an insistence on the reality of universal salvation. This reality is grounded upon God's undefeatable love: "In the universe of love there can be no heaven which tolerates a chamber of horrors, no hell for any which does not at the same time make it hell for God. He cannot endure that, for *that* would be the final mockery of his nature. And he will not."[82]

According to Robinson, these myths were created by the ancient church in order to speak to its current situation and in order to "embody *present* realities within the life of the New Age."[83] This bit of redaction criticism allows Robinson to argue that when these myths are held together they compose two sides to the same eschatological coin that the church was trying to convey. The key to ironing out the seeming contradiction between the two views is a matter of perspective. Seen from man's view the salvation decision is real. Seen from God's view universalism is real. In this way Robinson sought to say that it is not actually a case of either an eternally binding choice or universalism, but rather that both realities could be true at the same time based upon the perspective of the one who confronts them. Despite his effort to do justice to

---

[79] Although Robinson was sympathetic to Schweitzer's enterprise, he did not accept his conclusions. See John A.T. Robinson, *In the End God* (New York: Harper & Row, 1968), 32–33; 68–70.

[80] Robinson, *In the End God*, 130. Regarding Robinson's view of the use of myths in the Bible see *In the End God*, 44–46.

[81] Robinson, *In the End God*, 45.

[82] Robinson, *In the End God*, 133. See also 110–11.

[83] Robinson, *In the End God*, 77.

those passages in the Bible that speak of decision and eternal punishment, Robinson concludes that in the end it is universalism that will ultimately prevail. This conclusion begs the question of whether his solution has truly apprehended the real nature of human freedom and allowed for its full exercise—after all an important aspect of freedom is the uncertainty of the outcome.

Be this as it may, Robinson's resolution to the seeming contradiction created by various Bible passages illustrates how higher criticism can come to the aid of the universalist project. In fact, both form and redaction criticism seem to be tailor made for those who would like to strike uncomfortable references made to eternal punishment from Jesus' lips and from other areas of the Bible.[84] For instance, H.H. Farmer employs a bit of form criticism in his defense of universalism when he notes that New Testament passages speaking of eternal punishment may have been inspired by contemporary apocalyptic imagery or idiomatic Hebrew hyperbole.[85] Nels F.S. Ferré sees a redactional motive of self-righteousness reflected in some of the comments made by the New Testament writers related to the threat of eternal punishment.[86] Higher criticism, thus employed, has become an indispensable tool in the hands of many modern universalists and has greatly changed the parameter and terms of the ongoing debate.

2.2. Universalism and Dialectical Theology
The advent of the twentieth century also brought with it a revolt against nineteenth-century liberalism and its deconstruction of biblical revelation. Grounded in the ferment and upheaval created by the First World War, the dialectical movement began as a response made by a group of young German theologians to what they believed to be the ethical failure of their mentors.[87]
In August of 1914, ninety-three German intellectuals signed a public proclamation in support of the war policy of Wilhelm II. Among the signatories were such notable theologians as Adolf von Harnack and Wilhelm Herrmann. Particularly disillusioned by this turn of events was the Swiss theologian Karl Barth (1886–1968) who was a devoted student of Herrmann. In Barth's view, a theology that claimed divine support for an unjust war was bankrupt. In a 1957 retrospective, Barth reflected on his reaction to the proclamation and those who signed it:

---

[84] As we shall see shortly, this is the approach that John Hick takes toward the issue. See John Hick, *Death and Eternal Life* (London: Collins, 1976), 242–61.
[85] Herbert H. Farmer, *God and Men* (New York: Abingdon-Cokesbury Press, 1947), 175.
[86] In a comment that Ferré made in reference to Rev. 6:9–11 he said: "The scribes and Pharisees still murmur because Jesus receives sinners. Even those who wrote the Bible had to sponsor such attitudes, even to the point of making the saints clamor for revenge. How sad is such a state of the spirit reflected even in the New Testament." Nels F.S. Ferré, *The Christian Understanding of God* (New York: Harper & Bros., 1951), 233.
[87] The group included several notable twentieth-century theologians such as Karl Barth, Edward Thurneysen, Friedrich Gogarten, Rudolf Bultmann, Emil Brunner, and Günther Dehn.

Among these intellectuals I discovered to my horror almost all of my theological teachers whom I had greatly venerated. In despair over what this indicated about the signs of the time I suddenly realized that I could not any longer follow either their ethics and dogmatics or their understanding of the Bible and of history. For me, at least, 19th-century theology no longer held a future.[88]

In their efforts to break with the liberal theologies of their teachers, the dialectical theologians went down many disparate paths and it is for this reason that the movement was not long lived. By the 1930s most of the original alliances had shattered as a result of sharp theological disagreements. However, Karl Barth did succeed in achieving an entirely new synthesis in the arena of dogmatic theology. A byproduct of his work has been a renewal of the debate over universalism. As we shall see, Barth's new synthesis breathed new life into the doctrine and therefore has served as a lightning rod for discussion. Along with the widely read theology of Emil Brunner (1889–1966), Barth's work initiated a renewed interest in universalism among many theological circles in the twentieth century. It is therefore a significant subject for our study.

While it is generally acknowledged that Brunner put forward no more than a form of hopeful universalism, the same cannot be said for Barth.[89] Indeed, Brunner's criticism of Barth on this point was that his theology was too inflexible and that it had completely eliminated "the possibility of damnation."[90] While Barth adamantly denied that he had embraced *apokatastasis*,[91] there are two key aspects of Barth's theology that have combined to lead people to draw the opposite conclusion. The first was his

---

[88] Karl Barth, "Evangelical Theology in the Nineteenth Century," in Karl Barth, *The Humanity of God*, trans. Thomas Weiser (1960; Atlanta, Ga.: John Knox, 1978), 14.

[89] Heinrich Emil Brunner, *The Christian Doctrine of the Church, Faith, and the Consummation*, trans. Olive Wyon (Philadelphia: Westminster Press, 1962), 422. See also Gray, "Hell: An Analysis of Some Major Twentieth Century Attempts to Defend the Doctrine of Hell, 104–6; Bauckham, "Universalism," 52.

[90] Heinrich Emil Brunner, *Dogmatik: Bd. 1, Die christliche Lehre von Gott* (Zürich: Zwingli, 1946); English ed. trans. Olive Wyon, *Dogmatics, vol. 1, The Christian Doctrine of God* (Philadelphia, Penn.: Westminster, 1949), 348.

[91] Barth's denials may be found in Karl Barth, *Die kirchliche Dogmatik* (Zürich: Evangelischer Verlag, 1936–1977); English edition trans. G.W. Bromiley and T.F. Torrance, *Church Dogmatics* (Edinburgh: T. & T. Clark, 1936–1977), II/2, 417–18; *CD* IV/3, 478. The issue is well framed by J.D. Bettis who offers a defense of Barth's denials. See J.D. Bettis, "Is Karl Barth A Universalist?" *SJT* 20 (Dec. 1967): 423–36. More recently John Colwell has offered a defense of Barth's position. See John E. Colwell, *Actuality and Provisionality: Eternity and Election in the Theology of Karl Barth* (Edinburgh: Rutherford, 1989); John E. Colwell, "Proclamation As Event: Barth's Supposed 'Universalism' in the Context of His View of Mission," in Paul Beasley-Murray, ed., *Mission to the World: Essays to Celebrate the 50th Anniversary of the Ordination of George Raymond Beasley-Murray to the Christian Ministry* (Didcot, U.K.: Baptist Historical Society, 1991), 42–46; John E. Colwell, "The Contemporaneity of the Divine Decision: Reflections on Barth's Denial of 'Universalism,'" in Cameron, *Universalism and the Doctrine of Hell*, 139–160.

famous "No"—"Yes" dialectic. The second was his reformulation of the
Reformed doctrine of election.

In Barth's view, the divine "No" must always come before the divine "Yes."
Applying this idea to the sphere of salvation and judgment, judgment always
had to come first. However, Barth argued that this judgment—the divine "No,"
was always followed by an *equally powerful* salvation—or divine "Yes." This
meant that, for Barth, God's judgment would not get the better of his salvific
will. As Barth put it in his discussion of Romans 1:16–17: "Precisely because
the 'No' of God is all-embracing, it is also His 'Yes.'"[92] Similarly, in
discussing Romans 11:11, he concluded: "The 'No' of God is no more than the
inevitable turning to the man of this world of the reverse side of His 'Yes.'"[93]
Thus there was an equivalency between the two ideas in Barth's mind. He was
essentially saying that the divine "No" would not cancel out the divine "Yes";
judgment would not cancel out salvation. Therefore, it would seem that Barth's
affirmation of such a dialectical reversal would require nothing less than a
universalist outcome.

In addition to this fundamental principle, Barth also linked his "No"—"Yes"
dialectic directly into his view of divine election, which adds considerable
strength to the argument that Barth is much more than a hopeful universalist. In
an interesting modification to the Reformed doctrine of election, Barth made
the doctrine of predestination and election Christological, arguing that Christ
experiences the rejection for all on the cross and that all are universally elected
in Christ. After an extended discussion of the drawbacks of Reformed theology
Barth concluded that Jesus Christ is both "the electing God and the elected
man."[94] Barth elaborated on this mystery further when he said:

> In this free act of the election of grace there is already present, and
> presumed, and assured into unity with His existence as God, the existence
> of the man whom He intends and loves from the very first and in whom
> He intends and loves all other men, of the man in whom He wills to bind
> Himself with all other men and all other men with Himself.[95]

The net result of this complete Christological election is that Jesus
experiences the total rejection of all people: "He tasted Himself the damnation,
death and hell which ought to have been the portion of fallen man . . . He
elected our rejection. He made it His own."[96] So then, in effect, Jesus took on
the totality of our divine "No" in order that we might experience the
blessedness of the divine "Yes" that is communicated to us through Christ. The
election of all humanity in Christ rules out the possibility of a sustained and
unrelenting unbelief:

---

[92] Karl Barth, *The Epistle to the Romans,* 6th edition, trans. Edwyn C. Hoskyns (Oxford:
Oxford University Press, 1933), 38.
[93] Barth, *The Epistle to the Romans,* 401.
[94] *CD* II/2, 76.
[95] *CD* IV/1, 66.
[96] *CD* II/2, 164.

With the divine No and Yes spoken in Jesus Christ the root of human unbelief, the man of sin, is pulled out. In its place there is put the root of faith, the new man of obedience. For this reason unbelief has become an objective, real and ontological impossibility and faith an objective, real and ontological necessity for all men and for every man. In the justification of the sinner which has taken place in Jesus Christ these have both become an event which comprehends all men.[97]

It is interesting to note that in keeping with this view of election that Barth preferred to speak of hell in terms of the "No"—"Yes" dialectic. He wanted to say that there was a possibility that the recalcitrant might experience some form of hell, but he always seemed to fall back on the divine "Yes" as a response to it.[98] The best he could do in this regard was to speak to the hypothetical of damnation. Even in that case he affirmed, "[I]n hell we shall be in his hands. Even in its torments we shall be shielded with Him."[99] However, this was not the outcome that Barth really envisioned. His view was that, "Those whom He [God] will find and have for Himself He pursues to the remotest corner where their backs are to the wall and they can no longer escape Him."[100] When this pursuit is coupled to Barth's doctrine of universal election, it is hard to imagine any other outcome than universal salvation.

Although Barth denied embracing universalism,[101] it is hard to see how his theology could lead to anything else. His dialectical approach and retooling of the doctrine of election put universalism at the center of the theological equation in the early twentieth century and showed that biblically focused dogmatic theology was by no means dead. The contribution of Karl Barth points to a fluidity that is an essential characteristic of twentieth-century universalism. Freed from the rigid confessional structure of the church, Barth was able to pursue his theological inquiry to where ever it led him.

2.3. Universalism as a Response to Political Disillusionment
The unique circumstances of twentieth century politics brought with it a keen awareness of failures of human government to provide peace, safety, and prosperity for large portions of the human race. Nicholas Berdyaev is an example of a theologian whose theology was greatly influenced by the study of human history and recent political events. In his book *The Fate of Man in the Modern World* Berdyaev lamented the historic crisis that had befallen humanity in the early twentieth century.[102] He argued that through the tragedy of the First World War "the humanist myth about man was exploded" and the tragic situation that humankind faced was revealed.[103] Capitalism had failed and

---

[97] *CD* IV/1, 747.

[98] Cf. *CD* II/1, 274; 553.

[99] *CD* II/2, 609.

[100] *CD* II/2, 609.

[101] One of his main arguments against it was based in the freedom of God rather than the freedom of man. See *CD* IV/3, 477.

[102] Nicholas Berdyaev, *The Fate of Man in the Modern World* (London: Student Christian Movement Press, 1935).

[103] Berdyaev, *The Fate of Man in the Modern World*, 16.

dehumanized humanity, reducing people to mere elements of an economic process.[104] Communism, fascism, and national socialism had also failed and dehumanized people just as cruelly as capitalism had.[105] Collectivist schemes such as Russian Communism and German National Socialism had "cleansed culture of individualism" and created a dictatorship over the spirit of man.[106] Berdyaev's solution to these profound problems was found in a purified Christianity that had been cleansed of its human corruption including the "sadism" of endless punishment in hell.[107] Berdyaev believed that many of the elements that people found to be objectionable within Christianity had come about as a result of Christianity becoming "infected with all of history's temptations and imperfections."[108] This infection included the doctrine of endless punishment, which he believed to be an example of an unhealthy sado-masochistic complex adopted from human history that required complete excision.

However, this attitude of pessimism toward Christianity should not be misconstrued to imply that Berdyaev felt that it had become hopelessly corrupted. On the contrary, Berdyaev believed that a restored Christianity was the only answer to the world's problems. He declared, "Outside Christianity, or better, outside of Christ, there is no salvation for fallen man."[109] Despite the strong exclusivist sound to the declaration, what Berdyaev had in mind was universal salvation. He understood universalism to be the ultimate corporate remedy for the ultimate corporate problem. He concluded, "I cannot seek salvation individually, by my solitary self, such an interpretation of salvation destroys the unity of the cosmos."[110] Berdyaev's commitment to human solidarity led him to embrace the conviction that "salvation is inconceivable except in the company of all mankind."[111]

When taken as a whole, Berdyaev's universalism can be seen as both a philosophical and theological response to the corruption and failure of human government. His universalist solution was crafted within a keen awareness of the historic plight of all human beings. His universalism offered an all-embracing vision of deliverance for the entire human race. With Berdyaev we have a universalism conceived of in terms of the ultimate political deliverance.

2.4. The Growing Influence of Pluralism
A major phenomenon in the twentieth century that has contributed to the development of an entirely new expression of Christian universalism has been the growth and acceptance of a powerful socio-political movement known as pluralism. Grounded firmly in Enlightenment egalitarianism and a

---

[104] Berdyaev, *The Fate of Man in the Modern World*, 16.

[105] Berdyaev, *The Fate of Man in the Modern World*, 61–70.

[106] Berdyaev, *The Fate of Man in the Modern World*, 116.

[107] Berdyaev, *The Fate of Man in the Modern World*, 120.

[108] Berdyaev, *The Fate of Man in the Modern World*, 120.

[109] Berdyaev, *The Fate of Man in the Modern World*, 125.

[110] Nicholas Berdyaev, *The Destiny of Man*, trans. Natalie Duddington (London: G. Bles, The Centenary Press, 1945), 276–77.

[111] Nicholas Berdyaev, *Dream and Reality: An Essay in Autobiography* (London: G. Bless, 1950), 65.

postmodernist worldview that denies the existence of transcendent categories,[112] pluralism from the western perspective basically asserts that the West can no longer ignore any other culture or way of life and that it most certainly cannot maintain its superiority over them. Indeed, at the core of pluralist teaching is a pragmatic relativism that a priori sets all cultures and religions on equal footing.[113] On a societal level this fundamental organizing principle has in turn led to the general adoption of "tolerance," "diversity," and "multiculturalism" being pursued as moral ends through a myriad of social policies. In the United States these policies have taken on the form of affirmative action, diversity training, special studies programs, and a host of other strategies designed to promulgate pluralist ideals. At the religious level pluralism asserts that Christianity can no longer claim to be absolute and unique. Instead, Christianity must be viewed as just one religion alongside many others. From a theological point of view pluralism brings with it a demand that Christian theologians no longer practice theology on an intramural plane. If, as the pluralist claims, all religions are equal and have equal access to the truth, then all religions must be allowed a seat at the theological table. Veli-Matti Kärkkäinen summarized the consequences of pluralism by noting, "[I]t is no longer possible to limit the consideration of theological topics to the Christian sphere; we must take into account the questions and answers posed by other religions."[114]

---

[112] Postmodern psychologist and social critic Kenneth Gergen in his book, *The Saturated Self*, explained the phenomenon in this way: "With the spread of postmodern consciousness, we see the demise of personal definition, reason, authority. . . All intrinsic properties of the human being, along with moral worth and personal commitment, are lost from view" (Kenneth Gergen, *The Saturated Self: Dilemmas of Identity in Contemporary Life* [New York: Basic Books, 1991]), 228–29.

[113] It should be noted that this assumption is also an outgrowth of postmodernism. The postmodernist typically rejects the notion of the existence of absolute truth. Instead, truth is seen to be relativised within the "narrative" stories of the various cultures that created it. Thus, for the postmodernist, truth only exists within societal confines and cannot be taken out of that context and applied to another culture or society. The embrace of this viewpoint forces one into the pluralist camp in a defacto sort of way. Gergen sums up this point of view well along with its grave implications for truth: "[E]valuation can only take place from within a perspective. To favor one of these perspectives because it is 'objectively true' presupposes that I have a perspective in which 'objectively true' is an intelligible criterion of evaluation. If in my view 'objective truth' is a misleading term, I can scarcely condemn a theory because it is objectively false" (Gergen, *The Saturated Self*, 229).

[114] Veli-Matti Kärkkäinen, *An Introduction to the Theology of Religions: Biblical, Historical, and Contemporary Perspectives*, 17. On this point see also Paul A. Knitter, *No Other Name: A Critical Survey of Christian Attitudes Toward the World Religions*, 224. An interesting development along these lines is found in the "Pluralism Project" sponsored by Harvard University. The destinctives of the project may be explored at: http://www.pluralism.org. (Accessed on November 11, 2014.) Its stated mission is to ". . . help Americans engage with the realities of religious diversity through research, outreach, and the active dissemination of resources." The project was born out of the recognition that "how we appropriate plurality to shape a positive pluralism is one of the

While we have already noted the contributions that Guillaume Postel and Friedrich Schleiermacher made toward the development of pluralistic thought,[115] most trace the development of modern religious pluralism to the writings of the German theologian Ernst Troeltsch (1865–1923). Troeltsch struggled throughout his career with the issue of the relationship of God to the world and how God reveals himself within human history. He was particularly troubled by the popular notion that God, for the most part, left his creation alone and only interacted occasionally with it. His solution to the problem was to argue that God was not just present in bits and pieces of the unfolding story of human history, but rather that God was present in its entirety. In other words, Troeltsch believed that God was coterminous with human history and he argued for a unity between both the human and the divine: "Here 'human' and 'divine' are not antithetical terms. Instead, everything is human and divine at the same time."[116] If God was coterminous with all of human history, then it followed that all of human history must be of equal value and that all religions represented a unique and equally important expression of God. In speaking of Christianity, Troeltsch noted, "The Christian religion is in every moment of its history a purely historical phenomenon, subject to all the limitations of which any individual historical phenomenon is exposed, just like the other great religions."[117]

Interestingly enough, early in his career Troeltsch was unwilling to accept the unmistakably pluralistic implications of his reasoning and instead argued that Christianity was nevertheless the superior religion.[118] However, toward the end of his life it is clear that Troeltsch had finally made the pilgrimage into full-blown pluralism. His final lecture, which he had prepared for Oxford University but never delivered, was published posthumously. In it he finally accepted the logical conclusion toward which his life's work pointed:

> Thus the universal law of history consists precisely in this, that the Divine Reason, or the Divine Life, within history, constantly manifests itself in always—new and always—peculiar individualizations—and hence that its tendency is not towards unity or universality at all, but rather towards fulfillment of the highest potentialities of each separate department of life. It is this law which, beyond all else, makes it quite impossible to characterize Christianity as the reconciliation and goal of all the forces of

---

most important questions American society faces in the years ahead." (http://www.pluralism.org/about/mission.php. (Accessed on November 11, 2014.)

[115] The discussion of Postel may be found on pp. 99–101 of this study. The discussion of Schleiermacher may be found on pp. 117–20.

[116] Ernst Troeltsch, *Die Absolutheit des Christentums und de Religionsgeschichte* (Tübingen: J.C.B. Mohr [Paul Siebeck], 1929); English edition trans. David Reid, *The Absoluteness of Christianity and the History of Religions* (Richmond, Va.: John Knox, 1971), 53.

[117] Troeltsch, *The Absoluteness of Christianity*, 85.

[118] His title for chapter 4 in his book *The Absoluteness of Christianity* is particularly telling: "Christianity: Focal Point and Culmination of All Religious Developments." Troeltsch, *The Absoluteness of Christianity*, 5.

history, or indeed to regard it as anything else than a historical individuality.[119]

In this statement we have encapsulated the basic thesis of modern religious pluralism: God works separately with relative equality through all religions.

The broad embrace of pluralism in the western world has had a tremendous impact upon both its cultural and religious expression. On the popular level, the spirit of religious pluralism has been naïvely captured in the oft repeated slogan: "All paths lead to God."[120] Contained within this statement is an implied pluralistic universalism that can now be objectively measured within American religious culture. For instance, George Barna's research has found: "[A]bout four out of every ten adults strongly concurred that when Christians, Jews, Buddhists, and others pray to their god, all of those individuals are actually praying to the same god, but simply use different names for that deity. Only one out of every six adults strongly disagreed with this view."[121] The quantification of such sentiments reflects the influence that the pluralist movement has had upon religious consciousness in our own times and the contribution it has made towards popularizing universalist sentiments within western society. As we shall see, the promotion of pluralistic ideals has led to entirely new formulations of contemporary universalism.

3. Conclusion

The Age of the Enlightenment exerted an incredible influence over the development of universalism in the modern era. Enlightenment thought with its emphasis on the centrality of human reason provided the intellectual environment in which the hegemony of orthodoxy and biblical literalism could be easily challenged. Enlightenment humanitarianism with its emphasis on equality, tolerance, justice, material welfare, and religious pluralism provided the social environment in which the probity of the doctrine of eternal punishment could easily be attacked. In short, the Enlightenment provided an ideal environment for the further tearing down of the traditional eschatological paradigm and the promulgation of modern expressions of universalism.

To a large degree the agenda of the Enlightenment has became the agenda of modern universalism. Enlightenment appeals to compassion, egalitarianism, social justice, open-mindedness, and pluralism as well as other things have all resonated within the universalist camp and are often used to support and promote universalism. Enlightenment antipathy toward rigid orthodoxy and the

---

[119] Ernst Troeltsch, "The Place of Christianity among the World Religions," in John Hick and Brian Hebblethwaite, eds., *Christianity and Other Religions* (Philadelphia: Fortress, 1980), 17.

[120] Of course anyone who has attempted to prove this assertion has run into monumental problems in the translation of the concepts of divinity and salvation from one religion to the next. For a summary of the intractable problems encountered see the following articles written by Joseph A. DiNoia: "Christian Universalism: The Nonexclusive Particularity of Salvation in Christ," 37–48 and "Varieties of Religious Aims: Beyond Exclusivism, Inclusivism, and Pluralism," 249–74.

[121] George Barna, *What Americans Believe: An Annual Survey of Values and Religious Views in the United States* (Ventura, Calif.: Regal Books, 1991), 275.

notion of eternal punishment has also been assimilated and reason has been elevated as the master of revelation by many modern universalists. In short, the embrace of Enlightenment thought and assumptions have dominated universalist thinking for more than two centuries.

The influence of the Enlightenment continues into our own times and contemporary western culture is still largely driven by the Enlightenment agenda. Calls for equal rights, human rights, minority rights, and multiculturalism are all the direct offspring of the Enlightenment. Pluralism with its affirmation of the equality of all cultures and religions is also the direct descendent of the Enlightenment. Although we live in a post-modern world, it is a world that is still largely shaped and controlled by Enlightenment thinking and ideals. As we move forward to examine contemporary expressions of universalism we would do well to keep this fact in mind.

In the first part of this dissertation we have sought to trace the historical development of the doctrine of universalism as a means of setting the stage for understanding its contemporary expression. This analysis has clearly revealed that universalism has never existed in a purely theological vacuum. There has been a progressive evolution of the doctrine that has taken into consideration theological developments as well as socio-political influences and advances in cross-cultural awareness and technology. This evolution in universalist thought continues into our own times and, as we shall see shortly, contemporary universalism has continued to develop with a keen awareness of both its past and the present environment in which it operates.

PART 2

CONTEMPORARY EXPRESSIONS SINCE 1960

THE PROTESTANT CONTRIBUTION

CHAPTER 4

Christocentric Approaches

As the true heir of Enlightenment humanitarianism, contemporary Protestant theology has proven itself to be the pacesetter in the development of universalist thinking. Whereas earlier generations of theologians were generally constrained by church affiliation, the maintenance of doctrinal purity, and various threats of retribution for heresy, twentieth-century protestant theologians abandoned such constraints en masse and insisted on the right to exercise scholarly independence. This assertion of intellectual freedom has resulted in an environment in which theologians have felt much freer to explore alternative interpretations of scripture and doctrine.

The presentation of universalism in contemporary Protestant theology begins in earnest with an analysis of recent Christocentric proposals. By the word "Christocentric" it is meant that Christ remains at the center of the soteriological schema and that salvation is ultimately seen as being mediated through him in some significant way. The key feature of Christocentric universalisms is that they grant an indispensable role to Christ. However, precisely how that role is envisioned and played out can vary greatly.

Christocentric universalism stands in contrast to plurocentric approaches in which all religions and paths are accorded relative equality in the process of achieving salvation or unity with the divine. In plurocentric universalism the role of Christ in salvation is down played and he is usually viewed as not being a unique mediator. In these proposals Christ is typically accorded recognition as one great religious leader among many. Therefore, with plurocentric universalism the exclusivist claims for the uniqueness of Christianity and salvation in Christ must be dealt with and invalidated in some way. On the other hand, the claims of the various religions regarding communion with the divine must be established.

It should be noted that we will encounter some Christocentric universalisms that incorporate pluralistic ideas. What separates these Christocentric versions from their true plurocentric counterparts is that they still accord Christ a significant role in their soteriology despite the fact that they also reserve an honored place for other religions and religious expressions. In the interest of analyzing the issue of pluralism in a more comprehensive fashion we will put off examining these moderating forms until the next chapter, which will be devoted to the exposition of plurocentric universalism.

The focus of this chapter is on the analysis of recent Christocentric proposals. We will begin with an examination of the work of Thomas B. Talbott because he presents us with an extensive enunciation of Christocentric universalism that is paradigmatic of the classical position. The analysis of Thomas Talbott's universalism will be more detailed and comprehensive than most of the others that follow. The reason for this is that Talbott's extensive presentation serves as an ideal template against which several important issues regarding Christocentric universalism may be discussed. As we shall see, much of what is said regarding Talbott's proposal may be applied to others and therefore need not be restated. We will then move on to examine several other significant contributors to the contemporary scene.

The decision has been made to include an analysis of one contemporary universalist who is definitely outside of the mainstream of academic theology and is not typically mentioned within academic circles. Specifically, an analysis of the universalism Martin Zender has been incorporated into this section because he provides us with a window through which we may catch a glimpse of a historical vein of universalism of which many scholars are unaware: Ultra-dispensational universalism.

The section will end with an analysis of the universalism of Jürgen Moltmann who stands out because of how seamlessly he has integrated his universalism into the rest of his theology. Moltmann may well be the worthy successor to Origen in our own times.

1. Thomas B. Talbott—The Inescapable Love of God and the Victory of Christ

Thomas B. Talbott is emeritus professor of philosophy at Willamette University in Salem, Oregon.[1] He has emerged as perhaps the most prolific defender of Christocentric universalism in the contemporary debate and has authored a book as well as several important articles on the subject.[2] Although Talbott's main area of expertise is philosophy, the bulk of his writings regarding universalism engage the subject from a generally theological point of view and he devotes much time to the discussion of theology and the relevant passages found in the Bible. This incongruity between Talbott's chosen field of expertise and the focus of his discussions vis-à-vis universalism appears to be driven primarily by the fact that Talbott has a high regard for Scripture and considers it to be both determinative and authoritative over the issue at hand. A central feature of Talbott's universalism is his belief that universalism is the consistent message of the Apostles. Driven by this perspective, he goes to great lengths in his efforts to reconcile universalism with the text of the New Testament.[3]

---

[1] A brief biography may be found in Parry and Partridge, *Universal Salvation? The Current Debate*, ix. Dr. Talbott has posted some biographical information on his website at Willamette University. Point your browser to http://www.willamette.edu/~ttalbott/index.html. (Accessed on September 25, 2014.)

[2] The book is entitled *The Inescapable Love of God*. Many of Talbott's articles concerning universalism may be found online on his publications webpage: http://www.willamette.edu/~ttalbott/publications.html. (Accessed on September 25, 2014.) Due to the transient nature of web pages this study will refer to his articles in their official, published form whenever possible. Some of Talbott's work is unpublished and only available online through his website.

[3] Cf. Thomas Talbott, "A Case for Christian Universalism," in Parry and Partridge, *Universal Salvation?*, 10–13; Thomas Talbott, "Three Pictures of God in Western Theology," 79–81. In these articles Talbott discusses the hermeneutical problem faced by "those who believe that God has revealed Himself in the Bible." He then goes on to

The two most complete statements of Talbott's universalism are to be found in his book *The Inescapable Love of God* (1999) and in the symposium that focused on his theology entitled *Universal Salvation? The Current Debate* (2003). Because some important details concerning Talbott's universalism are to be found in his other writings—both published and unpublished—we will have to make reference to the broader range of his works, even though some of them are not easily accessible to all. Where there have been developmental changes in Talbott's view, we shall let his most recent writings govern.

Talbott's universalism had its impetus in his personal struggle to define the core meaning of Christianity. He describes a crisis of faith that was triggered when a philosophy professor presented an argument from evil that challenged the conservative Christian worldview in which he had been raised. His reaction to the challenge was profound:

> For I interpreted this quite rightly as a fundamental assault upon the very convictions that gave meaning to my life; in effect, I was being asked to believe that the idea of a loving God—an idea I had taken for granted throughout my childhood—is overly sentimental, too good to be true, just one more example of wishful thinking to be discarded as we mature into adults . . . I never for a moment doubted that my instructor's arguments were defective in a variety of ways, but neither did I doubt that I would have to find better ways to answer than I had at the time, answers that would at least have the virtue of satisfying me.[4]

Talbott's answer to his professor's argument would eventually lead him to the solution of universalism. Along the way the crisis of faith deepened as he found himself being shocked by the responses of Christian theologians—especially those of a Reformed persuasion—whom he concluded presented "a demonic picture of God" that was utterly incompatible with any sort of consistent expression of God's love.[5] Instead, what he found was "a theology of arbitrary power" that presented "a God who, though gracious (after a fashion) to some (the elect), refuses to will the good for others (the non-elect)."[6] Talbott's response to such an apparently unloving theology focuses on the centrality of God's love and a radical reformulation of our understanding of it.

In Talbott's view, God's moral nature is simple. He has one moral attribute: love. Other so-called moral attributes, such as mercy and justice, are not just *different forms* of love, but rather are *different names* for love.[7] Thus Talbot understands all of God's moral attributes to be identical with his love. This perspective results in a view of God in which love does not compete with or

---

offer some solutions to this problem that incorporate scriptures that pose some difficulty for his position. See also Talbott, "A Case for Christian Universalism," 3–6.

[4] Talbott, *The Inescapable Love of God*, 4–5.

[5] Talbott, *The Inescapable Love of God*, 8. "I found the writings of Christian theologians to be far more disturbing—and a far greater threat to my faith, as I understood it—than those of any atheistic thinker whom I had encountered" (Talbott, *The Inescapable Love of God*, 5).

[6] Talbott, *The Inescapable Love of God*, 8.

[7] Thomas Talbott, "Punishment, Forgiveness, and Divine Justice," *RelS* 29 (1993): 152.

balance out his other attributes, but rather that love is all that there is. Talbott sees this perspective as the logical conclusion to be drawn from the Apostle John's declaration in 1 John 4:8 and 16 that "God is love."[8] In defining what it means to be the object of God's love, Talbott further argues that, at its core, love must be characterized as God promoting that which is in a person's best interest—anything less that this would be unloving.[9] Extending the argument further, Talbott contends that "it is logically impossible that the person who is God should fail to love someone, or should act in an unloving way towards someone, or should do anything else that is incompatible with his love."[10] What is in a person's best interest includes the forgiveness of sins, and Talbott asserts that forgiveness is the "inalienable right" of all human beings:

> But if, according to our alternative picture, God's moral nature is simple—if all of his moral attributes are identical with his love—then his justice will be altogether merciful even as his mercy is altogether just; he will punish sinners, in other words, only when it is merciful to do so, and he will always forgive them because that is the most loving and therefore the just thing to do.[11]

When these assertions about the nature of God's love are coupled together, they lead to what Talbott believes to be an unavoidable universalist conclusion: "God loves all created persons only if it is his intention to secure blessedness—that is supremely worthwhile happiness—for each of them."[12]

Talbott offers his universalism as a solution to the centuries old conflict between Calvinism (which he prefers to call Augustinianism) and Arminianism. In setting up his universalist solution, Talbott offers three inconsistent propositions that he believes highlight the essential differences between Calvinism, Arminianism, and Universalism:

> 1. God's redemptive love extends to all human sinners equally in the sense that he sincerely wills or desires the redemption of each one of them.

> 2. Because no one can finally defeat God's redemptive love or resist it forever, God will triumph in the end and successfully accomplish the redemption of everyone whose redemption he sincerely wills or desires.

> 3. Some human sinners will never be redeemed but will instead be separated from God forever.[13]

---

[8] Talbott, *The Inescapable Love of God*, 113–14.
[9] Talbott, *The Inescapable Love of God*, 133–36.
[10] Talbott, *The Inescapable Love of God*, 113.
[11] Talbott, "Punishment, Forgiveness, and Divine Justice," 164.
[12] Thomas Talbott, "Craig on the Possibility of Eternal Damnation," *RelS* 28 (1992): 12.
[13] Talbott, "A Case for Christian Universalism," 7. The genesis of these three propositions may be found in Talbott's earlier writings. Prior to this updated version the three propositions appear in a form that spoke of (1) God's redemptive purpose and (2) his power to achieve his redemptive purpose, as opposed to the "redemptive love" of

Talbott explains the inconsistencies for each theological system in this way: The Calvinist rejects proposition #1 and accepts propositions #2 and #3; the Arminian rejects proposition #2 while accepting propositions #1 and #3; the universalist accepts both propositions #1 and #2, but rejects #3. According to Talbott, a naïve Bible reader can find support for all three propositions in the New Testament.[14] Talbott notes that from a hermeneutical point of view the inconsistencies set up the following fundamental interpretive conflicts: Either, (1) The Bible contradicts itself and therefore is not infallible, or (2) one of the propositions is false. Talbott's solution to the dilemma is to embrace the second hermeneutical choice. Taking the point of view of a universalist, he then rejects proposition #3 as false[15] and sets about the task of proving that the New Testament does not teach eternal punishment anywhere within its pages.[16]

Having accepted both propositions #1 and #2, Talbott believes that he has successfully reconciled Calvinism with Arminianism and preserved what is the strength of each system. In the case of Arminianism, it is the idea that God loves all sinners and desires their redemption. In the case of Calvinism, it is the idea that God is sovereign and can accomplish his will regarding the redemption of people. In affirming both propositions to be true, Talbott argues for a universal election of all people to salvation based upon God's redemptive love.[17] For Talbott, all inclusive love and all inclusive election are two sides to

---

God that is spoken of here. The recasting of the propositions in terms of "redemptive love" as opposed to "redemptive purpose" is a significant modification that puts the propositions more in alignment with Talbott's focus on the centrality of God's love while at the same time eliminating certain criticisms that might arise regarding the issue of divining God's purposes. Cf. Talbott, "Three Pictures of God in Western Theology," 79; and Talbott, *The Inescapable Love of God*, 43; 107–109. A variation of these propositions is advanced by Talbott as the basis of his argument in favor of universalism in his entry on universalism in *The Oxford Handbook on Eschatology*. See Thomas Talbott, "Universalism," in Jerry Walls, ed., *The Oxford Handbook of Eschatology* (New York; Oxford: Oxford University Press, 2007) 448–52. I must offer here my personal thanks to Dr. Talbott for graciously supplying me with a pre-release copy of this article so that I might include it in my original dissertation research.

[14] In support of proposition #1 he cites 2 Pet. 3:9, 1 Tim. 2:4, Ezek. 33:11, and Lam. 3:22, 3:31–3. In support of proposition #2 he cites: Eph. 1:11, Job 42:2, Ps. 115:3, Is. 46:10–11, Rom. 5:181 Cor. 15:27–28, and Col. 1:20. In support of proposition #3 he cites: Matt. 25:46, 2 Thes. 1:9, and Rev. 21:8. Cf. Talbott, "A Case for Christian Universalism," 9–10 and Talbott, "Three Pictures of God in Western Theology," 79–80.

[15] Talbott, "A Case for Christian Universalism," 10–11; Talbott, "Three Pictures of God in Western Theology," 81.

[16] Talbott, "A Case for Christian Universalism, 32–48; Talbott, "Three Pictures of God in Western Theology," 83–94; Talbott, *The Inescapable Love of God*, 55–106. Talbott's arguments against reading eternal punishment into the New Testament are traditional and familiar. In the interest of presenting a full overview of his universalism we shall offer a critique of them later.

[17] Talbott, "A Case for Christian Universalism," 11–13, 34–39; Talbott, "Three Pictures of God in Western Theology," 83–89; Talbott, *The Inescapable Love of God*, 113–29; Thomas Talbott, "The Love of God and the Heresy of Exclusivism," *CSR* XXVII/1 (1997): 109–112.

the same coin. He bases his view primarily upon his understanding of election in the Apostle Paul's writings:

> As Paul saw it, God does indeed elect or choose individuals for himself. But the election of an individual inevitably reaches beyond the elected person to incorporate, in a variety of ways, the community in which the person lives and, in the end, the entire human race. That is why the election of Abraham is ultimately a blessing to all nations (Galatians 3:8), including Esau and his progeny, and why the idea of a "remnant, chosen by grace" (Romans 11:5) plays such an important role in Paul's argument that God is merciful to all (11:32). The remnant is always a pledge on behalf of the whole; it is the proof that God has not rejected the whole (see 11:1–6) and also the proof that "the word of God" or his "purpose of election" has not failed (9:6).[18]

Building upon this understanding of universal election, Talbott, in his more recent writings, has argued that ultimately Augustine's view of unconditional election was right.[19] In his view, where the Augustinians went wrong was in placing limits on the number of people elected and in not including the entire human race in the doctrine. Talbott contends that once this adjustment is made to the doctrine, that unconditional election and irresistible grace come into their own and the eternal destiny of each human being and the entire human race is placed firmly in the hands of God—which is the biblical position. In an interesting mix of eschatological determinism and individual liberty, Talbott affirms: "Our free choices do not determine our eternal destiny, which, according to Paul, is wholly a matter of grace; instead, they determine the lessons we still need to learn in the present as we travel our own unique path in life." In elaborating on how God's sovereign election of the human race and personal freedom interact, Talbott states:

> Because our eternal destiny, as Paul understood it, lies in God's hands and not in our own, it is indeed secure. But Paul also provided a clear picture of how our choices, even if causally undetermined, could nonetheless play an essential role in a redemptive process whose end is foreordained and therefore secure. "Note then," he wrote in Romans 11:22, "the kindness and the severity of God: severity toward those who have fallen, but God's kindness toward you, provided you continue in his kindness; otherwise, you also will be cut off." As this text illustrates, Paul clearly believed that our own actions—even our free choices, if you will—determine how God will respond to us in the immediate future; they determine, in particular, the form that God's perfecting love will take. If we continue in disobedience, then God will continue to shut us up to our disobedience, thereby forcing us to experience the consequences of our

---

[18] Talbott, "The Love of God and the Heresy of Exclusivism," 107.

[19] Thomas Talbott, "Universal Reconciliation and the Inclusive Nature of Election," in Chad Owen Brand, *Perspectives on Election: Five Views* (Nashville: Broadman and Holman Publishers, 2006) 206–261.

choices and the very life we have chosen to live; in that way, we will experience God's perfecting love as severity. But if we repent and enter into communion with God, then we will experience his perfecting love as kindness.

Closely linked to the idea of universal election is Talbott's strong affirmation of the ultimate victory of Christ over all sin and all evil.[20] This too is based primarily in the teaching of Paul and along these lines Talbott argues that a key feature of Paul's theology was his unfaltering faith in the ultimate victory of Jesus Christ. In Talbott's view, Paul could not countenance the notion that evil would not be completely overcome and that the idea of an eternally existent place of punishment where un-purged evil could survive was antithetical to Paul's perspective. Two central passages that Talbott uses in support of universal election tied to the ultimate victory of Christ are Romans 5:18 and 1 Cor. 15:22, which convey Paul's doctrine of the two Adams. He translates Romans 5:18 thus: "Therefore just as one man's trespass led to condemnation for all [humans], so one man's righteous act leads to justification and for [them] all."[21]

In terms of his doctrine of hell, Talbott embraces the idea of a temporary hell where postmortem affliction leads eventually to salvation.[22] He understands the torment of hell to be an objective reality and argues that suffering in hell is a forcibly imposed punishment used by God "as a means of correction, or as a means of encouraging repentance."[23] He also argues that "damnation is *a process* whereby the damned *gradually* learn from experience the true meaning of separation from God."[24] In other words, God will increase the torment incrementally until the sufferer repents and embraces the bliss that God offers:

> Accordingly, though God's love no doubt does preclude positive *hatred* and does preclude a final rejection of the beloved, it in no way precludes our *experiencing* that love as punishment, or as harsh judgment, or even as divine wrath. For if God is love and his purifying love, like a consuming fire (see Hebrews 12:29), destroys all that is false within us, the very thing we *call* our self, then for as long as we cling to the false self we will continue to experience that love, not as kindness, but as harsh judgment and even wrath.[25]

---

[20] Talbott, "A Case for Christian Universalism," 18–28; Talbott, "Universalism," 448–49.

[21] Talbott, "A Case for Christian Universalism," 19.

[22] Talbott, "A Case for Christian Universalism," 46–47; Talbott, *The Inescapable Love of God*, 143–67.

[23] Thomas Talbot, "Misery and Freedom: Reply to Walls," *Religious Studies* 40 (2005): 218. Available online at: http://www.willamette.edu/~ttalbott/Reply-Walls2.pdf. (Accessed on July 10, 2014.)

[24] Talbot, "Misery and Freedom: Reply to Walls," 222 (my italics).

[25] Thomas Talbott, "The Love of God and the Heresy of Exclusivism," *CSR* xxvii (1997): 105.

Ironically, this view seems to be grounded in Talbott's respect for human freedom.[26] The torment of hell becomes a teaching tool whereby the resistant are taught the error of their sin and rebellion, eventually succumbing to the coercive effect of pain. In Talbott's view, the idea that a free, rational agent would reject God forever is inconceivable. He goes so far as to declare that "a *free and fully informed* decision to reject God forever is logically impossible."[27] Thus, the torments of hell serve as a corrective to self imposed illusion and deception and shall eventually "shatter" those lies that lead people to choose separation from God.[28] In the end, God will win out and no one will be able to remain eternally disobedient. Progressively painful torment imposed by God will insure a universal outcome. Even the most hardened rebel will eventually break under the onslaught.

The most recent development in Talbott's universalism has been his elaboration of his views regarding the issue of pluralism. His perspective remains thoroughly Christocentric although he endorses the idea that God uses other religions as stepping stones to universal salvation in Christ: "All who are being saved, regardless of their religious tradition in which their salvation is now taking place, are in the process of achieving a proper relationship with Jesus Christ, a relationship that may not become fully manifest in some cases until the Kingdom of God is fully realized."[29] Along these lines Talbott acknowledges that "moments of divine revelation" occur in other religious and cultural traditions and that there are varying degrees of truth to be found in the non-Christian religions.[30] He concludes that a loving, intimate, and wise creator "would know how to work with each of us in infinitely complex ways, how to shatter our illusions and transform our thinking when necessary, and how best to reveal himself to us in the end."[31] The plurality of religious expression in the world presents no obstacle to Talbott's universalism. God, the great teacher and grand chess master, will "undermine over time every possible motive for disobedience."[32]

From a historical point of view, Thomas Talbott offers us a contemporary version of universalism that is almost entirely a mirror image of the universalism of Friedrich Schleiermacher. To begin with, Schleiermacher centered his view of redemption in the notion that love—and love alone—was "the equivalent of the being or essence of God."[33] For Schleiermacher, as with Talbott, all of God's other attributes "merge for us in the divine love."[34] Based in this perspective of the radical unity of God's love, both men assert the universal election of all people to salvation and both men endorse a postmortem

---

[26] Cf. Talbott, "Misery and Freedom: Reply to Walls," 220–24.

[27] Thomas B. Talbott, "Universalism," 455. See also Thomas B. Talbott, "Freedom, Damnation, and the Power to Sin with Impunity," *RelS* 37 (2001): 417–34; Talbott, *The Inescapable Love of God*, 184–89; Talbott, "Misery and Freedom: Reply to Walls," 219.

[28] Talbott, "Misery and Freedom: Reply to Walls," 221; Talbott, "Universalism," 18–19.

[29] Talbott, "Universalism," 447.

[30] Talbott, "Universalism," 448.

[31] Talbott, "Universalism," 449.

[32] Talbott, "Universalism," 458.

[33] Schleiermacher, *The Christian Faith*, 730.

[34] Schleiermacher, *The Christian Faith*, 731.

salvation scheme in which God inexorably accomplishes his redemptive purpose.[35] Another similarity emerges in that both Schleiermacher and Talbott emphasize the total victory of Christ such that evil will be completely done away with and all people will partake in the triumph of the Second Adam.[36] Certain abstract arguments are also quite comparable. Both argue that bliss in heaven would not be possible if people were aware of eternal suffering going on elsewhere.[37] Both argue that Jesus' pronouncements regarding eternal punishment are to be taken "figuratively" rather than literally.[38] Finally, there is an amazing similarity between the two regarding the issue of pluralism. Both are firmly Christocentric in their soteriology with Christianity providing the ultimate expression of God's truth. However, both men also embrace the idea that other religions possess varying degrees of revelation and that a natural progression in the path of salvation will eventually be made by all people to the light that is found in Christ.[39] Therefore, in all the major details, Talbott offers us an interesting contemporary recapitulation of the universalism we have already encountered with Schleiermacher.

Talbott's greatest weakness lies in the New Testament exegesis he uses to support his universalism. From an exegetical point of view, Talbott's denial of his proposition #3 that "some human sinners will never be redeemed but will instead be separated from God forever" is problematic. As we have already seen, Talbott accepts the Bible to be authoritative regarding this matter and so in order to show that this proposition is false his burden is to prove that the New Testament is uniformly a universalist document while at the same time proving that the idea of eternal punishment is not countenanced within its pages. The exegesis that Talbott offers in support of this thesis does not deal adequately with the overwhelming evidence that is found in the New Testament in support of the doctrine of eternal punishment.

The first problem emerges with Talbott's decision to base his universalism almost entirely in the teaching of Paul while at the same time largely ignoring the teaching of Jesus. As the founder and central focus of the Christian faith, Christians from the apostles on down have always held Jesus' teaching to be definitive in those areas of doctrine that he personally addressed.[40] Regarding

---

[35] Cf. Schleiermacher, *The Christian Faith*, 547–50; Thomas Talbott, "The Love of God and the Heresy of Exclusivism," 109–112.

[36] Schleiermacher, *The Christian Faith*, 366–69; 720.

[37] Cf. Schleiermacher, *The Christian Faith*, 721; Talbot, "A Case for Christian Universalism," 15.

[38] Cf. Schleiermacher, *The Christian Faith*, 720; Thomas Talbott, "The Doctrine of Everlasting Punishment," *FP* 7 (1990): 20.

[39] Cf. Schleiermacher, *The Christian Faith*, 31–39; Talbott, "Universalism," 446–47.

[40] Scholars, such as A.N. Wilson (*Paul: The Mind of the Apostle* [New York: W.W. Norton & Co., 1997]), have argued that Paul was the true founder of Christianity rather than Jesus. An extensive rebuttal to this position may be found in David Wenham, *Paul: Follower of Jesus or Founder of Christianity?* (Grand Rapids, Mich.: Eerdmans, 1995). See also N.T. Wright, *What Saint Paul Really Said: Was Paul of Tarsus the Real Founder of Christianity?* (Grand Rapids, Mich.: Eerdmans, 1997). Regardless of one's view on this issue, few would deny the monumental impact that Jesus' teaching has had upon Christian doctrine.

the doctrine of eternal punishment, the gospel accounts appear to establish, in a rather definitive manner, that Jesus believed in and taught a doctrine of eternal punishment. To briefly review, we have already argued that there is an extremely powerful case to be developed between the parallel passages found in Mark 9:43–48 and Matthew 18:8–9 where Jesus discusses the horrors of being thrown "into the unquenchable/unending fire." [41] As we compare the two passages we discover that Mark chose to translate Jesus' words in verse 9:43 of his gospel with the phrase *eis to pur to asbeston* (εἰς τὸ πῦρ τὸ ἄσβεστον). As we have already established, *asbeston* (ἄσβεστον) speaks of a state of being that cannot be nullified or stopped—thus the phrase means "unquenchable/unending fire." In an interesting and significant variation, Matthew chose to translate the same declaration of Jesus with the phrase *eis to pur to aiōnion* (εἰς τὸ πῦρ τὸ αἰωνιον) in verse 18:8 of his gospel. This leads us to the crucial insight that Matthew felt free to use the phrase εἰς τὸ πῦρ τὸ αἰώνιον synonymously for the phrase εἰς τὸ πῦρ τὸ ἄσβεστον and thus we can definitively conclude that in Matt. 18:8 we have a clear case of the adjective *aiōnios* (αἰώνιος) being used to refer to eternal fire and thus we have a clear assertion of eternal punishment.

Pressing our case further we then linked Matthew's use of the phrase *to pur to aiōnion* (τὸ πῦρ τὸ αἰώνιον) in Matt. 18:8 to his use of it in Matt. 25:41, which occurs in the identical context of eschatological judgment and contains identical wording. In this case we argued that in order to remain consistent with Jesus' teaching and Matthew's use of the phrase in verse 18:8 that we have no other choice than to translate *aiōnion* (αἰώνιον) in v. 25:41 as "eternal":

> 41 "Then He will also say to those on the left hand, 'Depart from Me, you cursed, into the eternal fire [τὸ πῦρ τὸ αἰώνιον] prepared for the devil and his angels."

Given the fact that the context of eschatological judgment is the same, and that Matthew would want to remain consistent with his own usage and with Jesus' teaching, it was further argued that the double use of the word *aiōnion* (αἰώνιον) found in Matt. 25:46 should again be translated as "eternal":

> 46 "And these will go away into eternal punishment [κόλασιν αἰώνιον], but the righteous into eternal life [ζωὴν αἰώνιον]."

An additional link in this chain should be made to Matt. 3:12 where Matthew quotes John the Baptist as making this prediction regarding Jesus:

> 12 "And His winnowing fork is in His hand, and He will thoroughly clear His threshing floor; and He will gather His wheat into the barn, but He will burn up [κατακαύσει] the chaff with unquenchable fire" [πυρὶ ἀσβέστῳ].

---

[41] Cf. See the Introduction, section 4.3 on the meaning of *aïdios* (ἀΐδιος) and *aiōn/aiōnios* (αἰών/αἰώνιος).

Once again, given the context of eschatological judgment, and Matthew's use of the now familiar phrase "with unquenchable fire" (*puri asbestō*—πυρὶ ἀσβέστῳ), we argue that this phrase should be viewed as another reference to eternal punishment. Bridging over to Luke 3:17 from here we have Luke using the very same phrase that is used in Matt. 3:12: "[he] will burn up [*katakausei*, κατακαύσει] . . . with unquenchable fire [*puri asbestō*—πυρὶ ἀσβέστῳ]" and due to the exact correspondence in phrase, again we argue that it should be interpreted this as a clear reference to eternal punishment.

All of these parallel connections reveal that the concept of eternal punishment was taught by Jesus and that it was faithfully transmitted by his disciples. Given that the case we are making ties this doctrine back into Jesus himself as the originator, then we should not be surprised that we find references being made to eternal punishment by the Apostle's in their other writings. Certainly they would have wanted to remain true to Jesus' core theological teachings. Therefore, I would stretch the argument out even further and assert that when we encounter the words *aiōn/aiōnios* (αἰών/αἰώνιος) in the context of eschatological judgment in the Apostle's other writings, that it would be highly unusual that they would be using these words to mean anything other than "eternity/eternal." While a translation of "age/age long" is certainly a possibility, we would need a very good reason carry through such a translation when the words are used in the context of eschatological judgment.

This line of exegetical reasoning seems to provide an unassailable challenge to Talbott's task of having to prove that the New Testament is uniformly universalist in its outlook with no evidence of eternal punishment being revealed within its pages. Realizing the devastating blow that Jesus' teaching on eternal punishment in Mark 9:43–48 poses to his thesis, Talbott's response is to argue, in a manner similar to Moule, that Jesus' declarations are not to be taken literally. He contends that Jesus used hyperbole and exaggeration that was intended "to awaken the spiritual imagination of his disciples and to leave room for reinterpretation as they matured in the faith; it was not intended to provide final answers to their theological questions."[42] The problem with this line of reasoning is that Jesus never uses the Old Testament in a hyperbolic way. He always quotes the Old Testament with utmost amount of seriousness and, contrary to Talbott's assertion, he treats Old Testament teaching as the definitive last word on the topic at hand.[43] If there is hyperbole to be found in Mark 9:43–48 it is found in the command to cut off or to pluck out and not in the use of the imagery of judgment found in Isaiah 66:24 itself. The hyperbole of severing a limb or plucking out an eye is used by Jesus as a means of *enhancing the reality of the unending fire* spoken about in Isaiah's prophesy— not to minimize or reduce its impact. In addition to this, the theme of sinners being judged and subjected to a fiery penalty is used consistently throughout

---

[42] Talbott, "The Doctrine of Everlasting Punishment," 20.
[43] Cf. Matt. 4:1–11; 5:17–19; 9:10–13; 11:7–10; 12:1–8; 13:10–16; 15:1–16; 19:3–9; 21:14–16; 22:29–30; 22:41–45; 24:15; 24:29–31; 27:46. Mark 4:10–12; 7:5–13; 10:2–10; 11:15–17; 12:10–11; 12:18–27; 12:28–34; 12:35–37; 13:14; 14:27; 15:34. Luke 4:1–13; 4:16–21; 7:24–29; 8:9–10; 13:35; 19:45–46; 20:17–18; 20:37; 20:41–44; 23:30; 24:25–27. John 3:14; 5:46; 6:45; 7:37–39; 8:17; 10:34–38; 13:18; 15:25; 16:21; 16:32; 19:28.

Jesus' teaching regardless of the rhetorical style or device he employs. The theme of fiery judgment is affirmed by Jesus in declarative passages such as Mark 9:43–48 and Matt. 5:22; it is affirmed in parabolic passages such as Matt. 13:36–43 and Matt. 13:47–50; it is affirmed in prophetic passages such as Matt. 25:31–46. Jesus never taught any other outcome for unrepentant sinners. The doctrine of the eternal punishment was central to his eschatology.

Regarding the use of *aiōnios* (αἰώνιος) in Matthew 25:41 and 46, Talbott argues, in a manner quite similar to F.D. Maurice, that the word as used in those verses (as well as almost everywhere else in the New Testament) is to be understood as referring to a quality and not a duration.[44] In the Matthew 25 passage he believes αἰώνιος is being used as a qualifier of intensity, something akin to: "The dull after dinner speech simply dragged on forever!"[45] However, this interpretation is effectively rebutted by the fact that we find Matthew using *to pur to aiōnion* (τὸ πῦρ τὸ αἰώνιον) in Matt. 18:8 as a synonym for Mark's phrase *to pur to asbeston* (τὸ πῦρ τὸ ἄσβεστον) found in Mark 9:43. If Matthew's usage of *aiōnios* (αἰώνιος) is consistent in the context of its use regarding fiery judgment—and we have no reason to believe that it is not—then the best interpretation of Matt. 25:41 and 46 would be that of the goats being sent away into eternal fire.

The elegant parallel structure of v. 46 also weighs heavily against Talbott's interpretation. Although it is not an exact quote, the parallel structure of this sentence mirrors that found in Daniel 12:2: "And many of those who sleep in the dust of the ground will awake, these to everlasting life, but the others to disgrace *and* everlasting contempt." It is very likely that Jesus had this verse in mind as he concluded his discourse. We note in Dan. 12:2 the use of the Hebrew qualifier *olam* (עוֹלָם—"eternal"), which is translated in the LXX by the Greek word αἰώνιος. Jesus' use of the contrasting phrases κόλασιν αἰώνιον (eternal punishment) and ζωὴν αἰώνιον (eternal life) was surely intended to emphasize the *equivalent finality* of the separation in a similar fashion to that found in Daniel: "And these will go away into eternal punishment, but the righteous into eternal life." Talbott's exegesis would have us ignore the obvious connection and urge us to translate αἰώνιος in two different ways in a clearly parallel sentence. On the one hand he would like us to embrace the concept of eternal life, on the other hand he would like us to disregard the idea of eternal punishment. Such conceptual gymnastics do no justice to the simple logic and force of the conclusion that Jesus drew in Matt. 25:46.

In addition to his argument in favor of a limited extension for αἰώνιος, Talbott maintains that the word *kolasis* (κόλασις), as used in Matt. 25:46, is to be understood in terms of "correction" as opposed to "punishment." As a result Talbott believes that the proper translation of *kolasis aiōnion* (κόλασιν αἰώνιον) should be something like "an eternal means of correction"—eternal in the sense that the correction will be available for as long as people resist it and

---

[44] Cf. Talbott, "Three pictures of God in Western Theology," 89–92; Maurice, "On Eternal Life and Eternal Death," 302–32.

[45] Talbott, "Three pictures of God in Western Theology," 91–92.

that it will cease when all resistance is conquered.[46] In support of this view, Talbott quotes William Barclay as saying that "in all Greek secular literature, *kolasis* is never used of anything but remedial punishment . . . [kolasis] was not an ethical word at all. It originally meant the pruning of trees to make them grow better."[47] This assertion reveals more about Barclay's well known habit of stretching word meanings than it does to reveal the correct translation of *kolasis* (κόλασις) in the New Testament. As has already been discussed,[48] the analysis of Johannes Schneider in the *TDNT* links the word to an original etymology of maiming or cutting off and not that of pruning: "Punishment is designed to cut off what is bad or disorderly."[49] In the passive the word developed a sense of being robbed or to suffering loss through having something cut away or cut off—supporting Schneider's assertion that the focus is on the pain inflicted by removal as opposed to beneficial pruning or correction. Thus the primary meaning of punishment or even retribution comes to the fore as opposed to mere correction.[50]

In terms of putting forward a positive case for universalism, Talbott focuses most of his attention on the writings of the Apostle Paul. The idea that Paul was a universalist has been strongly challenged by several competent scholars and we will not repeat those discussions here.[51] Regarding Talbott's exegesis of Paul, Larry Lacy has noted that "the passages focused on by Talbott can be given reasonable interpretations consistent with the denial of universalism."[52]

---

[46] Talbott, "Three pictures of God in Western Theology," 91.

[47] Talbott, "Three pictures of God in Western Theology," 91.

[48] Cf. Introduction, Section 3.3.

[49] *TDNT*, 3:814; see also *NIDNTT*, 3:98.

[50] This perspective is also supported in BDAG (s.v. κόλασις), which focuses on punishment and divine retribution without any reference to correction at all. We do well to remember that in 4 Mac. 8:9 the tyrant uses the word as a warning of severe retribution: 9 "But if by disobedience you rouse my anger, you will compel me to destroy each and every one of you with dreadful punishments [δειναῖς κολάσεσιν] through tortures." (NRSA)

[51] Cf. Crockett, "Universalism and the Theology of Paul"; Crockett, "Wrath that Endures Forever," *JETS* 34/2 (June 1991): 195–202; Timothy George, Carl F.H. Henry, D.A. Carson, Scott Hafemann, and C. Ben Mitchell, "The *SBJT* Forum: Responses to the Inclusivist Challenge," *SBJT* 2/2 (Summer 1998): 50–60; Larry Lacy, "Talbott on Paul as a Universalist," *CSR* 21/4 (1992): 395–407; Douglas J. Moo, "Paul on Hell," in Morgan and Peterson, *Hell Under Fire*, 91–109; Stephen T. Pegler, "The Nature of Paul's universal language of salvation in Romans," (Ph.D. dissertation, Trinity Evangelical Divinity School, 2002); James E. Rosscup, "Paul's Concept of Eternal Punishment," *TMSJ* 9/2 (Fall 1998): 169–192; E.P. Sanders, *Paul and Palestinian Judaism: A Comparison of Patterns of Religion* (Philadelphia, Fortress, 1977), 442–74.

[52] Lacy, "Talbott on Paul as a Universalist," 395. I believe that it is on this point where M.E. Boring's interpretation of Paul also goes wrong. In his article "The Language of Universal Salvation in Paul" (*JBL* 105 [1986]: 269–292) Boring argues that Paul affirms both conditional and universal salvation in his writings. In Boring's view, these contradictory statements made by Paul cannot be subordinated or made to cohere with one another and so he concludes that Paul is simply irreconcilably inconsistent. However, as several scholars have demonstrated, there are reasonable ways to interpret Paul's statements in a consistent fashion.

In some cases Talbott's exegesis of Paul is simply incorrect. A key example of this may be found in Talbott's use of Paul's doctrine of the two Adams in support of universalism.[53] It is true that in Romans 5:18 Paul does draw a strong rhetorical analogy: "So then as through one transgression there resulted condemnation to all men, even so through one act of righteousness there resulted justification of life to all men." Taken in isolation, it would seem reasonable to conclude that Paul is teaching universalism in this verse. However, when taken in context it becomes abundantly clear that Paul intended no such thing. The central Pauline qualification of faith is laid down in v. 17: "For if by the transgression of the one, death reigned through the one, much more those who receive the abundance of grace and of the gift of righteousness will reign in life through the One, Jesus Christ." The substantival use of *hoi lambanontes* (οἱ λαμβάνοντες) in this verse refers to those who have literally "taken hold of" or "personally taken possession of" the gift of righteousness.[54] This idea is further emphasized by the fact that Paul sandwiches the phrase "the abundance of grace and of the gift of righteousness" between οἱ and λαμβάνοντες as a means of emphasizing precisely what these people have taken hold of. In light of this clear affirmation of justification by faith found in v. 17, we conclude that what we find in verse 18 is not a contradictory statement of universalism, but rather a statement regarding the scope and potential reach of salvation. The salvation will be applied, as it always is with Paul, to those who "receive" it. This interpretation is further confirmed in 1 Cor. 15:20–23, which Talbott also wrongly construes in universalist terms:

> [20] But now Christ has been raised from the dead, the first fruits of those who are asleep. [21] For since by a man *came* death, by a man also *came* the resurrection of the dead. [22] For as in Adam all die, so also in Christ all shall be made alive. [23] But each in his own order: Christ the first fruits, after that those who are Christ's at His coming . . .

The key interpretive question here is whether Paul is saying "all" in verse 22 in the sense of the entire world, or "all" in the sense of those who are "in Christ." The answer comes in v. 23 where Paul qualifies what he means: "But each in his own order: Christ the first fruits, after that those who are Christ's at His coming." In other words, those who partake in this resurrection are those who, once again, have met the Pauline standard of justification by faith in that they have become Christ's.[55]

---

[53] Cf. Talbott, "A Case for Christian Universalism," 18–22.

[54] BDAG s.v. λαμβάνω. Entry #6 notes that the word can even be rendered "choose."

[55] In a short article entitled "Will God Save Everyone in the End?", William V. Crockett, critiques universalism from the sociological perspective of group boundaries. He argues that the New Testament writings exhibit such boundaries in a striking way. In particular the writings of the Apostle Paul reveal, "There were only two classes of people: those who believed in Christ (insiders) and those who did not (outsiders). Insiders looked forward to a glorious future with Christ; outsiders would be destroyed in the eschaton." (p. 166) Crockett argues that the destruction of such clear boundaries in the New Testament by universalists is a clear misinterpretation of the text. See William

Conversely Paul is adamant about the fact that people who disobey God's law and reject salvation in Christ shall not be spared. Perhaps the strongest argument against Talbott's interpretation of Paul as a universalist is Paul's emphatic insistence that certain categories of people are permanently barred from participation in the Kingdom. In 1 Cor. 6:9–11 and Gal. 5:19–21 Paul provides a list of deadly transgressions and notes that anyone whose life is characterized by such transgressions "will not inherit the Kingdom of God." The warning that is laid down in Eph. 5:5–7 is particularly striking in that the denial of participation is coupled with the certainty of God's wrath:

> [5] For this you know with certainty, that no immoral or impure person or covetous man, who is an idolater, has an inheritance in the kingdom of Christ and God. [6] Let no one deceive you with empty words, for because of these things the wrath of God comes upon the sons of disobedience. [7] Therefore do not be partakers with them.[56]

In this passage we have an explicit denial of universal participation in the Kingdom as well as a denial of the idea of postmortem salvation through corrective punishment. People who persist in the behaviors described can only look forward to one thing: the wrath of God. Paul's parenesis hands down a clear warning to anyone who might fall in with them, saying in effect, "In the end you do not want to wind up in their shoes." It is hard to imagine a more definitive way in which the key tenets of Talbott's universalism could be denied. When these statements are coupled to Paul's repeated and consistent references to those who are perishing and/or those who will experience God's wrath and destruction, a much clearer view of Paul's soteriology emerges.[57] Although Paul does not talk explicitly about hell, he certainly enunciates the concept that a clean and permanent separation will be made between those who participate in salvation in Christ and those who do not. It is a telling fact that there are no statements to be found in the entire Pauline corpus that unambiguously endorse the idea of postmortem salvation. On the other hand there are numerous statements made by Paul that seem to affirm just the opposite. Justification by faith in Christ was central to Paul's theological thought: he was always careful to preserve a clear delineation between those who are in Christ and those who are not.

For those, like Talbott, who accept 2 Thessalonians into the Pauline corpus, 2 Thes. 1:3–12 is particularly difficult to deal with. It is worth quoting in its full context:

V. Crockett, "Will God Save Everyone in the End?" in Crockett and Sigountos, *Through No Fault of their Own? The Fate of Those Who Have Never Heard*, 159–166.

[56] Of course those who reject Paul's authorship of Ephesians will find this quote to be unimpressive. However, for these people there still remain the explicit denials found in 1 Cor. 6:9–11 and Gal. 5:19–21. Talbott himself does not reject Pauline authorship of Ephesians so for him this argument remains in force.

[57] Cf. Romans 1:18–32, 2:1–11, 2:12–16, 3:5–6, 5:8–9, 9:22; 1 Cor. 1:18, 3:17, 10:6–12; 2 Cor. 2:15–16, 4:3–4; Eph. 2:1–3, 5:3–7; Phil. 3:18–21; Col. 3:6–7; 1 Thes. 1:10, 2:16, 5:2–3; 2 Thes. 1:3–10, 2:9–12; 2 Tim. 4:1.

³ We ought always to give thanks to God for you, brethren, as is *only* fitting, because your faith is greatly enlarged, and the love of each one of you toward one another grows *ever* greater; ⁴ therefore, we ourselves speak proudly of you among the churches of God for your perseverance and faith in the midst of all your persecutions and afflictions which you endure. ⁵ *This is* a plain indication of God's righteous judgment so that you may be considered worthy of the kingdom of God, for which indeed you are suffering. ⁶ For after all it is *only* just for God to repay with affliction those who afflict you, ⁷ and *to give* relief to you who are afflicted and to us as well when the Lord Jesus shall be revealed from heaven with His mighty angels in flaming fire, ⁸ dealing out retribution to those who do not know God and to those who do not obey the gospel of our Lord Jesus. ⁹ And these will pay the penalty of eternal destruction, away from the presence of the Lord and from the glory of His power, ¹⁰ when He comes to be glorified in His saints on that day, and to be marveled at among all who have believed—for our testimony to you was believed. ¹¹ To this end also we pray for you always that our God may count you worthy of your calling, and fulfill every desire for goodness and the work of faith with power; ¹² in order that the name of our Lord Jesus may be glorified in you, and you in Him, according to the grace of our God and the Lord Jesus Christ.

The thrust of this passage is clearly encouragement in the face of difficult persecution for the sake of the Gospel. Paul's point is that the perseverance of the Thessalonians will be rewarded with entrance into the kingdom (v. 5), while the disobedience of those who rebel and persecute the faithful will result in "eternal destruction, away from the presence of the Lord" (v.8). Oddly, Talbott interprets this passage in terms of "eternal destruction of the old person or false self," arguing that "the very image of the Lord appearing in flaming fire suggests both judgment and purification."[58] The problem with this is that Paul's favorite word for the "old person," *sarx* (σάρξ), is not used here at all. Neither is there any hint that Paul intended to make a flesh/spirit distinction. A more literal and straight forward interpretation takes the word *ekdikēsin* (ἐκδίκησιν in v. 8 = retribution) very seriously: This is the meting out of justice, the infliction of reprisal, the imposition of righteous punishment upon wrong doers—even vengeance.[59] There is no remedial action or favorable outcome in view here. This in turn is tied to an even stronger statement regarding the reality of eternal punishment in v. 9: "And these will pay the penalty of eternal destruction [οἵτινες δίκην τίσουσιν ὄλεθρον αἰώνιον]." The noun *olethros* (ὄλεθρος) is typically used in the New Testament to refer to the destruction of life.[60] Coupling this with *aiōnios* (αἰώνιος) eliminates the prospect of annihilationism and focuses our attention on the permanent and ongoing nature of that destruction. Taken in total, this passage is indeed a powerful confirmation that Paul did indeed embrace the doctrine of eternal punishment.

---

[58] Talbott, "The New Testament and Universal Reconciliation," 393; 389–93.

[59] BDAG s.v. ἐκδίκησις; U. Falkenroth, ἐκδίκησις, *NIDNTT* 3:92–93.

[60] H-C Hann, ὄλεθρος, *NIDNTT* 1:465–66.

The teaching of both Jesus and Paul on the issue of eternal punishment is consistent with the witness of the entire New Testament. John the Baptist, the forerunner of Christ, presented a stark picture regarding the mission of the Messiah in Matt. 3:12: "He will gather His wheat into the barn, but He will burn up the chaff with unquenchable fire [πυρὶ ἀσβέστῳ]." In John 3:36 John the Baptist once again offers a bleak assessment: "He who believes in the Son has eternal life; but he who does not obey the Son shall not see life [οὐκ ὄψεται ζωήν], but the wrath of God abides on him." 2 Peter 3:7 discusses the fiery fate of the world in "the day of judgment and destruction of ungodly men." Jude 6 points to the destruction of Sodom and Gomorrah being "exhibited as an example, in undergoing the punishment of eternal fire [πυρὸς αἰωνίου]." Rev. 14:10–11 speaks of the eternal suffering of those who worship the beast: "He shall be tormented with fire and brimstone in the presence of the holy angels and in the presence of the Lamb. And the smoke of their torment ascends forever and ever [εἰς αἰῶνας αἰώνων]; and they have no rest [ἀνάπαυσιν = ceasing or interruption] day or night, who worship the beast and his image, and whoever receives the mark of his name." Rev. 20:11–15 speaks of the Day of Judgment and the fate of those whose names are not found in the Book of Life: [14]"And death and Hades were thrown into the Lake of Fire. This is the second death, the Lake of Fire. [15]And if anyone's name was not found written in the book of life, he was thrown into the Lake of Fire." Rev. 21:7–8 reiterates the finality of the separation that will be made on Judgment Day: [7]"He who overcomes shall inherit these things, and I will be his God and he will be My son. [8]But for the cowardly and unbelieving and abominable and murderers and immoral persons and sorcerers and idolaters and all liars, their part *will be* in the lake that burns with fire and brimstone, which is the second death."

In light of all this, we must conclude that Thomas Talbott has not adequately answered the exegetical challenge posed by the New Testament texts that focus on the issue of eternal punishment. There can be no doubt that Talbott takes the text of the Bible seriously and has come up with an interesting string of novel interpretations. However, there always seems to be an inherent eisegesis at work that ignores both the context and the most easily defended meaning. Nevertheless, Talbott's contribution to the debate is substantial. His considerable efforts serve to highlight and sharpen many important issues. The discussion is that much richer for his having entered into it.

2. Jacques Ellul—Predestined to be Saved

Jacques Ellul (1912–1994) was a French philosopher, sociologist, and theologian who was concerned primarily with the danger that modern technological methods pose to human freedom and the Christian faith.[61] Some

---

[61] Ellul was quite prolific and authored some forty books and many articles during his lifetime. His best known work on the subject of technology is his 1954 classic: *La technique; ou, L'en jeu du siècle* (Paris: Armand Colin, 1954); English edition trans. John Wilkinson, *The Technological Society* (New York: Knopf, 1964). A summary of his thought may be found in the following: Darrell J. Fasching, *The Thought of Jacques Ellul: A Systematic Exposition* (New York: Edwin Mellen Press, 1981) and David Lovekin, *Technique, Discourse, and Consciousness: An Introduction to the Philosophy*

have dismissed Ellul as a paranoid neo-Luddite, however this characterization is wholly inaccurate. Ellul was not so much anti-technology as he was concerned with the negative results brought about by modern technological methodology—something he called "technique." He defined technique as "the *totality of methods rationally arrived at and having absolute efficiency* (for a given stage of development) in *every* field of human activity."[62] His fear was the dehumanization of the race: "[W]hen technique enters into every area of life, including the human, it ceases to be external to man and becomes his very substance. It is no longer face to face with man but is integrated with him, and it progressively absorbs him."[63] Ellul's critique of the modern technological society had its genesis in his study of Karl Marx and his acceptance of the core of Marx's teaching. As David Menninger notes, "Marx represents for Ellul a model of the social theorist's personal resistance to impersonal social forces . . . Marx has provided Ellul with a sensitivity to the special significance of technique and technology as problems in contemporary social development."[64]

In developing his critique of the modern technological society Ellul steadily makes the case that technique is to be equated with sin and that the universal extension of technique is to be equated with the extension of rebellion against God.[65] In the end this rebellion must be done away with and humanity must be rescued from itself by the very power of God.[66] This is where Ellul's theology of universalism makes its appearance and converges with his philosophical critique of society. Given the starkness of Ellul's analysis and the seeming hopelessness of the human predicament he describes, one might conclude that Ellul has no option but to be a pessimist. To this assumption Ellul replies:

---

of Jacques Ellul (Bethlehem, Penn.: Lehigh University Press, 1991). See also Clifford G. Christians and Jay M. Van Hook, eds., *Jacques Ellul: Interpretive Essays* (Chicago: University of Illinois Press, 1981).

[62] Ellul, *The Technological Society*, xxv (italics in the original).

[63] Ellul, *The Technological Society*, 6.

[64] David C. Menninger, "Marx in the Social Thought of Jacques Ellul," in Christians and Van Hook, *Jacques Ellul: Interpretive Essays*, 18–19.

[65] This is especially noticeable in his works on morality, such as *Présence au monde moderne: Problèmes de la civilisation post-chrétienne* (Geneva: Roulet, 1948); English edition trans. Olive Wyon, *The Presence of the Kingdom* (Philadelphia: Westminster, 1951) and in his works that touch on eschatology, especially *L'Apocalypse: architecture en mouvement* (Paris: Desclée, 1975); English edition trans. George W. Schreiner, *Apocalypse: The Book of Revelation* (New York: Seabury Press, 1977). Ellul denies that "sin had any influence whatsoever on my analysis of technology" (Jacques Ellul, *Perspectives on Our Age: Jacques Ellul Speaks on His Life and Work*, trans. William H. Vandenburg, ed. Joachim Neugroschel [New York: Seabury Press, 1981], 104). This may be true in the sense that he did not start off with an a priori presupposition that technique is sin. However, in the end this seems to be the conclusion that is consistently drawn by him. Certainly the point of much of his critique is to expose the evil and the danger that is found in modern technical methodologies and systems.

[66] In discussing the destruction of Babylon the Great in Rev. 17 and 18, Ellul likens the harlot and the beast she is riding to the historic forms or expressions of humanity: "These forms are never a man; they are an organization, a society, a nation, a structure, an abstract specification such as money, the state, the city, technique, etc." Ellul, *Apocalypse*, 198.

So, am I a pessimist? Not at all. I am not pessimistic because I am convinced that the history of the human race, no matter how tragic, will ultimately lead to the Kingdom of God. I am convinced that all the works of humankind will be reintegrated in the work of God, and that each of us, no matter how sinful, will ultimately be saved.[67]

We see in this statement that Ellul's universalism is built upon total confidence in God's elective purpose and power—God's ability to have his way despite what humanity has done. People may choose to deny God, people may choose to resist God, people may choose to ignore God, but in the end it is God's decision that will count:

> It is inconceivable that the God of Jesus Christ, who gives himself in his Son to save us, should have created some people ordained to evil and damnation. There is indeed a predestination, but it can be only the one predestination to salvation. In and through Jesus Christ all people are predestined to be saved. Our free choice is ruled out in this regard. We have often said that God wants free people. He undoubtedly does, except in relation to this last and definitive decision. We are not free to decide and choose to be damned.[68]

Thus, in Ellul's theology, being saved or lost does not depend on human decision or ability. Instead, it is based totally and completely in God. It is God who, in his grace, extends salvation to all. People have no say in the matter. Grace comes as a free gift to all and all people are included in the grace of God. This all-inclusive aspect of God's election sets up his polemic against eternal punishment: "I believe that all the theologies that have made a large place for damnation and hell are unfaithful to a theology of grace. For if there is predestination to perdition, there is no salvation by grace . . . A theology of grace implies universal salvation . . . This grace covers all things. It is thus effectively universal."[69]

In discussing the roots of his universalism Ellul acknowledges the influence that the Swiss theologian Karl Barth (1886–1968) had upon his thinking. Although he is no mere parrot of Barthian theology, and in many ways pushes beyond Barth, there can be no doubt that Barth's reconstruction of the Reformed doctrine of election had a profound influence on his interpretation of universalism: "Once again, I have to credit Karl Barth with having seen that what the Bible announces is not sin, but salvation. It is only when people learn

---

[67] Ellul, *Perspectives on Our Age: Jacques Ellul Speaks on His Life and Work*, 104. Universalism is woven into the fabric of several of Ellul's works. His most extended exposition of it may be found in his book *Ce que je crois* (Paris: Grasset & Fasquelle, 1987); English edition trans. Geoffrey W. Bromiley, *What I Believe* (Grand Rapids, Mich.: Eerdmans, 1989), 188–209. See also Jacques Ellul, *Éthique de la liberté* (Geneva: Labor et Fides, 1976); English edition trans. Geoffrey W. Bromiley, *The Ethics of Freedom* (Grand Rapids, Mich.: Eerdmans, 1976), 79–83; Ellul, *Apocalypse*, 160; 176–77; 208–13; 220–25; 255.

[68] Ellul, *What I Believe*, 192.

[69] Ellul, *What I Believe*, 193.

that they are loved, forgiven, and saved—it is only then that they learn they were sinners."[70]

While God's elective purpose will stand in the end, in the meantime the rebellion against God continues with Satan as its principal instigator. In Ellul's view, Satan is a very real being who is still the prince of this world. At this time he is in control of human history and human institutions: "It is he who structures progress and makes it so fatal."[71] However, through the cross of Jesus Christ, Satan's power has been broken and he can no longer hope to win. At best Satan can merely fight a rearguard action until the inevitable victory of God is made manifest. In Ellul's eschatology Satan is the only sentient being to be thrown into the Lake of Fire—the Lake of Fire representing nothingness and total annihilation:

> The result of this gathering and assault is that, the last role of the divider being accomplished, he is in his turn annihilated (actually thrown into nothingness). And we must insist again upon the fact that in [Rev.] 20:10 it is once more the Devil and Satan who are thrown into the fire and the lake of brimstone: there is no question of men.[72]

In the end, death will swallow up death and nothingness itself is annihilated:[73]

> It is not theologically possible that there be damned men. That would mean, in a word, that there is an external limit to the love of God. Only the Nothingness is annihilated. And in the second death there are not men, there are not lives; there are evil works of man, there are Satan and the Devil, there are the incarnations (invented by man!) of these powers, there is death. Nothing more.[74]

Although Ellul rejects the idea that any human being will be cast into the Lake of Fire, even for rehabilitative purposes, it does seem that he allows for a limited form of judgment to fall upon the "beast worshipers" discussed in Rev. 14:10–11—the "beast" being defined as the State and political power.[75] These beast worshippers will experience the "cup of the wrath of God," which consists in God allowing them to become what they always wanted to be in their rebellion and, therefore, the suffering is self-inflicted. The duration of the suffering, "for eons of eons," (cf. Rev. 14:11) does not denote an unlimited timeframe and in the end the suffering will be terminated by the proclamation of God. Ellul draws this inference from Rev. 21:5 and 22:3: "'I make *all* things

---

[70] Ellul, *Perspectives on Our Age*, 104.

[71] Ellul, *The Ethics of Freedom*, 81.

[72] Ellul, *Apocalypse*, 210.

[73] Ramelli argues for this very same interpretation of Rev. 20:11–15. In v. 14, when death is thrown into the Lake of Fire—the Second Death—she interprets this as "the death of death." Ramelli, *The Christian Doctrine of Apokatastasis*, 47.

[74] Ellul, *Apocalypse*, 213. See also Ellul, *What I Believe*, 205: "The only outcome for death is that it must disappear in the death that slays death." See also Ramelli who argues for the very same interpretation of Rev. 20:10

[75] Ellul, *Apocalypse*, 176–77.

new,' and 'there will be no more curse' (chapter 22); then God puts an end to this impossible situation."[76]

Ellul was aware of the problems posed to his universalism by the scriptures in the New Testament that speak to the issue of eternal punishment and he made a short, but concerted effort to deal with them. Regarding the teaching of Jesus he essentially argued two things: (1) His parables were meant to communicate a single point and not factual data—"We cannot make dogmas out of the details," and (2) that Jesus' teaching was intended to communicate a warning that would result in a decision, rather than a threat that would result in damnation.[77] Regarding the teaching of the Epistles he argued that (1) the admonitions of potential punishment are aimed at believers and represent "a possible impossibility," and (2) that perdition is "a temporary situation of human life" in which hell is limited to our suffering here on earth.[78] Regarding the passages found in the Book of Revelation, the overall approach taken is to regard them as a metaphor for the judgment of a world system that is in rebellion to God: "[T]hose who are condemned in the final destruction are not men but the rebellious powers who are described for us in the central section, upon whom men depend and whom men represent only figuratively."[79]

On the affirmative side, Ellul's scriptural apologetic in favor of universalism centered on the vicarious atonement provided by Christ on the cross. In Ellul's view, the extension of the atonement could not be restricted in any way. In this he mirrors the thought of Barth:

> It seems to me that the universality of salvation is implied by the fact that the totality of condemnation fell on Christ. Since Christ was God, he did not assume a mere part of our condemnation, or the condemnation of a section of men. The measure of deity means that he bore the condemnation of all men. Hence there is no condemnation in Christ.[80]

In discussing Paul's doctrine of reconciliation in 2 Cor. 5:19 and Rom. 5:10–11, Ellul insists: "The 'us' sets no limit. It does not refer only to converts." All are wicked; all will be saved. God does not discriminate between believer or non-believer. The same sin issue plagues all. The same sin solution will be applied to all.

It should be noted that Ellul repeatedly observes that he does not hold to his universalism "dogmatically."[81] For him universalism is "a matter of faith."[82] He concludes his discussion in *What I Believe* by adding the ominous warning that "God is not mocked" (Gal. 6:6). His point is that there is a small possibility that he might be wrong regarding universalism. If he is wrong, Ellul wants to affirm that God would certainly hold those accountable who heard about his love and grace in Christ and scorned it. He wanted to make sure that his exposition of

---

[76] Ellul, *Apocalypse*, 177.
[77] Ellul, *What I Believe*, 195.
[78] Ellul, *What I Believe*, 196; 203.
[79] Ellul, *Apocalypse*, 65.
[80] Ellul, *The Ethics of Freedom*, 82. See also Ellul, *What I Believe*, 192.
[81] Ellul, *The Ethics of Freedom*, 82; Ellul, *What I Believe*, 188–89; 207; 209.
[82] Ellul, *What I Believe*, 188.

universalism did not facilitate a cavalier rejection of the gospel by those who were seeking an easy way out.

Ellul's universalism is somewhat of a mixed marriage between the old and the new. The idea of universal election goes back at least five centuries and can be found in the anonymous fifteenth-century book *Divine Light*, as well as in the writings of Friedrich Schleiermacher.[83] Is it possible that what we see here is Schleiermacher's influence on Barth showing up in Ellul's view of universal election? Barth's critique of Schleiermacher is well known[84] and yet Barth was in broad agreement with Schleiermacher on the notion of universal election. Of course Barth takes a radically different approach than Schleiermacher by making predestination Christological (Christ experiences the rejection for all and all are elected in Christ), but the net result was essentially the same—a recognition that all are elected to salvation.[85] As the basis behind the two constructions are so different, the connection will have to remain an open question. However, the possibility of such a connection remains an intriguing one.

Ellul's universalism is unique in that he ties it in so well with his critique of the modern technical society. For Ellul, theology comes to the rescue of his philosophy. Fasching has summarized his dialectical analysis of history: "That which desacralizes a given reality, itself in turn becomes the new sacred reality."[86] In his analysis, Ellul argues that science and reason have replaced the church and the Bible as the new reality. The technical society is the offspring of this paradigm shift. Therefore, people have left the church behind and become integrated into a technical world. Scientists are the high priests, technology is the new god in which all hope is placed. The dehumanization of humanity marches forward. Ellul finds the solution to this conundrum in God. Whereas his dialectical philosophy leads him almost into fatalism, his theology leads him into universalism. His comfort is drawn from the fact that in the end the all-powerful God will make *everything* come out right.

Several serious problems are found in Ellul's construction, not the least of which is his lack of serious exegesis. His approach to the Bible is more of a bird's-eye-view as opposed to a worm's-eye-view. Certainly both perspectives are needed, however Ellul seemingly has no patience for detail. His axiom, "We cannot make dogmas out of the details," does not ring true even when applied to the parables. Surely biblically sound dogmas can be constructed of nothing else but details. The beauty of a parable lies in how the details add up to say something important to us about reality. The more removed the details are from reality, the more distant the connection is to us and the more vague the point becomes. Jesus' parables cut to the heart because the details, if taken seriously, allow us little or no wiggle room. The easy dismissal of details, like

---

[83] Schleiermacher, *The Christian Faith*, 547–50.

[84] Karl Barth, *Die protestantische Theologie im 19. Jahrhundert: Ihre Vorgeschichte und ihre Geschichte* (Zollikon, Zürich: Evangelischer Verlag, 1947); English edition, *Protestant Theology in the Nineteenth Century: Its Background and History* (Valley Forge, Penn.: Judson Press, 1973).

[85] Barth's construction may be found in his *Church Dogmatics* (Edinburgh: T. and T. Clark, 1961), vol. 4, part 3, 477.

[86] Fasching, *The Thought of Jacques Ellul*, 35.

people being cast into unending fire (Mk. 9:43–48; Mt. 25:41–46) or the eternality of the second death (Rev. 14:10–11; 20:14; 21:8), is the Achilles' heel of Ellul's universalism. By not adequately dealing with the details, the edifice is greatly weakened.

On a theoretical level there is a problem with the interplay between Ellul's construal of divine election and human freedom. Most universalists posit the existence of hell as a means of giving recalcitrant people the necessary time and incentive to enter the kingdom. In Ellul's universalism hell is restricted to this world and the suffering we experience here—the Lake of Fire will admit no human beings. How then precisely does a rebellious person enter the kingdom? How is a rebellious person rehabilitated? How is their will turned? Ellul wants to say that we are free and unforced by God.[87] However, he offers us no means by which God could accomplish his goal of the salvation of the rebellious apart from coercion or divine fiat. For Ellul there is no place of remediation, no halfway house for the defiant. Without such a provision for reconciliation, it is hard to see how his universalism could accomplish all of the objectives he has set out for it without doing violence to God's benevolent character.

Ellul's focus on divine deliverance being the hope for humankind is a vision that virtually every Christian—universalist or not—has embraced. In a world that so often has taken the blessings of technology and used them for evil, Ellul's theology is a poignant reminder that this too will pass and that in the end we have the promise that God will usher in a glorious kingdom. Regardless of whether one agrees with Ellul's universalism or not, this is indeed an encouraging and enduring message.

3. Martin Zender—An Ultra-dispensational Approach

Martin Zender is a popular writer and speaker who has billed himself as "the world's most outspoken Bible scholar."[88] He has written several books that address a diversity of issues including the church, sin, prayer, and eternal punishment. Zender's style is decidedly brash and confrontational. He cultivates an anti-establishment persona often criticizing the clergy and accepted Christian orthodoxy.

Zender has been included in this study because his ultra-dispensational approach taps into a historical stream of universalism of which few people are aware. Developed in the late nineteenth and early twentieth centuries in both England and American, ultra-dispensationalism[89] provided the perfect

---

[87] Ellul, *The Ethics of Freedom*, 14ff.

[88] The appellation may be found in the banner at: http://www.martinzender.com. (Accessed on October 8, 2014.)

[89] Ultra-dispensationalists have also been called "Acts 28" dispensationalists in the literature. This is due to the fact that they reject the idea that the church was born on the Day of Pentecost as described in Acts 2. Instead they connect the birth of the church to the statement made by Paul to the Jewish elders in Acts 28:28. As a result of this view, most ultra-dispensationalists interpret everything that happened prior to Acts 28 as having to pertain rigidly to the *previous dispensation*. In turn, this prior dispensation is viewed as having to do exclusively with Israel. Therefore, all of Jesus' teaching in the Gospels would be viewed as applying to Israel and not to the church. In addition to this,

mechanism through which universalism could be advanced. By focusing rigidly on discrete dispensations or eras, a unique system of universalism was developed by a group of theologians who took dispensational arguments to the very extreme. As we shall see, Zender's universalism is simply a restatement of this more historical form. As such it provides us with a unique window through which we might view the extremes to which dispensational theology has been developed.

While certain aspects of Martin Zender's universalism are discussed on his website, www.martinzender.com, his most detailed exposition is found in his book, *Martin Zender Goes to Hell*.[90] In the book Zender begins his discussion of universalism by arguing that most English versions of the Bible have incorrectly translated key Greek terms involved in the debate and have thus added unnecessary confusion to the situation. Oddly, he understands this mistranslation to be a part of God's plan: "God purposely sends deception into the world—even in the form of mistranslated Scripture—to separate truth lovers from the lovers of injustice."[91] Furthermore he claims, "God actually wants a large segment of the populace believing wrong things, and then defending their ignorance out of a misappropriated Bible. Why does God want this? So that those who believe the right things from That Book will become apparent. It's about contrast."[92] The thrust of this argument ties into Zender's polemic against the clergy and traditional Christianity.[93] The implication being that God is using the debate over eternal punishment as a means of highlighting those teachers who should be followed and those teachers who should be abandoned.

Zender builds his universalism around a highly modified form of dispensational millennialism that focuses on Israel and her relationship to the thousand year reign of Christ. In elaborating his universalism Zender makes three key exegetical claims. The first is the assertion that Jesus' teaching on the kingdom always refers to the millennial reign of Christ.[94] By construing all references to the kingdom to be speaking of the millennial reign, Zender is able to compress all discussion of the kingdom, including the threats made regarding nonparticipation, into that limited time frame. Secondly, Zender asserts that Jesus was sent only to minister to the "lost sheep of the house of Israel" (cf. Matt. 15:24) and that everything that he said must be understood in the context of his dialogue with Israel. Regarding the import of these first two claims, he comments:

---

the applicability of Acts and the "Acts era" epistles to the church would be called into question.

[90] Martin Zender, *Martin Zender Goes to Hell* (Canton, Ohio: Starke & Hartmann, 2004).

[91] Zender, *Martin Zender Goes to Hell*, 18. See also 19–23, 35–37, 42, and 73.

[92] Zender, *Martin Zender Goes to Hell*, 20–21.

[93] He reduces the polemic to an axiomatic statement: "The religious majority is always wrong, always. Not sometime, but every time." Zender, *Martin Zender Goes to Hell*, 91. The title of one of his most popular books is also enlightening regarding this issue: *How to Quit Church without Quitting God: 7 Good Reasons to Escape the Box* (Canton, Ohio: Starke & Hartmann, 2002).

[94] Zender, *Martin Zender Goes to Hell*, 32–35; 53.

Appreciate what that means. It means that all of Jesus' words (the words printed in dark red in your New Testament) concern one people: Israel. And all the threats He directed toward those people—the fire, the worm, the curse of the goats, the separation of the bad fish, the uprooting of the tares, the burning of the branches—concerned the entrance or refused entrance in the coming millennial kingdom—*only*.[95]

A third key exegetical claim made by Zender ties up some loose ends regarding the language of judgment. He argues that the Greek adjective *aiōnios* (αἰώνιος) means "age long" as opposed to "eternal" and also always refers to the millennial kingdom of Christ.[96] Armed with these interpretive keys, Zender sets about the task of unlocking the universalism found in the New Testament.

To begin with, all references to eternal punishment are explained away as punishment occurring in the millennial age. References to Gehenna (γέεννα) are taken as literal references to the Valley of Hinnom in Jerusalem where criminals will be executed and burned during the millennium.[97] The word Hades (ᾅδης) is claimed to mean simply "unseen" as opposed to the world of the dead or the underworld. Thus Hades is understood to mean death in the sense of people going to the grave—a place where they are unseen.[98] The judgment of the sheep and the goats found in Matt. 25:31–46 is explained in terms of the nations being judged, as opposed to individuals. The criterion of judgment will be the nation's policy toward Israel: "If the nation helped Israel in her hour of trial ('Whatsoever you do to these, the least of My brethren, you do to Me'), that nation will be placed near the capital city, Jerusalem. If not, then off to one of the four corners of earth. Near nations will be blessed, far nations not so much. Here, at the far corners, we find the 'outer darkness' and the 'gnashing of teeth.'"[99]

Zender's soteriology is solidly Christocentric and he mirrors classic Reformed theology regarding the doctrines of election and salvation in Christ. The primary difference between the two systems lies in the fact that he believes that God will elect or "give faith" to all people in due time.[100] Zender accepts the notion of soul sleep and he believes that death puts a person into suspended animation until they are resurrected. He understands the punishment of the

---

[95] Zender, *Martin Zender Goes to Hell*, 34; 41.
[96] The sole exception to this rule is when αἰώνιος is repeated for intensity as in Rev. 11:15: τοὺς αἰῶνας τῶν αἰώνων. In these cases Zender argues that, "Eons are long periods of time during which God gradually reconciles all creation to Himself." Zender, *Martin Zender Goes to Hell*, 50. See also p. 48.
[97] "It may be a pleasant green valley today, but in the thousand-year kingdom it will function as a crematorium for corpses of criminals. Don't be shocked. Unlike today, judgment during the kingdom era will be swift and sure, and criminals will think twice before breaking laws" (Zender, *Martin Zender Goes to Hell*, 37).
[98] Zender, *Martin Zender Goes to Hell*, 62. The Parable of the Rich Man and Lazarus found in Luke 16:19–30 poses a particular difficulty for Zender's view, which he acknowledges. His explanation is that it is merely a parable that Jesus did not intend to be taken literally. See Zender, *Martin Zender Goes to Hell*, 68–71.
[99] Zender, *Martin Zender Goes to Hell*, 45.
[100] Zender, *Martin Zender Goes to Hell*, 80–81.

second death to be like the first, which for him means more soul sleep until "the second death is finally abolished."[101] In Zender's eschatology no human being will experience suffering in hell. People are saved through election and the gift of faith when God decides the timing is right. Those who suffer the second death were not given faith in their first lives on the earth and therefore they must wait for the eventual gift of faith that will come from God to them at some point as eternity progresses. In Zender's view, only three creatures suffer in the flames of the Lake of Fire: Satan, the Wild Beast (or antichrist), and the False Prophet. In the end even these will be saved. Regarding the deliverance of Satan he comments: "Am I suggesting that Satan himself shall be delivered from the Lake of Fire with a changed heart, to be granted an eternity of praising God at his Creator's throne. No. I am insisting upon it."[102]

When one considers Zender's single-minded focus on the timing of eschatological events it appears that he provides an expression of universalism that is part and parcel of that found in the universalist writings of Adolph Ernst Knoch (1875–1965) and Adlai Loudy (1893–1984). Knoch was an associate of the British ultra-dispensationalist E.W. Bullinger (1837–1913) and he wrote several books on universalism from a radically dispensational point of view in the early to mid-twentieth century.[103] Knoch was also the founder of Concordant Publishing Concern, which still publishes his books as well as the *Concordant Literal New Testament*.[104] Loudy was an associate of Knoch's who wrote articles and books on universalism from a similarly dispensational point of view. Although Zender makes no mention of the writings of Knoch or Loudy in his book, there can be little doubt that there is a strong connection between his work and theirs. This connection is made plainly evident by Zender's insistence upon using Knoch's *Concordant Literal New Testament* as the basis of his textual analysis. He claims that it is "the most accurate translation in the world."[105] Indeed, virtually all of the significant points made by Zender can be found in Knoch's writings and in Loudy's book, *God's Eonian Purpose*.[106] In embracing the ideas of Knoch and Loudy, Zender has embraced a rigid

---

[101] Zender, *Martin Zender Goes to Hell*, 81.

[102] Zender, *Martin Zender Goes to Hell*, 85.

[103] A summary of his universalist thought may be found in A.E. Knoch, *All in All: The Goal of the Universe* (Canyon Country, Calif.: Concordant Publishing Concern, 1978; no original date of publication indicated). See also A.E. Knoch, *Concordant Commentary on the New Testament* (Canyon Country, Calif.: Concordant Publishing Concern, n.d.); A.E. Knoch, *Salvation of the Unbeliever* (Canyon Country, Calif.: Concordant Publishing Concern, n.d.); A.E. Knoch, *Two Studies on Heaven and Hell* (Canyon Country, Calif.: Concordant Publishing Concern, n.d.); A.E. Knoch, *The Unveiling of Jesus Christ* (Canyon Country, Calif.: Concordant Publishing Concern, 1935).

[104] A.E. Knock, ed., *Concordant Literal New Testament* (Canyon Country, Calif.: Concordant Publishing Concern, 1983). A catalog of available works may be found at http://www.concordant.org/ catalog/index.html. (Accessed on October 20, 2014.)

[105] Zender, *Martin Zender Goes to Hell*, 93.

[106] Adlai Loudy, *God's Eonian Purpose* (Los Angeles: Concordant Publishing Concern, 1929). The book is out of print but is available online at: http://www.secret-evangel.site90.net/GodsEonianPurpose00.htm. (Accessed on October 20, 2014.)

dispensationalist approach to biblical interpretation that divides both the historical and prophetic narratives into discrete eras that do not overlap.

Zender himself emphasizes the centrality of this ultra-dispensational understanding when he notes: "Understanding the time aspect of Jesus' earthly ministry is the key to understanding the entire New Testament."[107] Thus, Zender provides us with a fascinating view into the world of radical dispensationalism and highlights the amazing flexibility that is latent within this system of theology. Not only can the system be used to eliminate large portions of New Testament Scripture from the contemporary Christian's agenda, but it can also be used to validate a belief in universalism. If one accepts the initial ultra-dispensational timing of events within the biblical scenario, along with its assertion of radically discrete divisions within this timing, then one has embraced an extremely powerful methodology by which Scripture may be systematically dismembered and reinterpreted. Zender's universalism also demonstrates the power of ultra-dispensationalism to fundamentally clarify and explain away the systemic problems and seeming contradictions that plague other universalist proposals. By hewing to rigidly defined dispensations, these problems can be easily dismissed or explained away on the basis of timing. To be certain, Zender's methodology is draconian and antithetical to most accepted notions of biblical hermeneutics, and yet it must be admitted that the system contains within itself an ingenious sort of internal consistency and that from the point of view of the system, the explanatory deviations that are proposed make sense.

From a soteriological point of view, Zender's theology mirrors that of Hosea Ballou and his "death and glory" theory of salvation. As we noted in chapter 3, Ballou essentially argued for a moral influence theory of the atonement. Related to this was his belief that death automatically brought an unregenerate soul to repentance and thus salvation was instantaneous and assured without the need for any postmortem remediation.[108] Zender puts forward a similar soteriology when he claims that salvation will come to every person through God's gift of saving faith. The gift may be withheld until after the second death, but in the end its administration by God to all is assured. Thus, with Zender as with Ballou, we have the elimination of the need for hell or any other coercive measures. Salvation is instantaneous as soon as God grants it.

Internal consistency aside, there are several serious problems to be found in Martin Zender's methodology and exegesis of scripture. The most significant has to do with his idiosyncratic claim that Jesus' teaching on the kingdom always refers to the millennial age. Most scholars have acknowledged that there is both a present and future aspect to Jesus' teaching on the kingdom.[109] The present aspect is emphasized in such scriptures as Mark 1:15 where Jesus calls for repentance and belief in the gospel because "the kingdom of God has drawn

---

[107] Zender, *Martin Zender Goes to Hell*, 55.

[108] Ballou, *A Treatise on Atonement*, 127–28; 140–41. See the discussion of Ballou on pp. 136–37.

[109] For a thorough examination of the major schools of thought regarding the kingdom in Jesus' teaching see Mark Saucy, *The Kingdom of God in the Teaching of Jesus in 20th Century Theology* (Dallas, Tex.: Word, 1997). Saucy's argument in favor of such an interpretation may be found on pages 309–47.

near." It is also seen in Matt. 12:28 where Jesus said to the Pharisees: "But if I cast out demons with the finger of God, then the kingdom of God has come upon you." A unique form of the present aspect of the kingdom is found in Luke 17:20–21 when Jesus declares to the Pharisees: "The kingdom of God is not coming with signs to be observed; nor will they say, 'Look, here it is!' or, 'There it is!' For behold, the kingdom of God is within you [or in your midst]." Regardless of how one interprets these verses, it strains credulity to think that in them Jesus is talking about a future millennium. Surely there is an immediacy about Jesus' comments that cannot be denied. If one wanted to find a reference to the millennium in these verses it seems that one would have to accept that the millennium was ongoing at the time that Jesus spoke. This in turn would logically preclude any interpretation that would hold the millennium to be a yet future event as Zender does.

In contrast, when Jesus discussed the difficulty of entering into the kingdom of heaven in verses like Matt. 5:20, 7:21, 18:3, 19:23 and their synoptic parallels, surely he had something far more expansive in mind than a millennial reign. For Jesus the fulfillment of the kingdom was the ultimate triumph in the history of the universe—not just a thousand year bump on the road to eternity. This point is perhaps best illustrated through the imagery he used in the kingdom parables found in Matthew 13. Jesus said the kingdom would grow like a mustard seed; it would spread like leaven through bread dough (vv. 13:31–33). Jesus said the kingdom would separate the wheat from the tares; the kingdom would act like a dragnet on the people of the earth (vv. 13:24–29; 36–43; 47–50). Jesus said that the kingdom was the treasure in the field and the pearl of great price for which he would give his all (vv. 13:44–46). For Jesus the kingdom was everything. It was the fulfillment of the very purposes of God for his creation. The fact that Jesus does not equate his kingdom to a millennial reign on earth is confirmed in some of the final words he spoke before his crucifixion. He said in John 18:36: "My kingdom is not of this world. If My kingdom were of this world, My servants would fight, so that I should not be delivered to the Jews; but now My kingdom is not from here." To reduce Jesus' teaching on the kingdom to the mere status of the millennium is to fail to recognize the richness and anticipation found in Jesus' comprehensive theology of the kingdom.

Another serious flaw in Zender's analysis is found in his insistence that all of Jesus' comments be interpreted as being directed solely and exclusively to the nation of Israel.[110] To be sure Jesus did understand his mission in broadly Jewish terms, after all, he did acknowledge that he was the Jewish messiah.[111] However, there is an aspect to Jesus' teaching that requires a broader extension than that. When one focuses on Jesus' teaching regarding "the world" it is easily demonstrated that Jesus understood his mission, and that of his disciples, in a much broader context. For instance, Jesus' temptation by Satan in the

---

[110] Here we may see Bullinger's influence at work through Knoch. Certainly there is a stream of ultra-dispensational thought here that taps into the timing and rigidity proposed by theologians like Bullinger.

[111] cf. Matt. 23:10; Mk. 8:29–31, 9:41, 14:61–62; Lk. 24:26, 24:46; John 4:25–26, 6:68–70, 10:24–30, 17:3.

wilderness (Matt. 4:1–11; Luke 4:1–13) sets the stage in which he will battle this implacable enemy not just for the nation of Israel, but for all "the kingdoms of the world." In Matt. 5:13–14 Jesus tells his disciples, "You are the salt of the earth . . . You are the light of the world," indicating that he understood their mission to have a much broader extension than to just Israel alone. In his explanation of the Parable of the Wheat and the Tares (Matt. 13:36–43) Jesus interprets the field of conflict as being nothing less than "the world" itself. In Matt. 24:14 Jesus affirms, "And this gospel of the kingdom will be preached in all the world as a witness to all the nations, and then the end will come." In each gospel there is found a form of the Great Commission through which Jesus sends his disciples forth into the world to declare his message (cf. Matthew 28:18–20; Mark 16:15; Luke 24:44–48; John 20:19–23; Acts 1:8). The Gospel of John is loaded with references that place Jesus' ministry into the broader context of the world. In vv. 3:16–21, 4:42 , 11:27, and 12:47 it is said by Jesus and others that he is the Savior of the world. In John 6:33 Jesus says that he is the bread that gives life to the world. In John 8:12, 9:5, and 12:46 Jesus says that he is the light of the world. Finally, in John 18:37, Jesus declares: "For this cause I have come into the world, that I should bear witness to the truth. Everyone who is of the truth hears My voice." By narrowing the extension of Jesus' message to just Israel, Zender ignores a wealth of scripture that places Jesus' mission into a broader context and he fails to see how Jesus' words were the driving force behind his disciple's move into the world with the good news. If Jesus had not had a broader vision for his ministry it is doubtful that it would have escaped the confines of Palestine and Judaism. Jesus' words provided the justification needed for the difficult task of world evangelism. Visionaries like the apostle Paul would have had no place in a backwater sect that was intentionally confined by its Master to the boundaries of Israel.

A final issue that should be touched upon is Zender's peculiar lexicography and how it is used in support of his interpretation. In case after case he seeks out a unique definition that ignores the context and the developed meaning of the word being discussed. For instance, in the case of the word *aiōnios* (αἰώνιος) he denies that "eternal" is a valid translation of the word, even going so far as to say: "To translate this word 'everlasting' or 'eternal' is to alter its meaning."[112] This assertion is rebutted simply and effectively by the fact that virtually every lexicon of first-century Greek lists both "age" and "eternal" as valid translational options.[113] Another example is seen in Zender's insistence that the word Gehenna, as used in the New Testament, be related literally to the Valley of Hinnom in Jerusalem. This claim ignores the etymological development of the word in Jewish usage from a specific location in ancient

---

[112] Zender, *Martin Zender Goes to Hell*, 48.

[113] Against Zender's focus on "age" is the view of Joachim Guhrt who, after an in-depth examination of the use of αἰών and αἰώνιος in the New Testament, concluded: "Surveying the usage of the word *aiōn*, aeon, and the connected eschatology, one can establish that, with all the varied accentuations, the NT speaks of eternity in the categories of time. Any dualism between two world-systems is thus foreign to it. The world is and remains God's creation, and Christ is the Lord of the worlds, even if his lordship is hidden. The expression *ho mellōn aiōn*, the future age, is used only with the greatest of caution." Joachim Guhrt, αἰών, *NIDNTT* 3:833.

times into a metaphor for fiery judgment in the first century.[114] His translation of Hades to mean "unseen" also ignores the centuries old usage of the word as an abode for the dead. This same usage is confirmed in the New Testament by Jesus himself in the Parable of Lazarus and the Rich Man (Luke 16:19–31) where Jesus paints a vivid picture of Hades as just such an abode for departed souls. The eccentric approach that Zender takes toward lexicography greatly diminishes the appeal of his interpretation and seriously detracts from the efficacy of his case.

For all of its weaknesses, Zender's ultra-dispensational universalism still serves as a reminder of the incredible diversity of thought that the issue of universalism has generated. Contemporary Christocentric universalism is far from monolithic. Zender's proposal is proof of this. It also reveals to us the extremes to which dispensational theology can be taken. Through the use of a rigid dispensational system, theologians such as Knock, Loudy, and Zender have been able to advance a coherent system of universalism that effectively places a wall of separation between seemingly contradictory Scriptures while at the same time providing an explanatory framework for those Scriptures. In the end, there can be no doubt that this system fails to do justice to the entire sweep and scope of the New Testament, and yet it must be acknowledged that it provides a unique addition to the contemporary scene.

4. Marilyn McCord Adams—Therapeutic Universalism

Marilyn McCord Adams (b. 1943) is an American philosopher of religion who is currently Distinguished Research Professor of Philosophy at Rutgers University.[115] She is an ordained Episcopal priest and from 2004–2009 was the Residentiary Canon of Christ Church Cathedral at Oxford. Adams has wide-ranging interests including Medieval theology, philosophical theology, and the problem of evil. She has written several articles concerning universalism over the years, however it is in her formulation of a response to the question of theodicy that Adams enters into the contemporary discussion in her most forceful way.[116]

In her books, *Horrendous Evils and the Goodness of God* and *Christ and Horrors: The Coherence of Christology*, Adams explores the issue of evil with an eye toward providing a solution to how horrendous evil might be mitigated and corrected in the lives of individual human beings as well as in humanity as

---

[114] See Duane Watson's discussion on the etymology of the word in his article, "Gehenna," *ABD* 2:926–928.

[115] A brief biography of Marilyn McCord Adams may be located on her web page at Rutgers University. http://www.philosophy.rutgers.edu/recurring-visitng-faculty/754-adams-marilyn-mccord. (Accessed on September 22, 2014.)

[116] Her most concise and systematic presentation of universalism may be found in her article "Divine Justice, Divine Love, and the Life to Come," *Cx* 13 (1996–1997): 12–28. See also Marilyn McCord Adams, "The Problem of Hell: A Problem of Evil for Christians," in Eleonore Stump ed., *A Reasoned Faith* (Ithaca, N.Y.: Cornell University Press, 1993), 301–327; Marilyn McCord Adams, "Hell and the God of Justice," *RelS* 11 (December 1975): 433–47; Marilyn McCord Adams, "Universal Salvation: A Reply to Mr. Bettis," *RelS* 7 (September 1971): 245–249.

a whole.[117] Her focus is on the victim's point of view and she defines horrendous evils as "evils the participation in which (that is, the doing or suffering of which) constitutes a prima facie reason to doubt whether the participant's life could (given their inclusion in it) be a great good to him/her on the whole."[118] In her book, *Christ and Horrors: The Coherence of Christology* Adams describes three stages of horror-participation by which God can defeat the horrendous evils that individuals experience.[119] *Stage I horror-defeat* involves God's participation in the horrors of human history on an individual level such that it brings about "occasions of personal intimacy with God."[120] *Stage II horror-defeat* involves God providing "healing and coaching" to what Adams refers to as the "meaning-making capacities" of individuals, which have been destroyed by the onslaught of evil. In calling them "meaning-making" she means those capacities that enable individuals to make sense of their lives. Evil often destroys these capacities and these capacities must be restored.[121] *Stage III horror-defeat* involves a change of relationship to our environment so that we are "no longer radically vulnerable to horrors."[122]

Adams' solution to the problem of horrendous evil focuses on God and his unlimited benevolence: "If divine Goodness is infinite, if intimate relation to It [i.e. divine Goodness] is thus incommensurately good for created persons, then we have identified a good big enough to defeat horrors in every case."[123] She argues that in order for God to truly value and love each person, that he must show his goodness to each one. This goodness must include the defeat of evil with good: "At a minimum, God's *goodness* to human individuals would require that God guarantee each a life that was a great good to him/her on the whole by balancing off serious evils."[124] In Adam's view, only God is capable of truly defeating the horrors that are experienced in this world and only God has the power and ability to truly reverse their affects in a person's life: "*My conclusion is that the only currency valuable enough to make good on horrors is God, and the horror-participant's overall and eventual beatific intimacy with God.*"[125]

Adams proposes two primary processes through which God will accomplish this goal: (1) identification, and (2) universalism. Adams argues that it is through identification with our suffering that God makes our experience of evil meaningful. In a manner similar to Moltmann (whom we shall discuss shortly), Adams contends that it is through the incarnation of Christ, and especially his suffering and passion, that God identifies with human misery and the

---

[117] Marilyn McCord Adams, *Horrendous Evils and the Goodness of God* (Ithaca, N.Y.: Cornell University Press, 1999); *Christ and Horrors: The Coherence of Christology* (Cambridge: Cambridge University Press, 2006)

[118] Adams, *Horrendous Evils*, 26.

[119] , Adams, *Christ and Horrors*, 47.

[120] Adams, *Christ and Horrors*, 47.

[121] Adams, *Christ and Horrors*, 48.

[122] Adams, *Christ and Horrors*, 48.

[123] Adams, *Horrendous Evils*, 82–83.

[124] Adams, *Horrendous Evils*, 31. See also her discussion in, "Divine Justice, Divine Love, and the Life to Come," 20.

[125] Adams, *Christ and Horrors*, 47 (italics in the original).

horrendous evils that people perpetrate and are subjected to.[126] This divine identification endows the horrors "with a good aspect" making them "so meaningful that one would not retrospectively wish it away."[127] This identification with the suffering of human beings forms a very real part of a meaningful relationship with God and insures that "each person's earthly antemortem career has deep positive significance for her/him."[128]

Adams acknowledges that identification alone is not able to counteract the horrendous evil that people often experience in this life. This is where her universalism enters the equation. Her essential argument is that through universal salvation God guarantees that each individual's experience of evil is overwhelmed by an ever expanding experience of good. In discussing the scope of salvation she concludes, "First, my criterion is universalist in insisting that God be good to each created person. Given the ruinous power of horrors, I think (contrary to Hartshorne and Griffin) that it would be cruel for God to create (allow to evolve) human beings with such radical vulnerability to horrors, unless Divine power stood able, and Divine love willing, to redeem."[129] Thus, universalism is deployed in a therapeutic response to the conundrum of theodicy. Evil is defeated through the application of good. The arithmetic of human suffering is cancelled out through an incontestably positive outcome:

> My own estimate is that for an omnipotent, omniscient, and perfectly good God, success with an elite isn't good enough; universal salvation is required. To be true to Godself, God must accomplish God's purpose in creation for each and every created person God has made.[130]

Regarding the apocalyptic imagery and the discussion of eternal suffering found in the New Testament, Adams accepts that such things are a part of the text. However, she dismisses them as "sharing . . . the aesthetic defects of a grade B Western" that pits the righteous against the wicked.[131] In her view, the apocalyptic scenario offers a two-dimensional balancing in which the righteous ultimately receive their just reward and the wicked receive their just punishment. In this scenario there are positional reversals, but the essential character of the two groups remains the same. In looking for scriptural support,

---

[126] "In the crucifixion, God identified with all human beings who participate in actual horrors—not only with the victims (of which he was one), but also with the perpetrators" (Adams, *Horrendous Evils*, 166). "Christ's human nature allows Christ to join us in horror participation. This identification with us in horrors is essential to Stage I horror-defeat . . ." (Adams, *Christ and Horrors*, 79).

[127] Adams, *Horrendous Evils*, 167.

[128] Adams, *Horrendous Evils*, 168.

[129] Adams, *Horrendous Evils*, 157.

[130] Adams, *Christ and Horrors*, 206.

[131] Adams, *Horrendous Evils*, 138. This comment affirms a previous position she took regarding the authority of the New Testament: "Because I do not regard Scripture as infallible on any interpretation, I do not feel bound to translate into theological assertion some of the apocalyptic imagery and plot lines of the New Testament" (Adams, "The Problem of Hell," 325).

Adams prefers to focus on the passion narrative. As with Moltmann, she finds in the cross of Christ both universal identification and universal forgiveness.

In formulating her universalism, Adams argues that a universalist outcome is fully compatible with an unrestricted notion of human freedom. In her view, God will not be defeated by human rebellion. She argues that the creator has "enormous resourcefulness to enable human agency to work (Chapter 4) not only to 'grow it up' in the first place, but to rehabilitate it with new environments and therapeutic exercises."[132] Adams views such intervention by God as "agency-enabling" and not coercive. This line of reasoning is in keeping with some statements she made previously in which she affirmed her view that a loving God would not condemn any person to hell but rather that he might place persons who are not ready for heaven at death into alternate worlds.[133] On the other hand, Adams speculates that God might use a dramatic conversion or a "sudden change" scenario to move people into his kingdom immediately following their demise. She sees no problem with God transforming a person's character to affect an attitude of receptivity.[134] She envisions this reconstitution of the character in such a way that it does not operate to force a positive decision upon a person. The choice between instant and gradual change would have to be made by God on a cost/benefit analysis based upon what is most beneficial for the person.

Adams' proposal of using universalism as a solution to the problem of theodicy had been suggested previously by John Hick.[135] Thomas Talbott puts forward a similar argument, although his solution includes an actual reversal of evil deeds as opposed to a mere overbalance of good.[136] Adams' suggestion that God might use a "sudden change" scenario to move people into heaven has close parallels to the "death and glory" theory of salvation advocated by Hosea Ballou in the early nineteenth century as well as the soteriology of Martin Zender. As we have noted, both Ballou and Zender have advocated a variety of universalism that provides a form of instantaneous salvation. Adams' proposal seems to recapitulate this idea fairly closely, although she is not dogmatic about God's use of such a strategy.[137] Thus, the core of Adams' universalism has antecedents in history and has been explored by other contemporary

---

[132] Adams, *Horrendous Evils*, 157.

[133] Adams, "Divine Justice, Divine Love, and the Life to Come," 21.

[134] Adams, "Divine Justice, Divine Love, and the Life to Come," 21.

[135] John Hick, *Evil and the God of Love* (New York: Harper & Row, 1966), 373–400. Hick's universalism will be discussed in the next chapter, which is devoted to plurocentric proposals.

[136] Talbott, *The Inescapable Love of God*, 157–61; 212–13.

[137] In his article "Three Versions of Universalism," Michael J. Murray calls this view "naïve universalism" and asserts that to date "no one has endorsed such a position." He acknowledges Adams' tentative proposal, although he seems to be unaware of Ballou's more ancient advocacy. He also seems to be unaware of the fairly recent universalist proposals that seem to require such a direct translation of individuals into heaven such as that of Jacques Ellul. As we shall see, the universalist theologies of Karl Rahner, Hans Urs von Balthasar, Ninian Smart and Steven Konstantine, Raimundo Panikkar, and Hans Küng all point in the direction of a direct translation into heaven. See Michael J. Murray, "Three Versions of Universalism," *FP* 16/1 (January 1999): 56.

universalists as well. Her unique contribution lies in her application of these ideas to the defeat of horrendous evil.

Several important issues are raised by Adams' discussion, not the least of which is a theoretical one that has been raised in the past. In the words of J.D. Bettis, "Does the goodness and greatness of God's love depend on what it does for men?"[138] Bettis argues that the idea that God's love and goodness must be measured by what he does for people is an inherently man-centered philosophy and false.[139] The idea treats God as a means to an end and turns him into just another man-created idol that could be easily cast away once the goal of universal salvation is obtained. In her response to Bettis, Adams essentially argued that love and goodness should still be measured by behavior. If God truly loves human beings he will do what is best for them—which is to save them.[140] However, this response ignores several key points. Theologically speaking, God is loving and good in and of himself, regardless of what he does for people. God is not good because he saves; God is good because he is good. God is not loving because he saves; God is loving because he is love. The declaration טוֹב יְהוָה (the LORD is good), that is made in Ps. 34:8, Ps. 100:5, Ps. 135:3, Jer. 33:11, Nah. 1:7, is unqualified—it is a statement of fact. So is the declaration, ὁ θεὸς ἀγάπη ἐστίν (God is love), which is made in I Jn. 4:8 and repeated in I Jn. 4:16. We are also told in Is. 61:8 that אֲנִי יְהוָה אֹהֵב מִשְׁפָּט (I, the LORD, love justice) and in Ps. 45:8 it is said of God that אָהַבְתָּ שֶּׁדֶק (You love righteousness).[141] How God relates his love for justice, righteousness, and people is inscrutable. One could posit many situations where love for justice and what is right must stand in conflict with what is "best" for a person (from their point of view)—even though we love them. One can love a mass murderer and still opt for the death sentence or life imprisonment without parole because one loves justice and righteousness also. Thus the notion that God can only be good if he saves human beings still suffers from the problem of looking at the issue from a man-centered perspective. It fails to recognize God's transcendent sovereignty and the balance that he must strike between all the things that he loves.

There are several other issues that are raised by Adams' presentation. We will focus the balance of our comments on her hermeneutics and her exegesis of scripture since these things cut to the heart of her case. In dismissing the "apocalyptic scenario" because she judges that it has "the aesthetic defects of a grade B Western," it appears that she approaches the scriptures as if she were a film critic and not an exegete. Aesthetics have nothing to do with establishing the truth or falsity of a particular claim. A particularly ugly truth is still true regardless of how ugly it appears. In saying something to the effect that, "I believe this story to be false because I do not like how it looks," Marilyn Adams has bypassed the issue of truth all together and introduced an untenable subjectivity into her argument.

---

[138] Joseph Dabney Bettis, "A Critique of the Doctrine of Universalism," *RelS* 6 (December 1970): 336.

[139] Bettis, "A Critique of the Doctrine of Universalism," 338–39.

[140] Adams, "Universal Salvation: A Reply to Mr. Bettis," 246–47.

[141] Numbered as verse 7 in the English translations.

Another issue that arises in connection to this is that it appears that Adams has grossly mischaracterized the apocalyptic scenario as it is presented in the New Testament. Her claim is that what we have in the scenario is the righteous vs. the wicked, with each receiving their just reward and no essential change being made to the character of either group. However, it is the consistent testimony of the New Testament that the righteous *were once a part of the wicked* and that the righteous are simply wicked people who have been saved and transformed by grace through faith in Christ. This is a far more complicated plot line than the one that Adams alleges. The witness of the tribulation saints found in Rev. 12:11 is that they overcame Satan through "the blood of the Lamb and by the word of their testimony"—not that they overcame Satan because they were righteous. In Rev. 20:4, we see the souls of the tribulation saints who had been beheaded "because of the testimony of Jesus and because of the word of God"—again, not because of their righteousness. In speaking of his parousia in Luke 18:8, Jesus himself asks: "However, when the Son of Man comes, will He find *faith* on the earth?"—he does not ask, "will He find *righteousness* on the earth?" Therefore we see that the simplistic apocalyptic scenario that Adams presents is not consistent with the one found in the New Testament and that her version misunderstands the consistent witness of the New Testament regarding the transformation of sinners through the grace of God.

Finally, in choosing to prefer the passion narrative to the apocalyptic scenario as a means of justifying her universalism, Adams seems to be saying that certain parts of the Bible are inspired and provide a reliable source of information, while others are not. The problem with this is that she does not offer us any criterion (other than that of aesthetics) by which she makes such weighty decisions. The context here is that we are talking about issues of eternal destiny. If Adams wants us to embrace her universalism and abandon a belief in the eternal punishment that she finds in the apocalyptic scenario, then should she not offer us some very good reasons for making such a move? As things are, we have little more than an appeal to relative beauty. The subjectivity of such an appeal is laid bare by the old saying, "Beauty is in the eye of the beholder."

In spite of these drawbacks, Adams' perspective is important because it draws our attention to the issue of theodicy and the inherent problems that the doctrines of hell and eternal punishment pose to the resolution of that issue. Her concern for the sufferers of horrendous evil is certainly admirable and something that must be taken into account in the eschatology of every serious theologian.

5. Robin Parry [Gregory MacDonald]—
Return from Exile and the Restoration of All Things

"Gregory MacDonald" is a pseudonym used by the British theologian Robin Parry who has written a book entitled *The Evangelical Universalist*.[142] According to Parry, his penname was formed by making a composite out of the names of two well known Christian universalists—the patristic theologian Gregory of Nyssa and the nineteenth century poet/novelist, George MacDonald.[143] Parry chose to use the penname until August 29, 2009 when he revealed his identity to the world through his internet weblog.[144]

Parry's explanation for using a pseudonym is two-fold: (1) he did not want to cause his employer—a Christian book publisher—any undeserved criticism, and (2) he did not want the issue of his universalism to distract from the message of his book *Worshipping Trinity*, which he feels is a more important book.[145] The fact that Parry felt the need to use a pseudonym at all is, in and of itself, a timely commentary on the harsh divide that still attends the issue of universalism in our own day, especially among the more conservative enclaves of Christianity. The recent controversy in the United States over megachurch pastor Rob Bell's book *Love Wins: A Book About Heaven, Hell, and the Fate of Every Person Who Ever Lived* is confirmation that Parry is essentially right in his assessment of the evangelical community at large and the fact that the evangelical world is not ready at this point—nor may it ever be—to accept universalism or to abandon the doctrines of hell and eternal punishment.[146]

Parry's book, *The Evangelical Universalist*, is an amazingly compact treatise that bundles a relatively large amount of intricate argumentation into a relatively small space (177 pages—not counting the appendices). It is written

---

[142] Gregory MacDonald, *The Evangelical Universalist* (Eugene, Or.: Cascade Books, 2006).

[143] This information was provided by Parry himself through some biographical notes he posted on his web log located at: http://evangelicaluniversalist.blogspot.com. (Accessed on September 28, 2009.)

[144] http://theologicalscribbles.blogspot.com/2009/08/i-am-evangelical-universalist.html. (Accessed on September 28, 2009.) The base page for Parry's weblog may be found at: http://evangelicaluniversalist.blogspot.com In addition to his web log, he also hosts a discussion group located on the internet at: http://www.evangelicaluniversalist.com. (Accessed on Decemeber 27, 2014.)

[145] Robin Parry, *Worshipping Trinity: Coming Back to the Heart of Worship* (Carlisle, U.K.: Paternoster, 2005).

[146] Rob Bell, *Love Wins: A Book About Heaven, Hell, and the Fate of Every Person Who Ever Lived* (New York: HarperOne, 2011). In the book Bell questions the traditional view of hell as eternal conscious suffering and made some positive statements about universalism. It should be noted that Bell has denied being a universalist on several occasions. In a few interviews Bell revealed that the controversy over the book caused 3,000 parishioners to leave his church and eventually led to his stepping down from the pastorate in September of 2011. See Katherine Weber, "Rob Bell Tells How 'Love Wins' Led to Mars Hill Departure," *Christian Post* (12/3/12). http://www.christianpost.com/news/rob-bell-tells-how-love-wins-led-to-mars-hill-departure-5995/#oFZ3ZEYqY JehcLaq.99. (Accessed Dec. 27, 2014.) See also Kelefa Sanneh, "The Hell-Raiser: A megachurch pastor's search for a more forgiving faith," *The New Yorker* (November 26, 2012): 56–60.

from the perspective of a man who claims to be a classic evangelical in all things save for the doctrine of universal salvation.[147] In elaborating on what he means by this he affirms that he believes in the inspiration and authority of the Bible as well as "those crucial Christian doctrines such as Trinity, creation, sin, atonement, the return of Christ, salvation through Christ alone, by grace alone, through faith alone."[148] He also believes in the reality of hell with the exception that he rejects the idea that it will be a place of eternal, conscious suffering. Instead he argues that hell is a "terrible, but temporary fate"[149] that is "educative."[150] A place where "God does not torture anybody," but rather "allows the painful reality of sin to hit home."[151]

Parry begins his book on a personal note with an autobiographical account of his gradual embrace of universalism. He describes a time in his spiritual life when he entered into a doxological crisis—a time when he could no longer worship God because he wavered in his belief that God truly loved all people.[152] At the heart of the problem was the issue of hell and the implications it had for God's omnibenevolence. In reading William Lane Craig's book *The Only Wise God*,[153] Parry concluded that Craig's argument in favor of God's "middle knowledge" implied that God could save everyone *if he wanted to.*[154] The fact that God did not do so undermined Parry's confidence in God's love

---

[147] Of course Parry believes that the doctrine of universal salvation is sonorous with evangelicalism, hence the title of his book, nevertheless he recognizes that universalism has been broadly rejected by the evangelical world at large.

[148] MacDonald, *The Evangelical Universalist*, 6.

[149] MacDonald, *The Evangelical Universalist*, 135.

[150] MacDonald, *The Evangelical Universalist*, 136.

[151] MacDonald, *The Evangelical Universalist*, 136.

[152] MacDonald, *The Evangelical Universalist*, 1.

[153] William Lane Craig, *The Only Wise God: The Compatibility of Divine Foreknowledge and Human Freedom* (Grand Rapids, Mich.: Baker, 1987).

[154] MacDonald, *The Evangelical Universalist*, 2–3. I believe that Parry has fundamentally misunderstood Craig's middle knowledge argument in drawing such a conclusion. See William Lane Craig, "'No Other Name': A Middle Knowledge Perspective on the Exclusivity of Salvation Through Christ," 172–188. It seems that one of the main points that Craig is trying to make is not that, given the right set of circumstances, God can save everyone; but rather that God knows or has "middle knowledge" that in each and every world that he could *feasibly create* that certain people would always choose against receiving salvation and thus be lost—feasibility being defined by Craig in terms of the baseline goals that God desires to obtain including free agency, a certain population size in heaven, etc. . . This ties into his concept of "transworld damnation"—the idea that it is possible that a person could be lost in all feasible worlds and thus no matter which world is actualized the outcome is still the same. The same people are saved and the same people are lost. As Craig hypothesizes, "It is possible, then, that although God, in order to bring this many persons to salvation, had to pay the price of seeing this many persons lost, nevertheless He has providentially ordered the world such that those who are lost are persons who would not have been saved in any world feasible for God in which they exist." (Craig, "A Middle Knowledge Perspective," 184). Parry's extended rejoinder to Craig, found in Chapter 1 and Appendix 1, does not blunt the force of Craig's logic in any significant way and seems to amount to an "I just don't like what he is saying" sort of argument (See MacDonald, *The Evangelical Universalist*, 26–32; 178–83).

and led him into "the most anguishing period of reflection on my faith I have ever experienced."[155] Eventually, Parry encountered arguments in favor of universalism and was greatly influenced by the work of Thomas Talbott. He gradually became convinced that universalism was not only plausible but that it also "yields a theology of hope, of divine love, and presents a vision of the victory of God that has significant advantages over the tradition, with its eternal hell."[156] Before launching into a presentation of his views, Parry adds the following disclaimer:

> I am a hopeful dogmatic universalist. . . . The theology outlined in this book is one that espouses a dogmatic universalism, but I must confess to not being 100% certain that it is correct. Thus I am a hopeful dogmatic universalist, a non-dogmatic dogmatic universalist, if you will.[157]

Parry's argument in favor of universalism begins with philosophy rather than biblical exegesis. In his view, Christian theology is guided by scripture, tradition, reason, and experience. When it comes to the traditional view of hell he believes that there is a conflict between tradition and reason and that "philosophical attempts to defend the tradition to date have failed to present a convincing case."[158] On the other hand, Parry finds the philosophical arguments in favor of universalism to "have considerable force."[159] Therefore Parry argues that in the conflict between reason and tradition that reason should win out. He concludes:

> The reflective Christian should re-examine the Bible and theology to see if they are not, in fact, compatible with some form of universalism. If such an attempted re-reading fails, then they must return to philosophy and try again to make reason fit the Bible. I, however, shall argue in the following chapters that a universalist interpretation of the Bible can work; and if it does, reason will have played a crucial role in exposing our misinterpretations and pointing us to truer understanding of Scripture.[160]

Parry's philosophical attack is focused on the typical defenses that are offered in support of the doctrine of hell and eternal punishment. He notes problems with the idea of infinite retribution, arguing that the penalty of eternal punishment appears to be overkill for the sorts of crimes that people commit in

---

[155] MacDonald, *The Evangelical Universalist*, 3.

[156] MacDonald, *The Evangelical Universalist*, 8.

[157] MacDonald, *The Evangelical Universalist*, 4.

[158] MacDonald, *The Evangelical Universalist*, 10.

[159] MacDonald, *The Evangelical Universalist*, 10.

[160] MacDonald, *The Evangelical Universalist*, 10. This is similar to the approach taken by John Kronen and Eric Reitan in their book *God's Final Victory: A Comparative Philosophical Case for Universalism*: "[O]ur goal is to show that central Christian teachings render DU [the Doctrine of Universal Salvation] *more reasonable* than DH [Doctrine of Hell], and this requires a comparative approach." John Kronen and Eric Reitan, *God's Final Victory: A Comparative Philosophical Case for Universalism* (New York; London: Bloomsbury Academic, 2011; 2013), 9; 4–9.

a finite lifetime. He notes problems with the idea that eternal bliss could co-exist in the shadow of an eternally present hell. He notes problems with the Calvinists' reduction of God's all-loving nature. He notes problems with the free-will theists' insistence that God will not step in to override a libertarian freedom that is exercised to the eternal detriment of his beloved children. He notes problems with the middle knowledge perspective on freedom and the idea that God would actualize worlds in which anyone is lost. All of this is offered in an effort to show that, from a philosophical perspective, the Church's teaching on hell is incoherent and indefensible. Parry believes that if this thesis can be proven that the only rational recourse open to a theologian would be to return to the scriptures to see if they have in fact been misinterpreted.

Parry's biblical exegesis is built upon a meta-narrative that links the Old and New Testaments together into a panorama that he believes supports the doctrine of universal salvation. By relying on a meta-narrative Parry seeks to avoid a proof-text debate and to show that the Bible is essentially "the story of God's creating and then redeeming His world."[161] He asserts that, "It is only within the broader context of biblical theology that we can address the specific texts pro and contra adequately."[162] Thus the meta-narrative provides an overarching framework into which Parry can place any confusing or awkward text. He argues that "all Christians are prepared to tolerate some problematic texts without surrendering their beliefs. . . . I suggest that the universalist should behave no differently in this respect: Only if problem texts are significantly serious or numerous should they start to worry."[163] So then Parry's exegesis of his biblical meta-narrative has certain curative properties that allow him to rehabilitate difficult texts that, on the surface, would appear to contradict his universalism.

Parry's biblical meta-narrative essentially traces a creation-fall-restoration pattern that he believes is found woven into the fabric of the Bible. The Edenic story of Adam and Eve serves as the prototype—Adam representing a humanity that lost its blessing and relationship with God and was expelled from Eden. Eventually humanity will be restored and all that Adam lost will be regained. In Parry's view, the story of Israel's exile and restoration provides a parallel to the Edenic account and connects Israel to the overall struggle that humanity faces for restoration. Following closely the work of N.T. Wright, Parry argues that "Genesis sets up Abram as the new Adam and Israel as the new humanity in him."[164] The land of Canaan is viewed as a symbol of Eden. Israel's exile becomes a metaphor for humanity's expulsion from the garden. Israel's return from exile is said to correspond to humanity's future restoration.

Taking this pattern one step further, Parry then introduces a final parallel in which Jesus' life story is connected to the Edenic account and the history of Israel. Using Paul's Adam-Christ Christology (cf. Rom. 5:12–21; 1 Cor. 15:20–28), Parry connects Jesus' role as the new Adam to a universalist outcome

---

[161] MacDonald, *The Evangelical Universalist*, 36.
[162] MacDonald, *The Evangelical Universalist*, 37.
[163] MacDonald, *The Evangelical Universalist*, 37.
[164] MacDonald, *The Evangelical Universalist*, 55; cf. 54–73. See N.T. Wright, *The New Testament and the People of God* (Minneapolis: Fortress, 1992), 262–68.

including the restoration of all creation.[165] His conclusion is typical of the standard argumentation that universalists employ on this issue: "Adam's sin brought condemnation and death to *all* people (compare [Rom.] 3:23). Christ's act brings justification and eternal life to *all* people." It is in making the connection between Jesus' life story and the history of Israel that Parry offers an interesting new twist on things. Once again closely following the work of N.T. Wright, Parry argues that Jesus "embodies in his own story Israel's exilic suffering and restoration in the imagery of death and resurrection."[166] He accepts Wright's controversial assertion that most 1st century Jews thought of themselves as still living in exile even though they had returned to the land of promise many years earlier.[167] This return-from-exile theology becomes a central focus of Parry's meta-narrative. In his view Jesus becomes the true and faithful Israel and those who receive him by faith, both Jews and Gentiles, "are the transformed, end-time Israel in him."[168] The magnitude of these associations is made clear when Parry delivers the following summary of Jesus' central role:

> In conclusion, we have argued that in Jesus Christ God has acted to save Israel and, thus, to save the world. On the cross he takes upon himself Israel's exile and humanity's expulsion, both conceived of in terms of a divine curse. His resurrection anticipates the return from exile the Jews longed for and the restoration of humanity and creation. Christ is thus, on the one hand, the Messiah representing the nation of Israel and, on the other, the Messiah representing the whole of humanity. In his representative role nobody is excluded. Christ does not merely represent a limited group of people within Israel and the nations. Christ's death is not merely on behalf of some elect grouping with the wider family of humanity. He represented all, and his death was for all without any exceptions. In his resurrection, the whole of creation is reconciled, and the whole of humanity redeemed.[169]

How does the church fit into this picture? Parry views the church as the eschatological Israel as well as "the anticipation in the present age of a future salvation for Israel and the nations in the new age."[170] In an effort to clarify all the connections, Parry offers the following master diagram:[171]

---

[165] MacDonald, *The Evangelical Universalist*, 78–90; 139.

[166] MacDonald, *The Evangelical Universalist*, 66. See Wright, *The New Testament and the People of God*, 268–72; N.T. Wright, *Jesus and the Victory of God* (Minneapolis: Fortress, 1996), 126–31; 202–209; 244–46; 268–74; 363; 428–30; 445; N.T. Wright, *The Resurrection of the Son of God* (Minneapolis: Fortress, 2003), 253–63.

[167] MacDonald, *The Evangelical Universalist*, 76. See N.T. Wright, *The Climax of the Covenant: Christ and the Law in Pauline Theology* (Minneapolis: Fortress, 1991), 22–23, 137–56; Wright, *The New Testament and the People of God*, 268–72.

[168] MacDonald, *The Evangelical Universalist*, 90.

[169] MacDonald, *The Evangelical Universalist*, 104–105.

[170] MacDonald, *The Evangelical Universalist*, 105.

[171] MacDonald, *The Evangelical Universalist*, 105.

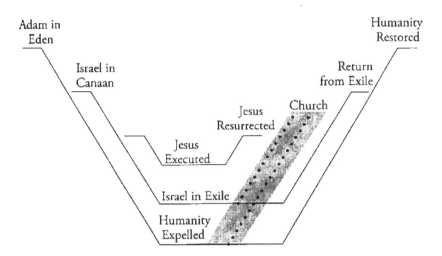

In this diagram we clearly see the creation-fall-restoration pattern and how Parry envisions the biblical meta-narrative parallels between Adam, Israel, and Christ. The grayed box representing the church actually represents all of humanity. The parallel dotted lines respectively connected to Israel and humanity show that in the end both Jewish and Gentile Christians will reside in one unified body, which is the church. Therefore, in the end, all people will become members of Christ's eschatological church.

Biblical texts that are problematic for Parry's perspective are dealt with after his meta-narrative is laid out in full. He does this so that the "biblical theological web" of the meta-narrative can be used as an interpretive tool.[172] He begins his defense by laying out a universalist interpretation of the Book of Revelation with its well known references to the seemingly endless punishment of wrongdoers. The explanation he offers of these texts is an eclectic compilation of several arguments. Some are methodological while others attempt to make rather intricate exegetical points. The net sum of them is aimed at proving that the Book of Revelation may be plausibly interpreted along universalist lines, especially given the "hermeneutical bias" that is presupposed by Parry's meta-narrative.[173]

In discussing the teaching of Jesus and his many references to fiery judgment, Parry's approach is to argue that (1) none of Jesus' teaching affirms the notion of eternal punishment, and (2) that none of Jesus' teaching rules out the possibility of postmortem salvation.[174] Since Parry's theology places a substantial emphasis on the idea that God will use the suffering of hell as the operative means of persuading obdurate sinners to receive Christ, he does not feel compelled to try to significantly mitigate or contradict Jesus' statements. It is sufficient for him to attempt to show that Jesus' teaching is commensurate

---

[172] MacDonald, *The Evangelical Universalist*, 106.

[173] MacDonald, *The Evangelical Universalist*, 131–32.

[174] MacDonald, *The Evangelical Universalist*, 145.

with classic Christian universalism and that it does not contradict the idea that *in the end* all will be saved.

Parry handles the teaching of the Apostle Paul on eternal punishment in a manner similar to how he handles the teaching of Jesus. He does not deny that Paul makes statements that clearly teach that a separation will occur between the saved and the lost. Nevertheless, Parry argues that Paul never envisions such a separation as being final and eternal. In Parry's view, Paul is simply endorsing the reality of hell, which is something that many Christian universalists also embrace. Given the fact that Paul seems to make some statements that can be interpreted along universalist lines, Parry argues that Paul "saw the division as one that would eventually be overcome."[175]

From a historical perspective, Parry offers us a contemporary version of what would best be described as classical Christian universalism. His universalism has a timeless quality to it that flows out of his evangelical heritage and his efforts to remain faithful to the Bible and to maintain doctrinal purity. By hewing to a strongly Christocentric perspective Parry has contributed a contemporary variation of universalism that would probably have been well received by the patristic universalists. On the other hand, his extraordinary efforts to place the story of Jesus within the historical context of Jesus' Judaism owes much to the scholarship inaugurated by the Third Quest of the Historical Jesus. Within that movement, of which Tom Wright has played an important part, there has been a recognition that the essential Jewishness of Jesus must be recovered in order to convey a more accurate picture of him and his ministry. Thus Parry's unique vision owes much to both the old and the new, and it offers us a distinctive combination of both.

Since Parry's grand meta-narrative stands at the center of his universalism and stands out as his unique contribution to the field, we will focus our critique upon it. Parry's defenses of the problem passages he finds in the Bible have already been largely dealt with in previous discussions and we will not repeat those arguments here. We begin our critique with a few comments about the hermeneutics that he employs.

In spite of the attractiveness of Parry's comprehensive meta-narrative and his all-encompassing vision of universal salvation and apokatastasis, there are several serious problems that bring his high-flying proposal to earth. To begin with there is his decision to promote philosophy over pure biblical exegesis as the starting point for his case. For one who claims to be a classic evangelical in all things save universalism, this is indeed an odd choice given the well known evangelical preference for sola scriptura. Indeed, what seems to irritate liberals the most about evangelicals is what they perceive to be a narrow minded focus on "the Bible, the whole Bible, and nothing but the Bible."[176] Although Parry claims to be an "evangelical universalist," his initial hermeneutical decision will more than likely raise serious questions regarding the validity of this claim among the evangelicals whom he is seeking to convince. More seriously, by placing his philosophical arguments first Parry appears to be attempting to stack the deck in his favor before the serious exegetical work begins and the

---

[175] MacDonald, *The Evangelical Universalist*, 151.
[176] To quote the motto of a well known evangelical church in my home town.

philosophical arguments that he makes seem to amount to little more than a poisoning of the pond before the divers enter the water.[177] Parry's claim that his failure to discover a philosophical justification for the doctrine of eternal punishment that he finds acceptable should "lead us to *prefer* a universalist interpretation if a plausible one is available" has nothing to do with a serious examination of the biblical evidence and will gain little or no traction with those who are more interested in where the hard data leads.[178] The fact that one cannot conceive of a personally acceptable reason for the existence of the doctrine of eternal punishment within the Bible has nothing to do with whether that doctrine is actually taught in the Bible. There are a great many things that the Bible teaches that are not explained and are left within the purview of God's own inscrutable will. Therefore a criterion of philosophical plausibility can be no substitute for a criterion of biblical credibility.

It is on this very point that Parry's grand meta-narrative fails. For while it may offer a plausible biblical framework into which he may fit his universalism, it lacks the biblical credibility necessary to make a convincing case. In particular, his basic Edenic schema and the connections that he forges to it in an effort to link it with the history of Israel and the life of Christ do not pass muster. To begin with, the basic outline that Parry offers of the biblical story seems to be inordinately focused on the *expulsion of humanity* from paradise as opposed to the *fall of humanity* into sin. Although the initial outline that Parry offers follows a creation-fall-restoration pattern,[179] the final form that his meta-narrative takes on is something entirely different: Adam in Eden—Humanity Expelled—Humanity Restored.[180] Thus a significant shift in focus is made in the development of Parry's meta-narrative away from the fall into sin and on to the expulsion from Eden. In the end, Parry argues that it is these three crucial features that form the essential framework of the biblical story.

The problem here is that this is not how the writers of the New Testament viewed things. Uppermost in their mind was the presentation of Jesus the Christ as being the savior of human beings from sin as opposed to being the deliverer of humanity from Edenic expulsion. The synoptic gospels very clearly enunciate Jesus' mission to bring salvation to his people. The Gospel of Matthew begins essentially with an angel declaring to Joseph the purpose of

---

[177] The Bible itself offers a withering critique of human philosophy and reason. In rejecting David's brother Eliab, the LORD said to Samuel in 1 Sam. 15:6: "The LORD does not look at the things man looks at." (NIV) In Isaiah 55:8–9 we find this declaration: "For My thoughts are not your thoughts, nor are your ways My ways," says the LORD. [9] "For as the heavens are higher than the earth, so are My ways higher than your ways, and My thoughts than your thoughts." The Apostle Paul, in his famous critique of human reason found in 1 Cor. 1:18–25, tells us that in Christ God has "made foolish the wisdom of this world" and in Col. 2:8 he warns us: "See to it that no one takes you captive through philosophy and empty deception, according to the tradition of men, according to the elementary principles of the world, rather than according to Christ."

[178] MacDonald, *The Evangelical Universalist*, 35 (italics in the original).

[179] See his discussion of Col. 1:15–20 in MacDonald, *The Evangelical Universalist*, 41–53.

[180] MacDonald, *The Evangelical Universalist*, 105.

Christ's coming into the world. In Matt. 1:21 he is told: "And she will bear a Son; and you shall call His name Jesus, for it is He who will save His people from their sins." Mark 10:45 quotes Jesus as saying: "For even the Son of Man did not come to be served, but to serve, and to give His life a ransom for many." The Gospel of Luke closes with Jesus reiterating his mission to his disciples in Luke 24:46–47: "Thus it is written, that the Christ should suffer and rise again from the dead the third day; and that repentance for forgiveness of sins should be proclaimed in His name to all the nations, beginning from Jerusalem." The Gospel of John is rife with allusions to Jesus' special mission, vis-à-vis deliverance from sin (cf. John 1:29, 3:16–17, 8:24, 8:34–36, 12:47, 20:21–23, etc…). Thus it is clear from the presentation found in the Gospels themselves that the writers' attention was focused upon the deliverance from sin that Jesus brings as opposed to the restoration of an expelled humanity.

The same is true of the writings of Paul and of the general epistles: the focus is consistently upon salvation from sin rather than the reversal of Edenic eviction. In 1 Cor. 15:3–4 the Apostle Paul presents an incredibly compact version of his gospel message: [3] "For I delivered to you first of all that which I also received: that Christ died for our sins according to the Scriptures, [4] and that He was buried, and that He rose again the third day according to the Scriptures." Surely if deliverance from Edenic expulsion were a central element of Paul's theology he would have included it here, but there is no mention of it at all and it is not mentioned in the rest of the chapter, which comprises the single most detailed theological discussion found in the New Testament regarding the resurrection of Jesus Christ and its ramifications for the Christian life. Instead we find a single minded focus upon the reversal of the ultimate consequence of sin, which is death. Not once does Paul mention in his discussion a return from exile or a reversal of Edenic expulsion. In fact, nowhere in Paul's writings do we have a clear and unambiguous link made between Jesus' death and resurrection and the exile and restoration of Israel or between Jesus' death and resurrection and the expulsion of Adam and Eve from the Garden. Even a careful reading of the much discussed Adam/Christ passages found in Rom. 5:12–21 and 1 Cor. 15:20–28 yields absolutely no conceivable hint of the expulsion from Eden or the Exile of Israel. Instead, one finds a discussion of the reversal of the affects of sin that Christ brings. This is also true of Paul's definitive discussion of Israel's rejection of the Messiah in Romans 9–11. If ever there was a passage of Scripture in which Paul could have made the linkages clear, this would be it—but he does not, and instead focuses on how God's election of Israel will lead to its ultimate salvation in Christ. The same may be also said of all the other New Testament writings. Nowhere do we find an in-depth discussion that explicitly supports or proves Parry's fundamental thesis. Nowhere is there a clear and indisputable statement made in support of the connections he has forged in his meta-narrative. Nowhere do we find an irrefutable link or declaration.

In fact, the Garden of Eden is not mentioned one time in the New Testament. To be sure, Paul does lay out his Adam Christ analogy in Rom. 5:12–21 and 1 Cor. 15:20–28. He also discusses Adam's fall into sin in 1 Tim. 2:13–15 as well as Eve's deception (cf. 2 Cor. 11:3). Nevertheless, we receive no discussion at all of Adam and Eve's expulsion from the Garden or the broader ramifications for salvation history that Parry pours into the event. Similarly, the exile of Israel is not discussed in any great detail even once in the entire New Testament.[181] Surely, if the connections that Parry is making are so vital and important, then the writers of the New Testament would have made that point abundantly clear. They would have taken the time to underscore the analogy. They would have taken the time to forge the links. They would have taken the time to make the connections clear to all. Instead, they say nothing—and their silence is perhaps the most poignant critique of Parry's thesis.

The essential problem here is that Parry has relied on N.T. Wright for his return from exile theology and in so doing he has incorporated all the problems that Wright himself has encountered. In my view (and in the view of many others) Wright has not proven his return from exile hypothesis—namely, the theory that most of the Jews in Jesus' day saw themselves as still being in exile and that Jesus' teaching was primarily aimed at announcing the end of that exile.[182] In a withering critique of Wright's exposition, James D. G. Dunn argues that Wright has exaggerated the importance of the theme in Palestinian Judaism and has presented "no real evidence that *those who actually were living in the land* thought of themselves as still in exile."[183] In contravention of Wright's thesis Dunn goes on to quote from several contemporary first-century

---

[181] Only a few unambiguous references to the exile of Israel are to be found in the New Testament. In Matthew's genealogy of Christ we have a reference to the members of David's lineage being "carried away to Babylon" and being held in "captivity" there— see Matt. 1:11–12, 17. In this case the exile of Israel is used as a general timing marker in Jewish history. In Acts 7:43 Stephen makes a brief reference to God prophesying against Israel: "I will remove you beyond Babylon." A case might be made that references made to διασπορά in the New Testament actually embrace the idea of Israel's exile. Both the Epistles of James and 1 Peter begin by addressing those who are in διασπορά. However, in both cases it would appear that the addressees are those Jewish Christians who have been "dispersed" among the nations through persecution as opposed to being a group of people who are held captive in a forced exile—see Acts 11:19 and the description of persecuted Christians as being διασπαρέντες. This interpretation is further supported 1 Pet. 5:13 where Peter concludes: "She who is in Babylon, chosen together with you, greets you." Most scholars interpret this verse as a veiled reference to the church in Rome (see the discussion of J. Ramsey Michaels in *1 Peter*, Word Biblical Commentary, vol. 49 [Waco, Tex.: Word, 1988], s.v. 5:13) since there is no evidence that either Peter or first-century Christianity came remotely close to establishing a presence in the area of Babylon. In John 7:35 the Jews ask this question regarding Jesus: "Does he intend to go to the Dispersion (εἰς τὴν διασποράν) among the Greeks and teach the Greeks?" Here we clearly see that the idea of διασπορά was connected by first-century Jews to those Jews who willingly decided to live among the Gentiles as opposed to those who were forced into such a circumstance. For a more detailed discussion of the diaspora see William R. Stegner, "Diaspora," in Hawthorne, Martin, and Reid, eds., *Dictionary of Paul and His Letters*, 211–13.

[182] Wright, *New Testament and the People of God*, 268–72; Wright, *Jesus and the Victory of God*, 245, 576–77.

[183] James D. G. Dunn, *Jesus Remembered, Christianity in the Making*, vol. 1 (Grand Rapids, Mich.: Eerdmans, 2003), 473 (emphasis in the original). For an argument that would seem to contradict Dunn on this point see J. Julius Scott, Jr., "Restoration of Israel," in Hawthorne, Martin, and Reid, eds., *Dictionary of Paul and His Letters*, 796–805.

Jewish sources that imply that just the opposite was true. In addition to this, Dunn notes several other key themes that are important motifs in Jesus' preaching that Wright's grand meta-narrative must of necessity ignore.[184]

The weakest part of Wright's case is to be found in his exposition of Scripture. Here the dearth of unambiguous references to a return from exile theology in the New Testament reduces him to the having to find it in such unlikely passages as the Parable of the Prodigal Son[185] and the Parable of the Sower.[186] Wright's exegesis of the Parable of the Prodigal Son is representative of his handling of the Scriptures as a whole and reveals the strained nature of his approach. First, the context in which the parable is told militates against Wright's interpretation. Luke makes it clear in the beginning of chapter 15 of his gospel that Jesus told this parable as a means of defending his ministry against the self-righteous accusations made by the Pharisees and Scribes who did not like the fact that Jesus fellowshipped with tax collectors and sinners (cf. v. 2: "This fellow welcomes sinners and eats with them."). Thus we have a story about two sons—one a reprobate (representing the tax collectors and sinners) and one who is faithful (representing the Pharisees and Scribes). Wright's claim that the faithful son represents "the mixed multitude, not least the Samaritans"[187] with which Israel had to contend upon her return, does not square with the fact that both of the boys came from *the same father and family*. Thus Jesus' point is just the opposite of what Wright claims—Jesus is really saying that they are from the same nation and serve the same God. As Wright's exposition proceeds, similar incongruities rise to the surface. For instance, in the parable the son is sent away *with his inheritance in his hand*— he was given blessing and reward even as he went. Israel, in a contrast that is completely ignored by Wright, was *mauled by Babylon* and sent away empty and stripped of everything she had. In the parable, the salvation of the faithful son is never in question (cf. v. 31: "Then the father said to him, 'Son, you are always with me, and all that is mine is yours.'") In Wright's view the faithful son is turned into an enemy: "those who oppose are the enemies of the true people of God."[188] And so it goes. On virtually every important point Wright ignores the clear meaning of the text in favor of an interpretation that allows him to force the text into the mold and contours of his grand meta-narrative.

Therefore, what we have in Wright's exposition is an interpretation of Scripture that is very heavily driven by an external idea—his grand meta-narrative. This is the very definition of eisegesis. Parry's exposition of Scripture suffers from the very same flaw. In accepting Wright's meta-narrative and basic interpretation he has incorporated all of Wright's weaknesses into his own and made his meta-narrative, and not the biblical text, the driving force behind his thesis.

In spite of its shortcomings, Parry's proposal does present a challenge to all interpreters of the Bible. Is the Bible a unified whole? Does the Bible attempt to

---

[184] Dunn, *Jesus Remembered*, 475.

[185] Wright, *Jesus and the Victory of God*, 125–31.

[186] Wright, *Jesus and the Victory of God*, 230–39.

[187] Wright, *Jesus and the Victory of God*, 127.

[188] Wright, *Jesus and the Victory of God*, 127.

tell a unified story? If so what is that story? Dunn argues that "we should heed postmodernism's warning against uncritical dependence on grand narratives, against the superimposition of a unitary meta-narrative on much more complex data."[189] Nevertheless, there is an undeniable attractiveness to be found in an integrated theory that has the power to unite and explain. The problem lies in the difficulty of constructing a theory in such a way that accounts for all of the data. In the end such a theory may well turn out to be as complicated and incomprehensible as God himself.

6. Jürgen Moltmann—Apokatastasis as the Culmination of Christology

Jürgen Moltmann (b. 1926) is considered by many to be one of the most influential theologians of the twentieth century. His theology was profoundly influenced by his experiences as a young man growing up in war torn Germany.[190] He describes an incident that occurred in July of 1943 that would

---

[189] Dunn, *Jesus Remembered*, 477.

[190] Moltmann's body of work is quite large and the literature on him is enormous. His autobiography provides an extensive discussion of his life and a chronology of the development of his theology. See Jürgen Moltmann, *Weiter raum: Eine Lebensgeschichte* (Gütersloh: Gütersloher Verlagshaus, 2006); English edition trans. Margaret Kohl, *A Broad Place: An Autobiography* (Minneapolis, Minn.: Fortress Press, 2008). An extensive bibliography of Moltmann's work as well as a bibliographic biography and a listing of known dissertations and monographs up to the year 2002 may be found in James L. Wakefield, *Jürgen Moltmann: A Research Bibliography* (Lanham, Md.: Scarecrow Press, 2002). Perhaps his best and most prolific interpreter has been Richard Bauckham. For an introduction into Moltmann's thought see the following works by Bauckham: *Moltmann: Messianic Theology in the Making* (Basingstoke: Marshall Pickering, 1987); *The Theology of Jürgen Moltmann* (Edinburgh: T. & T. Clark, 1995); (as editor and contributor), *God will be All in All: The Eschatology of Jürgen Moltmann* (Minneapolis, Minn.: Fortress, 2001). Moltmann describes Bauckham's first two studies as "far and away the best accounts of my theology" (Jürgen Moltmann, "The World in God or God in the World," in Bauckham, *God will be All in All*, 35). A shorter summary of Moltmann's thought may be found in Bauckham's article, "Jürgen Moltmann," in David F. Ford and Rachel Muers, eds., *The Modern Theologians: An Introduction to Christian Theology Since 1918*, 3rd ed. (Oxford: Blackwell, 2005), 147–62. Earlier introductions may be found in M. Douglas Meeks, *Origins of the Theology of Hope* (Philadelphia: Fortress, 1974) and Christopher Morse, *The Logic of Promise in Moltmann's Theology* (Philadelphia: Fortress, 1979); Hermann Deuser, Gerhard Marcel Martin, Konrad Stock, and Michael Welker, eds., *Gottes Zukunft—Zukunft der Welt. Festschrift für Jürgen Moltmann zum 60 Geburstag* (Munich: Christian Kaiser, 1986). Recent analyses include Brock Bingaman, *All Things New: The Trinitarian Nature of the Human Calling in Maximus the Confessor and Jürgen Moltmann* (Eugene, Ore.: Pickwick Publications, 2014) and Isaiah Nengean, *The Imago Dei As the Imago Trinitatis: Jürgen Moltmann's Doctrine of the Image of God* (New York: Peter Lang Publishing, Inc., 2013). The work of Nicholas Ansell provides the most extensive discussion of Moltmann's universalism. See Nicholas Ansell, *The Annihilation of Hell: Universal Salvation and the Redemption of Time in the Eschatology of Jürgen Moltmann* (Milton Keynes, U.K.: Paternoster Press, 2013); "The Annihilation of Hell and the Perfection of Freedom," in MacDonald, *"All Shall Be Well,"* 417–39. The theme of apokatastasis is woven throughout the entire fabric of Moltmann's theology. The most concentrated discussions of it may be found in two

change the direction of his life forever. He was manning a flak battery in Hamburg along with his high school classmates when the British Royal Air Force struck. Forty thousand people perished in the raid and his classmates were wiped out—including the friend standing next to him. In the darkness he cried out to God for the first time: "My God, where are you? Why am I alive and not dead like the others?"[191] Moltmann was eventually taken to England and kept as a prisoner of war for three years. In that time he began to search for answers to his questions. Eventually he found them in the form of Jesus' dying cry from the cross as recorded in the Gospel of Mark: "When I came to Jesus' dying cry, I knew, 'There is your divine brother and redeemer, who understands you in your godforsakenness.'"[192] This affinity for the cross and suffering of Christ would become the central focus of his theology and his universalism:

> The Gentile-Christian proclamation concerns all men, because confronted with the cross all men, whatever the differences between them and whatever they may assert about each other, "are sinners and fall short of the glory of God" (Rom. 3:23). "Here there is no distinction" (Romans 3:23a). Gentile-Christian proclamation must therefore essentially be the proclamation of the crucified Christ, i.e. the word of the cross (1 Cor. 1:18). . . . *The theology of the cross is the true Christian universalism.* There is no distinction here, and there cannot be any distinctions. All are sinners without distinction, and all will be made righteous without any merit on their part by this grace with has come to pass in Christ Jesus (Rom. 3:24).[193]

Moltmann's theology is built around a Christological center. In his first three books, *Theology of Hope* (1964), *The Crucified God* (1972), and *The Church in the Power of the Spirit* (1975), he explores his now familiar dialectic between the cross and the resurrection and what it means for both the present time and the eschatological trajectory of the universe. In the cross of Christ Moltmann sees God's total identification with humanity and the present world, including all the attendant ugliness of this reality: sin, suffering, and death. Through the cross, the Triune God truly experiences the depths of our godlessness,

---

books: *Das Kommen Gottes: Christliche Escatologie* (Gütersloh: Christian Kaiser, Gütersloher Verlagshaus, 1995); English edition trans. Margaret Kohl, *The Coming of God: Christian Eschatology* (Minneapolis, Minn.: Fortress, 1996), 235–55 and *Im Ende der Anfang* (Gütersloh: Christian Kaiser, Gütersloher Verlagshaus, 2004); English edition trans. Margaret Kohl, *In The End The Beginning: The Life of Hope* (Minneapolis: Fortress, 2004), 137–64.

[191] Jürgen Moltmann, ed., *Wir ich mich geändert habe* (Gütersloh: Christian Kaiser, 1997); English edition trans. John Bowden, *How I Have Changed: Reflections on Thirty Years of Theology* (Harrisburg, Penn.: Trinity Press International, 1997), 13.

[192] Moltmann, *How I Have Changed*, 13.

[193] Jürgen Moltmann, *Der gekreuzigte Gott; Das Kreuz Christi als Grund und Kritik christlicher Theologie* (Munich: Christian Kaiser, 1972); English edition trans. R.A. Wilson and John Bowden, *The Crucified God: The Cross of Christ as the Foundation and Criticism of Christian Theology* (Minneapolis, Minn.: Fortress, 1974; 1993), 194–95 (italics added).

godforsakenness, and transitoriness: "God did not become man according to the measure of our conceptions of being a man. He became the kind of man we do not want to be: an outcast, accursed, crucified . . . God's Incarnation 'even unto the death on the cross' is not in the last resort a matter of concealment; this is his utter humiliation, in which he is completely with himself and completely with the other, the man who is dehumanized."[194] In the resurrection of Christ Moltmann sees God's eschatological promise for a new creation and the restoration of all things: "It is still outstanding, has not yet come about, has not yet appeared, but it is promised and guaranteed in his resurrection, and indeed is given along with his resurrection as a necessary consequence: the end of death, and a new creation in which amid the life and righteousness of all things God is all in all. Thus the future of the risen Lord involves the expectation of a creative act."[195]

Therefore, for Moltmann, apokatastasis is the inevitable outcome of the Christological dialectic that God sets up between the cross and the resurrection. God's total identity with the fallen world entails his promise to deliver the fallen world from its current plight. A key feature of Moltmann's view is the total participation of the Trinity in the process of identity and redemption.[196] As Bauckham notes, this leads Moltmann into an interesting form of panentheism: "The goal of the Trinitarian history of God is the uniting of all things with God and in God: A Trinitarian and eschatological panentheism."[197]

Taking his cues from the theology of Joachim of Fiore (1135–1202), Moltmann develops a Trinitarian doctrine of the kingdom in which he argues that each member of the Trinity has impressed a unique "form" upon human history.[198] Each of these kingdoms is viewed as a "continually present strata"[199] in history and thus are absorbed into one another and in this sense are coextensive with one another: (1) "The kingdom of the Father consists of the creation of a world open to the future, and the preservation both of existence

---

[194] Moltmann, *The Crucified God*, 205. This theme is developed more fully in several places. See for instance Jürgen Moltmann, *Der Weg Jesu Christi: Christologie in messianischen Dimensionen* (Munich: Christian Kaiser, 1989); English edition trans. Margaret Kohl, *The Way of Jesus Christ: Christology in Messianic Dimensions* (London: S.C.M. Press; San Francisco: HarperSanFrancisco, 1990), 160–71, 178–81, 192–95; Moltmann, *In The End—The Beginning*, 147. See also Jürgen Moltmann, *Trinität und Reich Gottes: Zur Gotteslehre* (Munich: Christian Kaiser, 1980); English edition trans. Margaret Kohl, *The Trinity and the Kingdom: The Doctrine of God* (San Francisco: Harper & Row, 1981), 47–52, 75–83.

[195] Jürgen Moltmann, *Theologie der Hoffnung: Untersuchungen zur Begründung und zu den Konsequenzes einer christlichen Eschatology* (Munich: Christian Kaiser Verlag, 1964); English edition trans. James W. Leitch, *Theology of Hope: On the Ground and Implications of a Christian Eschatology* (New York: Harper and Row, 1967), 88.

[196] Moltmann, *The Crucified God*, 205–206, 265–66, 274–78.

[197] Bauckham, "Jürgen Moltmann," 156. In *The Way of Jesus Christ*, Moltmann argues that God's ultimate desire for the creation is "the deification of the cosmos" with its ground being "the cosmic incarnation of God." Cf. *The Way of Jesus Christ*, 302. See also his defense of perichoresis in "The World in God or God in the World: Response to Richard Bauckham," in Bauckham, *God will be All in All*, 35–42.

[198] Moltmann, *The Trinity and the Kingdom*, 202–12.

[199] Moltmann, *The Trinity and the Kingdom*, 209.

itself and of its openness for the future of the kingdom of glory."[200] (2) "The kingdom of the Son consists of the liberating lordship of the crucified one, the fellowship with the first-born of many brothers and sisters. The Son liberates men and women from servitude to sin through his own servitude (Phil. 2)."[201] (3) "The kingdom of the Spirit is experienced in the gift conferred on the people liberated by the Son—the gift of the Holy Spirit's energies."[202] A fourth and final kingdom is added to these three by Moltmann out of recognition that Joachim included it in his original formulation. It is called the "kingdom of glory": (4) "Finally, the kingdom of glory must be understood as the consummation of the Father's creation, as the universal establishment of the Son's liberation, and as the fulfillment of the Spirit's indwelling."[203]

While, for Moltmann, the goal of a Trinitarian panentheism neatly ties together God's work with human beings from beginning to end, especially in regard to freedom, the cross and the resurrection remain at the center of his concept of apokatastasis. Based upon the profound impact that Christ's passion has upon history and the world, and will have upon eternity going forward, he develops what he calls a "cosmic Christology"—a Christology that entails the reconciliation of all things: "The *ontological foundation* for cosmic Christology is Christ's death. In light of the cosmic dimensions of his resurrection, his death on the cross takes on a universal significance . . . Christ did not die for the reconciliation of men and women. He died for the reconciliation of the cosmos (II Cor. 5:19)."[204]

In keeping with this perspective, Moltmann does not believe in the existence of a literal hell or a place for the "performance of penitential acts" such as purgatory.[205] In his book, *In the End, the Beginning* he dismisses the traditional idea of a literal hell with eternal torments awaiting condemned sinners and he also rejects the softened versions of hell embraced by modern churches, which define hell as "inescapable distance from God."[206] These ideas, he contends, are not Christian: "General concepts of this kind and similar vividly embroidered images of the negative can be found in all religions. They are not Christian, even if Christian churches have taken them over."[207] Inspired by comments

---

[200] Moltmann, *The Trinity and the Kingdom*, 209.

[201] Moltmann, *The Trinity and the Kingdom*, 210.

[202] Moltmann, *The Trinity and the Kingdom*, 211.

[203] Moltmann, *The Trinity and the Kingdom*, 212.

[204] Moltmann, *The Way of Jesus Christ*, 282–83 (italics in the original). Moltmann explains that resurrection of the human race is tied in with a restoration of all living things: "In a 'resurrection of the flesh' human beings will be redeemed together with the whole interwoven fabric of all the living, and the living space of the earth." Jürgen Moltmann, *Sein Name is Gerechtigkeit: Neue Beiträge zur christlichen Gotteslehre*, (Gütersloh: Gütersloher Verlagshaus, 2009); English edition translated by Margaret Kohl, *Sun of God Arise! God's Future for Humanity and the Earth* (Minneapolis, Minn.: Fortress, 2010), 60.

[205] Jürgen Moltmann, "Is there life after death?" in John Polkinghorne and Michael Welker, *The End of the World and the Ends of God: Science and Theology on Eschatology* (Harrisburg, Penn.: Trinity Press International, 2000), 253; Moltmann, *In The End—The Beginning*, 145–48.

[206] Moltmann, *In the End, the Beginning*, 147.

[207] Moltmann, *In the End, the Beginning*, 148.

made by Luther and Calvin, Moltmann argues that hell is bound up with Christ's suffering and passion:

> Hell is not some place in the great beyond, in the underworld or in the abyss of evil. It is an experience of God. It is the experience of God-forsakenness. What Jesus suffered from Gethsemane to Golgotha—that was his descent into hell. . . . What we can with certainty call hell can be seen solely in Christ's passion. In his suffering from God, all assailed and God-forsaken men and women can find themselves again when they suffer the torments of hell here before they die.[208]

We see here that the "God-forsakenness" of which Moltmann speaks is synonymous in his theology with hell itself. Interestingly enough, as we dig deeper into Moltmann's thought we find that this God-forsakenness/hell is related to the entire space-time continuum of creation and that he views its existence as a necessary byproduct of the actions that God had to take in order to create the universe. To comprehend how all this comes together for Moltmann, we must first understand that he equates God-forsakenness/hell with what he calls the "*nihil*" ("nothingness")—an empty space opened up by God prior to creation. In his book, *God in Creation: A New Theology of Creation and the Spirit of God* Moltmann argues that in order to create the world, God had to vacate enough space to allow for it to come into being.[209] This idea has its origins in the Kabalistic doctrine of "zimzum" (צמצום = "contraction") taught by Isaac Luria (1534–1572). Luria argued that the first creative act of God resulted in a divine exile in which God contracted his infinite light so as to allow space for spiritual and physical worlds to exist. Luria tied this space also to the potentiality of freedom. Without this space, the argument went, these things could not exist because God's totality would overwhelm them all. Moltmann explains the first step in the process of creation in this way:

> 1. God makes room for his creation by withdrawing his presence. What comes into being is a *nihil* which does not contain the negation of the creaturely being (since creation is not yet existent), but which represents the partial negation of the divine Being, inasmuch as God is not yet Creator. The space which comes into being and is set free by God's self-limitation and is literally God-forsaken space. The *nihil* in which God creates his creation is God-forsakenness, hell, absolute death: and it is against the threat of this that he maintains his creation in life. Admittedly the *nihil* only acquires this menacing character through the self-isolation of the created beings to which we give the name of sin and godlessness. Creation is therefore threatened, not merely by its own non-being, but also by the non-being of God its Creator—that is to say, by Nothingness

---

[208] Moltmann, *In the End, the Beginning*, 147.

[209] Jürgen Moltmann, *Gott in der Schöpfung: Ökologische Schöpfungslehre*, (Munich: Christian Kaiser, 1985); English edition translated by Margaret Kohl, *God in Creation: A New Theology of Creation and the Spirit of God,* The Gifford Lectures 1984–1985. (Minneapolis, Minn.: Fortress Press, 1985; 1994), 87.

itself. The character of the negative that threatens it goes beyond creation itself. This is what constitutes demonic power. Nothingness contradicts, not merely creation but God too, since he is creation's Creator. Its negations lead into that primordial space which God freed within himself before creation. As a self-limitation that makes creation possible, the *nihil* does not yet have this annihilating character; for it was conceded in order to make independent creation "outside" God possible. But this implies the possibility of the annihilating of Nothingness.[210]

So then we must be careful to understand that, to a great degree, the concept of hell in Moltmann's eschatology is tied to the idea of a divine exile of God from his creation that was dictated by the need for a God-forsaken space sufficiently large enough to bring about the creation of our world. By allowing the space for the creation to exist, God allows space for human freedom, and human freedom—exercised wrongly—leads to sin and the victory of God-forsakenness over large portions of the human race and the creation of God. These ideas in turn have great impact upon Moltmann's eschatology. For if God is going to emerge victorious in the end over sin, hell, and God-forsakenness, then what will be required is the re-entrance of God into the space of his creation. This, in turn, will have a powerful impact upon the freedom of human beings. Moltmann explains:

> If God himself enters into his creation through his Christ and his Spirit, in order to live in it and arrive at his rest, he will then overcome not only the God-forsakenness of sinners, but also the distance and space of his creation itself, which resulted in isolation from God, and sin; for redemption can only mean that with sin itself the potentiality for sin has also been surmounted; otherwise redemption would not be final.[211]

For Moltmann the true destruction of God-forsakenness/hell comes when God reclaims and indwells the space he vacated in the first step of creation. With God indwelling this area then God-forsakenness/hell are truly destroyed and God becomes "all in all," which Moltmann has pointed to throughout his writings as God's ultimate goal in creation. The indwelling of God in his creation is not a pantheism, but rather a high nuanced panentheism:

> To the transcendence of the Creator towards his creation is added the immanence of his indwelling creation. With this the whole creation becomes *the house of God*, the *temple* in which God can dwell, the *home country* in which God can rest. All created beings participate directly and without mediation in his indwelling life and live in it eternally. Once God finds his dwelling place in creation, creation loses its space outside God and attains to its place in God. Just as at the beginning the Creator made himself the living space for his creation, so at the end his new creation will be his living space. A mutual indwelling of the world in God and

---

[210] Moltmann, *God in Creation*, 87–88. (Italics in the original.)
[211] Moltmann, *The Coming of God*, 306–307.

God in the world will come into being. For this it is neither necessary for the world to dissolve into God, as pantheism says, nor for God to be dissolved in the world, as atheism maintains. God remains God, and the world remains creation. Through their mutual indwellings, they remain unmingled and undivided, for God lives in creation in a God like way and the world lives in God in a world like way. [212]

This victory is, of course, tied to the cosmic dimensions of the resurrection of Christ:

> To sum up what has happened through the living God in the raising of Jesus form the dead, and to express it philosophically:
> Nonbeing has been annihilated, death has been abolished, sin—the separation from God—has been overcome, and hell destroyed. These negations of the negative are the presupposition for a positive position which is indestructible. Out of the surmounting of nonbeing by being, new being emerges.[213]

Given that Moltmann rejects the traditional concept of hell and has replaced it in his theology with a radically different version, the question then naturally arises as to the kind of punishment that God might inflict upon those who continue to rebel and commit sin in order to bring it about that they stop sinning. To that question Moltmann responds, "Transforming grace is God's punishment for sinners."[214] Rather than accepting the idea of a literal hell that may be used to rehabilitate and correct the obdurate, in Moltmann's view there will be a sort of "intermediate state" between life on earth and eternal life in God's kingdom: "I conceive of that 'intermediate state' as a wide space for living, in which the life that was spoiled and cut short here can develop freely."[215] This concept is developed primarily out of Moltmann's desire for justice. He wants to allow room for people to regain what was lost, to correct what was in error, and to develop into their full potential before entering into the kingdom. Therefore, he posits a postmortem salvation: "God's history with our lives will go on after our deaths, until that completion has been reached in which a soul finds rest."[216] In Moltmann's view, the Last Judgment is not about bringing down condemnation upon the heads of sinners, but rather it is aimed at redemption and putting all things right.[217]

---

[212] Moltmann, *The Coming of God*, 307.

[213] Moltmann, *Sun of Righteousness, Arise!*, 57.

[214] Jürgen Moltmann, "The Logic of Hell," in Bauckham, *God Will be All in All*, 47.

[215] Moltmann, "Is there life after death?" 252. See also the near identical wording of these ideas in Moltmann, *In The End—The Beginning*, 116–18.

[216] Moltmann, "Is there life after death?" 252. Moltmann, *In The End—The Beginning*, 117.

[217] "It is quite clear that the divine righteousness which is under discussion here has nothing to do with rewards and punishments. It is a righteousness that creates justice and puts people right, so it is a redemptive righteousness (Isa. 1:27). 'The day of the messiah', like the day of Yahweh, is ultimately not *dies irae*, a day of wrath" (Moltmann, *The Way of Jesus Christ*, 335). "'The Last Judgment' is not a terror . . . The

All of this ties in well with Moltmann's affirmation of universal election. He believes in human freedom, but cannot accept the idea that God allows human beings to be the ultimate masters of their own destiny: "God's decision 'for us', and our decisions for faith or disbelief no more belong on the same level than do eternity and time."[218] Given that in the end, God will take over the God-forsaken space that made the true exercise of freedom possible, it would seem that God's reentrance into this space would reverse this and therefore preclude true freedom of the will from operating. All of this would seem to imply that Moltmann stands ready for coercive measures to be applied to the recalcitrant, but he is careful in his writing to avoid admitting this.[219] Moltmann's failure to deal adequately with this issue is one of the most glaring defects in his theology.

Moltmann's doctrine of apokatastasis is all inclusive. The entire creation shall be remade, transformed, and indwelt by God.[220] This transformation includes Satan and the fallen angels.[221] Nothing will be wasted or allowed to slip past God's declaration that he will become "All in All." Based in his reverence for the creation and the high place he accords it in his eschatology, Moltmann argues for ecological conservation in the current age. God confers dignity on all creatures through his love, the sacrifice of Christ, and the indwelling of his Holy Spirit. All creatures, plants, and the earth itself have "rights" that should be respected.[222] Applied to the political realm, Moltmann argues the church should become actively involved in politics and should take up the cause of righting wrongs, working for the liberation of all downtrodden

---

eschatological doctrine of the restoration of all things has these two sides: *God's Judgment*, which puts things to rights, and *God's kingdom*, which awakens to new life" (Moltmann, *The Coming of God*, 255). See also Moltmann, *The Coming of God*, 250–51; Moltmann, *In The End—The Beginning*, 140–51.

[218] Moltmann, *The Coming of God*, 245. "There is rejection and there is one who is rejected: Christ, who on the cross became sin for us and a curse, as Paul says, so that we might be saved. The resurrection of Christ manifest that universal rejection has been overcome by election, which applies equally universally to all human beings" (Moltmann, *The Coming of God*, 245). See also his discussion of human freedom in his article, "The Logic of Hell," 44–45.

[219] Nicholas Ansell agrees that such references are few and far in between in Moltmann's writings and are typically rendered intentionally vague. Cf. Ansell, "The Annihilation of Hell and the Perfection of Freedom," 476, fn. 76.

[220] Moltmann, *God in Creation*, 276–97. Jürgen Moltmann, *Zukunft der Schöpfung: Gesammelte Aufsätze* (Munich: Christian Kaiser, 1977); English edition trans. Margaret Kohl, *The Future of Creation: Collected Essays* (Philadelphia: Fortress, 1979), 124–27; Moltmann, *Theology of Hope*, 221–22; Moltmann, *The Way of Jesus Christ*, 282–85, 291; Moltmann, *The Coming of God*, 274; Moltmann, *In The End—The Beginning*, 149–51.

[221] "In the cosmic Christology of the Epistles to Ephesians and the Colossians, not only all human beings and earthly creatures but the angels too—evidently the disobedient ones, since for the others it is unnecessary—will be reconciled through Christ" (Moltmann, *The Coming of God*, 240).

[222] Moltmann, *The Way of Jesus Christ*, 307–309; Jürgen Moltmann, *Ethik der Hoffnung* (Gütersloh: Gütersloher Verlagshaus, 2010); English edition trans. Margaret Kohl, *Ethics of Hope* (Minneapolis, Minn.: Fortress, 2012), 147–57.

and oppressed people, and defending the ecology of earth on which we live.[223] In short, knowledge of the glorious future awaiting the creation should cause the church to be working to make the world a better place in the here and now. In all this we see that Moltmann's millenarian eschatology is no mere escapist mechanism and that he will not countenance any attitude of defeatism or apathy.

Moltmann is aware of the difficulties posed to his position by the text of the New Testament. He examines the evidences found therein and concludes: "Universal salvation *and* a double outcome of judgment are therefore both well attested biblically. So the decision for the one or the other cannot be made on the ground of 'scripture.'"[224] Although Moltmann offers an apologetic against eternal punishment in the form of the familiar *aionios* = "age long" argument, he is not satisfied with it. In his view, the only adequate way of resolving the conflict is to return to Christology—to return to the theology of the cross. *"The true Christian foundation for the hope of universal salvation is the theology of the cross, and the realistic consequence of the theology of the cross can only be the restoration of all things."*[225] Rather than denying the reality of damnation or hell, Moltmann prefers to accept these concepts in the fullness of their horror:

> The *Christian* doctrine about the restoration of all things denies neither damnation nor hell. On the contrary: it assumes that in his suffering and dying Christ suffered the true and total hell of God forsakenness for the reconciliation of the world, and experienced for us the true and total damnation for sin. It is precisely here that the divine reason for the reconciliation of the universe is to be found. It is not the optimistic dream of a purified humanity, it is Christ's descent into hell that is the ground for the confidence that nothing will be lost but that everything will be brought back again and gathered into the eternal kingdom of God.[226]

Thus, it is in his theology of the cross that Moltmann grounds his doctrine of apokatastasis. The dialectic between suffering and death and resurrection and life guarantees the deliverance of all. In the end, the incalculable depths of sin are matched by the incalculable heights of eternal life in Christ.

Moltmann's doctrine of apokatastasis appears to be the worthy successor of no less than Origen himself. It is in every way equal to the vision of Origen and, in several ways, even larger. While Origen had a colossal perspective regarding the restoration of all things, Moltmann has been able to incorporate even contemporary politics and worldwide ecological responsibility into his grand vision. Whereas for Origen apokatastasis was a somewhat speculative doctrine, the theme of apokatastasis runs through Moltmann's theology from stem to stern and serves as an essential unifying feature. Moltmann's Christology as related to apokatastasis is also larger than that of Origen and is

---

[223] Moltmann, *Theology of Hope*, 329–38; Moltmann, *The Crucified God*, 291–338.
[224] Moltmann, *The Coming of God*, 241.
[225] Moltmann, *The Coming of God*, 251 (italics in the original); Moltmann, *In The End— The Beginning*, 147.
[226] Moltmann, *The Coming of God*, 251 (italics in the original).

truly massive in its conceptual scale. The size of Moltmann's vision can be seen in his expansion of the doctrine of the atonement to include the creation itself as well as in his extension of God's identification and empathy to all things.

The magnitude of Moltmann's perspective on the resurrection is also equally imposing. While the idea of incorporating the remaking of creation itself into the power and promise of the resurrection of Christ was first hinted at by Gregory of Nyssa,[227] Moltmann's advocacy of such an expansive view is unparalleled in the contemporary literature. In an era when the historical Jesus is so often reconstructed in a way that minimizes or completely vitiates the theology of the cross, Moltmann has managed to place the cross back into the center of the theological debate and to even expand its horizons. This focus on the centrality of Christ and his salvific work will remain Moltmann's enduring theological challenge and legacy.

Despite Moltmann's soaring proclamation, there are several problems that arise in his presentation, the first being that his sweeping vision does not suffer the details well. In other words, what we have with Moltmann is more of a theology built upon a theoretical construct as opposed to a theology built upon careful exegesis of the Bible and a consistently applied hermeneutic. Take for instance Moltmann's claim that "Christ did not die for the reconciliation of men and women. He died for the reconciliation of the cosmos."[228] This claim is central to his thesis, which extends the benefits of Christ's death to the fallen universe itself. Moltmann cites 2 Cor. 5:19 in support of it, which reads: 19 ". . . namely, that God was in Christ reconciling the world to Himself [κόσμον καταλλάσσων ἑαυτω], not counting their [αὐτοῖς] trespasses against them [αὐτῶν], and He has committed to us the word of reconciliation." Obviously, Moltmann interprets the word *kosmon* (κόσμον) in this verse in the broadest sense possible as referring to the universe, as opposed to the more limited possibility of it referring to the human world or humanity. The problem is that the context and the grammar of the passage will not permit Moltmann's interpretation. Going back to verse 18 we see that Paul is clearly talking about people, and not the universe, when he says: 18 "Now all *these* things are from God, who reconciled us to Himself through Christ [τοῦ καταλλάξαντος ἡμᾶς ἑαυτῷ], and gave us the ministry of reconciliation . . ." The fact that Paul continues to talk about people, and not the universe, in verse 19 is verified in that he uses the plural (αὐτοῖς/αὐτῶν) to refer to people as opposed to the singular (αὐτῷ/αὐτοῦ), which would refer to the universe. If Paul was using *kosmon* (κόσμον) in verse 19 in the sense of a unified creation or universe we would expect him to use the singular, rather than the plural, to refer back to it. However, Paul chose to use the plural as a means of completing his thought, indicating that he was thinking of people ("them") as opposed to the universe ("it"). When taken out of context, 2 Cor. 5:19 would seem to lend strong

---

[227] In his *De hominis opificio* Gregory linked the resurrection to the doctrine of restoration: "The grace of the resurrection promises to us nothing other than the restoration of the fallen to their original state" (Gregory of Nyssa, *De hom. opif.*, PG 44:188c–d).

[228] Moltmann, *The Way of Jesus Christ*, 282–83.

support to Moltmann's thesis. Placed back into context, the support that 2 Cor. 5:19 lends to his thesis evaporates. We find this sort of problem consistently throughout Moltmann's work: Verses are frequently taken out of context; thorough exegesis on the most important biblical connections is never performed; contradictory passages are all too often ignored.

Moltmann's conjecture regarding an "intermediate state" between temporal life on earth and eternal life in the kingdom brings the issue into sharper focus. Here we have an essential element of his eschatology—what happens to us immediately after we die—for which absolutely no scriptural support is given. Instead, Moltmann appeals to the vague notion of God's justice: "I think all this not for selfish reasons, neither for the sake of a personal completion nor in the interests of a moral purification, but for the sake of the justice which I believe is God's own concern and his first option."[229] The detail that Moltmann goes into in fleshing out this proposition is quite striking. The intermediate state is a "wide space for living"; it is a place in which "the life that was spoiled and cut short here can develop freely"; it is a "time of new life"; it is a place in which "God's history with a human being can come to its flowering and consummation"; it is a place where "the handicapped and the broken can live the life that was meant for them."[230] The problem with all of this is that it is based simply upon conjecture. It is a theoretical construct. For Moltmann, the intermediate state fills a similar void that purgatory does in Catholic theology and it suffers from the same basic deficiency: there is no scriptural support for it.

The same is also true of Moltmann's use of the Kabalistic doctrine of zimzum and the contraction of God in order to generate a necessary space in which the universe could be created. This space—which Moltmann identifies with nothingness, God-forsakenness, and hell—stands at the center of his eschatological thinking such that its ultimate elimination is viewed by him as the great victory that brings God and his universe together, and yet there is not one shred of biblical support for such a doctrine. Moltmann mentions in passing that he understands the contraction to be similar to the empting of Christ found in Philippians chapter 2, but again there is no direct evidence in the Bible indicating that the Creator went through such a kenosis at the time of the creation. There is no evidence in the Bible that God retreated out of this world. There is no evidence in the Bible that hell is directly correlated with the space within which this world resides.

There are also problems with the leap that Moltmann makes regarding the resurrection of Christ and its application to the apokatastasis. In Moltmann's view, the resurrection of Christ carries with it the prototype and guarantee of the restoration and remaking of all things. For him, the resurrection has "cosmic dimensions."[231] This too, however, is a theoretical construct that is by no means conclusively testified to in scripture. Indeed, a thorough investigation of the concept of the resurrection in the New Testament reveals that it is always carefully related to the raising of the dead and is never connected to the idea of

---

[229] Moltmann, "Is there life after death?" 253.
[230] Moltmann, "Is there life after death?" 253.
[231] Moltmann, *The Way of Jesus Christ*, 282.

God remaking the universe.[232] The idea of resurrection in the New Testament is unanimously testified to be a bodily event and not a cosmic one. Moltmann consistently uses Romans 8:18–25 to justify his position (where else can he go?), but here Paul uses none of the words that would indicate resurrection (ἀνάστασις, ἐγείρω) and instead he carefully uses other terminology that avoids such a metaphor being applied to the remaking of the creation. In verse 21 Paul declares: 21 ". . . that the creation itself also will be set free [ἐλευθερωθήσεται] from its slavery to corruption into the freedom of the glory of the children of God." Here the deliverance of the creation is spoken of in terms of liberation or being set free (*eluetherōthēsetai–*ἐλευθερωθήσεται) from the slavery of decay. In verse 23, where Paul discusses the human desire for glorification, he again carefully avoids resurrection imagery. Instead Paul prefers to speak in terms of adoption (*huiothesian–*υἱοθεσίαν) and redemption (*apolutrōsin–*ἀπολύτρωσιν) and not resurrection: 23 "And not only this, but also we ourselves, having the first fruits of the Spirit, even we ourselves groan within ourselves, waiting eagerly for *our* adoption as sons [υἱοθεσίαν] the redemption [ἀπολύτρωσιν]of our body." One could argue that the redemption of the body speaks by analogy of its transformation at the resurrection, however this argument does not hold up on two important grounds: (1) redemption and resurrection are two entirely different concepts in the New Testament, and (2) the word *apolutrōsin* (ἀπολυτρωσιν) describes a release or deliverance or manumission achieved by a ransom payment or *lutron* (λύτρον).[233] Thus, Moltmann's reliance on this passage to justify his position is misguided at best. If anything, upon close inspection, the passage seems to disprove his point rather than support it.

In all of this we see that Moltmann's theological method poses serious problems for the efficacy of his doctrine of universal salvation and apokatastasis. His doctrine of creation is sheer speculation. His concept of the intermediate state is put forward with little more than a philosophical justification. His famous dialectic between the death and resurrection of Christ is interesting as a theoretical construct—as a scriptural proposition it has little or no standing when applied to the eschatology of the universe.

These issues aside, it is the sheer scale and magnitude of Moltmann's theology of the cross that catches our attention. Its attractiveness lies in its ability to role all things together into Christ and the Godhead in which he participates. Moltmann makes no apologies for the focus of the New Testament upon the wounding and suffering of Christ. He does not dismiss or tiptoe around an atonement theology written in blood. Instead, Moltmann celebrates the sacrifice and sees in it nothing less than the glory of God revealed. This is

---

[232] Cf. Mt. 16:21, 17:23, 20:19, 22:23, 22:28, 22:30, 22:31, 26:32, 27:32, 27:53, 27:63; Mk. 6:16, 8:31, 9:31, 10:34, 12:18–27, 14:28; Lk. 2:23, 7:22, 9:22, 14:14, 16:31, 18:33, 20:27, 20:33, 20:35, 20:36–37, 24:37, 24:46; Jn. 5:29, 11:23–25, 12:1, 12:9, 12:17, 20:9, 21:14; Acts 1:22, 2:24, 2:31, 2:32, 3:15, 3:26, 4:2, 4:10, 4:33, 5:30, 10:40, 13:30–34, 13:37, 17:3, 17:18, 17:32, 23:6, 23:8, 24:15, 24:21, 26:23; Rom. 1:4, 4:23–35, 6:1–11, 7:4, 8:11, 10:9; 1 Cor. 15:1–58; 2 Cor. 4:14; Gal. 1:1; Eph. 1:20, 2:6; Phil. 3:10, 3:11, 3:20–21; Col. 2:11–12, 3:1; 1 Thes. 1:10, 4:16; 2 Tim. 2:8, 2:18; Heb. 6:2, 11:35; 1 Pet. 1:3, 1:21, 3:2; Rev. 20:4–6.

[233] BDAG s.v. λύτρον; Colin Brown, λύτρον, *NIDNTT* 3:189–200.

no cheapening of the cross, but rather a profound meditation on its enduring meaning.

7. Conclusion

What stands out in this examination of contemporary Protestant universalism is how well most of it was anticipated in history. As we have seen, virtually every contemporary proposal has antecedents in the past with some of the parallels presenting an almost point by point agreement. These similarities reveal that Christian thinkers throughout history have been capable of an incredible diversity of thought and were in every way the equals of contemporary theologians.

On the other hand, we also see the influences of contemporary thought and culture at work within these proposals. In particular, there is a willingness to employ universalism as a solution to contemporary problems and challenges. For instance, scholars like Talbott and Adams find in universalism an answer to the unique problems posed by the question of theodicy and our ever increasing awareness of the evils perpetrated by humankind. Zender finds in his universalism an apologetic that allows him to evangelize a nation. Ellul and Moltmann find in universalism nothing less than the ultimate solution to the world's problems and a call for political engagement in the here and now. The result of all this has been a unique merging of the historical and the contemporary. The synthesis that has emerged in these proposals has left us with a resurgent doctrine of universalism that attempts to apply an ancient solution to contemporary issues.

CHAPTER 5

Plurocentric Approaches

We now turn our attention to an innovative form of universalism that can be rightly counted as a unique contribution made by contemporary theology to the expansion of the doctrine. As we have seen, most contemporary expressions of Christocentric universalism have antecedents that reach back into the past—whether the proponent is aware of them or not. However, when it comes to plurocentric universalism no such antecedents exist and we are confronted with an entirely new theological development.[1]

To be sure, plurocentric universalism did not develop in a vacuum. There was the general influence of Enlightenment thought and ideals. There was the development of postmodern relativism. There were the early contributions of people such as Guillaume Postel and Friedrich Schleiermacher.[2] There were the extremely influential pluralist theories of Ernst Troeltsch.[3] Nevertheless, there are no examples of true plurocentric universalism prior to the mid-twentieth century. Plurocentric universalism stands out as a paradigm shift in universalist thinking. It represents a quantum leap in universalist thought.

1. Moderating Positions
As we noted in chapter 4, some proposals that are arguably Christocentric also incorporate pluralistic ideas. The problem is what to do with such moderating positions. On the one hand these proposals still accord Christ a significant role in their soteriology. However, on the other hand, they also reserve a significant role for other religions and religious expressions. The result is a sort of hybrid inclusivistic universalism that in some way affirms the centrality of Christ, albeit in a highly modified form. In the interest of analyzing the issue of pluralism in a more comprehensive fashion the decision was made to discuss these moderating proposals along with the fully plurocentric proposals in the same chapter. It is hoped that by incorporating these two categories into the same chapter that a deeper understanding of plurocentric universalism will emerge. It should be kept in mind that the two moderating proposals presented here could just as easily be labeled "Christocentric" as opposed to

---

[1] By way of review, we regard plurocentric universalism to be the concept that universal salvation will be mediated through many different religions and/or, in many cases, through no religion at all. On this view, Christianity is considered to be just one religion among many and just one path among many. In plurocentric universalist soteriology, Christ is not required for salvation and the deliverance of all people does not occur through him. Plurocentric universalism asserts that all paths eventually lead to salvation.

[2] The discussion of Postel may be found in chapter 2, section 2.2 of this study. The discussion of Schleiermacher may be found in chapter 3, section 1.1 of this study.

[3] The discussion of Troeltsch may be found in chapter 3, section 2.4 of this study.

"Plurocentric." In this regard they do truly occupy a sort of middle ground in the debate.

1.1. Keith Ward—Cosmic Unity in Christ

Keith Ward (b. 1938) is a British theologian and an ordained Anglican priest who has held several prestigious posts in British academia.[4] Ward's work has focused on topics as diverse as the interface between science and religion, the relationship between various religious faiths, and the development of a pluralist theology of religions. In the context of these pursuits, he has developed a consistent universalist theology over the years. Ward is a confirmed religious pluralist who advocates what he calls "convergent pluralism."[5] However, in an interesting twist he holds to a highly modified form of Christocentric universalism and a belief that in the end all things will be united in Christ.

In order to better understand Ward's universalism we must begin by gaining an understanding of his view of cosmic purpose. According to Ward, the overarching goal of God in creation is to move the universe into a "conscious unity" with himself:

> The Christian vision of God is one of breathtaking scope. It extends to the whole created universe, with its millions of galaxies and its immense solitudes of space. It prompts one to see the universe as a growing, organic whole, moving from a primal chaos, the "great deep", unconscious, without freedom or feeling, towards a completed and conscious unity with the Pure Spirit who is the creator of all. The history of the cosmos is, in the Christian perspective, the history of a material universe that is being transfigured, over millions of years, into a perfected sacrament of Infinite Spirit.[6]

Christ fits into this panentheistic (pantheistic?) vision in that he is "the deliverer and ruler of the whole cosmos" and the one who "invests the process with its true meaning and significance."[7] Ward's concept of Christ is cosmic in its scope and is not restricted to the human Jesus. In his view, Christ is

---

[4] Keith Ward was Lecturer in Logic at the University of Glasgow from 1964–1969. He was Lecturer in Philosophy at the University of St Andrews, 1969–1971. He was Lecturer in Philosophy of Religion at the University of London from 1971–75. From 1975–83, he was Dean of Trinity Hall, Cambridge. In 1982 he was appointed the F. D. Maurice Professor of Moral and Social Theology at the University of London. He was appointed Professor of History and Philosophy of Religion at King's College London in 1985. He was appointed the Regius Professor of Divinity at Oxford in 1991; he retired from that position in 2004. He was the Gresham Professor of Divinity at Gresham College in London from 2004–2008.

[5] According to Ward, "convergent pluralism" is intended to convey the idea that "most, and probably all traditions will need to be revised to approximate more nearly to a fuller unitary truth which none of them yet fully encapsulates" (Keith Ward, *A Vision to Pursue: Beyond the Crisis in Christianity* [London: SCM Press, 1991], 175).

[6] Keith Ward, *God, Faith & The New Millennium: Christian Belief in an Age of Science* (Oxford: Oneworld Publications, 1998), 38–39.

[7] Ward, *God, Faith & The New Millennium*, 34; 42.

synonymous with the eternal Word of God and in the future "Christ will be manifest as the pleroma, in whom all finite realities will be fulfilled and brought to their proper function."[8] Humanity fits into this cosmic purpose by assisting God in the realization of his panentheism: "The vocation of humanity is to co-operate with God in working towards the full realization of matter as an embodiment and personal manifestation of the life of God."[9] In expanding his cosmic vision, Ward argues that extra-terrestrial beings (if they exist) would probably have their own incarnation of Christ, the universal liberator, and thus it would not be necessary for them to receive Jesus as savior.[10] He also speculates that humanity may eventually create machines that obtain actual consciousness. He sees no reason that these machines would not be incorporated into the universal program of God and "have as much reason to hope for immortality."[11] Ultimately, the final unity of all things will be realized in the "pleromal Christ": "In the pleromal Christ, all personal beings, of whatever life-form or galaxy, will be sharers."[12]

In keeping with his pluralism, Ward contends that divine revelation has occurred in many diverse cultures and histories apart from Christianity. In these extra-biblical revelations he discerns a common structure of religion that he identifies as (1) "liberation from self," and (2) "union with a reality of supreme intrinsic value."[13] In terms of biblical revelation, Ward argues that it is "implausible to see Christian revelation as the provision of inerrant information on irrefutable evidence. It is more properly seen as a historical disclosure of divine reality, articulated in imaginative and symbolic forms."[14] Along these lines he argues against a "naively literal interpretation" of the apocalyptic passages in the New Testament and instead prefers to spiritualize their meaning.[15] Thus, temporal symbols such as eternal punishment are interpreted as looking beyond historical time and speaking to God's eternal judgment on evil.[16] The cosmology of the end of the world is interpreted as speaking of the ultimate victory of the cosmic Christ. Ward warns against pressing "too far for literal truths about things we can scarcely envisage."[17]

The nuts and bolts of Ward's universalism is based upon what he perceives to be the real fundamentals of the Christian faith: love (1 Tim. 2:4) and unity (1 Cor. 15:22). As has already been seen, Ward's universalism is strongly wedded to his cosmic Christology and the notion that all things will be brought into unity through Christ. Regarding the salvation of those who resist God's will in this life, Ward argues for the reality of hell and the extension of a postmortem

---

[8] Ward, *God, Faith & The New Millennium*, 42.
[9] Ward, *God, Faith & The New Millennium*, 39.
[10] Ward, *God, Faith & The New Millennium*, 210–211.
[11] Ward, *God, Faith & The New Millennium*, 209–210.
[12] Ward, *God, Faith & The New Millennium*, 211.
[13] Keith Ward, *Religion and Revelation: A Theology of Revelation in the World's Religions* (Oxford: Clarendon Press, 1994), 341. As we shall see, these themes recapitulate the conclusions drawn by John Hick.
[14] Ward, *Religion and Revelation*, 281.
[15] Ward, *God, Faith & The New Millennium*, 206.
[16] Ward, *God, Faith & The New Millennium*, 206–207.
[17] Ward, *God, Faith & The New Millennium*, 207.

salvation to all who will receive it.[18] The existence of hell will be limited to the time it takes for each resistant person to embrace Christ.[19] Ward argues against the idea of there being literal flames in hell. Instead, he maintains that the pain one experiences in hell comes about as a result of the knowledge of the loss of a relationship with God.[20] He understands the suffering in hell to be both retributive and redemptive. In terms of election, Ward contends that the church itself has been chosen, but not to exclusive salvation. The election of the church serves as a "foreshadowing and a model for the glorification of the whole creation of God."[21]

Ward is circumspect about the possibility that someone might be able to resist God's will for his or her salvation. In affirming the sovereignty of human freedom he acknowledges, "We cannot know that all will come to repentance."[22] On the other hand, Ward is upbeat about God's ultimate ability to overcome all resistance:

> If God is omnipotent love, therefore, the divine purpose can be frustrated in many particulars, since divine love will not compel. But it cannot be frustrated in its final outcome, since God's power in its ultimately irresistible attraction, will not suffer love to be defeated. One cannot positively guarantee that this will happen. Yet it is an outcome one can rightly hope for and pray for, if God's universal love indeed wills the salvation of all created beings.[23]

Ward's vision of universalism linked to cosmic unity in the "pleromal Christ" has some striking similarities to certain forms of ancient Gnosticism.[24] Of course, the idea of the pleroma was developed heavily by the gnostics as a central element of their understanding of both deity and cosmology. The pleroma was typically envisioned as embodying the totality of all that is divine, which included the True God and the aeons, or eternal beings, who were said to self-emanate from the pleroma. While it is true that the gnostics believed that our world was fashioned into its current state by evil demiurges intent on separating people from the True God, it is also true that they believed that ultimately all things emanated from the divine pleroma. Jesus was generally identified as an aeon who was sent as an intermediary to the earth to bring the

---

[18] Keith Ward, *Morality, Autonomy, and God* (London: One World Publications, 2013), 206–07.

[19] Keith Ward, *Religion and Human Nature* (Oxford: Clarendon Press, 1998), 321. "It is the process of bringing a soul to see what its choices really entail, in the long run for itself and for others" (Ward, *Religion and Human Nature*, 250).

[20] Ward, *Religion and Human Nature*, 318–19.

[21] Keith Ward, *Religion and Creation* (Oxford: Clarendon Press, 1996), 49.

[22] Ward, *God, Faith & The New Millennium*, 213. See also Keith Ward, *Ethics and Christianity* (London: George Allen & Unwin, 1970), 250, as well as Ward, *Morality, Autonomy, and God*, 207.

[23] Ward, *Religion and Creation,* 265.

[24] A brief review of the essential doctrines of Gnosticism may be found in Kurt Rudolph's article in the *Anchor Bible Dictionary*, "Gnosticism," 2:1033–40.

knowledge of the True God to the people and to assist them in finding their way back to him.

When Ward talks about the divine Christ not being restricted to the human Jesus and the possibility of the divine Christ being manifested in several places and forms (even as an extra-terrestrial), he seems to be embracing the gnostic concept of emanation. His discussion about the divine Christ ultimately being "manifest as the pleroma" appears to confirm the conclusion.[25] On this view, Christ is capable of multiple emanations from the pleroma and in the end will become the embodiment of the pleroma. Ward fleshes out these ideas by talking about the gradual deification of matter itself through which the world evolves toward a sort of pleromic pantheism.[26] One could argue that in deifying matter that Ward has left Gnosticism behind. However, in the bigger picture it appears that he has provided a way for matter to be made holy and be reclaimed by the pleroma from which it originally emanated.[27] Thus, Ward's perspective may actually offer an improvement to the original gnostic formulation in that the true God's victory is total and complete.

The problem with this pleromal Christology is that it is antithetical to the incarnational Christology found in the New Testament. Ward argues that the essential character of the incarnation is that "Jesus has a unique form of relationship to God." In Ward's view he did not embody the "full reality" of God that transcends any finite form.[28] However, this is not the confession of the New Testament. In John 1:14 we are told that the divine Word *became* (ἐγένετο) flesh, not merely that the Word had a special relationship with a human being. In John 10:30 Jesus declared: "I and the Father are one." In Phil. 2:5 Paul speaks of the pre-incarnate Christ as existing in "the form of God." Col. 2:9 tells us that in Jesus all the fullness (*pan to plērōma*—πᾶν τὸ πλήρωμα) of the deity took on bodily form. Hebrews 1:3 indicates that Jesus is the exact representation of God's being (*charaktēr tēs hupostaseōs*—χαρακτὴρ τῆς ὑποστάσεως αὐτοῦ).

The idea of a limited relationship with an emanation from the pleroma does not do justice to these sorts of full-blown incarnational characterizations. Furthermore, the incarnational Christology found in the New Testament creates a problem for the notion that all people and all matter will eventually be unified into the being of the pleromal Christ. According to the New Testament, the Lord Jesus Christ already has a physical body that God went through great pains to resurrect. In the future, matter will exist apart from him, just as it always has. The Christian hope of the eschaton focuses on people in relationship with the Triune God (cf. Rev. 21:3–4). The new creation, as glorious as it will be, is just the backdrop against which that relationship shall be developed and explored.

---

[25] Ward, *God, Faith & The New Millennium*, 42.

[26] Ward, *God, Faith & The New Millennium*, 39.

[27] "The history of the cosmos is, in the Christian perspective, the history of a material universe that is being transfigured, over millions of years, into a perfected sacrament of Infinite Spirit" (Ward, *God, Faith & The New Millennium*, 39).

[28] Ward, *God, Faith & The New Millennium*, 189.

1.2. Ninian Smart and Steven Konstantine—Pluralism Embodied in the Trinity

Roderick Ninian Smart (1927–2001) was a university professor and an Anglican theologian who was a pioneer in the field of religious studies. Smart wrote extensively on the practices, patterns, and relationships of world religions. Steven Konstantine (b. 1957) is a Greek Orthodox theologian who has a profound interest in Trinitarian theology. Together Smart and Konstantine (hereafter referred to collectively as SK) produced a pluralistic systematic theology entitled *Christian Systematic Theology in a World Context*.[29] In this book they explore the concept of the Social Trinity as it relates to other religions in the world. Their thesis is that "if the divine is a Social Trinity then it is a Social Trinity that lies at the center of the world's religions."[30] Thus their pluralist hypothesis is linked to a strongly Christocentric core.

Our focus here will be primarily upon SK's unique version of universalism but it will help to first understand how they relate their doctrine of the Social Trinity to the revelations and practices of other religions. They identify three aspects of the divine life that come about as the result of the Triunity of God and the unique interactions that occur among the members of the Godhead: (1) the "infinity of the divine life," (2) the "plurality of the three persons," and (3) the "shared ego of the three."[31] These unique aspects of divine life are then used to explain various experiences of the divine that are found in other religions. The infinite quality of the Godhead is equated to a non-relational, impersonal sense of connection or oneness with the divine life that is so often spoken of in eastern religions such as Hinduism or Buddhism.[32] The plurality aspect of the Godhead is equated to various three-fold qualities found in other religions. For instance, in Hinduism it is related to the qualities of being, consciousness, and bliss. SK acknowledge that some of the resemblances in this area might be rather superficial. Finally, the shared ego or common will aspect of the Trinity is equated with the *bhkatism* or devotionalism found in various religions.[33] Tied into this aspect are personal experiences such as prophetic visions, conversion events, etc. that are experienced as an encounter with the unified, personal God.[34] Taken as a whole, this Trinitarian approach to pluralism provides a means of incorporating into the Triune Godhead the various experiences of the divine found in the world religions.

In elaborating their pluralism, SK are careful to note that while they acknowledge that all other religions retain a measure of divine revelation in their tradition, they believe that not all religions are created equal: "Not everyone comes into the world with equal access to any sacrament." In their view, Christianity takes pride of place among the religions of the world due to the fact that they believe that unique aspects, such as historical process and the idea of the atonement, could not have been incorporated into eastern

---

[29] Ninian Smart and Steven Konstantine, *Christian Systematic Theology in a World Context* (Minneapolis, Minn.: Fortress, 1991).
[30] Smart and Konstantine, *Christian Systematic Theology*, 296.
[31] Smart and Konstantine, *Christian Systematic Theology*, 174.
[32] Smart and Konstantine, *Christian Systematic Theology*, 174.
[33] Smart and Konstantine, *Christian Systematic Theology*, 176.
[34] Smart and Konstantine, *Christian Systematic Theology*, 176–77.

revelation.[35] SK are unapologetic for granting to Christianity a certain primacy over the other religions. In their view, not all cultures offer the ideal soil for the development of revelation. Along these lines, they contrast their view to the egalitarian tendencies of the pluralist trailblazer, John Hick. They understand Hick's insistence on religious equality to be myopic and they conclude that he is "asking for a kind of 'justice' that is unimaginable."[36]

Despite their rejecting the Bible as having any "doctrinal or narrative authority," SK spend a fair amount of time elaborating their unique understanding of the doctrines of the Trinity and of the Atonement.[37] The Trinity, as we have seen, is viewed as being the key to understanding God's interaction with humanity. The atonement of Christ on the cross is important for SK's theology in that it provides for the purification of sin as well as a re-establishing of communion with God.[38] Christ's death on the cross is pictured as a gift of love from God rather than a dying "in place of" individual sinners.

SK's universalism is constructed around a panentheistic view of the eschaton that focuses on union in the cosmic Christ:

> Universal *mokṣa* will on our view have as its focus the social Trinity. The liberated self will be assimilated to the loving relations of the divine Brahman. All will be adopted children of Christ, and will live within his organic body. To them the divine will be all in all.[39]

The path to this cosmic unity will include "other levels of existence beyond death in which spiritual growth can take place."[40] The doctrine of eternal punishment is emphatically denied. For those who have been "especially wicked in this life" there will be a "purgatorial purification" in which divine love will meet with the cruelest human being: "Even Hitler and Stalin will feel the outpouring of the Lord's love."[41] In putting forward their hypothesis of other levels in the afterlife, SK hint at the possibility of reincarnation, however, their phraseology on this point remains vague and difficult to interpret.[42] In considering the possibility that alien life has evolved on other planets, SK speculate that this would not change the centrality of Christ in the eschaton. In their view self-conscious alien beings would be drawn into world unity in which "the Spirit of the one Saviour would rule."[43]

SK offer us an interesting interpretation of universalism that combines a Christocentric core with a pluralistic embrace. No doubt, a hard pluralist like John Hick would look in askance at such a scheme. However, it can be

---

[35] Smart and Konstantine, *Christian Systematic Theology*, 293–94.
[36] Smart and Konstantine, *Christian Systematic Theology*, 294. This aspect of Hick's plurocentric universalism will be examined at the end of this chapter.
[37] Smart and Konstantine, *Christian Systematic Theology*, 47; 149–99; 284–88.
[38] Smart and Konstantine, *Christian Systematic Theology*, 287.
[39] Smart and Konstantine, *Christian Systematic Theology*, 296.
[40] Smart and Konstantine, *Christian Systematic Theology*, 294.
[41] Smart and Konstantine, *Christian Systematic Theology*, 296.
[42] Smart and Konstantine, *Christian Systematic Theology*, 295.
[43] Smart and Konstantine, *Christian Systematic Theology*, 283–84.

appreciated that SK have tried to remain true to their Christian roots, while at the same time expanding their vision of God to include all other expressions.

From a historical point of view, SK's unique approach of folding all experiences of the divine into the various expressions of the Triune Godhead has certain parallels to the approach taken by Marcellus of Ancyra (d. c. 374) and later on by the Brothers and Sisters of the Free Spirit who followed in the footsteps of Amaury of Bène (d. c. 1207). Both Marcellus and Amaury divided world history into three ages that corresponded to the three persons of the Trinity.[44] In essence both were attempting to incorporate the entire history of humanity into the Godhead. What we have with SK is a similar approach, however, rather than the incorporation of human history into the Godhead, we have the incorporation of the human experience of the divine. Marcellus and Amaury were driven by the desire to emphasize God's immanence in all human history. SK are driven by the desire to emphasize God's immanence in all religious experience.

The Achilles' heel of SK's approach has to do with theological justification. At the beginning of their exposition they declare:

> It happens that critical enquiry into the Biblical texts has reached such a point that there is no general agreement on precisely what Jesus said, or what the early church believed about him. The liberal-academic solvents have gnawed away at the rusts of Biblical certainty. It therefore seems nonsense to pretend that the Bible has doctrinal or narrative authority . . . [W]e shall not, in this attempt at a Christian *darśana*, cite Biblical proof texts as if the critical work of the last century and a half did not exist, nor will we cite them as if there were any kind of absolute agreement as to what they reveal about Jesus.[45]

Given this dim view of Scripture, their elaborate exposition of the Christian doctrine of the Trinity and their intricate defense of the doctrine of the atonement seems to be a non-sequitur. If it is really true that we cannot know what Jesus said or what the early church believed about him, then how can he be incorporated into the Triune Godhead and become the central figure in their panentheistic eschaton? It is as if they have sawed off the limb of biblical authority and then climbed back out on thin air, pretending that it still exists. The doctrines of the Trinity and of the atonement have posed monumental difficulties for theologians who held the entire Bible to be inspired (witness the titanic clashes in the early church as these doctrines were established) let alone

---

[44] Of course there are parallels here also to the theology of Joachim of Fiore (c. 1135–1202) who was not a universalist. As we saw in the last chapter, more recently Jürgen Moltmann has taken up Joachim's view of the kingdoms with the addition of a fourth, the Kingdom of Glory: "Finally, the kingdom of glory must be understood as the consummation of the Father's creation, as the universal establishment of the Son's liberation, and as the fulfillment of the Spirit's indwelling . . . The kingdom of glory is the goal—enduring and uninterrupted—for all of God's works and ways in history" (Moltmann, *The Trinity and the Kingdom: The Doctrine of God*, 212).

[45] Smart and Konstantine, *Christian Systematic Theology*, 47.

for theologians who claim that none of it is inspired. Without the authority of the Bible to under gird their doctrinal claims it seems that the rest is just speculation or wishful thinking.

It does not help matters when SK invokes the metaphor of biography to claim that there is a "developing revelation" within the churches and among believers today that might actually relate a clearer picture of Jesus now than the one found in the New Testament.[46] Mystical experiences and ecstatic visions are no substitute for eyewitness accounts. The fact remains that the Jesus event occurred some 2000 years ago. It seems an unassailable proposition that those who are most qualified to speak about it are those who actually witnessed it and had first-hand knowledge of what actually happened. Even in our own lifetimes, the irresistible march of time dims our memories and fogs our recollections. In terms of establishing precisely who Jesus is and what happened in his life, it would seem that our best source remains the closest source, which would be the New Testament.

These issues aside, we can appreciate SK's desire to stress the immanence of God in his relationship with human beings. This is much the same point that is made in John 16:8 where Jesus tells his disciples that the Holy Spirit will be sent into the world to convict the world "of sin, and of righteousness, and of justice." The Bible presents to us a God who interacts with his creation and with his creatures. In the bigger picture, SK's proposal is an effort to affirm this important aspect of Christian theology.

2. Plurocentric Universalism

As we have already noted, true plurocentric universalism dispenses entirely with an orthodox soteriology that focuses on the centrality of Christ. Instead, pluralists accept the idea that salvation will be mediated through many different means and religions. A key issue for true plurocentric universalists is how they deal with the concept of salvation itself. The problem can be summarized by asking this important question: In what way can we say that people are universally saved by various religions if those religions are aiming at entirely different goals and outcomes? Some approach the problem in a rather naïve fashion, simply assuming that all religions are automatically aiming at the same thing. This is the sort of over-simplified approach taken by a pair of Quaker pastors, Philip Gulley and James Mulholland, who have co-written two popular books advocating a naïve form of plurocentric universalism.[47] In their version of pluralism it is just assumed that all religions are aiming for the same goals and outcomes and it is for this very reason that their plurocentric universalism fails. Gulley and Mulholland betray a keen lack of awareness of the rich diversity of tradition and purpose that exists in other religions and just how imperialistic their perspective may appear to the adherents of other religions.

---

[46] Smart and Konstantine, *Christian Systematic Theology*, 48–49.
[47] Philip Gulley and James Mulholland, *If Grace Is True: Why God Will Save Every Person* (San Francisco: HarperSanFrancisco, 2003); Philip Gulley and James Mulholland, *If God Is Love: Rediscovering Grace in an Ungracious World* (San Francisco: HarperSanFrancisco, 2004).

On the other hand, there are those who realize that the world religions are aiming at many disparate objectives and make efforts to deal with that difficult reality. Those pluralists who understand the difficulty of synchronizing the various salvific claims made by the world religions have advanced two essential approaches to the problem. The first is harmonization. With this solution an effort is made to show that the disparate salvific objectives do actually correspond or harmonize together in some meaningful way. This is the approach taken by Protestant theologian John Hick and Catholic theologians Raimundo Panikkar and Paul Knitter. The second approach taken to the problem is acceptance. In this case the diversity of objectives is accepted as a brute fact of life that must be dealt with straight up without any effort being made to strip the religions of their uniqueness. This is the approach taken by Catholic theologian Hans Küng.

In this section on Protestant plurocentric universalism we will be examining the harmonizing approach of John Hick.

2.1. John Hick— **Pluralism and the Copernican Revolution of the Real**
There can be no doubt that the most prolific and influential contributor to the concept of plurocentric universalism has been the British philosopher John Hick (1922–2012). Hick is considered by many to be one of the most influential philosophers of religion in the twentieth century. He held teaching positions in both Britain and the United States[48] and he wrote numerous books and articles that elaborate in great detail the various aspects of his plurocentric universalism.[49]

Hick's journey toward pluralistic conclusions began with his conversion to conservative Christianity while he was studying at University College, Hull. He then moved on to Edinburgh University in 1940 where his studies were interrupted by the war. During the war Hick became a conscientious objector

---

[48] The best source of biographical information on John Hick may be found in his autobiography, *John Hick: An Autobiography* (Oxford: Oneworld, 2002). What I discuss here is taken primarily from that source. The official website for John Hick may be found at: http://www.johnhick.org.uk/jsite/. (Accessed on November 28, 2014.)

[49] The corpus of John Hick's work is substantial and the literature it has spawned is huge. What is greatly needed at this point is the creation of a research bibliography. Critical introductions to Hick's thought may be found in the following: David Cheetham, *John Hick: A Critical Introduction and Reflection* (Aldershot, UK: Ashgate, 2003); Gavin D'Costa, *John Hick's Theology of Religions: A Critical Evaluation* (Lanham, Md.: University Press of America, 1987); Paul Rhodes Eddy, *John Hick's Pluralist Philosophy of World Religions* (Aldershot, UK: Ashgate, 2003); R. Douglas Geivett, *Evil and the Evidence for God: The Challenge of John Hick's Theodicy* (Philadelphia: Temple University Press, 1993); Lindsay Hall, *Swinburne's Hell and Hick's Universalism: Are We Free to Reject God?* (Aldershot, UK: Ashgate, 2003); Terry Richard Mathis, *Against John Hick: An Examination of His Philosophy of Religion* (Lanham, Md.: University Press of America, 1985); John Mesle, *John Hick's Theodicy: A Process Humanist Critique* (London: Macmillan, 1991); David S. Nah, "A Critical Evaluation of John Hick's Theology of Religious Pluralism" (Ph.D. dissertation, Claremont Graduate University, 2005); Kenneth Rose, *Knowing the Real: John Hick on the Cognitivity of Religions and Religious Pluralism* (New York: Peter Lang, 1996); Stetson, *Pluralism and Particularity in Religious Belief.*

and served as an ambulance driver; after the war he returned to Edinburgh and to his studies in philosophy. It was at this time that he became generally dissatisfied with fundamentalist Christianity and began a gradual slide toward liberalism. By the mid-1950s Hick had earned a doctorate in philosophy of religion from Oxford and had abandoned belief in the verbal inspiration of the Bible as well as the literal interpretation of much of what it says. Hick worked in America for several years after obtaining his doctorate, teaching at Cornell University (1956) and Princeton Theological Seminary (1959). In 1963 he moved back to England and took up a lectureship at Cambridge.

In 1967 Hick was appointed to the H.G. Wood professorship at the University of Birmingham. Birmingham was one of the most ethnically diverse cities in England and, due to his chosen field of study, Hick found himself getting increasingly involved with the multi-cultural community. As a result of this, he had a great deal of personal interaction with people from many other religious faiths. He wrote: "It was not so much new thoughts as new experiences that drew me, as a philosopher, into issues of religious pluralism, and as a Christian into inter-faith dialogue."[50] These experiences led Hick to write his groundbreaking book, *God and the Universe of Faiths*, which in many ways prefigures and anticipates the later trajectory and development of his thought.[51] In *God and the Universe of Faiths* Hick asserted that a "Copernican revolution" needed to occur in Christian theology. The problem, according to Hick, was that if Christian exclusivism was true then the large majority of the human race, who were born outside of Christendom, were eternally doomed: "Can we accept the conclusion that the God of love who seeks to save all mankind has nevertheless ordained that men must be saved in such a way that only a small minority can in fact receive this salvation?"[52] In other words, could God hold an accident of geography against the majority of people? Hick saw this as both illogical and immoral. It was Hick's rejection of such a conclusion that gave rise to his embrace of pluralism and the development of his unique expression of plurocentric universalism.

In demanding his "Copernican revolution" Hick analogized the Christocentric theology that existed within Christianity to the old Ptolemaic cosmology that had the universe revolving around the earth. What was needed was a paradigm shift to a theocentric view that allowed the religions, including Christianity, to revolve around God. He explained the Copernican revolution in this way: "It involves a shift from the dogma that Christianity is at the center to the realization that it is *God* who is at the center, and that all the religions of mankind, including our own, serve and revolve around him."[53]

In reviewing world-wide religious history, including the development of the major religious traditions, Hick concluded that "from the standpoint of religious faith the only reasonable hypothesis is that this historical picture represents a movement of divine self-revelation to mankind." These revelations were

---

[50] John Hick, *Disputed Questions in Philosophy of Religions* (New York: Palgrave, 2001), 141.

[51] John Hick, *God and the Universe of Faiths: Essays in the Philosophy of Religion* (London: Macmillan, 1973).

[52] Hick, *God and the Universe of Faiths*, 122.

[53] Hick, *God and the Universe of Faiths*, 131.

responded to by people based upon "ethnic, geographical, climatic, economic, sociological, and cultural circumstances."[54] In these circumstances lies the answer to the differences found in the world religions. Humanity had responded in "imperfect human analogies, but none of that is 'the truth, the whole truth, and nothing but the truth.'"[55] Thus no religion had the right to claim possession of the absolute truth; each one is viewed as possessing only an incomplete and imperfect revelation.

In rounding out his concept of the Copernican revolution, Hick argued for universal salvation mediated through many religions and conditions.[56] Because the circumstances of a person's life (e.g. geographical, chronological, cultural, biological, etc . . .) virtually guarantee that it will be impossible for God to fulfill his purposes for that person in this life, Hick argues, "It would thus be intolerably unjust for the victim of adverse circumstances to be eternally penalized. From the Christian premise of the goodness and love of God we must accordingly infer continued human life beyond death leading eventually to the far-distant fulfillment of the purpose for which we exist."[57] In the eschaton, Hick envisioned the doing away with all religious systems. When eternal life had been obtained, there would be no need for "a way" as the pilgrim had finally "arrived."[58]

The above outline represents the initial stage in Hick's development of plurocentric universalism.[59] In an effort to expand the vision of his Copernican revolution, Hick elaborated his meaning in much greater detail as time progressed—sometimes making significant changes to his theology as he developed his thought and as he sought to answer an ever-growing chorus of hostile critics. Perhaps, the most obvious and most significant modification that Hick made to his initial theology had to do with his concept of God. Some of the sharpest criticisms of Hick pointed to the fact that the Christian concept of a God of love did not correspond to the concept of the divine found in other religions. For instance, the Hindu concept of an ultimate reality, which is bereft of personal attributes, seems to have no correspondence to the personal, Christian God. Similarly, the ultimate enlightenment, which is pursued by most

---

[54] Hick, *God and the Universe of Faiths,* 138.

[55] Hick, *God and the Universe of Faiths*, 140.

[56] Hick had already put forward a case for universal salvation related to solving the problem of theodicy in his book *Evil and the God of Love*, 377–88. In this presentation, Hick endorsed the idea of a postmortem salvation combined with a hell of limited duration that was both purgatorial and remedial. Here we see this view beginning to undergo the change necessary to bring it into alignment with his newly found pluralism. As we shall see shortly, Hick will develop this idea of progress towards God's goal for our perfection in terms of a possible progression of many lives through which the goal can be gradually obtained.

[57] Hick, *God and the Universe of Faiths*, 192.

[58] Hick, *God and the Universe of Faiths*, 147.

[59] We must be careful to make a distinction between the theology of the later and much more mature John Hick, and his earlier preliminary work. Along these lines, Lindsey Hall's analysis of Hick's universalism in the book *Swinburne's Hell and Hick's Universalism* is a bit anachronistic in that it reconstructs Hick's universalism primarily from his earlier writings. Hick's later views underwent significant changes that modify some of his earlier declarations.

Buddhists, does not seem to correlate in any way to the Christian concept of God. Hick was criticized for being ignorant of other religions and even of cultural imperialism—the notion that he was trying to force other religions to fit his western mold. Faced with the monumental problem of correspondence, Hick put forward his famous theory of "the Real" (a new name for deity) in which he posited a Kantian influenced epistemology that differentiates between the perceived world (*phenomena*) and the world as it actually is (*noumena*). In Hick's view, the seeming contradiction between a personal and impersonal deity can be explained through the fact that we do not comprehend the transcendent Real as it really is.[60] We experience the Real through a distorted perception, mediated by the trappings of this life and our historical and cultural attachments. If we could see the Real in its fullness, Hick was sure that we would see that there is no contradiction.

Carrying this distinction between perception and reality into the realm of explaining incompatible truth claims between religions, Hick makes a distinction between what is mythological truth and literal truth.[61] In his view, all religions engage in mythological talk about the Real. These myths are not to be discounted in that they have the power to evoke potent personal transformations and responses to the Real. However, the myths are not to be taken literally either. The value of the myths lie in their ability to bring connection and change. Mythological truth claims about the Real are not to be taken literally in that they represent the *phenomena* not the *noumena* regarding talk about the Real.[62] Thus, the seeming incompatibility between certain truth claims about the Real can be attributed to our imprecise perception rather than an irresolvable contradiction.

The development of this perspective in Hick's theology and Christology was gradual. Already in *God and the Universe of Faiths* Hick had made the claim that "it is extremely unlikely that Jesus thought of himself, or that his first disciples thought of him, as God incarnate."[63] In support of this, Hick accepted the standard liberal interpretation that the doctrine of the incarnation was "a doctrine developed by the church."[64] This idea was elaborated on in a series of books and articles in which the concept of the divinity of Christ was systematically attacked.[65] In 1977 Hick edited a symposium entitled *The Myth of God Incarnate*, which called into question the deity of Christ and examined whether such a doctrine was essential to Christianity.[66] In his contribution to the book, Hick argued that the incarnation of Christ was put forward in the New Testament in mythological and metaphorical language and must be recognized

---

[60] John Hick, *An Interpretation of Religion: Human Responses to the Transcendent*, 2nd edition (1989; New Haven, Conn.: Yale University Press, 2004), 9–11; 240–49.

[61] Hick, *An Interpretation of Religion*, 343–61.

[62] Hick, *An Interpretation of Religion*, 348; 350.

[63] Hick, *God and the Universe of Faiths*, 114. See also John Hick, *God Has Many Names* (Philadelphia: Westminster, 1980), 72–75.

[64] Hick, *God and the Universe of Faiths*, 115.

[65] For a chronological account of the development of Hick's Christology see Chester Gillis, *A Question of Belief: John Hick's Pluralistic Theory of Salvation* (London: Macmillan, 1989), 72–85.

[66] John Hick, ed., *The Myth of God Incarnate* (Philadelphia: SCM Press, 1977).

for what it is. He insisted that Christianity must "outgrow its theological fundamentalism, its literal interpretation of the idea of incarnation, as it has largely outgrown its biblical fundamentalism."[67] These ideas were greatly expanded and elaborated in his book *The Metaphor of God Incarnate: Christology in a Pluralistic Age*. In the book Hick maintains that if we accept the incarnation as being metaphorical, then "it becomes entirely natural to say that all the great religious figures have in their different ways 'incarnated' the ideal of human life lived in response to divine Reality."[68] In Hick's view, Jesus is just one great religious leader among many and biblical revelation is just one mythological revelation among many. As he put it in *The Myth of Christian Uniqueness*: "Christianity is not the one and only way of salvation, but one among several."[69]

Hick's theological justification for such an assertion is really an exercise in comparative religions and what he calls the religious "experience-of."[70] Granting that each religion has validity, Hick looks for common themes among them all. He discerns two primary goals: (1) salvation/liberation as human transformation, and (2) unity with the Real.[71] With these goals in mind he wants to ask, how can we distinguish between which revelations are "veridical" and which are "delusory"? The answer is found in religious experience: "The central criterion can only be the long-term transformative effect on the experiencer."[72] By looking at how the revealer's life was changed and transformed "from natural self-centeredness to a re-centering in God, the Real, the Ultimate" we can judge the validity of what they have to say.[73] Thus, inspiration is judged through the lens of common features and transformational power.

Related to this perspective is Hick's opinion that the exclusivist claim of Christianity is extremely myopic and dangerous—something that must be systematically rebutted and essentially eliminated. He argues that this claim, taken literally, has led to a multitude of evils:

> This conviction was used to validate Europe's conquest of most of what we call today the Third World, carrying off many of its inhabitants as slaves, exploiting its economies and destroying its cultures. The idea that Jesus was God likewise validated the Christian persecution of the Jews, who were held guilty of deicide, thus creating a deep-seated prejudice within the European psyche which continued in secular anti-Semitism of the nineteenth and twentieth centuries, culminating in the holocaust of the

---

[67] Hick, "Jesus and the World Religions," 183–84.

[68] John Hick, *The Metaphor of God Incarnate: Christology in a Pluralistic Age* (Louisville, Ky.: Westminster/John Knox, 1993), 98.

[69] John Hick, "The Non-absoluteness of Christianity," in John Hick and Paul F. Knitter, eds., *The Myth of Christian Uniqueness: Towards a Pluralistic Theology of Religions* (Maryknoll, N.Y.: Orbis, 1987), 33.

[70] Hick, *God has Many Names*, 79.

[71] Hick, *An Interpretation of Religion*, 32–50.

[72] Hick, *The Fifth Dimension*, 169; 173. See also John Hick, *Between Faith and Doubt: Dialogues on Religion and Reason* (New York: Palgrave McMillian: 2010), 39–61.

[73] Hick, *The Fifth Dimension*, 179.

1940s. When taken literally, the Christian myth becomes a supremacist ideology which, in conjunction with human greed, pride and prejudice, has used the name of Christ to justify profoundly unchristlike acts.[74]

The goal of Hick's symposium, *The Myth of Christian Uniqueness: Towards a Pluralistic Theology of Religions*, was to argue for a re-interpretation of Christian uniqueness, "one so different that, perhaps, some will say that the word 'uniqueness' is no longer appropriate."[75] In Hick's view, the myth of Christian uniqueness has to be done away with for the betterment of the world. This leads Hick into an us-against-them attitude when it comes to dealing with conservative Christians. Here his tolerance turns to intolerance and much of what he has to say about conservative Christianity is pejorative and filled with deprecatory polemic.

The net result of Hick's system of pluralism has been the production of a strain of universalism that plays no favorites among world religions and argues against Christian particularism of any kind. Hick affirms that in the end all will be saved; the path that people start out on makes little difference as all paths are useful to God. In his book *Death and Eternal Life* Hick maintains that human nature is basically oriented toward God and that it is this basic orientation that guarantees the eventual salvation of all in full accordance with human freedom.[76] In speaking of the afterlife, Hick speculates that after death a soul will enter into the *bardo* stage, a stage of bodiless existence and intense reflection on the life just lived.[77] From the bardo realm, a soul emerges ready for a new life experience and continued growth. He reasons that next step in the process will involve "many lives in many worlds."[78] The essential idea is that through these additional lives God will continue his work within each person, moving them toward perfection.[79] He also speculates that our additional lives may be lived out in other worlds, some of them, perhaps, quite different from the present one.[80] What will be the eventual end of this process? What will be the final destination of humanity? One cannot know with certainty. It seems that Hick favors the Eastern solution where individuality melts into the Real, leaving "the wholeness of ultimately perfected humanity beyond the existence of separate egos."[81] However, he allows for the possibility that individuality is maintained: "As to whether even this deeper self will have an endless separate appearance, or will finally become one with the eternal Reality, we at present neither know nor need to know."[82] In arriving at this uncertain conclusion, Hick

---

[74] Hick, *The Fifth Dimension*, 243.

[75] Hick and Knitter, *The Myth of Christian Uniqueness*, vii.

[76] Hick, *Death and Eternal Life*, 254.

[77] Hick, *Death and Eternal Life*, 399–414. In constructing the bardo stage, Hick synthesizes the teachings of the *Bardo Thödol* (the *Tibetan Book of the Dead*) and the works of H.H. Price.

[78] Hick, *Death and Eternal Life*, 414–24, 456–58; Hick, *The Fifth Dimension*, 250–55.

[79] "And if one is not enough, then more than one, perhaps a long succession of future lives" (Hick, *The Fifth Dimension*, 251).

[80] Hick, *The Fifth Dimension*, 251. Hick, *Between Faith and Doubt*, 150–58.

[81] Hick, *Death and Eternal Life*, 464; Hick, *The Fifth Dimension*, 260.

[82] Hick, *The Fifth Dimension*, 255; 260.

maintains the ambiguity between a personal and non-personal Real and between personal and non-personal ends.

Many have argued that in developing his pluralistic hypothesis that John Hick has left the realm of Christianity entirely.[83] However, Hick's view is that he writes as a Christian and that his pluralism is an attempt at offering a Christian contribution to global theology.[84] Whether it is valid for him to claim the mantle of Christianity or not, one cannot deny that he honestly believes himself to be a Christian philosopher/theologian. His inclusion in this study recognizes the fact that he wishes to be recognized as such and that he has always been taken to be a serious dialogue partner within Christian theological circles.

Hick's theology is distinctive primarily because of its egalitarian approach towards soteriology. In many ways it is the ultimate expression of Enlightenment philosophy and ideals. Religious pluralism, the equality of all people, a reliance on human reason to pass judgment on divine revelation—all of these things were essential features of the Enlightenment, and they are also essential features of Hick's vision. In a very real sense, Hick's project is the ultimate Enlightenment project and it is perhaps in this point that Hick's plurocentric universalism is at its most vulnerable.

An important part of his argument has to do with providing a rational means by which religious systems might be compared and assigned a greater or lesser relative value. Hick argues that "the generic concept of salvation/liberation, which takes a different specific form in each of the great traditions, is that of transformation of human existence from self-centeredness to Reality-centeredness."[85] Therefore, he contends that the function of "post-axial" religions is to "create contexts within which the transformation of human existence from self-centeredness to Reality-centeredness can take place."[86] He then concludes that religious systems, including their specific revelations, "have greater or lesser value according as they promote or hinder the salvific transformation."[87] Thus Hick is really saying that the relative level of divine presence within a religious system is to be judged through its relative effectiveness vis-à-vis a this-worldly transformation from self-centeredness to Real-centeredness: "For although we cannot describe absolute Reality as it is in itself, we *can* describe its effects on the lives of men and women."[88]

Aside from the fact that there are considerable problems with Hick's assertion that the great religious traditions in the world are all aiming at this same transformational goal,[89] there is the issue of his confusing basic human nature with divine presence. The Apostle Paul argues in Rom. 2:14–15 that the Gentiles "who do not have the Law do instinctively the things of the Law" because, he says, they "show the work of the Law written in their hearts, their

---

[83] Cf. Parry and Partridge, *Universal Salvation*, xxi.

[84] Hick, "The Non-absoluteness of Christianity," 18; Hick, *Death and Eternal Life*, 27.

[85] Hick, *An Interpretation of Religion*, 36.

[86] Hick, *An Interpretation of Religion*, 300.

[87] Hick, *An Interpretation of Religion*, 300.

[88] Hick, *The Fifth Dimension*, 171.

[89] On this see J. A. DiNoia's critique in his article "Varieties of Religious Aims: Beyond Exclusivism, Inclusivism, and Pluralism," 249–74.

conscience bearing witness, and their thoughts alternately accusing or else defending them." In other words, Paul argues that all human beings have a certain common instinct or impulse to do what is right and this is coupled to a common conscience or moral center that has been built into them by God. If this is true, is it unusual that we find that people universally have a sense of right and wrong and that certain behaviors such as murder, rape, and the torture of innocent children are collectively viewed as evil behaviors by the entire human race? Is it unusual that we find that people have an almost universal desire for change, for righteous living, for self-transformation? Paul says that people desire these things because God made them that way. This is their instinct; this is their nature. Is it then unusual that we find people trying to act on this instinct?[90]

When Hick says that he finds a common feature among major world religions in that they attempt to affect a transformation away from selfishness in their adherents, he has simply confirmed what the Apostle Paul asserted so long ago about the essential constitution of human nature. The problem is that Hick has mistakenly confused this desire and impulse for change with the notion of divine presence. He mistakes the essential *design* of humanity for a divine *communion or communication* with humanity. From the Apostle Paul's point of view, these two things were mutually exclusive. To know that people universally desire change and are pursuing it says nothing about whether God is actually present in their religious system. It says nothing about whether God has actually spoken to them, if indeed he has.

Furthermore, in speaking of the desire for a deeper meaning in life, Solomon declared in Ecc. 3:11 that God has "set eternity in their heart." Thus, it is natural for human beings to desire something better than this life, something beyond this life—even for human beings to desire unity with deity—because, as Solomon declares, God has "set" just such a desire for something beyond us in our hearts. This natural inclination of human nature, which Hick himself acknowledges exists, leads people to pursue a relationship with the divine. Hick sees in this pursuit another means of measuring divine presence, but again, he has confused the essential *design* of humanity for a divine *communion or communication* with humanity. To know that people universally seek unity with the divine says nothing about whether God is actually present in their religious system. It says nothing about whether God has actually spoken to them, if indeed he has. The relative level of the "transformation" that Hick speaks of can just as easily be viewed as instinct driven as opposed to divinity driven. If people have been designed by God to desire change and transformation and to desire something greater than themselves, then, from a biblical point of view, the instinctive seeking of these things is the confirmation of the inherent design of human nature and not proof of God's presence. In reality these things just confirm what the Bible has said about human nature. They are misapplied when

---

[90] We note here the store shelves full of self-help books and video presentations as well as the huge sums of money spent on psychiatrists and psychologists. On any given day or weekend there are a myriad of classes and meetings and conferences in any large city that one might attend to affect a transformation in one's life. The existence of these things also serve to validate Paul's observations.

used as a measuring rod by which divine presence can be validated. If this is true, then the primary criterion that Hick uses as justification for his theological method is called into serious question.

Another problem loosely related to the above is Hick's insistence that most religious discourse is presented in the language of myth. Hick claims to be a "critical-realist,"[91] however his insistence on relegating many essential religious truth claims to the status of myth seems to call this claim into question and to move him much closer to the anti-realist camp. His opposition to the incarnational theology found in the New Testament is a notable example of this. He argues for an interpretation that denies that God's incarnation in Christ has "a literal physical, psychological, or metaphysical meaning."[92] However, it appears that the writers of the New Testament had already encountered similar sorts of arguments in the first century and had already countered them by restating the doctrine of the incarnation in the most literal terms possible. For instance, in 1 John 4:1–3 the writer declares: "Beloved, do not believe every spirit, but test the spirits, whether they are from God; because many false prophets have gone out into the world. By this you know the Spirit of God: Every spirit that confesses that Jesus Christ has come in the flesh [I read it as "incarnated"] is from God, and every spirit that does not confess that Jesus has come in the flesh is not from God." And again this point is confirmed in 2 John 7: "For many deceivers have gone out into the world, those who do not acknowledge Jesus Christ *as* coming in the flesh [incarnated]. This is the deceiver and the antichrist."

Finally, S. Mark Heim in his book *Salvations: Truth and Difference in Religion* has put forward a criticism of pluralism that is really an objection to the heavy-handed approach that most pluralists take toward the religions they study.[93] In essence Heim notes that pluralists like Hick are not pluralistic enough. They want to grant equality to all religions and their various expressions, but they also want to eliminate the exclusivist elements in these religions so that they comport well with pluralism. However, Heim wants to ask, is this not yet another from of exclusivism parading as pluralism? It appears that what Hick has really come up with is a pluralistic exclusivism that will not countenance any other option but pluralism. Understood in the context of true pluralism, Hick's consistent attacks on traditional Christianity and his deep seated desire to eliminate certain fundamentals of the faith appears to be far less pluralistic than he makes it out to be. A true pluralist would recognize the fundamental importance of the teachings of the New Testament, as the majority of Christians have understood them for close to two millennia. A true pluralist would take seriously the early creeds and the long confessional history of the church. A true pluralist would celebrate the diversity that historical Christianity brings to the religious world without feeling compelled to try to assail it and fundamentally change it.

---

[91] Hick, *An Interpretation of Religion*, 172–75.
[92] Hick, *The Metaphor of God Incarnate*, 104.
[93] S. Mark Heim, *Salvations: Truth and Difference in Religion* (Maryknoll, N.Y.: Orbis, 1995), 129–57.

The value of Hick's work lies in his desire to examine the role of Christianity in the universe of faiths. While many might not agree with his conclusions, there can be no doubt that John Hick has moved this issue to the center of the contemporary theological debate and forced theologians to formulate a cogent response to it. This is a good thing in an ever shrinking world where a well-reasoned response to other religions is vital. Hick's enduring legacy will be that of a pioneer who helped to open up an entirely new frontier of research and discussion.

3. Conclusion

All three of the universalist proposals placed before us in this chapter are notable for their efforts to redefine the very nature and composition of God. Keith Ward presents to us a vision of the pleromal Christ that is more of an all absorbing reality than an actual personal being. Ninian Smart and Steven Konstantine expand the notion of the Godhead to cosmic proportions, presenting us with a social Trinity that participates in every religious expression of man. John Hick posits "the Real" as a new conception of God that not only captures the essence of man's limited and imperfect efforts to define it, but also embraces the entirety of all possible reality.

In contemplating each of these reconstructions it becomes clear that the real issue at hand is what to do with Jesus Christ. Classic Trinitarian formulations that have Jesus participating in the Godhead are philosophically at odds with pluralism and so we note that what these approaches all have in common is the significant redefinition of Jesus' role vis-à-vis the Godhead. As we move away from the moderating forms and into full-blown plurocentric universalism, what we get is not just a reformulation, but rather the complete elimination of Jesus from the Godhead. This makes sense from a pluralistic perspective in that all forms of particularism must be eradicated in order for the proposal to truly work. From a biblical point of view, however, such an exercise raises important questions about the true nature of Christianity.

In the end, it remains an open question as to whether what is left over after such a maneuver can rightly be called "Christian." Certainly John Hick believes that his reconstruction is a faithful one. However, when one eliminates virtually every major doctrine taught by the Apostles in the New Testament regarding Christ, the question must be pondered. How much of a car can one eliminate before it is no longer a car? How much of a house can one remove before it is no longer a house? How far can one chop away at the essentials of the faith before the chopping results in an entirely new religion?

As we move on now to examine the Catholic contribution to the debate, these sorts of questions will come to the fore. As a church with a long history of confessional orthodoxy the Catholic Church is supremely interested in maintaining doctrinal purity and a consistent self-image. The resurgence of universalism, especially since the Second Vatican Council, has been a cause for both conflict and debate as well as a catalyst for the further clarification of Church dogma.

PART 3

CONTEMPORARY EXPRESSIONS SINCE 1960

THE CATHOLIC CONTRIBUTION

CHAPTER 6

Christocentric Approaches

In convening the Second Vatican Council in 1962 Pope John XXIII called for an "aggiornamento" (refreshing/renewal) within the heart and soul of the Catholic Church. The Council met for two months at a time over the next four years and produced a series of documents that have had a profound and lasting effect upon the Church and that have, by and large, brought in to being the aggiornamento that Pope John XXIII had so passionately hoped for. For many within the Church, the renewal has been a welcome one—a fresh infusion of life and movement into a body that had long languished within the straightjacket of unyielding tradition. For others the renewal has been a disturbing development—an opening of Pandora's Box that has turned loose a host of ills upon the Church, ills that had in the past been subdued and safely contained.[1]

Karl Rahner called the Second Vatican Council "the beginning of the beginning" and by that he meant that it was the beginning of a theological renewal movement within the Church that would concern itself with a multiplicity of issues, both old and new.[2] For Rahner, anything less than this would be unworthy of the mandate of the Council and answering the clarion

---

[1] Many read into the promulgation of a new church catechism an effort to tamp down the theological excesses unleashed by Vatican II. Certainly Pope John Paul II and Joseph Cardinal Ratzinger (who would succeed Pope John Paul II as Pope Benedict XVI) were inspired to update the catechism in an effort to define Catholic orthodoxy in a post-Vatican II world. In his Christmas Address given to the Roman Curia on Dec. 22, 2005, Pope Benedict XVI decried those who applied a "hermeneutic of discontinuity and rupture" to the Vatican II documents, which he warned "risks ending in a split between the pre-conciliar Church and the post-conciliar Church." Quoting from John XXIII's 1962 speech inaugurating the Second Vatican Council, Benedict XVI called the church back to John XXII's original purpose: "[T]o transmit the doctrine, pure and integral, without any attenuation or distortion." The text of Benedict XVI's address may be found online at the Vatican website: http://www.vatican.va/holy_father/benedict_xvi/speeches/2005/december/documents/hf_ben_xvi_spe_20051222_roman-curia_en.html. (Accessed on October 10, 2014.) The text of the new catechism may be found in: The Catholic Church, *Catechism of the Catholic Church: With Modifications from the Editio Typica* (New York: Image Books/Doubleday, 1995). A large companion volume that contains the full wording in English to all the various texts quoted and footnoted to in the Catechism has been published under the title *The Companion to The Catechism of the Catholic Church: A Compendium of Texts Referred to in The Catechism of the Catholic Church* (San Francisco: Ignatius, 1994).

[2] Rahner, *The Church After The Council*, 19–20.

call of the Council meant nothing less than a new exploration of all the ancient questions. Questions of

> how theology can speak of God, and His existence in the midst of mankind, in such a way that the words can be understood by the men of today and tomorrow; how it can so proclaim Christ in the midst of an evolving universe that the world of the God-man and the incarnation of the eternal Logos in Jesus of Nazareth do not sound like myths which men cannot any longer take seriously; . . . how it can show that love of God and love of neighbor always form in a new and epochal way an absolute unity, love which one without the other is incomprehensible and unattainable, especially since God is manifested for us through Christ in mankind and thus is for us only so attainable; . . . These and similar eternal, old, ever radically new, never-solved questions will be the questions for the theology of tomorrow which will be worthy of the Council.[3]

In other words, according to Rahner, Vatican II was nothing less than a mandate for the Catholic Church to renew and refresh its theological discourse and to relate that renewal to the challenges of the modern world.

With the theological renewal brought on through Vatican II came a re-examination of Roman Catholic soteriology, particularly as it related to other religions and non-Christians. For centuries the Church had proclaimed the axiom *extra ecclesiam nulla salus*, but in the Vatican II documents we see that this stance is considerably moderated.[4] In fact, in the Vatican II documents Christocentric inclusivism—as opposed to the ancient expressions of exclusivism—becomes codified as the official position of the Catholic Church regarding non-believers.[5] The Dogmatic Constitution of the Church, *Lumen gentium*, promulgated on November 21, 1964, offers this affirmation of inclusivism:

> There are others who search for the unknown God in shadows and images; God is not far from people of this kind since he gives to all life

---

[3] Rahner, *The Church After The Council*, 25.

[4] Or perhaps just given a clearer enumeration. In an interesting article entitled "'Extra ecclesiam nulla salus' revisited," Gavin D'Costa has argued that the doctrine was intended to deal with heretics and schismatics and that it is misapplied when related to non-Christian religions. In his view, "Non-Christians can be saved while remaining explicit non-Christians. The religion of the non-Christians may thereby contain the instrumental means of grace in varying degrees." See Gavin D'Costa, "'Extra ecclesiam nulla salus' revisited" in Ian Hamnett, ed., *Religious pluralism and unbelief: Studies critical and comparative* (London: Routledge, 1990), 142. For a more in-depth discussion see Francis Aloysius Sullivan, *Salvation Outside the Church? Tracing the History of the Catholic Response* (New York: Paulist, 1992).

[5] Interestingly, the idea of inclusivism has a long history in Catholic theology. In the *DEC* Alberigo, Tanner, et al. provide references to Aquinas' *Summa Theologiae* (III, quest. 8, art. 3), a letter from the Holy Office to the archbishop of Boston (D 3869–72), and Eusebius' *Praeparatio evangelica* (1, 1: PG 21). See *DEC* 2:861.

and breath and everything (See Ac 17, 25–28), and the Saviour wishes all to be saved (See 1 Tm 2, 4). There are those who without any fault do not know anything about Christ or his Church, yet who search for God with a sincere heart and, under the influence of grace, try to put into effect the will of God as known to them through the dictate of conscience: these too can obtain eternal salvation. Nor does divine Providence deny the helps that are necessary for salvation to those who, through no fault of their own, have not yet attained to the express recognition of God yet who strive, not without divine grace, to lead an upright life.[6]

In keeping with other definitions of inclusivism, the Catholic Church affirms that the key to salvation is a sincere desire to find God and have a relationship with him, which is indicative of a primitive faith. The Pastoral Constitution on the Church in the World of Today, *Gaudium et spes*, promulgated on December 7, 1965, goes even further in acknowledging a secret work of grace operating among nonbelievers. It speaks of non-Christians "sharing in this paschal mystery," explaining that this sharing, "applies not only to Christians but to all people of good will in whose hearts grace is secretly at work."[7]

In the Declaration of the Church to Non-Christian Religions, *Nostra aetate*, promulgated on October 28, 1965, the Church added additional support for inclusivism by affirming its respect for non-Christian religions as sources of truth: "The Catholic Church rejects nothing of those things which are true and holy in these religions. It regards with respect those ways of acting and living and those precepts and teachings which, though often at variance with what it holds and expounds, frequently reflect a ray of that truth which enlightens everyone."[8] The Declaration goes on to encourage all Catholics to dialogue and collaborate with the followers of other religions in an effort to "recognize, preserve and promote those spiritual and moral good things as well as the socio-cultural values which are to be found among them."[9]

This inclusivist stance has been confirmed and elaborated on most notably by Pope John Paul II. On December 7, 1990 Pope John Paul II issued an encyclical entitled *Redemptoris missio* in which he affirmed the essential role of the Church in the process of salvation: "The Council makes frequent reference to the Church's role in the salvation of mankind. While acknowledging that God loves all people and grants them the possibility of being saved (cf. 1 Tm 2:4), the Church believes that God has established Christ as the one mediator and that she herself has been established as the universal sacrament of salvation."[10] However, John Paul II also noted that salvation outside of the Church did not automatically turn a person into a Catholic. In discussing the possibility of salvation for people outside of the witness of the Church he noted: "For such people salvation in Christ is accessible by virtue of

---

[6] *DEC Lumen gentium*, §16.
[7] *DEC Gaudium et spes*, §22.
[8] *DEC Nostra aetate*, §2.
[9] *DEC Nostra aetate*, §2.
[10] Pope John Paul II, *Redemptoris missio*, §9, http://www.vatican.va/holy_father/ john_paul_ii/encyclicals/documents/hf_jp-ii_enc_07121990_redemptoris-missio_en.html. (Accessed on October 10, 2014.)

a grace which, while having a mysterious relationship to the Church, does not make them formally part of the Church but enlightens them in a way which is accommodated to their spiritual and material situation. This grace comes from Christ; it is the result of his Sacrifice and is communicated by the Holy Spirit. It enables each person to attain salvation through his or her free cooperation."[11]

On August 6, 2000, Joseph Cardinal Ratzinger issued a declaration as the Prefect of the Congregation for the Doctrine of the Faith that was entitled "*Dominus Iesus*: On the Unicity and Salvific Universality of Jesus Christ and the Church." In the declaration Cardinal Ratzinger sought to clarify the Church's position regarding its view of other religions and salvation outside the Church. The concern was that Catholic inclusivism was being misunderstood by many to imply an egalitarian pluralism. Cardinal Ratzinger cautioned:

> With the coming of the Saviour Jesus Christ, God has willed that the Church founded by him be the instrument for the salvation of *all* humanity (cf. *Acts* 17:30–31). This truth of faith does not lessen the sincere respect which the Church has for the religions of the world, but at the same time, it rules out, in a radical way, that mentality of indifferentism "characterized by a religious relativism which leads to the belief that 'one religion is as good as another.'" If it is true that the followers of other religions can receive divine grace, it is also certain that *objectively speaking* they are in a gravely deficient situation in comparison with those who, in the Church, have the fullness of the means of salvation.[12]

Thus the Catholic Church has been careful to preserve a central role for both Christ and the Church in the process of salvation. Catholic inclusivism has been enunciated within clearly defined boundaries.

It should be understood that in embracing Christocentric inclusivism that the Catholic Church has not abandoned the doctrine of hell or eternal punishment. On the contrary, these doctrines are still endorsed in the strongest terms:

> The teaching of the Church affirms the existence of hell and its eternity. Immediately after death the souls of those who die in a state of mortal sin descend into hell, where they suffer the punishment of hell 'eternal fire.'[13]

The Church has also reiterated its teaching on purgatory:

> All who die in God's grace and friendship, but still imperfectly purified, are indeed assured of their eternal salvation; but after death they undergo

---

[11] Pope John Paul II, *Redemptoris missio*, §10.

[12] Joseph Cardinal Ratzinger, "Declaration '*Dominus Iesus*': On the Unicity and Salvific Universality of Jesus Christ and the Church," *The Congregation for the Doctrine of the Faith*, Aug. 6, 2000, http://www.vatican.va/roman_curia/congregations/cfaith/ documents/rc_con_cfaith_doc_20000806_dominus-iesus_en.html, §22. (Accessed on October 10, 2014.)

[13] The Catholic Church, *Catechism of the Catholic Church*, §1035; See also *DEC Lumen gentium*, §48.

purification so as to achieve the holiness necessary to enter the joy of heaven.[14]

Thus, the embrace of inclusivism has not altered the teaching of the Church as it is related to the more negative aspects of its soteriology. However, in officially endorsing a position of inclusivism the Church has opened the door to interreligious dialogue and to interreligious collaboration on a scale never thought to be possible in the past. In order to achieve these ends, at the close of the Second Vatican Council in 1965, Pope Paul VI made permanent the secretariats for the Promotion of Christian Unity, for Non-Christian Religions, and for Non-Believers. Today Catholic clergymen regularly participate in all sorts of ecumenical activities including, prayer, worship services, ecumenical organizations, and political collaboration with leaders of other religions. Vatican II inclusivism has opened up a new pluralistic universe to modern Catholicism.

Nevertheless, as we have seen, there are still clearly defined limits to the inclusivist stance the Church has taken. Furthermore, historically, the Catholic Church has been the implacable enemy of universalism, condemning the apokatastasis of Origen and the other early church fathers and zealously persecuting the Free Spirit heretics and the Cathars. The question for our own day is has the stance of the Church softened? If so, how far can a Catholic theologian go in endorsing the notion of universal salvation without running afoul of the keepers of orthodoxy? As we now move on to examine universalism in contemporary Catholic theology, these issues once again become of paramount importance.

1. Christocentric Universalism Expressed as a Hope
We begin our analysis by examining two hugely influential Catholic theologians who incorporated the idea of universal salvation into their theology in terms of it being *a supreme hope*: Karl Rahner and Hans Urs von Balthasar. In Section 4.1 of the Introduction we made a distinction between "strong universalism" and "hopeful universalism" by noting that the former expressed a certainty about universal salvation in the final state of affairs while the latter expressed a hope that things will be so while allowing for the regrettable possibility that some may remain alienated from the Kingdom. In Protestant theological circles, the idea of someone being a hopeful universalist is fairly non-controversial and would not merit much mention in a study like this one, which is primarily directed toward examining contemporary expressions of strong universalism. However, in Catholic theological circles hopeful universalism—although steadily gaining support—is still viewed by many as a radical departure from orthodoxy and therefore naturally draws the attention of this study. Indeed, due to the dogmatic restrictions placed upon the Catholic theological enterprise by the Church, it turns out that hopeful universalism has made a significant contribution to the Catholic landscape regarding this issue. It is my contention that one cannot understand the development of strong forms of universalism within Catholic theology without also understanding the impact

---

[14] The Catholic Church, *Catechism of the Catholic Church*, §1030.

that hopeful universalism has made upon the field. For this reason a study of hopeful universalism has been integrated into this section.

The choice to incorporate a discussion of the universalist leanings of Rahner and von Balthasar may well prove to be the most controversial decision taken in this dissertation. Because both men are by no means dogmatic about their universalist hopes it could easily be argued that they do not qualify for inclusion. In light of this, the key threshold question that must be explored is that of eligibility. In the case of von Balthasar the fact of his hopeful universalism is fairly transparent. Indeed, even the title of his book on the subject *Dare We Hope "That All Men Be Saved?" with a Short Discourse on Hell* is intended to imply an endorsement of the idea.[15] In Rahner's case, however, the issue becomes a bit murkier. Within the body of Rahner's work— which is amazingly large—one can find endorsements of both universalism and standard Catholic inclusivism. These seeming contradictions introduce a level of ambiguity into Rahner's writings that we do not find with von Balthasar. Morwenna Ludlow, perhaps the leading expert on Rahner's universalism, believes that the solution to the issue lies in Rahner's embrace of eschatological tension. In other words, he was comfortable with eschatological incongruities. In Ludlow's view, this places Rahner firmly in the hopeful universalist camp. Certainly, she finds more in Rahner's eschatology than mere Catholic inclusivism. On the other hand, one cannot say that Rahner was dogmatic about his universalist leanings. At the end of her lengthy examination of Rahner's universalism Ludlow concluded:

> In sum then, Rahner's view of universal salvation is coherent and attractive when expressed in terms of hope; but because he sometimes goes further than this and speaks both of the possibility of hell and of the certainty of God's world-wide victory in love, he leaves a tension in his eschatology with which it is difficult to deal.[16]

It is this tension in Rahner's eschatology that makes it difficult for some to accept the label "universalist" being applied to him. However, this is where the distinction we have made between strong and hopeful universalism offers us some assistance. This study recognizes that Rahner was by no means a dogmatic universalist. On the other hand, it cannot be said that he had no universalist expectations. The same is true of Hans Urs von Balthasar. Therefore, what we offer here regarding both men is an analysis of a hope that they both held in their hearts that flirted with the dogmatic but in the end took on the form of an optimistic dream.

---

[15] Hans Urs von Balthasar, *Dare We Hope "That All Men Be Saved?" with a Short Discourse on Hell*, trans. David Kipp and Lothar Krauth (San Francisco: Ignatius, 1988).

[16] Ludlow, *Universal Salvation: Eschatology in the Thought of Gregory of Nyssa and Karl Rahner*, 247.

1.1. Karl Rahner—Orthogenesis and Hope for the Anonymous Christian

Karl Rahner (1904–1984) began his theological study as a novitiate of the Society of Jesus.[17] He was originally trained in philosophy at the University of Freiburg where he came under the influence of Martin Heidegger (1889–1976) and Joseph Maréchal (1878–1944). His dissertation at Freiburg on Thomas Aquinas' doctrine of perception was entitled *Geist in Welt* and was rejected by his mentor Martin Honecker for being too much Heidegger and too little Catholic.[18] This episode proved to be a preview of coming attractions, as controversy would follow Rahner throughout his theological career. Eventually, Rahner moved to Innsbruck where he completed a doctorate in theology and became a member of the faculty of the university.

Rahner desired to restate the traditional Catholic faith in existential and transcendental terms and his efforts along these lines got him trouble with the Catholic authorities. In 1962, the Vatican placed him under "pre-censorship" meaning that he had to ask permission to publish or to lecture. This status was soon removed and Rahner served as a *peritus* (theological expert and advisor) at the Second Vatican Council. After becoming a noted professor at the University of Munich in 1964, Rahner again became embroiled in controversy over his theology. Some professors in the theology faculty refused to let Rahner's students submit doctoral dissertations. In 1966 he moved to the University of Münster. He retired from teaching in 1971.

Rahner's endorsement of hopeful universalism must be understood against the backdrop of his theory of the transcendental self-communication of God to the world. Rahner saw the need to develop an ascending Christology—from the historical Jesus to the incarnation of the Divine Logos—and to marry it to a descending Christology, which comes from God down to humanity. His understanding of God's self-communication helped him to do this as well as to resolve several other anthropological issues. It also assisted him in developing his own unique theory of epistemology. Beginning from what he calls "an evolutionary world view," Rahner argued that matter was endued with developmental power that progressed toward consciousness and spirituality: "[I]t is of the intrinsic nature of matter to develop towards spirit."[19] Steps along

---

[17] Biographical information was taken from the following: Declan Marmion and Mary E. Hines, *The Cambridge Companion to Karl Rahner* (Cambridge: Cambridge University Press, 2005); William V. Dych, *Karl Rahner* (Collegeville, Minn.: Liturgical Press, 1992); and Herbert Vorgrimler, *Understanding Karl Rahner* (London: SCM, 1986). An evaluation of Rahner's universalism may be found in Ludlow, *Universal Salvation: Eschatology in the Thought of Gregory of Nyssa and Karl Rahner*, 115–277.

[18] Today the work is considered by many to be a *tour de force*. See Karl Rahner, *Geist in Welt: zur Metaphysik der endlichen Erkenntnis bei Thomas von Aquin* (Innsbruck: F. Rauch, 1939); English edition trans. William Dych, *The Spirit in the World*, 2nd edition (New York: Herder & Herder, 1968).

[19] Karl Rahner, *Grundkurs des Glaubens: Einführung in das Begriff des Christentums* (Freiburg im Breisgau: Herder, 1976); English edition trans. William V. Dych, *Foundations of Christian Faith: An Introduction to the Idea of Christianity* (New York: Crossroad, 1978), 179; 184. Rahner preferred to use the essay as the vehicle through which his theology was communicated. Therefore his famous *Schriften zur Theologie* amounts to a loosely organized collection of miscellany. Since *Foundations of Christian*

the path of this development included consciousness and then self-consciousness. Man as a self-conscious development in this process was seen as the definitive expression of the "self-transcendence of matter." In light of this understanding of man, Rahner asserted that matter therefore reached its ultimate objective in the history of man's spirit.[20]

In answering the question of why matter was endued with such developmental power, Rahner pointed to God's purpose in creation and explained that "the goal of the world is God's self communication to it."[21] Consciousness is required in order for this communication to happen on a meaningful level and thus we can understand why matter was developmentally empowered. Rahner asserted that the cosmos becomes conscious of itself through spiritual beings who possess true freedom. To accept God's self-communication is called justification; to reject it is called sin.[22]

This idea of evolutionary development led Rahner to the concept of "absolute savior." If God's goal for the world is his self-communication to it, and if the world was created in such a way that it develops the means necessary to receive this self-communication, then the world must be waiting for the absolute self-communication of God. According to Rahner, this is what the incarnation of Jesus Christ is all about. The absolute savior embodies the perfect self-communication of God. To truly communicate himself to the world God had to enter it; he had to become a part of it; he had to become matter.[23] According to Rahner, the Word assumed a human nature and in this way became a man. The problem with understanding this event is that it is impossible to fully and accurately define just who or what man is. Rahner declares that man is a mystery because of his conscious orientation toward God who in and of himself is the ultimate mystery. Rahner commented: "Seen from this perspective, the incarnation of God is the unique and *highest* instance of the actualization of the essence of human reality, which consist in this: that man is insofar as he abandons himself to the absolute mystery whom we call God."[24] This, for Rahner, was the essence of the hypostatic union of Christ.

According to Rahner, the value of a creature finds its deepest expression in the fact that it could be assumed by God and become the "grammar" for God's self-expression. To Rahner's way of thinking, man is the "cipher of God"— "the utterance in which God could express himself."[25] The development of man anticipated the incarnation of Christ. Man is the container into which God would pour himself. Rahner asserted that Christ is fully man "in the most radical way." For Rahner, "He is the union of the historical manifestation of the

---

Faith is Rahner's most systematic presentation we will use it as the backbone of our presentation, augmenting it with other writings when appropriate. See Karl Rahner, *Schriften zur Theologie*, 16 vols. (Einsiedeln: Benziger & Co., 1954–1972); English edition trans. Boniface Kruger, et al., *Theological Investigations*, 23 vols. (Baltimore, Md.: Helicon Press, 1961–1979).

[20] Rahner, *Foundations of Christian Faith*, 187.
[21] Rahner, *Foundations of Christian Faith*, 192.
[22] Rahner, *Foundations of Christian Faith*, 193.
[23] Rahner, *Foundations of Christian Faith*, 196–97.
[24] Rahner, *Foundations of Christian Faith*, 218.
[25] Rahner, *Foundations of Christian Faith*, 223–25.

question which man is and the answer which God is. He is the union of a question which as a question about God is the manifestation of the answer. This is the union which is meant in Christology."[26] Thus, for Rahner, God's goal for his self-communication to the world was fulfilled in Christ who is a union of the ultimate development of the self-transcendence of matter (which is man) and the communication of the absolute savior (which is God). Therefore Christ stands at the center of all things.

Several important features of Rahner's hopeful universalism flow from this thesis. To begin with, Rahner believed that because God pre-programmed all matter to move toward consciousness and spirituality, that all human beings had a latent or "unthematic" awareness of God within themselves. God's self-communication in terms of grace and revelation are present in all human beings in an unthematic way, driving them forward toward consummation (a word often used by Rahner as a synonym for salvation) with God. This proto-revelation is the basis for the later recognition of special revelation, such as the gospel message. It can also lead people who have never heard about Jesus Christ to salvation in him:

> According to the Catholic understanding of the faith, as is clearly expressed in the Second Vatican Council, there can be no doubt that someone who has no concrete, historical contact with the explicit preaching of Christianity can nevertheless be a justified person who lives in the grace of Christ. He then possesses God's supernatural self communication in grace not only as an offer, not only as an existential of his existence; he has also accepted this offer and so he has really accepted what is essential in what Christianity wants to mediate to him: his salvation in that grace which objectively is the grace of Jesus Christ. Since transcendental self-communication of God as an offer to man's freedom is an existential of every person, and since it is a moment in the self-communication of God to the world which reaches its goal and its climax in Christ, we can speak of "anonymous Christians."[27]

---

[26] Rahner, *Foundations of Christian Faith*, 225.

[27] Rahner, *Foundations of Christian Faith*, 176. Some have thought the phrase "anonymous Christians" was actually adopted by Rahner from a book by Anita Röper entitled *De anonieme Christen* (Hilversum: Brand, 1964). Nevertheless, Rahner acknowledged that the phrase is his creation. See Karl Rahner, *Karl Rahner in Dialogue: Conversations and Interviews, 1965–1982,* ed. Paul Imhof and Hubert Biallowons, trans. John J. O'Neill (New York: Crossroad, 1986), 218–19. Rahner cited Matt. 25:31–44 as scriptural support for the doctrine (Rahner, *Karl Rahner in Dialogue,* 218). However, it must be noted that in this passage it is the recipients of the good works who represent Jesus, not the practitioners. Rahner discussed the issue of anonymous Christianity in several of his essays in his *Theological Investigations*. See Rahner, "Anonymous Christians," in *Theological Investigations,* 6:390–398; Rahner, "Anonymous Christianity and the Missionary Task of the Church," in *Theological Investigations,* 12:390–98; Rahner, "Observations on the Problem of Anonymous Christians," in *Theological Investigations,* 14:280–94; Rahner, "Anonymous and Explicit Faith," in *Theological Investigations,* 16:52–59; and Rahner, "The One Christ and the Universality of Salvation," in *Theological Investigations,* 16:199–224.

Thus we see that Rahner's concept of "anonymous Christians" is linked closely to the unthematic awareness of God that innately exists in every person. Does this mean that all people will automatically be saved? No. For Rahner it meant that all people *might* be saved:

> The salvation which God, of his will to save all men, offers and effectively bestows upon the individual, is present now in its first principles and as a seed which is still undeveloped. (At this stage it is called "justifying and sanctifying grace"). In the future this will be brought to its fullness in the form of eternal life (this is called the "vision of God"). It can only fail to be brought to this fullness if man of his own free will sinfully rejects it.[28]

Interestingly enough, Rahner significantly shrank the definition of sinful rejection by noting that explicit rejection of the gospel by members of other religions did not necessarily mean that they had sinfully rejected it. In Rahner's view such a rejection may be nothing more than a matter of conscience developed through contact with a foreign culture and religion. He spoke of those "who consciously and explicitly believe that they are required by their conscience to refuse the Gospel of Christ as this is presented to them. In this last case it is not a case of sin offering a threat to salvation . . . their rejection does not mean an existentially serious sin."[29] In other words, a culturally conditioned rejection was not fatal to salvation. Such a rejection showed that a person was acting on his or her conscience, something that God could respect as an effort to hold onto the truth as they had been taught it. Along these lines, Rahner acknowledged that Jesus Christ could be present in non-Christian religions.[30] He also argued the Holy Spirit could be active within their structures. In his view, the unthematic awareness of God latent in humanity was seeking for the absolute savior, although humanity was not consciously aware of it. This explained for Rahner the phenomenon of humanity's overwhelmingly religious orientation and the possibility of there being anonymous Christians:

> Now God and the grace of Christ are present as the secret essence in every reality we can choose . . . Consequently, anyone who, though still far from any revelation explicitly formulated in words, accepts his existence in patient silence (or, better, in faith, hope and love), accepts it as the mystery which lies hidden in the mystery of eternal love and which bears life in the womb of death, is saying "yes" to Christ even if he does not know it.[31]

It is this formulation of the theory of the anonymous Christian that seems to open the door most widely to the prospect of universal salvation. When we see

[28] Rahner, "Church, Churches, and Religions," in *Theological Investigations*, 10:33–34.
[29] Rahner, "The One Christ and the Universality of Salvation," in *Theological Investigations*, 16:216.
[30] Rahner, *Foundations of Christian Faith*, 311–21.
[31] Rahner, *Foundations of Christian Faith*, 228.

how Rahner links this formulation to an unthematic awareness of God found in all people, it seems that such a universalist outcome becomes a very real possibility.

These aspects of Rahner's theology tie into something he labeled "collective eschatology."[32] He argued that the eschatology of human beings must be considered both individually and collectively as a part of humanity in total. It was when Rahner was discussing the collective fate of all humanity that he made his most forceful statements in favor of universal salvation. In particular, it seems that for him a collective fate of universal salvation had a higher level of probability than did the eternal loss of a single individual. He commented:

> In the doctrine of hell we maintain the possibility of eternal loss for every individual, for each one of us, because otherwise the seriousness of the free history would be abolished. But in Christianity this open possibility is not necessarily the doctrine of two parallel ways which lie before a person who stands at the crossroads. Rather the existence of the possibility that freedom will end in eternal loss stands alongside the doctrine that the world and the history of the world as a whole will *in fact* enter into eternal life with God.[33]

What Rahner seems to be saying here is that the possibility of hell is necessary for the operation of human freedom: Without real consequences there can be no real choices. However, the existence of such possibilities appears to be trumped by the "fact" that the entire world will experience eternal life. In Rahner's view, the two ideas stand side by side in Christian theology. Nevertheless, it would appear that he is trying to artfully say that the possibility of eternal loss will yield to the fact of eternal life. This is as close as Rahner will come to endorsing the idea of universal salvation. He is satisfied with a level of ambiguity in his discussion that effectively avoids a definitive resolution of the issue.

Despite such a sweeping vision, as Rahner noted, hell and eternal punishment are indeed a very real possibility in his eschatology. In his view, no one could make absolute statements about the fate of any particular person.[34] Therefore, in the end he denied *apokatastasis* (which he characterized as the assertion that all people are actually saved as opposed to a total restoration of the universe).[35] On the other hand, Rahner interpreted the scriptural warnings regarding hell as "'threat discourse' and hence not to be read as a preview of something which will exist some day."[36] In keeping with this interpretation he believed that New Testament discussions of hell fire were the "mental furniture

---

[32] Rahner, *Foundations of Christian Faith*, 444 ff.

[33] Rahner, *Foundations of Christian Faith*, 444. (Italics in the original.)

[34] Rahner, "The Hermeneutics of Eschatological Assertions," in *Theological Investigations*, 4:338–39.

[35] Karl Rahner, "Hell," in Karl Rahner, et al., ed., *Sacramentum Mundi: An Encyclopedia of Theology*, trans. W.J.O'Hara, et al. (New York: Herder and Herder, 1968–1970), 3:8. See also Rahner, "Christian Dying," in *Theological Investigations*, 8:236, 241.

[36] Rahner, "Hell," 7.

of contemporary apocalyptic" and metaphorical in nature.[37] The visions found in the Bible of people being cast into hell fire were understood by him to be "statements about the possibilities of human life" and "the absolute seriousness of human decision."[38] They did not, however, require a literal interpretation. Therefore he concluded, "The Christian message, says nothing about whether in some people or in many people evil has become an absolute reality defining the *final end and result* of their lives."[39]

Rahner affirmed the doctrine of purgatory in a highly modified form as a means of fashioning completely integrated human beings.[40] However, he also had a problem with the generally accepted understanding of purgatory as a temporal reality. Time seemed to him to be an enemy that raised many more problems than it solved. In the end his preferred answer to the issue seemed to be "the consummation of the whole person in the moment of death."[41] Purgatory, it appeared, would be an instantaneous occurrence, although how it was experienced by the soul may be a quite different matter.

The consummation of all things involved the entire cosmos being incorporated back into God to form a sort of panentheistic whole. In this process God's self-communication to matter was made complete:

> [T]he whole cosmos as a whole, whose meaning and goal is the fulfillment of freedom, will one day be subsumed into the fullness of God's self-communication to this material and spiritual cosmos, and that this will happen through many histories of freedom which do not only take place on our earth.[42]

Hopeful universalism has a long history that stretches back to the time of the Patristic writers. Like many others before him, Rahner was unwilling to affirm a dogmatic universalism because of two seemingly intractable problems: (1) scriptural assertions regarding the reality of hell and eternal punishment, and (2) a respect for human freedom. Thus, for him, the hope of universal salvation became his next best option—although it would seem that his theory regarding the ultimate consummation of all things in God required a universalist outcome.

Rahner's theory of orthogenesis (the idea of matter evolving in a predestined, purposeful direction or "straight-line evolution" as it is sometimes called) is not unique and has antecedents in the work of another Jesuit, Pierre Teilhard de Chardin. In his book, *The Phenomenon of Man*, Teilhard argued that inorganic matter contains pre-life and pre-consciousness within itself.[43] While not all of Teilhard's speculations line up with Rahner's, his idea of the

---

[37] Rahner, "Hell," 7–8.

[38] Rahner, *Foundations of Christian Faith*, 104.

[39] Rahner, *Foundations of Christian Faith*, 104; 443–44.

[40] Rahner, "Purgatory," in *Theological Investigations*, 9:184–85.

[41] Ludlow, *Universal Salvation: Eschatology in the Thought of Gregory of Nyssa and Karl Rahner*, 197. For an in-depth discussion of this aspect and Rahner's view of the "intermediate state" see pp. 195–207.

[42] Rahner, *Foundations of Christian Faith*, 445–46.

[43] Pierre Teilhard de Chardin, *Le phénomène humain* (Paris: Du Seuil, 1955); English edition trans. Bernard Wall, *The Phenomenon of Man* (New York: Harper, 1959).

Omega Point is somewhat similar to Rahner's goal of all things becoming the fulfillment of the self-communication of God. Teilhard argued that when the Omega Point is reached that all consciousness will merge into a final unity. Although Rahner spoke in terms of God realizing his self-communication to matter, he foresaw a day when the universe would be "subsumed into the fullness of God's self-communication to this material and spiritual cosmos." In other words, Rahner spoke of a sort of all encompassing Omega Point in which matter and spirituality would merge into God. Granted that Teilhard saw this as an evolutionary process and Rahner understood it to be primarily the product of freedom, there is still a striking similarity in the outcome—the achievement of a final all-encompassing unity.

For Rahner, orthogenesis was essential to his thesis. He used orthogenesis to explain the development of humankind and human consciousness. He used orthogenesis to explain humanity's unique unthematic orientation towards God. He used orthogenesis to explain the salvation of anonymous Christians. He used orthogenesis as a key element of his universalist hope and his theory of eschatological consummation. "It is of the intrinsic nature of matter to develop towards spirit," declared Rahner.[44] This was his orthogenic claim. However, the problem with the notion of orthogenesis is that it has been repudiated by contemporary scientists on at least two substantial grounds: (1) the disjointed nature of the fossil record, which shows no smooth teleologically linear development,[45] and (2) DNA heredity, which makes it clear that only random mutations to the DNA code can alter a creature's form and thus rules out the possibility of material purposefulness in the evolutionary process.[46] Based on these facts, the theory of orthogenesis has been strenuously attacked and rebutted in the scientific literature.[47] After presenting his case against

---

[44] Rahner, *Foundations of Christian Faith*, 184.

[45] This observation serves as an anchor to Stephen Jay Gould's "punctuated equilibrium" hypothesis of evolutionary development. He comments: "The history of life is a story of massive removal followed by differentiation within a few surviving stocks, not the conventional tale of a steadily increasing excellence, complexity, and diversity" (Stephen Jay Gould, *Wonderful Life: The Burgess Shale and the Nature of History* [New York: W.W. Norton & Co., 1989], 25). Ernst Mayr argues that the fossil record shows frequent changes in evolutionary direction as well as complete course reversals. See Ernst Mayr, *What Evolution Is* (New York: Basic Books, 2001), 82. On this point see also the comments of Bruce J. MacFadden in his book *Fossil Horses: Systematics, Paleobiology, and Evolution of the Family Equidae* (Cambridge: Cambridge University Press, 1992). MacFadden devotes an entire chapter to refuting the naïve and inaccurate presentation of evolution as a smooth march of progress from simplicity to complexity that would imply some kind of purposefulness. See MacFadden, *Fossil Horses*, 27–37. Both MacFadden and Gould sharply criticize and dismiss as inaccurate the standard "iconography" of evolution, which shows a smooth, uninterrupted development of organisms such as the monkey to man drawings, the rudimentary limb to hand drawings, etc . . . See Gould, *Wonderful Life*, 21–52; MacFadden, *Fossil Horses*, 27ff.

[46] Mayr, *What Evolution Is*, 73–82; 121.

[47] Mayr defines orthogenesis as: "The refuted hypothesis that rectilinear trends in evolution are caused by an intrinsic finalistic principle" (Mayr, *What Evolution Is*, 288). An earlier refutation of orthogenesis may be found in George Gaylord Simpson, *Tempo*

orthogenesis, Bruce MacFadden concluded that the hypothesis is essentially dead within the scientific community: "In summary, few scientists today would consider evolution to be an orderly, directed process resulting in perfectly adapted species."[48]

Where does this leave Rahner, with his almost utter reliance on his theory of orthogenesis? It leaves him with no scientific grounds upon which to rest his thesis. Rahner's science has in effect become an anachronistic pseudo-science and, in the end, the evolutionary science that Rahner sought to affirm and justify has turned out to be his greatest enemy. On the other hand, from a theological point of view, what is so striking about Rahner's theory is the utter lack of any reference whatsoever to Scripture in his presentation.[49] It is possible that Rahner could have based his claim upon Scripture and then turned to science secondarily as his handmaiden. However, this is not what he did. Instead, he built his case for orthogenesis upon scientific claims alone and these claims have now been effectively refuted by the evidence. As a result, what we have in Rahner's orthogenesis and the account of God's self-communication to matter is an inventive cosmic fable that attempts to provide a theory of everything. It is a just-so story that turns out to be grounded upon nothing other than Rahner's fertile imagination.

A major problem related to Rahner's orthogenic claim is the issue of faith. Rahner maintained that the orthogenic nature of matter drove people to embrace God and salvation outside of explicit Christianity. This idea became a central consideration in his development of the concept of the "anonymous Christian." However, in order to make such a concept work Rahner had to do serious injury to the language of faith both from a conceptual point of view and from how it is construed in the New Testament. According to Rahner

> anyone who, though still far from any revelation explicitly formulated in words, *accepts his existence in patient silence* (or, better, in faith, hope and love), accepts it as the mystery which lies hidden in the mystery of eternal love and which bears life in the womb of death, *is saying "yes" to Christ even if he does not know it.*[50]

---

and Mode in Evolution (New York: Columbia University Press, 1944), 161–63. See also Gould, *Wonderful Life*, 21–52 and MacFadden, *Fossil Horses*, 27–37. In terms of theologians who have embraced orthogenesis, Teilhard's theory of orthogenesis has been subjected to the most severe criticism because he claimed to be writing primarily from a scientific point of view. Perhaps Teilhard's fiercest critic has been the Nobel Prize winner Peter B. Medawar who wrote an essay debunking *The Phenomenon of Man* and concluded that the book is "nonsense, tricked out with a variety of metaphysical conceits, and its author can be excused of dishonesty only on the grounds that before deceiving others he has taken great pains to deceive himself." See Peter B. Medawar, "The Phenomenon of Man," in Peter B. Medawar, *The Strange Case of the Spotted Mice and Other Classic Essays on Science* (Oxford: Oxford University Press, 1996), 1–11.

[48] MacFadden, *Fossil Horses*, 37.
[49] Rahner, *Foundations of Christian Faith*, 178–202.
[50] Rahner, *Foundations of Christian Faith*, 228. (Italics added.)

From the point of view of logic and grammar, this is a nonsense sentence. In theory, a rational human being cannot *say* "yes" to a proposition that has not been explicitly communicated to him/her. A rational human being cannot *say* "yes" to something without knowing he/she has done so. A basic legal principle regarding the law of contracts is what we call "genuineness of assent." This principle holds that an assent to a contract or an agreement of any kind must be "genuine." In other words, a party must knowingly and explicitly assent to the terms of an agreement in an un-coerced fashion in order for it to be valid. What Rahner proposes is the opposite of what we all understand an assent to be. It is an agreement without agreement. It is an assent without an assent. It is a "yes" forced upon the ignorant. This is the world turned upside down where the common conventions of language that make modern life possible do not apply. If Rahner had tried to enforce such an agreement in any industrialized nation of the world he would have been laughed out of court.

Furthermore, Rahner's construction flies in the face of how saving faith is defined in the New Testament. In the New Testament faith is presented as an explicit, knowing consent to Christ. For instance, Jesus himself affirms in Matt. 10:32–33: "Therefore whoever confesses Me before men, him I will also confess before My Father who is in heaven. But whoever denies Me before men, him I will also deny before My Father who is in heaven." Likewise, the Apostle Paul affirms in Romans 10:9–10: "that if you confess with your mouth Jesus as Lord, and believe in your heart that God raised Him from the dead, you shall be saved; for with the heart man believes, resulting in righteousness, and with the mouth he confesses, resulting in salvation." Orthogenesis aside, the New Testament does not countenance the idea of someone coming to faith without consciously knowing about it and assenting to it.

The collapse of Rahner's thesis provides a warning regarding the danger of forcing theology to accommodate what seems to be the latest scientific understanding. Scientific knowledge is not fixed—it is fluid and always developing. Scientific models that seemed unassailable have been displaced many times. Ptolemaic cosmology gave way to the Copernican model. The theory of the ether gave way to molecular chemistry. Particle physics is being challenged by string theory. The idea of an eternal, steady state universe has yielded to the big bang theory and the unavoidable notion that the universe had a beginning. In wedding his theology so closely to a scientific claim, Rahner sowed into his thesis the seeds of its own destruction. There can be no doubt that Rahner's vision for humanity and the universe is all-embracing. The problem is that a major component of his theology has been built in large part around a non-theological claim that he felt compelled to defend and that was subject to external falsification.

1.2. Hans Urs von Balthasar—Hope Through the Depths of Christ's Suffering

Hans Urs von Balthasar (1905–1988) was an incredibly talented and prolific Swiss theologian who wrote over one hundred books in his lifetime.[51] Although

---

[51] A brief introduction to von Balthasar's thought was written by himself and offers some key insights into his overall focus. See Hans Urs von Balthasar, "A Résumé of My

von Balthasar's primary focus was on theology, his doctoral work was done in German literature. He never took a professorship in his long career, preferring instead to maintain an itinerant lecture schedule while at the same time establishing a foundation named *Johannes Gemeinschaft*, which helped lay people to serve in the Church. Von Balthasar's interests ranged over a broad spectrum of topics including theology, philosophy, patristics, saints, mystics, literature, poetry, music, art, and theater. Because of the breadth of his knowledge, he was known as "the most cultured man in Europe."[52] Long recognized for his conservative theology and unwavering support for Catholic distinctives, von Balthasar was said to be the favorite theologian of Pope John Paul II. On the occasion of the centennial anniversary of his birth, Pope Benedict XVI issued a letter to an international convention gathered in Balthasar's honor, praising his work and encouraging its study.[53]

The core of von Balthasar's theology is found in his famous trilogy, which forms an extensive and profound meditation on God's self-revelation to humanity in Christ. Wolfgang Treitler summed up the purpose of the trilogy in this way:

> The trilogy, which realizes itself in the analogy of the series of transcendentals of truth, goodness, and beauty, conceived by von Balthasar in reverse order, unfolds God's one saving mystery *pro nobis* from the perspective of forms (*Gestalt*)—corresponding to the analogate of beauty; of its self-realization-in the analogy of good; and of its logic-analogous to truth. *The Glory of the Lord,*[54] *Theo-Drama,*[55] and *Theo-Logic,*[56] as well as the *Epilogue,*[57] which is an appendix rather than a

---

Thought," *Communio* 15 (Winter 1988): 468–473. An introduction to von Balthasar may be found in a symposium edited by David L. Schindler, *Hans Urs von Balthasar: His Life and Work* (San Francisco: Ignatius, 1991). Balthasar's article, "A Résumé of My Thought," may also be found in Schindler's book on pages 1–5. See also Edward T. Oakes and David Moss, eds., *The Cambridge Companion to Hans Urs von Balthasar* (Cambridge: Cambridge University Press, 2000) and John O'Donnell, *Hans Urs von Balthasar* (Collegeville, Minn.: Michael Glazier/Liturgical Press, 1992).

[52] Edgardo Antonio Colón-Emeric, "Symphonic Truth: Von Balthasar and Christian Humanism," *CC* 122/11 (May 31, 2005): 30.

[53] Pope Benedict XVI, *Message of His Holiness Benedict XVI for The Centenary of the Birth of Fr Hans Urs Von Balthasar* (October, 6, 2005), http://www.vatican.va/holy_father/benedict_xvi/messages/pont-messages/2005/documents/hf_ben-xvi_mes_20051006_von-balthasar_en.html. (Accessed on October 25, 2014.)

[54] Hans Urs von Balthasar, *Herrlichkeit: Eine theologische Ästhetik*, 3 vols. (Einsiedeln: Johannes Verlag, 1961–1984); English edition trans. Erasmo Leiva-Merikakis, *The Glory of the Lord: A Theological Aesthetics*, 7 vols. (Edinburgh: T. & T. Clark, 1984–1991).

[55] Hans Urs von Balthasar, *Theodramatik*, 4 vols. (Einsiedeln: Johannes Verlag, 1973–1983); English edition trans. Graham Harrison, *Theo-Drama: Theological Dramatic Story*, 5 vols. (San Francisco: Ignatius,1988–1998).

[56] Hans Urs von Balthasar, *Theologik*, 3 vols. (Einsiedeln: Johannes Verlag, 1985–1987); English edition trans. Adrian J. Walker, *Theo-Logic*, 3 vols. (San Francisco: Ignatius, 2001–2005).

conclusion, constitute a methodically specified circling around God's absolute self-revelation in its distinct aspects.[58]

For von Balthasar Christology was the heart and soul of theology. Much of what he wrote reflected on the passion of Christ and humanity's response to it. For von Balthasar, the passion was the subject of the ages. He would return to it time and again to draw strength and meaning from it.

In the closing pages of his *Theo-Drama*, von Balthasar meditates on the tragedy that God would experience if he lost a part of humanity to the flames of hell. God has identified himself with our lostness through the drama of the Cross. He has experienced our pain and abandonment even unto death. Von Balthasar suggests that the real question to be answered is not, "What does man lose if he loses God?" but rather, "What does God lose if he loses man?"[59] In von Balthasar's view, the loss of any portion of humanity would be an incalculable misfortune for God who, in his all encompassing love, went to such great lengths to take salvation into the world. On the other hand, von Balthasar acknowledged that such a loss was a very real possibility in light of scriptural revelation regarding eternal punishment. Pressed between the two possibilities, von Balthasar opted to cling to the hope of the salvation of all rather than to affirm the damnation of any.

This position led von Balthasar into a theological conflict that came to a head in the mid-1980s with the publishing of the last volume of his *Theo-Drama*. In response to his critics he wrote two short books entitled *Was dürfen wir hoffen?*[60] and *Kleiner Diskurs über die Hölle*.[61] These two books have been combined into one English edition entitled, *Dare We Hope "That All Men be Saved"? With a Short Discourse on Hell*.[62] Von Balthasar's basic thesis is that hope for the salvation of all is consistent with the teaching of the New Testament, with teaching of the Church, and that it is an obligation for all Christians to hope for the salvation of every person.[63]

In discussing the New Testament evidence, von Balthasar argued that there are two irreconcilable series of statements to be found in the text:

It is generally known that, in the New Testament, two series of statements run along side by side in such a way that a synthesis of both is neither

---

[57] Hans Urs von Balthasar, *Epilog* (Einsiedeln-Trier: Johannes Verlag, 1987); English edition trans. Edward T. Oakes, *Epilogue* (San Francisco: Ignatius, 1992).

[58] Wolfgang Treitler, "True Foundations of Authentic Theology," in Schindler, *Hans Urs von Balthasar*, 169.

[59] Balthasar, *Theo-Drama: The Last Act*, 5:509. See the discussion of Nicolas J. Healy in "On Hope, Heaven, and Hell," *The University Concourse* 2/9 (May 6, 1997): 1.

[60] Hans Urs von Balthasar, *Was dürfen wir hoffen?* (Einsiedeln: Johannes Verlag, 1986).

[61] Hans Urs von Balthasar, *Kleiner Diskurs über die Hölle* (Einsiedeln: Johannes Verlag, 1987).

[62] Hans Urs von Balthasar, *Dare We Hope "That All Men be Saved"? With a Short Discourse on Hell*, trans. David Kipp and Lothar Krauth (San Francisco: Ignatius, 1988.)

[63] Balthasar, *Dare We Hope?* 29–46; 163–70; 211–21.

permissible nor achievable: the first series speaks of being lost for all
eternity; the second, of God's will, and ability, to save all men.[64]

In resolving this conflict von Balthasar made a distinction between pre-Easter
pronouncements regarding the possibility of eternal punishment and post-Easter
affirmations of universalism.[65] He noted that Jesus' comments regarding eternal
punishment are pre-Easter and as such were to be understood as being
presented in "a language and images that were familiar to the Jews of that
time."[66] Quoting Rahner, he agreed that such language presented an existential
choice that should not be "read as an anticipatory report about something that
will someday come into being."[67] In contrast, von Balthasar argued that the
post-Easter affirmations of universalism, found in the epistles, look back to the
cross and the resurrection and "formulate this totality from a post-Easter
perspective."[68] In his view, the post-Easter perspective naturally had a more
complete understanding of the situation at hand because it took into
consideration the redemption that had occurred on the cross.

Despite his assertion of a dichotomy between the pre and post-Easter
statements, von Balthasar softened his interpretation by observing that a certain
amount of overlap and mixture occurred between the two. Taking note of
certain negative statements made by Paul in the post-Easter era, he
acknowledged that even for Paul "judgment was not fixed."[69] Given that these
two mutually exclusive outcomes could be merged and that both outcomes
were discussed, von Balthasar concluded that bold statements of *apokatastasis*
were to be rejected and that one should "limit oneself to that Christian hope . . .
that God wills all men to be saved."[70]

In analyzing the traditional position of the Catholic Church on the issue, von
Balthasar quoted from Walter Kasper's *Katholischer Erwachsenen-
Katechismus* (1985), which was examined line by line in Rome before its
printing: "Neither Holy Scripture nor the Church's Tradition of faith asserts
with certainty of any man that he is actually in hell. Hell is always held before
our eyes as a *real possibility*, one connected with the offer of conversion and
life."[71] In von Balthasar's view, this fact turned the tables on his critics whom
he called "infernalists" for holding dogmatically to the absolute position that
some people will not escape hell fire.[72] He argued that this position of *de facto*
damnation was the one that was heterodox and out of step with the historical
teaching of the Church. In support of his claim he noted several prominent
Catholic theologians who were in agreement with this position including Erich

---

[64] Balthasar, *Dare We Hope?* 29.
[65] Balthasar, *Dare We Hope?* 21–23; 29–46.
[66] Balthasar, *Dare We Hope?* 29.
[67] Balthasar, *Dare We Hope?* 32. Cf. Rahner, "Hell," 8.
[68] Balthasar, *Dare We Hope?* 29.
[69] Balthasar, *Dare We Hope?* 33.
[70] Balthasar, *Dare We Hope?* 45; 166; 225–54.
[71] Balthasar, *Dare We Hope?* 164–65.
[72] Balthasar, *Dare We Hope?* 178.

Przywara, Henri de Lubac, Joseph Cardinal Ratzinger, Hermann-Josef Lauter, Walter Kasper, and Karl Rahner.[73]

It should be noted that von Balthasar did not believe that hell would be left empty: His hope was that it would be empty of *people*. Von Balthasar viewed the book of Revelation as metaphorical and argued that the things thrown into the Lake of Fire in the book were "everything in world history that appears as negative and incompatible with God's final new world."[74] Thus, there was the possibility of evil consuming itself in the Lake of Fire. This would tie into von Balthasar's discussion of the un-personhood of Satan, in which he speculated that Satan had become a malevolent force who had lost his true personhood.[75] In discussing the eternality of hell, von Balthasar argued that it could not be compared with the experience of eternal life. In his view, eternal life was the "highest-possible development of all duration within the vitality of God."[76] Hell, on the other hand, was a "complete withdrawal to the point of shriveling into the disconsolate immovable now."[77] In this von Balthasar seemed to be saying that hell would have an indefinite or timeless quality that would be experienced in a significantly different way than eternal life.[78] These time concepts seem to flirt with the idea that hell itself may be annihilated.

In the end von Balthasar urged caution regarding the embrace of universalism or eternal punishment. In his view, the two were held in tension by scripture and the two must be held in tension by us. He then reasoned that this leads us into the domain of hope. Von Balthasar found comfort in the words of Hermann-Josef Lauter: "Will it really be *all men* who allow themselves to be reconciled? No theology or prophecy can answer this question. But love *hopes all things* (I Cor. 13:7). It cannot do otherwise than to hope for the reconciliation of all men in Christ. Such unlimited hope is, from the Christian standpoint, not only permitted but *commanded*."[79]

Von Balthasar had a genuine love for the Patristic writers and it is only appropriate that we include in our analysis a discussion of his theology in the context of this setting. In von Balthasar's view, Origen and Gregory of Nyssa pushed their doctrine of apokatastasis beyond the permissible limits of scripture and were not willing to accept the ambiguity of what is found in the New Testament text. This overextension resulted in an overreaction that found its expression in Augustine's doctrine of eternal punishment.[80] According to von Balthasar, both sides bore culpability for the state of affairs that ensued.

---

[73] "My critics act as though I were alone in the limbo to which they banish me. But lo and behold, I discover myself in the best of company here" (Balthasar, *Dare We Hope?* 168).

[74] Balthasar, *Dare We Hope?* 134.

[75] Balthasar, *Dare We Hope?* 145–47.

[76] Balthasar, *Dare We Hope?* 133.

[77] Balthasar, *Dare We Hope?* 133.

[78] This idea shows up in vol. 5 of his *Theo-Drama.* For a discussion of it see Aidan Nichols, *No Bloodless Myth: A Guide Through Balthasar's Dramatics* (Edinburgh: T. & T. Clark, Ltd., 2000), 216–17.

[79] Balthasar, *Dare We Hope?* 213.

[80] Balthasar, *Dare We Hope?* 74.

Viewed against this backdrop, von Balthasar's hopeful universalism essentially serves as a corrective to both camps. His primary focus was to remain true to his reading of the New Testament, which he believed offered support for both sides of the issue. Von Balthasar was not troubled by this seeming contradiction in scripture and saw divine wisdom in the affirmation of both things. On the one side, the hope of universal salvation fit in well with von Balthasar's understanding of the supreme value of God's love and Christ's sacrifice. On the other hand, von Balthasar's understanding of the need for decision fit in well with his view of man's obligation in light of God's incredible gift.

Perhaps the central weakness in von Balthasar's argument lies in his assumption that the New Testament declarations regarding eternal punishment and universal salvation cannot be reconciled. Von Balthasar argued that this was the case even within the writings of the Apostle Paul himself and this perspective seems to have forced him into the position of saying something to the effect that Paul and the New Testament writers were simply being hopelessly inconsistent.[81] As we have already seen, there are several solutions to the issue of incompatibility, and many competent scholars have offered a myriad of alternatives. However, von Balthasar did not entertain or discuss any of these possibilities. Instead, in order to avoid the appearance of asserting such a contradiction von Balthasar argued that what we have in the New Testament declarations regarding eternal punishment were merely the announcement of a possibility as opposed to an absolute reality.[82]

Against this idea is the fact that Jesus never used the language of possibility when discussing the existence of hell and eternal punishment. Indeed, James T. O'Connor notes that the Theological Commission responsible for drafting *Lumen gentium* §48, which refers to those that "descend to eternal fire," made the point of noting that Jesus spoke of the damned in a form that was *grammatically future*: "The significance of that remark is that when the Church speaks of damnation of humans she speaks, as Christ himself did, not in a form of grammar which is *conditional* (i.e., speaking about something which *might* happen), but in the *grammatical future* (i.e., about something which *will* happen). And it was with this understanding that the bishops of Vatican II voted upon and accepted *Lumen gentium*."[83] Similarly, Paul never used the language of possibility when he discussed the issues of judgment,[84] exclusion from the kingdom,[85] destruction,[86] and wrath.[87] For Paul, the reality of these things was a given.

A problem related to this one is von Balthasar's claim that in the New Testament writings we see no human being absolutely consigned to hell. The New Testament characterizations of Judas Iscariot pose a major hurdle for this

---

[81] Balthasar, *Dare We Hope?* 31–34.

[82] Balthasar, *Dare We Hope?* 32.

[83] James T. O'Connor, "Von Balthasar and Salvation," *HPR* (July 1989): 10–21.

[84] Rom. 2:1–4; 3:7–8, 5:16, 8:1; 1 Cor. 11:32; 2 Cor. 3:9; 2 Thes. 2:12; 1 Tim. 5:24.

[85] 1 Cor. 6:9–11; Gal. 5:19–21; Eph. 5:5–7.

[86] Rom. 2:12, 9:22; 1 Cor. 1:18, 15:18; 2 Cor. 2:15, 4:3; Gal. 6:8; Phil. 1:28, 3:19; 1 Thes. 5:3; 2 Thes. 1:9, 2:10; 1 Tim. 6:9.

[87] Rom. 1:18, 2:5–9, 3:5, 5:9, 9:22; Eph. 2:3, 5:6; Col. 3:6; 1 Thes. 1:10, 2:16, 5:9.

perspective. Von Balthasar held out hope that Judas repented before he died: "Who can know the nature of the remorse that seized Judas when he saw the Christ had been condemned (Mt. 27:3)?"[88] However, the language of the New Testament offers us little or no reason to embrace such optimism. In Mark 14:21 Jesus ominously noted: "For the Son of Man is to go, just as it is written of Him; but woe to that man by whom the Son of Man is betrayed! It would have been good for that man if he had not been born." In referring to Judas in his high-priestly prayer in John 17:12, Jesus observed that none of his disciples are "destroyed" (*apollumi*—ἀπόλλυμι) except "the son of destruction" (υἱὸς τῆς ἀπωλείας). Acts 1:25 notes that Judas turned aside from his ministry that he might go to "his own place" (*poreuthēnai eis ton topon ton idion*— πορευθῆναι εἰς τὸν τόπον τὸν ἴδιον), a common first-century euphemism for one's own destruction.[89] All of these characterizations seem to indicate that Judas did indeed go into perdition. At a minimum it must be noted that we have no other verses in Scripture that contradict these unyielding declarations.[90]

In addition to Judas, there is the case of the Beast (the Antichrist) and his false prophet being summarily thrown into the Lake of Fire in Rev. 19:20. In Rev. 20:10 we see Satan also being thrown into the same Lake of Fire "where the beast and the false prophet are also" and we are told that "they will be tormented day and night forever and ever." Von Balthasar interpreted these things in metaphorical terms and thus attempted to escape the reality of two human beings being consigned to the flames of hell. However, a metaphorical interpretation of the lives of these men is difficult to maintain given the very

---

[88] Balthasar, *Dare We Hope?* 187.

[89] D.J. Williams, "Judas Iscariot," in Joel B. Green, Scot McKnight, and I. Howard Marshall, *Dictionary of Jesus and the Gospels* (Downer's Grove, Ill.: InterVarsity, 1992), 408.

[90] It should be noted that the recently published *Gospel of Judas* presents to us a Judas who carries out the will of Jesus in facilitating his death and is celebrated as a gnostic hero as opposed to being dismissed as a traitor. From the gnostic point of view, the human body was considered to be evil since it was a part of the physical world system. This system, they believed, was created by evil demiurges in an effort to trap human souls and keep them from migrating back to the one true God. In the context of discussing those who offer sacrifices to the angelic demiurge Saklas, Jesus tells Judas: "But you will exceed all of them. For you will sacrifice the man that clothes me." Thus, from a gnostic perspective, Judas' betrayal is cast in a positive light as Judas helped Jesus to escape from the injurious flesh. The *Codex Tchacos,* which contains the manuscript of *The Gospel of Judas,* is demonstrably a third to fourth-century work, although Irenaeus mentions a similar *Gospel of Judas* in his *Adv. Haer.* 1.31.1, which is dated to around 180 C.E. While the *Gospel of Judas* adds to our knowledge of Gnosticism, few scholars believe that it sheds any new light on Judas' actions or his relationship with Jesus because it is demonstrably a gnostic work that was composed at a much later date than the canonical gospels. The text of the *Gospel of Judas* may be found online at: http://www.nationalgeographic.com/lostgospel/_pdf/GospelofJudas.pdf. (Accessed on December 2, 2014.) The text may also be found in: Rodolphe Kasser, Marvin W. Meyer; and Gregor Wurst, eds., *The Gospel of Judas: From Codex Tchacos* (Washington D.C.: National Geographic, 2006).

detailed discussion we have in Rev. chapters 6–20 regarding their careers and their kingdom. At a minimum, one cannot deny that the image in Rev. 19:20 is that of *two human beings* being cast into the Lake of Fire. This is a fact that needs to be explained away rather than established.

In the final analysis, von Balthasar's presentation reminds us of the central role that hope plays in the Christian faith. His point about it being the responsibility of Christians to hope for the salvation of all people is well taken. If Christianity is anything, it is a religion of hope. It is the affirmation of the power of God to snatch life from the jaws of death.

2. Christocentric Universalism Expressed as a Certainty
Due to the official condemnation of universalism by the Church at the Second Council of Constantinople (553 CE) and the Church's aggressive persecution of those who have embraced it, very few Catholic theologians have been willing to publicly endorse a full-blown expression of universalism. While the documents generated by the Second Vatican Council raised the hopes of liberal Catholic theologians that there might be a wholesale loosening of doctrinal restrictions, these hopes have had to be moderated in light of the publishing of the new official catechism as well as the many corrective steps taken by the Congregation of the Doctrine of the Faith to rein in wandering theologians. Popes John Paul II and Benedict XVI turned out to be theologically conservative and fairly aggressive in their enforcement of Catholic doctrine. Their efforts had the desired effect of suppressing doctrinal deviations.

However, their successor Pope Francis has made some comments recently that appear to open the door to universal salvation and have created quite a controversy within the Church. On May 22, 2013, in a homily he delivered at a daily mass in the chapel of St. Martha hostel, Francis declared:

> The Lord has redeemed all of us, all of us, with the Blood of Christ: all of us, not just Catholics. Everyone! "Father, the atheists?" Even the atheists. Everyone! And this Blood makes us children of God of the first class! We are created children in the likeness of God and the Blood of Christ has redeemed us all! And we all have a duty to do good. And this commandment for everyone to do good, I think, is a beautiful path towards peace. If we, each doing our own part, if we do good to others, if we meet there, doing good, and we go slowly, gently, little by little, we will make that culture of encounter: we need that so much. We must meet one another doing good. "But I don't believe, Father, I am an atheist!" But do good: we will meet one another there.[91]

---

[91] Hendrik Hertzberg, "'Father, the Atheists?' Even the Atheists," *The New Yorker*, June 2, 2013; http://www.newyorker.com/news/hendrik-hertzberg/father-the-atheists-even-the-atheists. (Accessed December 10, 2014.) It should be noted that there is some difficulty encountered in accessing the text of Pope Francis' daily homilies, as the Vatican, at Francis' request, does not record or completely transcribe them. The limited quotes we have available from this particular sermon were first released by Vatican Radio and then picked up by the press. The summary and quotes from the homely are no longer available on the Vatican Radio website and are not available on the main Vatican

Within hours of the release of Francis' comments a controversy erupted over what he said with several commentators and news organizations arguing that Francis had embraced universal salvation as well as a theology of works-righteousness.[92] In order to quell the conflict, the Vatican had spokesman Fr. Thomas Rosica issue a clarification. In it Rosica affirmed several Church distinctives by quoting directly from the catechism including a confirmation of centrality of the Church in the plan of salvation: "[T]hey cannot be saved who, knowing the Church as founded by Christ and necessary for salvation, would refuse to enter her or remain in her."[93]

Given his focus upon redemption, the meaning of Francis' words surely hinge upon the Catholic doctrine of redemption, which has always held that all human beings are redeemed by Christ in the sense of having their sins paid for.[94] Nevertheless, the Church has also held that this redemption does not become salvation until it is received by the individual through faith.[95] Given that Vatican II inclusivism has greatly blurred the lines between those who consciously receive those who unknowingly receive redemption, one could argue that Pope Francis' comments seem to be pointing to a universalist outcome. However, such an argument appears to push things too far especially because Francis did not specifically address the related numbers of those who have actually received Christ's redemption.

The reaction of the Catholic Church to Pope Francis' words reveals how sensitive the Church is to doctrinal deviations even in our own day. Despite this sensitivity, there are still those theologians within the Church that are willing to take doctrinal risks. The most prominent of these in recent years have been the liberation theologians who have passionately challenged the status quo in many areas including eschatology. One liberation theologian in particular has made universalism a central element of his theology. This man is Gustavo Gutiérrez.

2.1. Gustavo Gutiérrez—Universalism as the Ultimate Liberation

"From the viewpoint of those who suffer." These words stand at the very heart of the theology of Gustavo Gutiérrez (b. 1928) and were selected by him to

---

website either. The *New Yorker* article cited above quotes directly from the original Vatican Radio summary.

[92] Dwight Longenecker, "Did Pope Francis Preach Salvation by Works??" *Patheos.com* (May 23, 2013); http://www.patheos.com/blogs/standingonmyhead/2013/05/did-pope-francis-preach-salvation-by-works.html. (Accessed December 10, 2014.) "Pope Francis Say Atheists Who Do Good Are Redeemed, Not Just Catholics," *Huffington Post*, May 23, 2013, http://www.huffingtonpost.com/2013/05/22/pope-francis-good-theists_n_3320757.html?view=print&comm_ref=false. (Accessed on December 10, 2014).

[93] Thomas Rosica, "Explanatory Note on the Meaning of 'Salvation' in Francis' Daily Homily of May 22," *Zenit* (May 23, 2013); http://www.zenit.org/en/articles/explanatory-note-on-the-meaning-of-salvation-in-francis-daily-homily-of-may-22. (Accessed on December 10, 2014.)

[94] The *Catechism of the Catholic Church* speaks of Christ's death providing "a mystery of universal redemption." Cf. *CCC*, § 601, p. 170.

[95] *CCC*, § 161–62, p. 50.

express the source from which his theology of liberation flows.[96] They are words that contain a philosophy as well as a call to action. They are words that have engendered a world-wide revolution in Christian thinking and—more importantly from Gutiérrez's perspective—they are words that have engendered a world-wide revolution in Christian practice. Born in the slums and abject poverty of Latin America, liberation theology has become a global force that has reached to the more opulent shores of North America and Europe and has had an impact that has carried far beyond the severely impoverished Latin American people that it was originally intended to serve.

A necessary result of the emergence of liberation theology on the world scene has been controversy and conflict.[97] As an intensely practical response to poverty and human suffering, liberation theology represents a potent threat to the existing structure and ordering of both society and religion, for one cannot demand total liberation for the poor and oppressed without challenging the existing machinery of societal power. At the center of it all are the writings of Gutiérrez, a Peruvian theologian, who is considered by most participants, both pro and con, to be the "father" of the movement.[98] Gutiérrez studied medicine, psychology, and philosophy before obtaining a doctorate in theology from the Institut Pastoral d'Etudes Religieuses, Université Catholique in Lyon. In addition to his academic work, Gutiérrez has spent a great deal of his time working among the poor in Lima, Peru.

In his classic book, *A Theology of Liberation*, Gutiérrez articulates three essential levels of "liberation."[99] The first level of liberation is political liberation: liberation from oppressive economic and societal conditions. The second level of liberation is historical liberation: liberation in the sense that humanity must take control of is own historical destiny. The third level of

---

[96] Gustavo Gutiérrez, *The Power of the Poor in History: Selected Writings* (Maryknoll, N.Y.: Orbis, 1983), xvi, 203, 231.

[97] The Catholic Church has experienced several epic battles over the issue of liberation theology. An important collection of documents and writings related to the conflict can be found in: Alfred T. Hennelly, *Liberation Theology: A Documentary History* (Maryknoll, N.Y.: Orbis, 1990). A concise discussion of the issues at hand may be found in: Rosino Gibellini, *The Liberation Theology Debate* (Maryknoll, N.Y.: Orbis, 1987), 42–60; Deane W. Ferm, *Third World Liberation Theologies: An Introductory Survey* (Maryknoll, N.Y.: Orbis, 1986), 100–117; and Arthur F. McGovern, *Liberation Theology and Its Critics* (Maryknoll, N.Y.: Orbis, 1989), 47–61. A more extended discussion may be found in Manfred K. Bahmann, *A Preference for the Poor: Latin American Liberation Theology from a Protestant Perspective* (Lanham, Md.: University Press of America, 2005).

[98] The bulk of Gutiérrez's writings and theological thought can be found in the following six volumes that have been translated from Spanish into English: Gustavo Gutiérrez, *A Theology of Liberation: History, Politics, and Liberation*, 15th anniversary edition (Maryknoll, N.Y.: Orbis, 1973; 1988); *The Power of the Poor in History*; *We Drink From Our Own Wells: The Spiritual Journey of a People* (Maryknoll, N.Y.: Orbis, 1984); *On Job: God-Talk and the Suffering of the Innocent* (Maryknoll, N.Y.: Orbis, 1987); *The Truth Shall Make You Free* (Maryknoll, N.Y.: Orbis, 1990); James B. Nickoloff, ed., *Gustavo Gutiérrez: Essential Writings* (Minneapolis, Minn.: Fortress, 1996).

[99] Gutiérrez, *A Theology of Liberation*, xxxviii–xl; 24–25; 103–105.

liberation is liberation from sin: liberation in the sense of "radical liberation" from all forms of oppression. Taken as a whole, these levels combine to provide a comprehensive soteriology that includes universal salvation.[100]

For Gutiérrez, salvation is an all-encompassing concept that "embraces the whole of humanity and all of human history."[101] His universalism is firmly Christocentric and is rooted in the documents of Vatican II. In particular it has been influenced by the "Dogmatic Constitution on the Church" *Lumen gentium* (November 21, 1964), which affirmed that the Church is "the universal sacrament of salvation."[102] Although he does not like the phrase "anonymous Christianity," Gutiérrez asserts that the process of salvation embraces all people whether they are aware of it or not. He comments:

> The rediscovery of this single convocation to salvation has caused the crumbling of barriers erected diligently but artificially by a certain kind of theology. It reaffirms the possibility of the presence of grace—that is, of the acceptance of a personal relationship with the Lord—in all persons, be they conscious of it or not. This in turn has led to the consideration of an anonymous Christianity, in other words, of a Christianity beyond the visible frontiers of the Church. The advent of a "Christendom without name" has been proclaimed. These expressions are equivocal and the choice of words poor. It will be necessary to refine them so that they will point with greater precision to a reality which is itself indisputable: all persons are in Christ efficaciously called to communion with God. To accept the historical viewpoint of the meaning of human existence is to

---

[100] Although Gutiérrez is not a Marxist, much of what he says comes clothed in Marxist terminology. In pursuing a solution for poverty in Latin America Gutiérrez spends quite a bit of time analyzing the causes of indigence and oppression. Along these lines he feels free to use several categories of analysis borrowed from Marxist and socialist schools of thought. He does this because he believes that Marx made substantial contributions toward constructing "a scientific understanding of historical reality" (*A Theology of Liberation*, 19). In *A Theology of Liberation* he comments: "Pointing the way towards an era in history when humankind can live humanly, Marx created categories which allowed for the elaboration of a science of history." I think to understand Gutiérrez as being a Marxist is to fundamentally misread what he has written. There can be no doubt that he embraces certain philosophical perspectives common to Marxism (e.g. a critique of capitalism, the principle of class struggle, and the abolition of the private ownership of the means of production) but Gutiérrez also rejects many essential aspects of the Marxist program (e.g. philosophical materialism, anti-religious bias, determinism, and violent revolution). For Gutiérrez's own defense against the charge of Marxism, see Gustavo Gutiérrez, "Theology and the Social Sciences," in James B. Nickoloff, ed., *Gustavo Gutiérrez: Essential Writings* (Minneapolis, Minn.: Fortress, 1996), 42–49. For an assessment of the use of Marxist analysis by liberation theologians see McGovern, *Liberation Theology and Its Critics*, 156–164.

[101] Gutiérrez, *A Theology of Liberation*, 91; Gutiérrez, *The Power of the Poor in History*, 10–12.

[102] *DEC Lumen gentium* §48; Gutiérrez, *The Power of the Poor in* History, 182; Núñez, *Liberation Theology*, 85.

rediscover the Pauline theme of the universal lordship of Christ, in whom all things exist and have been saved. [103]

This view ties in well with Gutiérrez's concept of soteriology, which is linked closely to his concept of liberation. Indeed, liberation itself is defined by Gutiérrez in this way: "Liberation is an all-embracing process that leaves no dimension of human life untouched, because when all is said and done it expresses the saving action of God in history."[104] In Gutiérrez's thought, true salvation is often equated with total liberation and the two terms are frequently used synonymously in his writings.[105] In completing his discussion of liberation and salvation in *A Theology of Liberation*, Gutiérrez draws this conclusion: "Salvation embraces all persons and the whole person; the liberating action of Christ . . ."[106] Thus, for him, salvation and liberation are one and the same concept: "[S]alvation history is a continuing process of liberation."[107]

Along these lines, it is important to come to an understanding of how the concept of utopia fits into Gutiérrez's thought. The achievement of utopia is linked by Gutiérrez to the goal of liberation. In his view, the creation of a utopia here on earth will be the "creation of a new humanity in a different society characterized by solidarity."[108] This utopia will be "the place of encounter between political liberation and the communion of all persons with God."[109] Thus, for Gutiérrez, utopia is defined very concretely as the human task of transforming the world and the future of human history into all that God desires it to be: "The term *utopia* has been revived within the last few decades to refer to a historical plan for a qualitatively different society and to express the aspiration to establish new social relations among human beings."[110] For Gutiérrez, the attainment of utopia is a part of the liberation process, and not the end of it: "The gospel does not provide utopia for us, this is a human work."[111] So then it is important that we understand that Gutiérrez's utopianism is not synonymous with his universalism. It is a step toward liberation; a real-world goal toward which human society should struggle.

As his focus is almost entirely upon the achievement of liberation, Gutiérrez does not spend much time elaborating the details of his universalism. For him it is enough to know that in the end all human beings will be liberated into a meaningful relationship with God. Therefore, there is virtually nothing said about heaven, hell, or eternal punishment. Liberation is his main focus and his declaration of universalism is an affirmation of his belief that this goal will eventually be obtained.

---

[103] Gutiérrez, *A Theology of Liberation*, 45.

[104] Gutiérrez, *We Drink From Our Own Wells*, 2.

[105] See Ferm's discussion of this in, *Third World Liberation Theologies*, 20.

[106] Gutiérrez, *A Theology of Liberation*, 97.

[107] Gutiérrez, *The Power of the Poor in History*, 33. See also J. Andrew Kirk, *Liberation Theology: An Evangelical View from the Third World* (Atlanta: John Knox, 1979), 26.

[108] Gutiérrez, *A Theology of Liberation*, 139.

[109] Gutiérrez, *A Theology of Liberation*, 139.

[110] Gutiérrez, *A Theology of Liberation*, 135.

[111] Gutiérrez, *A Theology of Liberation*, 139.

Most expressions of universalism are born out of a reaction against some theological assertion. Sometimes it is a reaction against the idea of hell and the doctrine of eternal punishment. Sometimes it is reaction against the idea of Calvinist election and predestination. Sometimes it is a reaction against the idea of exclusivism and the concomitant notion that many are destined to be lost. Gustavo Gutiérrez's universalism is interesting in that it is not so much a reaction against anything theologically, as it is an objection to a socio-political reality. It is a complaint leveled against a deadly status quo. It is a protest leveled against a system that consigns a great many people to a living hell on earth. In taking up the cause of human liberation Gutiérrez is trying to speak for a mass of human voices that all too often go unheard.

From a historical point of view Gutiérrez's universalism has a strong affinity to that of Nicolas Berdyaev, who crafted his universalist solution with a keen awareness of the historic plight of all human beings. Berdyaev's universalism was both a philosophical and theological response to the corruption and failure of human government. His universalism was conceived of in terms of the ultimate political deliverance. It too was a protest against all that exploits, all that dehumanizes, and all that destroys. By offering an all-embracing vision of the deliverance of the entire human race, Berdyaev envisioned an ultimate correction to the failure of human institutions. This sort of correction is also a central feature of Gutiérrez's presentation and his argument that in the end liberation will embrace all people.

A fundamental issue that tears away at the veracity of Gutiérrez's proposal is the theological method that he employs. In his view, theology is logically developed *after* experience. In his book, *A Theology of Liberation*, Gutiérrez describes theology as "a critical reflection on Christian praxis in light of the Word."[112] Thus, for Gutiérrez theology is logically secondary; it flows out of human experience:

> Theology must be critical reflection on humankind, on basic human principles. Only with this approach will theology be a serious discourse, aware of itself, in full possession of its conceptual elements . . . Theology is reflection, a critical attitude. Theology *follows;* it is the second step. What Hegel used to say about philosophy can likewise be applied to theology: it rises only at sundown.[113]

The problem with this approach is that it leads Gutiérrez to subordinate the Bible to socio-political concerns while at the same time elevating experience as the primary arbiter of the truth. For Gutiérrez this means that the Bible is treated as a manual on liberation. For instance, the exodus account is interpreted as paradigmatic of God's plan for human liberation. The liberation of Israel is declared to be "a political action."[114] Sin is interpreted as being "the breach of friendship with God and with other persons" and is said to be evident "in oppressive structures, in the exploitation of humans by humans, in the

---

[112] Gutiérrez, *A Theology of Liberation*, 11.
[113] Gutiérrez, *A Theology of Liberation*, 9.
[114] Gutiérrez, A Theology of Liberation, 88.

domination and slavery of people, races, and social classes."[115] It is argued that the work of Christ on the cross encompasses political liberation as well as liberation from hunger, oppression, misery, ignorance and injustice.[116]

All of these interpretations are problematic. A fair reading of the exodus account will reveal that the focus of scripture is on divine intervention and not on crude political calculations. A study of the doctrine of sin in the Bible will note that sin is always related to the violation of God's law and that it is definitively labeled as "lawlessness" in 1 John 3:4. If sin is defined primarily in terms of the oppression or exploitation of others, how does Gutiérrez deal with the Lord's acceptance of slavery in the Old Testament (Lev. 25:39–55) or Jesus' acceptance of bondservanthood in the New Testament (Lk. 17:7–10; see also Philemon 14; Tit. 2:9; 1 Pet. 2:18)? If Jesus' work on the cross was meant to heal a cornucopia of social ills, why does the New Testament not say so? Why does the New Testament focus so singularly on applying salvation in Christ to individuals as opposed to the deliverance of political organizations and oppressive human institutions? History records that the Roman Imperium was rife with institutionalized oppression, and yet both Paul and Peter advocate a submission to the ruling authorities (Rom. 14:1–7; 1 Pet. 2:13–17). Jesus himself endorsed submission to oppressive conquerors when he famously responded to the Herodians: "Then render to Caesar the things that are Caesar's; and to God the things that are God's" (Mt. 22:21). Jesus also commended the action of a poor widow who gave away her last pennies to a religious institution that was rife with corruption (Mk. 12:41–44). He did not stop her or reimburse her; he did not rail against an oppressive power structure. When people complained that expensive oil should have been sold to help the poor rather than used to anoint Jesus, he responded: "For the poor you have with you always . . ." (Mk. 14:3–9). All of these scriptures, as well as many others, cast serious doubt over the validity of Gutiérrez's interpretation. To the great detriment of his project, Gutiérrez makes no effort to deal with the evidence of scripture that contradicts his own peculiar construal of the text.

As we have seen already, the difficulty with an experience-driven interpretation of the Bible is that it is necessarily provisional and arbitrary. Thus the problem of interpretive subjectivity is a very real one for Gutiérrez. If interpretation is determined solely by one's experience of life then almost any interpretation of scripture is possible and justifiable as long as it meets that criterion. Those who are used to a more precise hermeneutical control (e.g. the application of the historical critical method) will find Gutiérrez's approach to interpreting the Bible to be entirely unacceptable.

Despite these shortcomings, the challenge that Gustavo Gutiérrez places before us is that of a theology that takes seriously the existence of an oppressed and poverty stricken humanity. While a universalist outcome is an important aspect of his faith, Gutiérrez is primarily concerned with attempting to bring about real change in our present day world. Western theological discussion has all too often devolved into an exercise of writing footnotes to footnotes. Gutiérrez reminds us that, no matter what our eschatological outlook may be,

---

[115] Gutiérrez, *A Theology of Liberation*, 103.
[116] Gutiérrez, *A Theology of Liberation*, 102–105.

our theology must engage the pressing and deadly problems that humanity faces every day.

3. Conclusion

The official stance of the Catholic Church regarding the salvation of non-Christians is inclusivism. Karl Rahner clearly tried to expand that envelope with the development of his concept of the anonymous Christian and his efforts to incorporate as many people as possible into the realm of the saved. In fact, when taken as a whole, Rahner's formulation of hopeful universalism comes about as close as one can come to an endorsement of dogmatic universalism while at the same time still staying within the extreme limits of the inclusivist camp. This leaves us to wonder what Rahner would have written had he not been placed under the constraints of Catholic orthodoxy.

Certainly Rahner's speculations go beyond the sort of inclusivism accepted by the Church hierarchy today. Joseph Cardinal Ratzinger's declaration *Dominus Iesus*, made before he became Pope, was intended to define the limits of Catholic inclusivism and appears to take a decisive step back from Rahner's optimistic assessment of those who are outside of the Church: "If it is true that the followers of other religions can receive divine grace, it is also certain that *objectively speaking* they are in a gravely deficient situation in comparison with those who, in the Church, have the fullness of the means of salvation."[117] This statement amounts to a corrective issued to those within the Church who would take either inclusivism or pluralism too far.

With this in mind, it is easy to understand why the tentative hope for universal salvation found in the theology of Han Urs von Balthesar is more paletable to the Catholic leadership. The ambiguity found in von Balthesar's proposal creates a space into which the current Church position may fit. On the other hand, the rejection of the more extreme aspects of Gustavo Gutiérrez's liberation theology is also made more explicable in light of recent Church pronouncements. As Pope Benedict XVI has stressed, the Church will not allow the Vatican II documents to be interpreted in such a way as they cause a "split" between the theologies of the pre-Conciliar and post-Conciliar Churches.[118]

In the view of the Catholic heirarchy, nothing less than the consistency of the theology and the tradition of the magisterium is at stake in these doctrinal debates. As we shall see, the Church has no compunction in dealing harshly with those who have over-stepped the doctrinal limits.

---

[117] Ratzinger, *Dominus Iesus*, §22.
[118] Benedict XVI, "Address of His Holiness Benedict XVI to the Roman Curia Offering Them His Christmas Greetings, Thursday, 22 December 2005."

CHAPTER 7

Plurocentric Approaches

We now turn our attention to plurocentric universalism as conceived of by Catholic theologians. As we noted in chapter five, this is an innovative form of universalism that can be rightly counted as a unique contribution made by contemporary theology to the expansion of the doctrine. This chapter will reveal that Catholic theologians have made a unique contribution of their own to this relatively new theological development.

As this perspective is definitely at odds with current Catholic inclusivist thinking, plurocentric universalism carries with it a much greater probability for provoking conflict within the Church. As we have already seen, recent Church declarations addressing pluralism, such as *Dominus Iesus*, have been condemnatory of any form of "religious relativism" that seeks to give equal weight to all religions and systems of salvation. Clearly, the Catholic Church wants to protect what it sees to be its unique status as "the sacrament of salvation." Therefore, there has been a gradual increase in the pressure brought to bear upon Catholic theologians who openly endorse the more radical forms of pluralism. The three theologians we will examine in this section are all notable for the fact that they have entered into open conflict with the Church and each of them has been denounced in some way by the keepers of orthodoxy. In the eyes of the Church, the theology of these men clearly violates present doctrinal standards and stands in need of correction.

1. Raimundo Panikkar—The Cosmotheandric Connection

Raimundo (or Raimon) Panikkar (1918–2010) was born in Barcelona to a Catalan Catholic mother and an Indian Hindu father. This distinctive ancestry and the diversity of the environment in which he was raised contributed greatly to his unique pluralist outlook on life.[1] Panikkar is an acknowledged pioneer in the development of a pluralist theology of religions. He was also one of the most educated men of his generation and held three earned doctorates: Philosophy (1945–Complutense University of Madrid), Science (1958–Complutense University of Madrid), and Theology (1961–Pontifical Lateran

---

[1] A brief biography of Raimundo Panikkar's life as well as a critical analysis of his thought may be found in Anthony Savari Raj, *A New Hermeneutic of Reality: Raimon Panikkar's Cosmotheandric Vision* (Bern; Berlin; Frankfurt/M.; New York; Paris; Wien: Peter Lang, 1998). Other analyses of Panikkar's thought may be found in: Jyri Komulainen, *An Emerging Cosmotheandric Religion? Raimon Panikkar's Pluralistic Theology of Religions* (Leiden, Brill, 2005); and Joseph Prabhu, ed., *The Intercultural Challenge of Raimon Panikkar* (Maryknoll, N.Y.: Orbis, 1996).

University in Rome). In addition to this education, Panikkar pursued advanced studies in Indian philosophy and religion at the Universities of Mysore and Varanasi. Panikkar was ordained a Catholic priest in 1946. He held several professorships in Europe, India, and America. Upon his retirement he moved to Tavertet, outside Barcelona, Spain. Panikkar once described himself as a Hindu-Buddhist-Christian. In commenting on his spiritual journey, Panikkar famously observed: "I 'left' as a Christian, I 'found' myself a Hindu and I 'return' a Buddhist without having ceased to be a Christian."[2] His devotional life represented an interesting blend of his own academic convictions and when it came to pluralism, Panikkar was an exceptional example of one who practiced what he preached.[3]

With over forty books and numerous articles to his credit, it would be impossible to plumb the depths of Panikkar's intricate synthesis of pluralist theology in the limited space that we have available here. Nevertheless, there is one overarching theme that makes his plurocentric universalism intelligible: his "cosmotheandric" vision or "cosmotheandrism." Panikkar developed this idea over an extended period of time as a means of encapsulating what he believed to be the ultimate metaphysical view of reality. Although the concept appears in several places in the 1981 revision of his classic book, *The Unknown Christ of Hinduism* (1964),[4] it finds its fullest and most mature elaboration in one of Panikkar's later books, *The Cosmotheandric Experience* (1993).[5] Perhaps the best way to begin to understand Panikkar's cosmotheandric vision is by dividing the word into its three constituent parts, *cosmos-theos-anêr*. He argued that these three Greek words represent the three irreducible and interconnected constituent elements of all reality: (1) the Cosmic, (2) the Divine, and (3) the Human. In positing this triadic formulation, Panikkar was essentially saying that there is a Trinitarian structure to everything that exists. If one removes one of these elements from the structure of reality, existence is not possible. On this point it is worth quoting Panikkar at length:

> The cosmotheandric principle could be formulated by saying that the divine, the human and the earthly—however we may prefer to call them—are the three irreducible dimensions which constitute the real, i.e., any reality inasmuch as it is real. It does not deny that the abstracting capacity of our mind can, for particular and limited purposes, consider the parts of reality independently; it does not deny the complexity of the real

---

[2] Raimundo Panikkar, *The Interreligious Dialogue* (Bangalore: Asian Trading Corp., 1984), 40.

[3] Panikkar describes his approach to life in his article "Philosophy as Life-Style," in A. Mercier and M. Svilar, eds., *Philosophers On their Own Work*, vol. IV (Berne: Herbert Lang, 1978), 193–228.

[4] Raimundo Panikkar, *The Unknown Christ of Hinduism*, revised and enlarged edition (Maryknoll, N.Y.: Orbis, 1981), 6, 20, 29, 93, 94. The revised edition signaled a radical change in Panikkar's thinking and is a window into the development of his thought. In light of the fact that the revised edition is so different from the original we will focus on it as a means of drawing closer to Panikkar's most mature theological development.

[5] Raimon Panikkar, *The Cosmotheandric Experience: Emerging Religious Consciousness* (Maryknoll, N.Y.: Orbis, 1993).

and its many degrees. But this principle reminds us that the parts are parts and that they are not just accidentally juxtaposed, but essentially related to the whole. In other words, the parts are real *parti*cipations and are to be understood not according to a merely spatial model, as books are part of a library or a carburetor and a differential gear are parts of an automobile, but rather according to an organic unity, as body and soul, or mind and will belong to a human being: they are parts because they are not the whole but they are not parts which can be "parted" from the whole without thereby ceasing to exist . . . They are constitutive dimensions of the whole, which permeates everything that is and is not reducible to any of its constituents.[6]

Panikkar argued that this cosmotheandric intuition is an "insight into the threefold core of all that is" and thus reality is to be viewed ultimately as an interdependent relationship among all things.[7] Panikkar stressed this relational aspect in an older formulation when he said: "There is no God without Man and the World. There is no Man without God and the World. There is no World without God and Man."[8]

In speaking of the divine dimension, Panikkar moved beyond God-talk and conceived of it as infinite, inexhaustible, and unfathomable. He also likened the divine dimension to "the mystery of Being and/or Non-Being" and therefore argued that there is room in his formulation for atheistic systems like Buddhism, which prefer to speak of a nothingness or an emptiness that makes everything else possible.[9] From these statements it can be seen that, for Panikkar, the divine dimension is not conceived of in terms of supreme being. *It is a dimension and not a person.* It is non-theistic rather than mono-theistic. As Panikkar stated, he wanted to "liberate the divine from the burden of being God."[10]

It seems that this conception of God developed early on in Panikkar's theology. We see in his little booklet, *The Trinity and World Religions* that Panikkar posited the radical transcendence of God the Father by positing that God gave his all in the generation of his Son and became literally nothing: "The Absolute, the Father, *is not.* He has no *ek-sistence,* not even of being. In the generation of the Son he has, so to speak, given everything . . . The Father *has* no being: the Son is *his* being."[11] He concludes: "The God of theism, thus, is the Son."[12] Into this profound nothingness of God he locates the dimension of

---

[6] Panikkar, *The Cosmotheandric Experience,* 60.

[7] Panikkar, *The Cosmotheandric Experience,* 61.

[8] Raimon Panikkar, "Ecology from an Eastern Philosophical Perspective," *Monchanin* 50 (June–December 1975): 27.

[9] Panikkar, *The Cosmotheandric Experience,* 61.

[10] As quoted in Gerhard Hall, "Multi-Faith Dialogue in Conversation with Raimon Panikkar," *Australian Association for the Study of Religions,* Annual Conference 4th–6th July 2003, Multi-Faith Centre, Griffith University, http://dlibrary.acu.edu.au/ staffhome/gehall/Hall_Panikkar.htm. (Accessed on October 30, 2014.)

[11] Raymond Panikkar, *The Trinity and the World Religions: Icon—Person—Mystery* (Madras: The Christian Literature Society, 1970), 46–47.

[12] Panikkar, *The Trinity and World Religions,* 51.

the divine. Into this profound nothingness he locates the *nirvāna* of the Buddhists and the *Brahman* of the Hindus.[13] Therefore, the divine dimension presents an ineffable mystery for Panikkar. It is nothing and everything at once. It should be noted here that Panikkar is careful to try to deflect an accusation of pantheism in his presentation and in point of fact he goes out of his way to make it clear that he believes that there is an independent aspect to the divine dimension. For him all things are not divine, but rather the divine is a "constitutive principle of all things."[14]

The human dimension of Panikkar's cosmotheandrism is the dimension of consciousness that entails the full range of reality. For Panikkar this includes not just the perceiver but also the object of perception. "In so many words, the waters of human consciousness wash all the shores of the real—even if Man cannot penetrate the *terra incognita* of the hinterland—and by this very fact, Man's being enters into relation with the whole of reality. The entire field of reality lives humanized in him. The transparent character of consciousness belongs not only to the Man who knows, but also to the object known."[15] By focusing on human consciousness, Panikkar is not saying that things exist only because human beings know them. He is saying instead that "thinkability and knowability as such are features of all that is."[16]

The cosmic dimension of Panikkar's cosmotheandrism draws the physical world into his formulation of reality in such a way that it is indissolubly linked to both the divine and conscious dimensions. Panikkar believes that the commonly held dualistic division of reality into the physical and spiritual realms leads to an insurmountable cleft that fails to see the interconnectedness of all things and essentially results in the propagation of two realities. For him reality cannot be divided. Everything must share in the secularity of the cosmos: "Again, this relation is not merely external or accidental: anything that exists has a constitutive relation with matter/existence . . ."[17] Even aphysical concepts such as truth and angels "have a worldly dimension" and "can only be meaningful within a World, i.e., within the range of worldly experience—even if we extrapolate afterwards."[18] For Panikkar, no matter how one looks at it, nothing that exists can escape a cosmic connection. At the conceptual level this means that Panikkar's formulation of the divine dimension necessitates the existence of the world. In his view, the divine space cannot exist in a vacuum— it must participate, it must be filled: "I am only saying that a God without the World is not a real God, nor does he exist. I am saying that the cosmic dimension is not a superfluous appendix to the other two dimensions, but equally constitutive, both of the whole and of each *real* part of the whole . . ."[19]

Thus, the cosmotheandric vision ties everything together for Panikkar and for him reality cannot be divided. Everything that exists participates in everything else. A rock, a bird, a human being—everything is interconnected.

---

[13] Panikkar, *The Trinity and World Religions*, 46.
[14] Panikkar, *The Cosmotheandric Experience*, 61.
[15] Panikkar, *The Cosmotheandric Experience*, 62.
[16] Panikkar, *The Cosmotheandric Experience*, 63.
[17] Panikkar, *The Cosmotheandric Experience*, 64.
[18] Panikkar, *The Cosmotheandric Experience*, 64.
[19] Panikkar, *The Cosmotheandric Experience*, 64–65 (italics in the original).

He concludes: "I am saying that there are no disembodied souls or disincarnated Gods, just as there is no matter, no energy, no spatio-temporal World without divine and conscious dimensions."[20]

In such a view of reality universalism is a *fait accompli*. Panikkar argues that, "An isolated individual is incomprehensible and also unviable." This leads naturally to the conclusion that there can be no individual fate apart from the fate of all things.[21] Each person participates in the cosmotheandric experience and cannot be separated from it or from the final outcome. As Panikkar puts it, "We are all in the same boat, which is not just this planet Earth but the entire mystery of life."[22] It is this interconnectedness found in Panikkar's cosmotheandrism that drives a universalist conclusion and insures, for him, a universalist outcome.

In addition to universalism, Panikkar's cosmotheandrism also entails a radically plurocentric orientation. He affirms, "God is at work in all religions."[23] In rejecting the exclusivist claims of Christianity he asserts: "Every religion deals with the salvation or liberation of Man, which means union with God, divinization of our being, the acquisition of truth, sanctity, light, and freedom from the bonds of injustice, slavery, passions of the worldly existence, and so on."[24] In support of this perspective Panikkar offers several arguments. First, he notes what he believes to be the essential desire of people to embrace the truth. He maintains that "very few human minds would choose falsehood over truth, darkness over light, and hence sin over sanctity, or damnation over salvation."[25] Related to this is an embrace of the notion of relativity when it comes to truth claims. He also commented on the absurdity of believing that a loving God would have confined his truth to one religion and left so many in so much darkness for so long a time.[26] Given the weight of these arguments, Panikkar believed that pluralism must be a foregone conclusion.

This embrace of pluralism does not mean, however, that the question of Jesus Christ is not important for Panikkar. Indeed, a profound Christological meditation lies at the center of his cosmotheandric program. Early on, he professed a rather Christocentric view of salvation, declaring: "Christ, manifest or hidden, is the only way to God. Even by definition the unique link between the created and the uncreated, the relative and the Absolute, the temporal and the eternal, earth and heaven, is Christ, the only mediator."[27] This perspective was expanded on in *The Unknown Christ of Hinduism* where Panikkar invested Christ with a universal significance: "This, then, is Christ: that reality from whom everything has come, in whom everything subsists, to whom everything

---

[20] Panikkar, *The Cosmotheandric Experience*, 66.
[21] Panikkar, *The Cosmotheandric Experience*, 75.
[22] Panikkar, *The Cosmotheandric Experience*, 128.
[23] Panikkar, *The Unknown Christ of Hinduism*, 168.
[24] Panikkar, *The Unknown Christ of Hinduism*, 72.
[25] Panikkar, *The Unknown Christ of Hinduism*, 72.
[26] Panikkar, *The Unknown Christ of Hinduism*, 72.
[27] Panikkar, *The Trinity and the World Religions*, 52.

that suffers the wear and tear of time shall return."[28] Already, at this earlier stage in Panikkar's thinking, Christ is the pluralistic center of all religions and is said to be "already present in every form of worship, to the extent that it is adoration directed to God."[29] From here Panikkar broadened his understanding of Christ into cosmic proportions. He enlarged his Christology to embrace all human beings and asserted that "each being is a Christophany, a manifestation of the christic adventure of all reality on its way towards infinite mystery."[30] This amounts to the delineation of a continuous incarnation of Christ into humanity. As Panikkar put it, "*Incarnatio continua.*"[31] For him, the Christ becomes the ultimate cosmotheandric symbol.[32] He believes that Christ occurs in all people and therefore is present in all religious expressions. This cosmic Christ can be called by many names, Rāma, Krishna, Īśvara, Purusha, or even Humanity—what matters is that he "stands for that centre of reality, that crystallization-point around which the human, the divine and the material can grow."[33]

Given the size of Panikkar's vision of the incarnation, it becomes obvious that the concept of the Christ cannot be limited to an expression located only in the man, Jesus of Nazareth. He states this point clearly when he says: "Christ the Savior is . . . not to be restricted to the merely historical figure of Jesus of Nazareth."[34] Indeed, Panikkar's cosmic Christ has little in common with the traditional Christology found in the New Testament and he has very little need for the historical Jesus. This is very likely the reason that he seldom makes reference to Jesus' death and resurrection. It is also probably the reason that he views Jesus' actions on the cross as largely metaphorical and not salvific in the classical sense.[35] It is telling that Panikkar has called for both the "dekerygmatization" and the "dehistoricizing" of Christ.[36] His transcendent view of christophany demands that the cosmic Christ be freed from the

---

[28] Panikkar, *The Unknown Christ of Hinduism*, 49. The same assertion occurs in the 1964 version with some minor variations: "That is Christ, from whom everything has come, in whom everything subsists, to whom everything that shall endure the bite of time will come." Raymond Panikkar, *The Unknown Christ of Hinduism* (London: Darton, Longman & Todd, 1964), 16.

[29] Panikkar, *The Unknown Christ of Hinduism*, 49. Cf. also the 1964 edition, p. 17.

[30] Raimon Panikkar, "A Christophany for Our Times," *ThD* 39 (1992): 7.

[31] Raimon Panikkar, "Indian Christian Theology," *Jeehvadhara* 27 (1997): 320, as quoted by Jyri Komulainen in *An Emerging Cosmotheandric Religion?* 132.

[32] "Christ is the Christian symbol of all reality . . ." (Panikkar, "A Christophany for Our Times," 6). "Christ is . . . a living symbol for the totality of reality: human, divine, cosmic" (Panikkar, *The Unknown Christ of Hinduism*, 27).

[33] Panikkar, *The Unknown Christ of Hinduism*, 27.

[34] Raimon Panikkar, *Salvation in Christ: Concreteness and Universality, The Supername* (Santa Barbara, privately published, 1972), 51, as quoted in Knitter, *No Other Name*, 155–56.

[35] Panikkar, *The Unknown Christ of Hinduism*, 4; 74–75.

[36] "Decades ago I called for the dekerygmatization of Christ in order to free him from any dogmatic proclamation. Today I would ask whether we have to also dehistoricize him" (Raimon Panikkar, "Can Theology Be Transcultural?" in Paul F. Knitter, *Pluralism and Oppression: Theology in World Perspective* [Lanham, N.Y.: University Press of America, 1988], 8).

limitations of the historical Jesus in order that the cosmic dimensions might be attained.

Just where, precisely, do these cosmic dimensions lead? What is humanity's purpose? Early on in his theological development, Panikkar stated in *The Unknown Christ of Hinduism*: "The thesis of the Unknown Christ is that, whether or not we believed in God or Gods, there is something in every human being that does not alienate Man but rather allows Man to reach fullness of being."[37] Thus, he views the ultimate goal of humanity as not the attainment of salvation from sin and the restoration of a relationship with God through Christ, but rather as the achievement of "fullness of being." This same goal is affirmed again in *The Cosmotheandric Experience* where Panikkar concludes: "[T]he meaning of human life no longer lies in the historical fulfillment of a mission but in the realization of the human being."[38] The achievement of this goal, in turn, will lead into a larger triumph:

> The "end of Man," then, is not individual happiness but full participation in the realization of the universe—in which one finds as well one's "own" joy (obviously not "owned" in the sense of private property). You need not worry about your own salvation or even perfection. You let live, you let be. You don't feel so much the need to interfere with Nature as to enhance, collaborate, and "allow" her to be.[39]

Panikkar's cosmotheandric project is reminiscent of the efforts of Arnold Toynbee in the 1950s to discern a common "spiritual presence" within all religions and all reality.[40] While Panikkar does not argue for an exact correspondence that is as uniform as that of Toynbee, his efforts nevertheless result in a sort of fuzzy equivalence among religions and religious concepts. Consider, for instance, the following parallels that he has drawn: Panikkar reduces the notion of the Father within the Christian Trinitarian formulation to a non-theistic nothingness that he equates with the *nirvāna* state of the Buddhists and the *Brahman* state of the Hindus;[41] the idea of the Christ in Panikkar's thought becomes a universal christophany that is experienced by all people and is a fundamental element in all religions;[42] Panikkar's vision of soteriology results in a rough equivalence between the ideas of *salvation from sin* as found in Christianity, the *nirvāna* state found in Buddhism, and the *Brahman* state found in Hinduism. Although Panikkar insists that he is by no means endorsing the "naïve and uncritical notion that 'there is' one 'thing' which Men call by many names," this seems to be precisely where he winds up.[43] To be fair, he does note the unique contributions that each religion contributes to the picture that is drawn—this is where the fuzziness is

---

[37] Panikkar, *The Unknown Christ of Hinduism*, 29.
[38] Panikkar, *The Cosmotheandric Experience*, 123.
[39] Panikkar, *The Cosmotheandric Experience*, 132.
[40] Arnold Toynbee, *An Historian's Approach to Religion* (New York: Oxford University Press, 1956).
[41] Panikkar, *The Trinity and World Religions*, 46–47; 51.
[42] Panikkar, "A Christophany for Our Times," 2–21.
[43] Panikkar, *The Unknown Christ of Hinduism*, 23.

introduced. However, in the end it seems that Panikkar's project is aimed primarily at creating a harmonization rather than the promotion of a truly pluralistic outlook that accepts the true diversity of each religion without resorting to some scheme of modification or linguistic semantics.

Given what Panikkar proposes, one cannot but conclude that his modifications of basic Christian doctrine create a vision of Christianity that would be altogether unrecognizable to the writers of the New Testament. His efforts to collapse the notion of God the Father into a non-theistic, non-personal, non-knowable divine space/non-space so distorts the image of the relational God whom Jesus called, "Abba," that one has to question whether such a reduction can really qualify to be called "Christian." The whole image of God that is presented in the New Testament is that of a relational being who has personality and is seeking to restore his relationship with lost people. Panikkar's reduction is a far cry from this picture and stands in direct contradiction to it.

The idea of Christ being a universal christophany experienced by all people is a gross distortion of both the biblical concept of the Messiah, and the affirmation of God's unique incarnation in the Messiah in the person of Jesus. What does it mean to say that we are all Christophanies? Does not this perspective eliminate the essential difference between the divine and the human and in so doing eliminate the possibility of any sort of a meaningful relationship between the creature and the creator? Between the individual and God? Panikkar has affirmed that, "The Father *has* no being: the Son is *his* being."[44] Furthermore, in Panikkar's view, Christ stands as a symbol of reality itself. Denials aside, does this not then lead to a form of pantheism, or as some have called it, panchristism?[45] What about the issue of human freedom and moral development through decision making? If I am a unique expression of the divine, does that mean that I can do no wrong? This was the conclusion drawn by the Free Spirit heretics as a result of their embrace of pantheism. Glaringly absent from Panikkar's theology is an extended discussion of the issue of sin and the development of an adequate hamartiology. It would seem that Panikkar's notion of ubiquitous christophany and plurocentric universalism has precluded the need for such doctrinal development.

This is also perhaps what makes it easy for Panikkar to equate the soteriological goals of Christianity, Buddhism, and Hinduism to one another. However, as we have noted already, this seems to be an impossible task. Salvation from sin and a restored relationship with God gained through faith in Jesus Christ and his work on the Cross just does not seem to correlate in any meaningful way to the Buddhist concept of *nirvāna*, which signals the attainment of the extinction of desire and individual consciousness. Similarly, the concept of Christian salvation seems to have no correlation to the Hindu idea of *Brahman*, which signals the absorption of a person into the absolute cosmic unity. In saying that all of these soteriological goals can be reduced to the idea of a person attaining "fullness of being" it appears that Panikkar is making an unwarranted reduction and not taking seriously the profound

---

[44] Panikkar, *The Trinity and World Religions*, 46–47.
[45] Komulainen, *An Emerging Cosmotheandric Religion?* 132.

soteriological differences found in these diverse religions. In fact his soteriological theory seems to be at odds with all of these concepts. The biblical Christian is not concerned so much with personal fulfillment as he or she is with obtaining a restored relationship with God. The orthodox Buddhist is not concerned with achieving a personal fulfillment, but rather with the elimination of emotion and individuality. The same is true of the Hindu who desires to shed personhood completely. So then the soteriological meeting place that Panikkar proposes is in reality no meeting place at all. It causes more problems and raises more questions than it resolves.

All of these things point to the fundamental conclusion that the basic problem encountered by Panikkar's cosmotheandrism is essentially the same problem that is encountered by John Hick: It turns out that his proposal is not pluralistic enough. Rather than accepting the hard diversity exhibited by the various religious traditions, both Hick and Panikkar have sought to find ways in which that diversity can be eliminated and the religious traditions of the world can be homogenized. In reality, this effort at homogenization represents the antithesis of true pluralism. Interestingly enough, both men seem to be unaware of just how un-pluralistic and intolerant their approaches appear and just how difficult it very likely would be to convince the serious adherents of the world's religions otherwise. Anyone who takes the claims of these religions seriously is bound to have grave reservations about accepting the interpretive reductions and eliminations made by both Hick and Panikkar.

These criticisms aside, Panikkar's approach does focus our attention on the important issue of syncretism. Is Panikkar's claim that one can be a faithful "Buddhist, Hindu, Christian" valid? To what extent can one embrace the beliefs of another religion and still remain true to one's original religion? What gets lost in such a marriage? What might be gained? As the world becomes a smaller place these issues will continue to grow in complexity and stature. The theology of Raimundo Panikkar challenges Christian theologians of all stripes to take seriously the Christian encounter of other religions and to consider carefully the impact that encounter will have upon the Christian faith.

2. Hans Küng—Plurocentric Relativism

Hans Küng (b. 1928) is a Swiss theologian who has generated a great deal of controversy both within the Catholic Church and outside of it.[46] Initially he studied theology and philosophy at the Pontifical Gregorian University in Rome and was ordained as a priest in 1954. In 1957 he received a doctorate in theology from the Institut Catholique in Paris. The title of his dissertation was

---

[46] Hans Küng has been quite prolific over his career and has written more than 40 books as well as numerous articles. In his memoirs Küng recites the story of his life and the development of his thought. See Hans Küng, *Erkämpfte Freiheit. Erinnerungen* (Munich: Piper Verlag, 2002); English edition trans. John Bowden, *My Struggle for Freedom: Memoirs* (Grand Rapids, Mich.: Eerdmans, 2003) and Hans Küng, *Umstrittene Wahrheit: Erinnerungen* (Munich: Piper Verlag, 2007); English edition trans. John Bowden, *Disputed Truth: Memoirs II* (London; New York: Continuum International Publishing Group, 2008).

"Justification. La doctrine de Karl Barth et une réflexion catholique."[47] In the dissertation he concluded that Barth's doctrine of justification was in substantial agreement with essential Catholic theology. The work was translated into German soon after its acceptance. This translation generated several negative reactions that were sent to Rome. The Holy Office responded by setting up a special file number on Küng in order to keep track of the criticisms.[48] It was a file that would grow ponderously large over the years.

In 1970, Küng published a book entitled *Unfehlbar? eine Anfrage*[49] in which he questioned the doctrine of papal infallibility. He was also quite outspoken about difficulties that he had with the Church's stance on birth control, mixed marriages, celibacy, the veneration of Mary, and various structural deficiencies within the Roman Curia.[50] The ensuing battle between Küng and the Church is well documented.[51] For ten years Küng and the Church faced off over the issues. More than a thousand pages of documents were generated in the exchange. On December 18, 1979 the Church delivered its final verdict to Hans Küng: his credentials to teach as a Catholic theologian were withdrawn. In 1980 a settlement was reached at the University of Tübingen, where Küng was a professor. He was allowed to continue to teach under secular rather than Catholic auspices. Küng was not excommunicated from the Church and he was allowed to remain a priest. Since that time Küng has continued to write and teach. He retired from Tübingen in 1996.

Küng's theology is built around a pluralistic core. Although certain statements he makes appear to be exclusivist at times, these are best understood as fitting beneath the pluralistic umbrella, which Küng extends over all religions. We see Küng's pluralism begin to take shape in his book *On Being a Christian* where he includes pluralistic universalism as an essential element of his theology.[52] In noting the ramifications for rethinking the Church's approach to world religions, Küng concludes: "In fact then there is salvation outside the Church. In addition to particular, there can be seen a general, universal salvation history."[53] This salvation history includes the major world religions, which Küng accepts as being salvific: "Not only Christianity, but also the world religions are aware of man's alienation, enslavement, need of redemption . . .

---

[47] Hans Küng, *Justification: The Doctrine of Karl Barth and a Catholic Reflection* (London: Burns & Oates, 1965).
[48] John Kiwiet, *Hans Küng* (Waco, Tex.: Word, 1985), 23.
[49] Hans Küng, *Unfehlbar? eine Anfrage* (Zuerich: Benziger, 1970); English edition trans. Edward Quinn, *Infallible? An Inquiry* (Garden City, N.Y.: Doubleday, 1971).
[50] Kiwiet, *Hans Küng*, 87.
[51] A large collection of documents may be found in Leonard Swindler, ed., *Küng in Conflict* (Garden City, N.Y.: Doubleday, 1981). See also The United States Catholic Conference, *The Küng Dialogue* (Washington, D.C.: United States Catholic Conference, 1980). Analyses of the situation may be found in Paul Collins, ed., *From Inquisition to Freedom: Seven Prominent Catholics and Their Struggle with the Vatican* (London; New York: Continuum, 2001) and Peter Hebblethwaite, *The New Inquisition: The Case of Edward Schillebeeckx and Hans Küng* (San Francisco: Harper & Row, 1980).
[52] Hans Küng, *Christ Sein* (Munich: R. Piper, 1974); English edition trans. Edward Quinn, *On Being a Christian* (Garden City, N.Y.: Doubleday, 1976), 89–116.
[53] Küng, *On Being a Christian*, 91.

Not only Christianity, but the world religions perceive the goodness, mercy and graciousness of the Divinity . . . Not only Christianity, but also the world religions rightly heed the call of their prophets."[54] In Küng's view, each of the major world religions is seeking the same mysterious deity, the same ultimate reality. They are involved in a "common quest for the truth."[55]

However, this does not mean that Küng embraces a naïve pluralism that tries to eliminate the unique distinctives that each religion possesses. In his view, such efforts are misguided and dangerous. "Together with exclusivistic absolutism, that crippling *relativism*, which makes all values and standards the same, must be avoided."[56] The problem with such efforts is that it makes a mockery of true pluralism by forcing religions to fit into a certain mold and worldview. Such an effort does not truly accept the rich diversity that is found in the world's religious systems. Therefore, as we shall see shortly, Küng's pluralism makes a concerted effort to avoid such pitfalls.

Küng is also dismissive of Catholic inclusivism and Karl Rahner's concept of the anonymous Christian, seeing them as a transparent effort to maintain the old status quo of *extra ecclesiam nulla salus*. In condemning the idea he notes: "What looks like tolerance proves in practice to be a kind of conquering through embrace, an assimilation through validation, and integration through relativisation and loss of identity."[57] He notes the theological weakness inherent in such a theory and the resistance that such inclusivist efforts are bound to engender:

> But is not the whole of good-willed humanity thus swept with an elegant gesture across the paper-thin bridge of a theological fabrication into the back door of the "holy Roman Church," leaving no one of good will "outside"? . . . Nor do they have a wish to be inside. And no theological sleight of hand will ever force them, against their will and against their desire to become active or passive members of the Church . . . it would be impossible to find anywhere in the world a sincere Jew, Muslim, or atheist who would not regard the assertion that he is an "anonymous Christian" as presumptuous.[58]

---

[54] Küng, *On Being a Christian*, 92. "Seen from *without*, viewed by the history of religion, there are *various true religions* . . . various paths of salvation toward a goal which to some extent overlap and in any case can mutually fructify each other" (Hans Küng, "What is the True Religion: Toward an Ecumenical Criteriology," *JTSA* 56 [September 1986]: 22).

[55] Küng, *On Being a Christian*, 112.

[56] Küng, "What is the True Religion" 9.

[57] Küng, "What is the True Religion" 9. See also Küng, *On Being a Christian*, 97–98.

[58] Küng, *On Being a Christian*, 112. See also Küng, "What is the True Religion? Toward an Ecumenical Criteriology," 9–10; Hans Küng, "Is There One True Religion? An Essay in Establishing Ecumenical Criteria," in John Hick and Brian Hebblethwaite, eds., *Christianity and Other Religions: Selected Readings*, revised edition (Oxford: Oneworld Publications, 2001), 122–24; Hans Küng, Josef von Ess, Heinrich von Stietencron, and Heinz Bechert, *Christianity and World Religions: Paths to Dialogue* (Maryknoll, N.Y.: Orbis, 1993; 1986), 110–11; 180–81.

In Küng's view, Christian inclusivism is a way of Christianizing the world without engaging it, while at the same time denying the true validity of other religious systems. Therefore, he rejects it.

Küng's solution to the issue of universal salvation is to propose what we will call a "plurocentric relativism."[59] He argues that each religion should be viewed through two "horizontal" dimensions: (1) the *outside or without* in which there are "*various true religions,* various paths of salvation*," and (2) the *inside or within* in which there is the unique experience of my own religion which is for me "*the true religion*."[60] Thus, viewed from *without,* religions are granted equal value and seen as *many paths* that can lead to salvation. Viewed from *within,* my own personal religion is allowed to be exclusivistic in that it is *my unique path* to salvation. In this way Küng seeks to embrace a plurocentric stance without compromising the unique distinctives of each religion. Each religion is allowed to be true *relative* to its own traditions and community. On the other hand, the religions viewed as a whole are allowed to form a pluralistic path to universal salvation. In proposing this solution, Küng wants to maintain pluralism while at the same time avoiding the pitfall of requiring people to give up their unique religion and community of faith.[61] His goal is not to force things or to change things, as, for instance, Hick and Panikkar seek to do. Instead, his goal is to embrace the unique expressions of a religion while allowing for the larger picture of pluralism to prevail.

It is important to note that Küng does not abandon the pursuit of truth in this endeavor. An important part of his program is to measure the truth that is found within each religion and thereby determine if they meet a minimum standard. In his view there is truth and untruth in every religion including Christianity.[62] The criteria he proposes by which the truth of a religion can be measured are pragmatic in that they must yield real results. The first is the ethical criterion he calls *humanum*: "A religion is true and good if and insofar as it is *human,* does not suppress or destroy humanness, but rather protects and fosters it."[63] The second is the religious criterion he calls, *authentic* or *canonical*: "A religion is true and good if and insofar as it remains true to its own *origin* or *canon.*"[64] The third criterion is what he calls *specific*. This criterion aims at internally quantifying a key feature that characterizes a true expression of that religion. In

---

[59] We do not use "relativism" here as Küng does in the sense of forcing all religions into an egalitarian mold. By relativism we mean it in the classic sense in which truth and value are viewed as being relative to a certain culture or religious system in which they were created.

[60] Küng, "Is There One True Religion?" 143–44; Küng, "What is the True Religion?" 9; Hans Küng, "Towards an Ecumenical Theology of Religions: Some Theses for Clarification," in Hans Küng and Jürgen Moltmann, eds., *Concilium: Christianity Among World Religions* (Edinburgh: T. & T. Clark: 1986), 120–22. It should be noted that these three articles essentially repeat each other with some minor appreciable differences.

[61] Küng, "Towards an Ecumenical Theology of Religions," 123.

[62] Küng, "Is There One True Religion?" 128–35; Küng, "What is the True Religion?" 11–12; Küng, "Towards an Ecumenical Theology of Religions," 120–22.

[63] Küng, "What is the True Religion?" 18. See pp. 12–16 for the justification.

[64] Küng, "What is the True Religion?" 18. See pp. 16–18 for the justification.

the case of Christianity Küng argues that a valid expression can be identified by the fact that "it lets the spirit of Christ be felt."[65] Of course, in another religion the specific criterion would be a distinguishing characteristic relevant to that religion. If all of these minimal standards can be met, Küng argues that we can know that the religion we are examining is a true religion.[66]

In discussing the issue of universalism from within the context of Christianity, Küng views universalism as the consummation of God's plan. It is "an all-embracing mercy."[67] He declares: "The true consummation and true happiness of humanity will exist only when not only the last generation but all human beings share in it."[68] In light of this perspective, Küng has a conceptual problem with the idea of a literal hell and he argues against any sort of literal interpretation. In his view, Jesus' pronouncements on hell were a *"time conditioned, time bound world vision"* adopted from first-century Jewish apocalypticism.[69] They are to be understood metaphorically, not literally. Jesus used them existentially to highlight the importance of decision.[70] In keeping with this view, Küng argues that hell should be interpreted "theologically as an exclusion from the fellowship of the living God."[71] Thus, hell becomes a metaphorical threat, but never an actual reality. He takes a similar stance regarding the doctrine of purgatory. In his opinion purgatory should not be taken literally either. Instead, "Purgatory is God Himself in the wrath of his place. Purification is encounter with God in the sense that it judges and purifies, but also liberates and enlightens, heals and completes man."[72]

In Küng's view, the eschatological end involves the final consummation of all things into God. Küng is ambivalent regarding the existence of an intermediate state. He maintains that we can know very little about dying "into the dimensions of God, where space and time are dissolved into eternity, nothing can be discovered, either about place and time or about the character of this purifying, sanctifying consummation."[73] The end is envisioned as a sort of pantheistic absorption of all things. God will dissolve temporality into finality. God will abolish the distinctions between subject and object.[74] In this final end the vision of nirvana, as espoused by eastern religions, may meet with Christian ideas about rebirth. The final, vertical dimension will be God. In the end there will be no more religion. No more Mohammad. No more Buddha. No more Jesus Christ. God will truly become *"everything to everyone."*[75]

---

[65] Küng, "What is the True Religion?" 18. See pp. 18–22 for the justification.

[66] Küng, "Is There One True Religion?" 143–44.

[67] Hans Küng, *Ewiges Leben?* (Munich: R. Piper, 1982); English edition trans. Edward Quinn, *Eternal Life? Life After Death as a Medical, Philosophical, and Theological Problem* (Garden City, N.Y.: Doubleday, 1984), 142.

[68] Küng, *Eternal Life?* 211.

[69] Küng, *Eternal Life?* 92 (italics in the original); 208–209.

[70] Küng, *Eternal Life?* 133–34.

[71] Küng, *Eternal Life?* 143.

[72] Küng, *Eternal Life?* 139.

[73] Küng, *Eternal Life?* 139.

[74] Küng, *Eternal Life?* 221; 233.

[75] Küng, "Is There One True Religion?" 145; Küng, "What is the True Religion?" 23.

Küng's plurocentric relativism offers us an interesting mixture of both the old and the new. On the one hand, Küng wants to embrace a comparatively orthodox understanding of Christianity, which is true to its internal distinctives. On the other hand, Küng wants to embrace a form of pluralism that allows for other religions to provide their own unique paths to salvation. This is an entirely different solution than that of John Hick who solved the pluralistic riddle by demanding that Christianity and all other religions abandon their claims to exclusivity. In Hick's view, exclusivism is an implacable foe that must be defeated before the goal of true pluralism can be realized. In Küng's view, exclusivism is a relative value developed within a community that can be safely contained behind the firewall of appropriate religious boundaries. His solution essentially amounts to a theological reversal of the old adage that "you can't have your cake and eat it too."

The question is, does this really work? Is it possible to embrace a limited Christian exclusivity while at the same time embracing a thoroughgoing pluralism? Can the two ideas be honestly held together without contradiction? It is on this point that it would seem that Küng's case falls apart. Küng argues that "exclusivistic absolutism" must be done away with because if it is held on to then "Christian theology has no answer to the question of the salvation of the majority of humanity."[76] According to Küng, "exclusivistic absolutism" can be eliminated simply by making a distinction between my personal religion and my broader embrace of a pluralism that denies ultimate exclusivistic claims. However, this distinction appears to be an artificial construct that turns a Christian into a religious schizophrenic rather than an enlightened pluralist.

To begin with there is the problem of the absolute nature of the exclusivistic claims found in the New Testament. Consider the declaration that Jesus makes in Matt. 7:21–23:

> [21] Not everyone who says to Me, "Lord, Lord," will enter the kingdom of heaven; but he who does the will of My Father who is in heaven. [22] Many will say to Me on that day, "Lord, Lord, did we not prophesy in Your name, and in Your name cast out demons, and in Your name perform many miracles?" [23] And then I will declare to them, "I never knew you; depart from Me, you who practice lawlessness."

Here we have an exclusivistic claim regarding entry into the kingdom that seems to be irreconcilable with Küng's vision of plurocentric universalism. Similarly, when Jesus says in John 14:6, "I am the way, the truth, and the life. No one comes to the Father except through Me," it does not appear that he allows any room for a pluralist interpretation to be brought to bear. When Peter declares in Acts 4:12, "And there is salvation in no one else; for there is no other name under heaven that has been given among men, by which we must be saved," it does not appear that Peter allows any room for a pluralist interpretation either. Küng wants to allow for a religion to maintain its unique distinctives. Indeed, one of his main criterion is that a religion stays true to its

---

[76] Küng, "What is the True Religion?" 8.

"origin and canon."[77] However, is he not denying a central feature of the Christian canon when he demands that Christians not hold to exclusivist claims in the absolute fashion in which they were originally made?

Küng is concerned that Christian theology present an answer to the "question of the salvation of the majority of humanity."[78] For him this answer includes the embrace of pluralism. However, in looking at the way that Christians dealt with the issue in the New Testament it appears that their answer was to proclaim an unyielding exclusivism. When Paul entered the city of Athens in Acts 17, we are told that "his spirit was being provoked within him as he was beholding the city full of idols. So he was reasoning in the synagogue with the Jews and the God-fearing *Gentiles,* and in the market place every day with those who happened to be present." The content of Paul's message was not that all paths lead to God and that idolatry was fine, but rather that all the people should repent of their idolatrous polytheism because God has "fixed a day in which He will judge the world in righteousness through the Man whom He has appointed, having furnished proof to all men by raising Him from the dead." The New Testament's answer to the lost is Christ—not pluralism. Regardless of whether one agrees with that answer, this is the honest conclusion we must draw if we are going to deal truthfully with the text.

In addition to this, Küng acts as if discovering the mass of lost humanity is a recent thing for Christians and he argues that in light of this new discovery that changes ought to be made to how Christians deal with New Testament exclusivism.[79] However, this ignores the common sense observation that the Apostles would have been well aware of the fact that they were dealing with a mass of lost humanity in the Roman world in which they lived. The city of Rome and its precincts is estimated to have had close to five million inhabitants in the first century. Surely the Apostles saw large gatherings of thousands of people assembled for religious festivals and holidays. Surely they would have also seen large gatherings at the amphitheaters assembled for theatrics, sporting events, and political purposes. What was their response to this phenomenon? Did they embrace the naïve pluralism popular in the Roman Empire of their day? No, they stuck doggedly to their message of exclusivism. This was what they understood the gospel of salvation to be.

Despite these serious problems, Küng is to be commended for his efforts to maintain the exclusivity of diverse religious traditions. Küng's plurocentric universalism is valuable in that it serves as a reminder of the difficulties that exclusivism poses for all sides of the debate. In a very real way, exclusivism is the *crux theologorum* of our own day. When it comes right down to it, how one deals with the issue of exclusivism will determine the shape and direction of one's theology—and even the shape and direction of one's life.

3. Paul F. Knitter—Plurocentric Liberation

Paul F. Knitter (b. 1939) is a Catholic theologian who has written extensively on the issue of pluralism. He also practices the pluralism he preaches in his own

---

[77] Küng, "What is the True Religion?" 18.

[78] Küng, "What is the True Religion?" 8.

[79] Küng, "What is the True Religion?" 6–9.

personal life through being an adherent of both Christianity and Buddhism.[80] Knitter is currently the Paul Tillich Professor of Theology, World Religions, and Culture at Union Theological Seminary in New York. He is Professor Emeritus of Theology at Xavier University in Cincinnati, Ohio, where he taught for twenty-eight years. He received a licentiate in theology from the Pontifical Gregorian University in Rome (1966) and a doctorate from the University of Marburg, Germany (1972).[81] In 1975 he joined the faculty at Xavier University and remained there until his retirement in 2002. Knitter describes a theological journey that he took in his life from the exclusivism of the Divine Word Missionaries (*Societas Verbi Divini*), which he joined in 1958, to the gradual development of his pluralist theology of religions. Steps along the way included a brief embrace of Catholic inclusivism and Karl Rahner's doctrine of the anonymous Christian.[82] In the end, this inclusivism became a bridge to pluralism and Knitter came to understand that he was now in uncharted territory: new theological maps were needed.[83]

His first major effort at providing one such map is contained in his book *No Other Name? A Critical Survey of Christian Attitudes Toward the World Religions*. In the book Knitter surveys and critiques the various proposals made toward establishing a pluralist theology of religions as well as the approaches taken toward other religions by the major schools of Christian thought. In the end he offers his own solution to the issue of pluralism, which includes a rethinking of the uniqueness of Christ and a call for Christians to move from a Christocentric orientation to a theocentric one.[84] This move is roughly analogous to John Hick's original proposal of a Copernican Revolution and, as with Hick, it would soon require considerable modification as the chorus of critics intensified.

In his book *One Earth Many Religions,* Knitter acknowledges the effect that relentless criticism has had upon his theology. He concludes: "I am still a pluralist—though a chastened one."[85] Criticism coupled to an increasing awareness of human suffering and the ecological plight of the planet Earth brought about a significant change in Knitter's pluralism especially as it relates

---

[80] Paul F. Knitter, *Without Buddha I Could not be a Christian* (Oxford: Oneworld Publications, 2009).

[81] Knitter has published three autobiographical accounts that are quite helpful in gaining an understanding of his life and theological thought. The first is entitled "My Dialogical Odyssey" and may be found in his book *One Earth Many Religions: Multifaith Dialogue and Global Responsibility* (Maryknoll, N.Y.: Orbis, 1995), 1–20. This same account is repeated with some minor variations in his book *Jesus and the Other Names: Christian Mission and Global Responsibility* (Maryknoll, N.Y.: Orbis, 1996), 1–21. Another autobiographical account may be found in an article he wrote on the occasion of his retirement from Xavier University in 2002. See Paul F. Knitter, "The Vocation of an Interreligious Theologian: My Retrospective on Forty Years in Dialogue," *Horizons* 31/1 (Spring 2004): 135–49.

[82] Knitter did his initial doctoral work under Rahner's guidance at the University of Münster before moving to Marburg. See Knitter, *One Earth Many Religions*, 5.

[83] Knitter, *One Earth Many Religions*, 7.

[84] Knitter, *No Other Name?* 145–204.

[85] Knitter, *One Earth Many Religions*, 16.

to the focal point of his religious dialogue. He began by calling for a theocentric focus, however, in his later theology this call has been greatly softened due the intractable problems related to translating the concept of divinity among the many disparate religions. Therefore the appeal for a theocentric focus as a point of agreement and dialogue has essentially been dropped. In its stead Knitter now advocates for a "soteriocentric" or "salvation-centered" focus—salvation being defined as a "global responsibility for eco-human well-being."[86]

In formulating this call, we see the increasing influence that liberation theology has had upon Knitter's thought. He quotes with approval the conclusion drawn by Aloysius Pieris: "Religion is *primordially* a liberation movement."[87] What started out as an effort on Knitter's behalf to remain in touch with a newly developing theology has led to an increasing involvement in the plight of poverty stricken Latin Americans and with the poor in general. This experience has had a profound effect upon Knitter and thus his theology has become an effort to bring together a *theology of liberation* and a *theology of religions*; it is an effort to bring together the "religious Other" and the "suffering Other."[88] In describing the impact that his experiences have had upon him, Knitter commented: "So people and events in my life have led me, sometime lured me, to what has become for me a moral obligation to join 'pluralism and liberation' or 'dialogue and global responsibility.'"[89] This, in turn, has led him to call for a "globally responsible, correlational dialogue of religions."[90]

This pragmatic call is rooted in Knitter's belief that "fidelity and faith are matters of *being* rather than *having*, of *living* rather than *affirming*."[91] He concludes: "Right belief (Orthodoxy) is Rooted in Right Action (Orthopraxy)."[92] This focus on orthodoxy being developed through experience, rather than being acquired through doctrinal formulation, forms the basis of Knitter's call for pluralistic dialogue. He maintains that the "*praxis of dialogue*" with peoples of other faiths is a necessary element for the discovery of truth in Christian revelation.[93] In other words, religious truth is mediated through interreligious dialogue.

In Knitter's view, the dialogue can only begin on an egalitarian playing field: "Only if Christians are truly open to the possibility (which, I will argue below, is for Christians a probability bordering on a necessity) that there *are* many true, saving religions and that Christianity is one among many ways in which God has touched and transformed our world—only then can authentic dialogue take place."[94] A corollary of this perspective is the embrace of

---

[86] Knitter, *One Earth Many Religions*, 16–17; 36–37; 98–102.

[87] Knitter, *One Earth Many Religions*, 100.

[88] Knitter, *One Earth Many Religions*, 14.

[89] Knitter, *One Earth Many Religions*, 11.

[90] Knitter, *Jesus and the Other Names*, 23–45.

[91] Knitter, *Jesus and the Other Names*, 64.

[92] Knitter, *Jesus and the Other Names*, 65.

[93] Knitter, *No Other Name?* 206.

[94] Knitter, *One Earth Many Religions*, 30. Cf. Knitter, *Jesus and the Other Names*, 24; 30.

plurocentric universalism. For Knitter, the logic behind God's declared love for all people must lead to both a pluralist and a universalist outcome:

> Theologically, Christians say they believe in a God who truly wishes to save all people; this is the God of Jesus Christ, a God of "pure unbounded love," who embraces all beings and wishes all of them to have life and salvation . . . . Our Christian experience of the God of love revealed in Jesus Christ tells us that despite our own sinfulness, despite the corruptions in our Church, this God has embraced us in and through the ecclesial community. It seems to me that if I doubt that God can do the same thing for other people through other communities, I have reason to doubt that God has really done so for me. A loving God who loves only some people or who can overcome sinfulness and corruption in only some religions is somehow not a trustworthy God of love (Gilkey 1987, 38–39). Therefore, Christians can and must approach other religions expecting not just that they might *possibly* find much that is true and good but that they *probably* will.[95]

As can be readily anticipated, the major obstacle looming in the path of Knitter's program is the exclusivist claim of Christianity. He takes a two-pronged approach to dealing with this issue. First, he argues that all truth is necessarily relative and therefore no one religion can claim to have the sole deposit of truth. Second, he argues that we must redefine what it means to say that Jesus is unique.

Regarding relativism, Knitter accepts the post-modern argument that all truth is "contextually conditioned," "theory laden," and "socially-constructed." Based upon these claims he maintains that "Christians (and all religious persons) have to admit honestly that within our human condition, there can be no final word, no one way of knowing truth that is valid for all times and all peoples."[96] Absolutism is an enemy that must be done away with because it can lead to the "idolatry" of confining and limiting deity; the "idolatry" of insisting that there is only "one way, one norm, one truth."[97] Furthermore, Knitter contends that truth can only be discovered through dialogue with others. Truth is always changing based upon new cultural developments. "There is no fixed place of truth outside the fray of historical processes and continuous dialogue (see also Omann 1986), which means that Christianity is one of *many, limited* religions."[98] In light of the weight of these arguments, Knitter concludes that Christianity can no longer cling to absolute truth claims.

Regarding the uniqueness of Christ, Knitter maintains that it must be redefined based upon recent New Testament scholarship that insists that the titles and images of Christ given in the New Testament are "literary-symbolic" as opposed to "literal-definitive."[99] He argues that the image of Christ as the

---

[95] Knitter, *One Earth Many Religions*, 32–33. See also Knitter, *Jesus and the Other Names*, 41; 91; 96; 98; 111; 118.
[96] Knitter, *Jesus and the Other Names*, 30.
[97] Knitter, *Jesus and the Other Names*, 38; 73.
[98] Knitter, *Jesus and the Other Names*, 30.
[99] Knitter, *Jesus and the Other Names*, 43.

exclusivist savior found in the New Testament is couched in the language of love as one would speak to a lover: "You are my one and only."[100] This does not mean that there are literally no others; it means that there are no others for me. This language then is seen as an affirmation of fidelity as opposed to a strict assertion of exclusivism. He also argues that the image of Christ as the exclusive savior found in the New Testament is couched in the language of dedication; it is "performative, a call to action."[101] It is an affirmation of discipleship and commitment for those within the Christian community. Based upon these arguments, Knitter would like to redefine Jesus' uniqueness away from absolute terminology. Jesus is not the "full, definitive, and unsurpassable" revelation of God; he is instead affirmed to be "universal, decisive, and indispensable."[102] Jesus is not "solely unique," he is "truly unique."[103] He is not "solely God's universal saving Word," he is "a saving Word."[104] Jesus' uniqueness is defined as "a matter of distinctness, of specialness that will surely be different from, but not necessarily better than others."[105] Through this process of redefinition Knitter seeks to eliminate the scandal of exclusivity that isolates Christianity from other religions and thwarts attempts at egalitarian dialogue. This process of redefinition, in turn, will allow for the embrace of pluralism within the Christian community.

In terms of salvific mediation, Knitter denies that Jesus brings salvation in the classic Christian sense. Instead of dying on the cross to provide salvation for sinners, Jesus came to bring a fuller life to his followers.[106] People on other religious paths will be unfulfilled without Christ—not in a salvific sense—but rather because they will lack the unique insights that Christ taught regarding the human condition. This view of the salvific aspects of Jesus' ministry is in keeping with Knitter's reclassification of Jesus to a mere human being who had an incredibly rich relationship with God. In Knitter's view, the deity of Christ was a secondary development in which Jesus' own theocentric orientation was overlaid with the Christocentric theology that is found in the New Testament.[107] Accepting conclusions drawn from the Third Quest for the historical Jesus,[108] Knitter argues that "Jesus was a *spirit-filled mystic* and a *social prophet.*"[109] Jesus' primary message was not simply God, but more properly "the Reign of

---

[100] Knitter, *Jesus and the Other Names,* 196–97. See also Paul F. Knitter, "Toward a Liberation Theology of Religions," in Hick & Knitter, *The Myth of Christian Uniqueness,* 196–97.

[101] Knitter, *Jesus and the Other Names,* 67–69; 107.

[102] Knitter, *Jesus and the Other Names,* 73–76; 76–80.

[103] Knitter, *Jesus and the Other Names,* 76.

[104] Knitter, *Jesus and the Other Names,* 104.

[105] Knitter, *Jesus and the Other Names,* 105.

[106] Knitter, *Jesus and the Other Names,* 76–79; 90.

[107] Knitter, *No Other Name?,* 177–82.

[108] Primarily those of Marcus Borg and John Dominic Crossan. See Marcus Borg, *Jesus, A New Vision: Spirit, Culture, and the Life of Discipleship* (San Francisco: HarperSanFrancisco, 1987) and John Dominic Crossan, *The Historical Jesus: The Life a Mediterranean Jewish Peasant* (San Francisco: HarperSanFrancisco, 1991).

[109] Knitter, *Jesus and the Other Names,* 93 (Italics in the original).

God."[110] This Reign was to embrace all people but was especially aimed at "those who needed it most: those suffering needlessly, the many victims of social oppression resulting from foreign domination working through local elites."[111] The open commensality of Jesus' table, through which he embraced the outcasts, the sinners, the tax collectors, was meant to symbolize a society that was structurally transformed through the Reign of God. According to Knitter, liberation is the "hermeneutical key" to understanding Jesus' message and mission.[112]

In light of this understanding, Knitter believes that the missionary task should be restructured to reflect a pluralistic focus. Efforts toward achieving conversions are to go forward, however, they are not to be driven by "concerns that 'eternal salvation' is hanging in the balance."[113] Instead, the goal of conversion is to seek "a return of the heart to God and to God's truth."[114] Thus, missionary activity should still carry with it the aspiration to transform human lives, but this transformation is now to be defined in pluralist terms. Ultimate religious affiliations do not matter. A Hindu is to be assisted in becoming a better Hindu. A Buddhist is to be assisted in becoming a better Buddhist. The Christian missionary him/herself is to be profoundly changed through the pluralistic dialogue. The focus of that dialogue is to be on Knitter's overarching soteriological concern: "global responsibility for eco-human well-being." Knitter argues that when this central issue is promoted and addressed that true liberation will be the result.

This restructuring of the missionary task away from a focus on conveying eternal salvation through the gospel message ties into Knitter's rejection of hell and eternal punishment. In his most recent book, *Without Buddha I Could not be a Christian*, Knitter gives his most detailed and mature explanation of his eschatology. He begins by connecting his rejection of hell and eternal punishment to his embrace of God's love:

> As I have already candidly confessed, I simply don't believe in hell because I simply can't. The square peg of God's eternal punishment just doesn't fit into the round hole of God's love. If the "use of reason" means anything in the Christian life, then we've got to make a choice between a God who administers or allows eternal pain or a God who loves and never gives up on that love.[115]

Given the fact that Knitter draws such a strong dichotomy between eternal punishment and God's love, one would think that he would have no use for the doctrine of eternal punishment at all. However, this is where he uses his Buddhism to bring what he believes to be greater light to his Christianity. In particular, Knitter believes that the Buddhist doctrine of karma and rebirth is speaking to the same issue that the Christian doctrine of eternal punishment

---

[110] Knitter, *Jesus and the Other Names,* 90.

[111] Knitter, *Jesus and the Other Names,* 91.

[112] Knitter, *Jesus and the Other Names,* 91.

[113] Knitter, *Jesus and the Other Names,* 123.

[114] Knitter, *Jesus and the Other Names,* 122.

[115] Knitter, *Without Buddha I Could Not Be A Christian,* 82.

does—karma being defined by Knitter as "the law of cause and effect: what you do is what you get."[116] Thus karma visits good things upon those who do good, and bad things upon those who do bad. Rebirth works with karma to enforce the effect—whether good or bad—into the next life. If one commits a great deal of sin in this life then the law of karma can even make one regress away from human rebirth into a lower form of animal as a sort of cosmic punishment.

> I believe that the underlying, practical meaning of the Buddhist teachings on *karma* and rebirth are fundamentally the same as the underlying, practical meaning of traditional Christian teachings on heaven and hell: the heart of both these teachings is that our free will is no joke. It's not to be taken lightly. There are grave, lasting consequences of the choices we make. And the Buddhist image of being reborn as a slug or other apparently lower forms of life, as well as the Christian image of hellfire, inform us that when those choices are selfish and harmful to others the consequences are so serious that they can extend into the reality of what comes after our individual death. . . . the message of "hell" or "rebirth" is that what may not have haunted us in this life will do so in the next. The results of our free choices are so serious that they will extend beyond the grave and affect, for better or for worse, what comes next. . . The "evil that men do" during the few years they strut upon this earth can be such that it carries on even after their footprints have long disappeared. That, I believe, is the central message of the Christian doctrine of hell. This message, even though it does not take "eternal" literally can still affect and guide our lives the way the traditional belief in hell was supposed to.[117]

For Knitter, the Buddhist doctrine of rebirth replaces the Christian doctrine of hell. Whereas traditional Christocentric universalists envision hell as a temporary place of correction/retribution that will eventually be emptied of all inhabitants as the last rebels give up their rebellion, Knitter envisions Buddhist rebirth as the means through which correction is brought upon sinners and entrance is eventually made into eternal life: "The good we do, or can do, will outlive, or offset, the evil we have done. But it may take more than what we define as one, single lifetime! *That* this is true I trust firmly. *How* it works I cannot say clearly."[118]

In a further assimilation of Buddhist eschatology, Knitter affirms that eternal life will consist of a very different life from the one we have lived here on earth. In an embrace of the eastern perspective, he argues that individuality will be done away with and each individual will become one with the divine spirit: "I think we can say, simply and profoundly, that life after death will no longer be lived as individuals. . . . The 'you' you thought you were is no longer

---

[116] Knitter, *Without Buddha I Could Not Be A Christian*, 82

[117] Knitter, *Without Buddha I Could Not Be A Christian*, 85.

[118] Knitter, *Without Buddha I Could Not Be A Christian*, 86–87.

around. *What you find is not what you lost.* That is the "good news" about heaven!"[119]

Knitter's universalism includes at its core a unique marriage of a theology of liberation and a pluralistic theology of religions. His desire for the deliverance of both humanity and nature has parallels in the most ancient constructions of apokatastasis found in the writings of the early church fathers. While Knitter does not posit a final eschatological apokatastasis, he is nevertheless concerned with the transformation of all things related to our world. His call for the bringing about of "eco-human well-being" on the earth can therefore be seen as a call for a sort of realized eschatology of apokatastasis in the here and now. The timing may be different than the traditional model of apokatastasis, but the goal is largely the same. The concern is not just for human liberation, but rather the liberation of nature itself. This is the sort of all-embracing vision that is found in the writings of Origen and Gregory of Nyssa as well as Moltmann and other contemporary proponents. Knitter gives it a uniquely contemporary twist that is drawn from liberation theology's focus on improving present circumstances.

Of course, with the widespread success of his books, Knitter has not been able to avoid the gaze of the keepers of doctrine within the Catholic Church, which, as we have noted, is becoming increasingly concerned with religious relativism. In May of 1996 the Church officially took note of Knitter's writings as Joseph Cardinal Ratzinger, acting as the Prefect of the Congregation for the Doctrine of the Faith, delivered a message in Guadalajara, Mexico, to the Doctrinal Commissions of the Bishops' Conferences of Latin America. The message was entitled, "Relativism: The Central Problem for Faith Today." In the message Cardinal Ratzinger singled out the pluralism of both John Hick and Paul Knitter for criticism. In reacting to Knitter's work, he took issue with Knitter's claim that orthodoxy should be developed out of orthopraxis. He likened this approach to that of the Marxist communists who tried to change the world while denying the knowability of absolute truth. He commented: "The failure of the communist regimes is due precisely to the fact that they tried to change the world without knowing what is good and what is not good for the world, without knowing in what direction the world must be changed in order to make it better. Mere praxis is not light."[120] In essence Cardinal Ratzinger expressed a very real concern that Knitter's theology has no conceptually valid foundation.

This sort of criticism also carries over to the justification that Knitter offers for his plurocentric universalism, which focuses on a philosophical relativism that is linked to a redefined Christology. It is on each of these points that he encounters serious structural difficulties. To begin with, an assertion of relativism is self-refuting in that it carries the seeds of its own destruction in its

---

[119] Knitter, *Without Buddha I Could Not Be A Christian*, 89.

[120] Joseph Cardinal Ratzinger, "Relativism: The Central Problem for Faith Today," *Origins* 26/20 (October 1996): 309–16. This article may also be found online at: http://www.ewtn.com/library/CURIA/RATZRELA.HTM, *Eternal Word Television Network*. (Accessed on December 11, 2014.)

very declaration.[121] To say something to the effect that "there are absolutely no absolute truths" is to make an absolute claim about truth that cannot stand up to its own standard, for in the process of claiming there is no absolute truth, one has just asserted that one knows absolutely that this is so. Thus one has asserted an absolute (the existence of relativism) when one just said that there are no absolutes. This sort of claim is similar to saying something self-refuting like, "There are no English sentences." The statement is self-refuting because I just asserted this claim in English, the very thing that my English sentence tried to deny. Notice in the following quote how Knitter absolutely asserts the relativist position:

> Given the context-conditioned, "theory-laden," socially-constructed interpretative limitations of every grasp and statement of truth, and given also the ever-changing, always-confining flow of history, Christians (and all religious persons) have to admit honestly that within our human condition, there can be no final word, no one way of knowing truth that is valid for all times and all peoples.[122]

This statement amounts to an absolute claim that there are no absolutes. What Knitter knows absolutely—what he gives the "final word" on—is that "there can be no final word." In affirming such an absolute claim regarding the existence of relativism, Knitter has just contradicted the very relativism that he asserts. In short, Knitter's statement is self-refuting.

Furthermore, if Knitter was true to his own relativism he would not be able to draw concrete conclusions about any matter of significant truth because, according to him, all such assertions cannot be extracted from the fog of human social constructs. However, this is exactly what Knitter proceeds to do. Having claimed "there can be no final word," he goes on to declare a final word regarding the pursuit of "eco-human well-being." He is absolutely sure that all religions should be pursuing this goal or they are "not from God."[123] Knitter is not relativistic on this point at all. He does not hedge his bets or equivocate. He knows absolutely that this goal should be pursued by all religions and thus contradicts his own relativism. Is Knitter a relativist or an absolutist? This seems to depend on what truth he is discussing. If it is the exclusivist claims of Christianity, he is a relativist; if it is his exclusivist claims regarding eco-human well-being, he is an absolutist.[124]

Knitter attempts to defend his truth claims by arguing that they are "absolute though speaking through relative forms." However, this amounts to little more

---

[121] A definitive refutation of the relativist position may be found in J.P. Moreland and William Lane Craig, *Philosophical Foundations for a Christian Worldview* (Downers Grove, Ill.: InterVarsity, 2003), 131–34; 143–54; 406–23.

[122] Knitter, *Jesus and the Other Names*, 29–30.

[123] Knitter, *Jesus and the Other Names*, 36.

[124] This is just one contradiction among many that we find in Knitter's work. He makes other absolutist sounding claims regarding the pursuit of love, justice, and kingdom values—to name a few. See Knitter, *Jesus and the Other Names*, 99; 101; 123; Knitter, *One Earth Many Religions*, 97–117; 124–29.

than another contradictory, self-refuting statement.[125] At least Knitter's definition of relativism will not allow for such double-talk. For him relativism is an all-or-nothing proposition. He said that there can be "no final word," yet he ventures to offer just such a word. It would seem that something has to give ground here: Knitter cannot have it both ways. He cannot be an absolutist/relativist any more than one can be an artist who draws square circles.

In addition to these difficulties, there is the issue of his re-interpretation of New Testament Christology. His relativizing approach to this issue does not work either. Knitter wants to say that the exclusivist claims regarding Christ were developed within the confines of a social situation, a "big-bang experience" of transformation that the disciples encountered as "salvation."[126] Seen in this way, exclusivist language can then be done away with by dismissing it as love language or the language of commitment and devotion that was never truly intended to isolate or separate. However, this approach does not seem to take seriously the actual social situation that existed at the time that such exclusivist claims were formulated and asserted. If this exclusivist language was really intended to be relativistic, why did the Apostles risk their lives to affirm its absoluteness? Why did they go to jail declaring an exclusivist Christology? Why were they willing to die for it? Why did so many Christian martyrs lay down their lives for these claims? Why were so many Christians so unwilling to bow to the genius of Caesar? To say that somehow the writers of the New Testament did not really mean what they said, is to ignore not only what they wrote, but also a long history of persecution and suffering that confirms that the early Christians, from the Apostles on down, were willing to die for precisely that exclusivist interpretation that Knitter is attempting to deny. All the early Christians had to do was to endorse a pluralist perspective and they would have been left alone by the Romans. Instead, the charge of "atheism" was leveled against them for refusing to bow down and worship the gods of Rome. The fact that they refused to do so gives us a clear indication of how they interpreted their own writings and how they intended other Christians to interpret them.

Furthermore, Knitter claims that the early Christians rejected the pluralism of their age, not out of Christocentric or monotheistic motivations, but rather because "it could not be reconciled with the right action or with the ethical-social vision contained in the Jesus' message about the Kingdom of God."[127] He argues that if the early Christians had been exposed to a pluralism that was "working for the eco-human justice that constitutes the heartbeat of Jesus' kingdom—then we can expect that the early Christians might have been all for it."[128] Along these lines, Knitter says that he prefers the "Logos/wisdom" Christology of John as opposed to the "Paschal/Easter" Christology of Paul because "Wisdom Christology views Jesus as *representative* of divine love" and locates the *"particularity* of Jesus *within the universality* of God's self-

---

[125] Knitter, *One Earth Many Religions*, 129–32.
[126] Knitter, *Jesus and the Other Names*, 175.
[127] Knitter, *Jesus and the Other Names*, 71.
[128] Knitter, *Jesus and the Other Names*, 71.

revelation, rather than locating God's universality *within the particularity* of the historical Jesus."[129] This leads Knitter to conclude that Logos/Wisdom theology opens the door to the idea that such a manifestation did not happen "*only* here."[130]

The problem is that such an interpretation of John's Incarnational theology does not seem possible in light of the on-going recovery of the Gospel of John's profoundly monotheistic, Jewish context. For instance, Peder Borgen has argued that the prologue of John's Gospel forms an independent unity that can be characterized as a Jewish midrash like exposition of Gen. 1:1–5.[131] Based upon both philological and thematic parallels such as God, the Word, creation, light, darkness, and life, Borgen contends, "Jn 1:1–5 is the basic exposition of Gn 1:1–5, while Jn 1:6ff. elaborates upon terms and phrases from Jn 1:1–5."[132] While one might not agree with Borgen's midrashic hypothesis, the parallels he notes are compelling from the aspect of understanding that the points of contact between the two passages extend far beyond the first few words of John 1:1. Although there may be Hellenistic overtones to the concept of the Logos,[133] the context of the passage itself is the strongest argument for the fact that the author intended it to be read primarily through monotheistic, Jewish lenses. Based on the obvious Genesis 1 context in which the prologue is located, Herman Ridderbos concludes:

> This backward look at Genesis 1 is proof that the Evangelist did not wish to subsume the glory of Christ under some other heading and explain it in that other way. Instead, he sought to identify the presence of God in the advent and work of Jesus of Nazareth, on the basis of the Old Testament, as the presence of the God who from "the beginning" showed himself to be, not a self-sufficient, immutable, silent God, but the God who "extended" himself and spoke: "Let there be light in the darkness." Of *that* beginning the "in the beginning" of the prologue is a continuation, and in that "beginning" it also has its most fundamental basis.[134]

Given the strong connection made to Gen. ch. 1 in the prologue of John's Gospel, the argument seems to be compelling that what we have in Johannine Christology is the exact opposite of what Knitter contends. Far from being a mystical Christology that allows for a sort of panentheistic pluralism (at least as it relates to multiple manifestations in other religious leaders), Johannine Christology confirms an exclusivistic monotheism that extends back to the very beginning and creation of all things. John's prologue does not set the stage for

---

[129] Knitter, *Jesus and the Other Names*, 42 (Italics in the original).

[130] Knitter, *Jesus and the Other Names*, 42 (Italics in the original).

[131] Peder Borgen, "Observations on the Targumic Character of the Prologue of John," *NTS* 16 (1970): 288–95. See also Peder Borgen, *Logos Was the True Light, and other essays on the Gospel of John* (Trondheim, Norway: Tapir, 1983).

[132] Borgen, *Logos Was the True Light*, 13.

[133] George R. Beasley-Murray, *John*, Word Biblical Commentary, vol. 36 (Waco, Tex.: Word, 1987), 6–10.

[134] Herman Ridderbos, *The Gospel According to John: A Theological Commentary* (Grand Rapids, Mich.: Eerdmans, 1997), 26.

wild speculation; its goal was to remove all doubt about the monotheistic identity of the God who was made flesh in Jesus Christ.

Taking up Knitter's unique marriage of Christian and Buddhist theology we encounter perhaps his greatest theological weakness: his resorting to a works-righteousness scheme in order to open a way for people to gain access to eternal life. The problem Knitter is trying to solve has its root in the fact that his theology has reduced Jesus Christ to the status of a mere man. Having stripped Jesus of his divinity and power, Knitter is not then able to utilize the divine work of the Savior on the cross to atone for the sins of humanity. This in turn forces him to find an alternative solution to the problem of sin and in the end he chooses a works-righteousness system of atonement to try to get the job done. In his book *Without Buddha I Could not be a Christian* he puts forward his essential works-righteousness thesis: "The good we do, or can do, will outlive, or offset, the evil we have done. But it may take more than what we define as one, single lifetime!"[135] Here then we see why Knitter finds the Buddhist doctrine of rebirth so attractive, because it would in theory allow each individual an unlimited number of lifetimes to atone for their own sins through the accumulation of good deeds.

However, the basic problem that Knitter's scheme faces is the same basic problem that has plagued all other works-righteousness schemes down through history: good works cannot possibly pay off our debt of sin because good works are not the currency of payment demanded by God. According to the Bible only shed blood can atone for sin: "For the life of the flesh is in the blood; and I have given it to you for making atonement for your lives on the altar; for, as life, it is the blood that makes atonement" (Lev. 17:11, NRSA). This demand for the recompense of life for sins committed, as symbolized by the shedding of blood, ties into the death sentence that was announced upon sinners by the LORD God in Gen. 2:16–17 and is confirmed in several places in the New Testament.[136] This is why the theology of atonement found in both the Old and New Testaments is built upon blood sacrifice and not good works. The stance of the scriptures is that a death sentence can only be expunged by a death. Either the blood of a substitutionary sacrifice or the blood of the violator will have to be shed, for sin can only be atoned for by the sacrifice of a life, which is symbolized by shedding of blood. Therefore, at the heart of the gospel message is the shedding of Christ's blood for our sins:

---

[135] Knitter, *Without Buddha I Could Not Be A Christian*, 86–87.

[136] Romans 6:23: "For the wages of sin is death . . ." Hebrews 9:7: ". . . but into the second only the high priest *enters*, once a year, not without *taking* blood, which he offers for himself and for the sins of the people committed in ignorance." Hebrews 9:18–22: [18] "Therefore not even the first *covenant* was dedicated without blood. [19] For when Moses had spoken every precept to all the people according to the law, he took the blood of calves and goats, with water, scarlet wool, and hyssop, and sprinkled both the book itself and all the people, [20] saying, '*This* is *the* blood of the covenant which *God has commanded you.*' [21] Then likewise he sprinkled with blood both the tabernacle and all the vessels of the ministry. [22] And according to the law almost all things are purified with blood, and without shedding of blood there is no remission."

[11] But when Christ appeared *as* a high priest of the good things to come, *He entered* through the greater and more perfect tabernacle, not made with hands, that is to say, not of this creation; [12] and not through the blood of goats and calves, but through His own blood, He entered the holy place once for all, having obtained eternal redemption. [13] For if the blood of goats and bulls and the ashes of a heifer sprinkling those who have been defiled, sanctify for the cleansing of the flesh, [14] how much more will the blood of Christ, who through the eternal Spirit offered Himself without blemish to God, cleanse your conscience from dead works to serve the living God? [15] And for this reason He is the mediator of a new covenant, in order that since a death has taken place for the redemption of the transgressions that were *committed* under the first covenant, those who have been called may receive the promise of the eternal inheritance.

Hebrews 9:11–15

By eliminating the substitutionary atonement of Jesus Christ from his theology, Knitter has put himself between a rock and a hard place when it comes to dealing with the issue of sin and the death sentence that God has pronounced upon sinners. To his credit Knitter recognizes to a certain degree the severity of the issue at hand and he makes a feeble effort to deal with it. The problem is that his solution falls far short of kind of expiation that the LORD God demands from sinners in the Bible. In the end, Knitter has hollowed out the Christian faith to the point where its ultimate collapse under the weight of the burden of sin was inevitable. Without the work of the Savior he has no meaningful solution to offer us to the problem of sin.

Despite these serious flaws, Knitter's work still provides a valuable contribution to the current debate and the focus of theology in general. To begin with, Knitter is to be commended for his scrupulous honesty regarding the positions taken by his opponents and the changes that he has made to his own theology. Knitter goes to great lengths to treat his critics fairly and in so doing provides a great deal of penetrating summary and analysis. He has a knack for highlighting key features and issues. Secondly, Knitter's focus on a sort of realized eschatology serves as a reminder that even in our modern age a great many of our fellow human beings live lives that are marked by incredible suffering and misery. Knitter's work is essentially a call for Christians to engage this issue. It is a reminder that there is a responsibility on the part of all Christians to take actions that will lead to the elimination of the dire circumstances faced by so many of our fellow human beings. Finally, Knitter's focus on the liberation of the earth underscores the close connection that humanity has to this special and unique planet. This focus, in turn, reminds us of our God-given responsibility to be wise stewards of the resources that God has placed into our hands.

4. Conclusion
Contrary to what one might expect, the Catholic Church has succeeded in producing a more diverse expression of plurocentric universalism than has been developed within the Protestant tradition. The approaches of Panikkar, Küng, and Knitter represent radically different solutions to the same problem, albeit

from a uniquely Catholic perspective. Interestingly enough, this diversity in thought appears to have been spurred on by the unique circumstances that the contemporary Church finds itself in.

To begin with, it must be noted that the sheer size and geographical scope of the Catholic Church has brought the Church into direct contact with more cultures and religious systems than any other organization on the face of the earth. This contact has often resulted in efforts at religious harmonization and syncretism such as that found in the Caribbean (e.g. Voodoo and Santeria) and Africa. Panikkar's proposal is surely illustrative of the sorts of solutions that can simply arise out of the Catholic collision with the religions of the world. Secondly, due to its size and influence, the Church cannot avoid the political ramifications of its policies and actions. Liberation theology is in large part a reaction against Church policies that supported a deadly status quo in much of Latin America. Knitter's proposal is rooted and grounded in this protest movement and its call for reform. It is essentially an expansion on this theme. Thirdly, and perhaps most importantly, we cannot ignore the tremendous influence that the Vatican II reforms have had upon the Church. The embrace of inclusivism and the recognition of the potential for salvation in other religious traditions has encouraged a move on the part of some towards a robust universalism. Küng's proposal seems to be representative of those who would like to expand upon Vatican II or think that Vatican II did not go far enough. In their view, Vatican II is an invitation to walk through the wider door of universalism.

In light of these factors it seems reasonable to conclude that the Catholic contribution to the debate is indeed uniquely Catholic. Outside influences have certainly affected the positions taken. However, the core issues addressed and the approaches taken toward them remain uniquely Catholic in both their expression and resolution.

CHAPTER 8

Findings and Conclusions

So far in this study we have surveyed the universalist proposals made by sixteen contemporary theologians. In addition to this we have provided a historical review of the development of the doctrine, which has supplied us with the context in which our discussion has taken place. This final chapter will be devoted to making sense of the mosaic that now lies before us. We will begin by attempting to provide a solution to the problem of categorization. The study will then conclude with a discussion of the key insights that have emerged from our analysis.

1. The Problem of Categorization

The contemporary landscape of universalism presents to us an interesting mixture of both the old and the new. In the struggle to adapt universalism to our current age, contemporary theologians have taken several paths. Some have opted for more traditional approaches to the issue and have done little more than update the arguments and ideas put forward by patristic proponents such as Origen. Others have felt free to combine several time honored solutions with some new propositions. Still others have opted to create entirely new expressions of the doctrine. These disparate approaches have in turn led to a bit of a crisis in the field regarding categorization. Simply put, recent developments in the field have added a level of complexity that makes it quite difficult to create a meaningful framework that would provide a simple way of categorizing and sorting the field. Without such a framework in which to view contemporary proposals, key connections and linkages might be overlooked or ignored and crucial insights might remain hidden. Therefore, the development of a satisfactory representation of the current state of affairs would be a helpful step to take in order to gain a deeper understanding of contemporary universalism.

In the study of historical universalism there has been little or nothing done in terms of an effort to graphically represent the various positions held. Typically, studies have been organized by era rather than by characteristic, with common features usually being collated and evaluated at the end. To the best of my knowledge, there has been no chart published that specifically seeks to categorize and graphically depict the various positions held by contemporary universalists. The closest thing to such a chart was produced by David Powys in his article, "The Nineteenth and Twentieth Century Debates about Hell and Universalism." In that chart Powys sought to delineate "The Fate of the Unrighteous" as it was developed in eighteenth century theology through to the present.[1] The chart is not focused specifically on universalism and due to the wide-ranging nature of the subject matter, it is fairly large and cumbersome. Powys' approach illustrates the difficulty of striking the proper balance between complexity and usefulness. What is needed is a chart that will provide a simple yet informative overview of the field with the capability for expansion and addition as the field moves forward.

2. The Universalism Matrix

In examining contemporary proposals that we have encountered it seems abundantly clear that two fundamental issues divide the field. The first is the position that the proponent takes on the relative importance of Jesus Christ in their scheme of salvation. The second is the position that the proponent advances on the question of hell. It is these two factors that differentiate the field more than any others and therefore these two factors represent a unique opportunity to provide us with a meaningful visual representation of the field.

If we take each the two issues on an individual basis they present each proponent with a binary decision that essentially eliminates any gray areas and thus adds to the attractiveness using these to formulate a chart. In the case of the relative importance of Jesus Christ, the decision is between his absolute necessity as a provision of salvation and his being essentially unnecessary to the overall scheme. In the case of the question of hell, again we have basically a binary choice between the absolute necessity of hell being used to inflict the coercive suffering necessary to extract an endorsement of faith and the notion that such a heavy handed method is unnecessary.

In combining these two factors and the binary choices involved it appears that the problem of categorization can be effectively resolved through the use of a chart arranged as a four-quadrant matrix. Such a matrix is simple enough to provide us with some major, easily recognizable categories while at the same time providing us with enough intricacy to supply a useful portrayal of the current state of scholarly development. It also has the advantage of categorizing the field in such a way that any foreseeable future proposals will easily fit on to the grid in as much as any future proponents will have to deal with these two essential issues that clearly delineate the various varieties of contemporary Christian universalisms from one another.

As a technical matter, it should be understood that this matrix is offered strictly as a heuristic device as opposed to a more scientifically developed tool. Nevertheless, it is hoped that it will fill a gap that has long existed in the field and provide a convenient and useful template that may be used in the future to categorize universalist proposals and the discussion of what separates them from one another and what unites them. With this said, the proposed matrix is as follows:

---

[1] David J. Powys, "The Nineteenth and Twentieth Century Debates About Hell and Universalism," in Nigel M. de S. Cameron, ed., *Universalism and the Doctrine of Hell*, Carlisle, U.K.: Paternoster, 1992, 137–38.

Universalism Matrix
Contemporary Expressions in Western Theology since 1960

Eschatological Means

Hell
Temporary Remedial—Corrective—Retributive Punishment

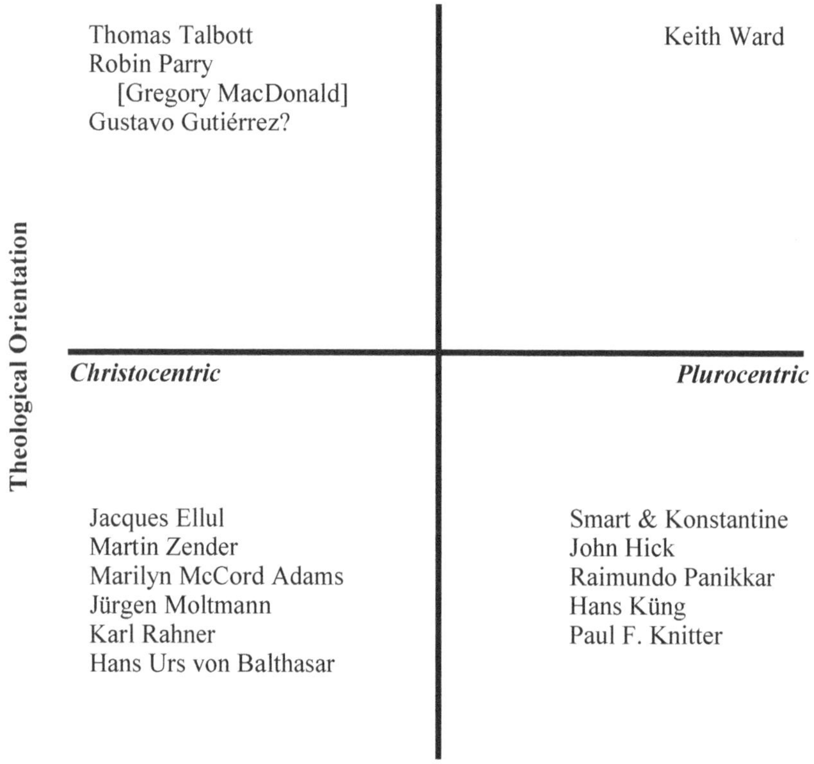

Thomas Talbott Robin Parry [Gregory MacDonald] Gustavo Gutiérrez?	Keith Ward

Christocentric   *Plurocentric*

(vertical axis label: **Theological Orientation**)

Jacques Ellul Martin Zender Marilyn McCord Adams Jürgen Moltmann Karl Rahner Hans Urs von Balthasar	Smart & Konstantine John Hick Raimundo Panikkar Hans Küng Paul F. Knitter

No Hell
Translation / Re-embodiment / Intermediate State(s) / Reincarnation

To better understand this matrix let us begin by discussing the horizontal axis that delineates "Theological Orientation." This is the axis that takes up the question of the relative importance of Jesus Christ. On the left side is a "Christocentric" approach and on the right side we have a "Plurocentric" approach. These divisions are by now quite familiar to us with a Christocentric universalist being someone who understands universal salvation to be entirely mediated through Jesus Christ and thus places the highest level of importance on Christ in their scheme of salvation. Before the advent of religious pluralism in the twentieth century virtually all universalists were of the Christocentric variety.

On the right side of the horizontal axis is the category "Plurocentric." A Plurocentric universalist is, of course, a religious pluralist who understands universal salvation to be mediated through many different faiths and thus places a substantially reduced emphasis on the relative importance of Jesus Christ in their scheme of salvation. This view would hold that all the major religious systems provide relatively equal access to salvation and that the net result is that in the end all people will be saved regardless of their religious affiliation.

It should be kept in mind that we have argued that both Karl Rahner and Hans Urs von Balthasar fall into the "hopeful universalism" camp although Rahner leans much more closely to the dogmatic end of that scale. As such they could have been eliminated from the matrix. However, in recognition of their importance for Catholic theology it was decided to include them in the grid. The reader should keep in mind that the position that they take should be qualified as being only a possibility and is by no means a dogmatic one.

The problems created by moderating positions have already been discussed in the introduction to chapter five. It should be noted that along these lines Keith Ward presents a particularly difficult case to categorize. It will be recalled that Ward advanced a theory of universal salvation through what he called the "pleromal Christ." Based strictly on the semantics of Ward's proposal, he might very well be included on the Christocentric side of the matrix. However, when one examines the particulars of Ward's "pleromal Christ" it rapidly becomes clear that Ward's conception of this impersonal, pantheistic deity is so divergent from the orthodox view that it makes better sense to include it on the pluralist side of the grid.

The vertical axis of the matrix is labeled "Eschatological Means." This is the axis that takes up the question of hell. As such it is focused on categorizing universalists based upon their view of the means through which those who die in an unregenerate state will be brought into the kingdom. The top half of the matrix labeled "Hell" is reserved for universalists who argue that hell will play an important postmortem role in reconciling the lost to God. For this group, hell always entails at a minimum a temporary, remedial/corrective punishment allowed by God or inflicted by God upon recalcitrant sinners. In some cases hell is even viewed as being retributive or purgatorial in nature. In all cases hell is viewed as a temporary evil that will be done away with when the last sinner submits to God's will for his or her salvation.

The bottom half of the matrix is labeled "No Hell" and is reserved for those who argue that hell will not be necessary for anyone. In this case the actual means of deliverance employed varies greatly, but the result is the same: all people will enter the kingdom without having to experience the anguish of hell.

Of those who would argue for the "No Hell" outcome, theologians like Ellul, Zender, Rahner, von Balthasar, Smart & Konstantine, Panikkar, Küng, and Knitter take positions that seem to require a sort of instantaneous translation of the individual into the kingdom upon death. However, caution must be exercised when evaluating these individuals as some of them make conflicting statements, or remain intentionally vague about this aspect of their theology. Jürgen Moltmann is notable for his advocacy of a benign intermediate state through which God will allow a re-embodied person to work up to their full potential.[2] John Hick seems to agree with this point of view, although he envisions "many lives in many worlds"[3] and his work also seems to open the door to a form of reincarnation.[4] Smart and Konstantine also seem to hint at the possibility of reincarnation, although they are by no means clear on this point.[5]

It should be noted that Gustavo Gutiérrez presented a particular challenge when it came to categorizing his eschatological outlook. This is because he does not appear to discuss the issue of hell or eternal punishment anywhere in his writings. Because Gutiérrez seems to be fairly traditional in those areas of theology that do not touch upon the issue of liberation, it was assumed that he would probably endorse the standard Catholic eschatological schema with the exception that he embraces the notion of a universalist outcome. I have placed a question mark after Gutiérrez's name in order to indicate that this categorization is only a tentative one.

Taken as a whole, the Universalism Matrix highlights two very important trends that have occurred within contemporary universalism. The first is a shift away from an orthodox Christology that focuses on the centrality of Jesus Christ in the process of salvation. Here we have the influence of pluralism leaving its mark upon the field. The startling statistic is that 44% of those theologians we have examined have adopted a pluralist position and are advocating a Christology that essentially reduces Jesus to one great religious leader among many. For centuries Christocentrism was assumed to be a given within universalist circles. Even sixty years ago the centrality of Christ went virtually unchallenged. What we have here is a sea change in theology that has occurred within just the last fifty-five years. When one takes into account that trends in Christian theology are often measured in terms of centuries, this is indeed a truly amazing development. If this trend continues as it has, it may well be that within the next two decades Christocentric universalism will become the exception rather than the rule. If this happens we will have witnessed a complete paradigm shift in universalist thinking in which the time honored model that has existed for two millennia has been displaced in a matter of several decades.

The second important trend highlighted by the Universalism Matrix is a shift away from the eschatological necessity of hell and the infliction of coercive punishment. In this case, a more startling statistic reveals that 75% of the contemporary universalists that we have studied have abandoned a belief in any form of hell. This is an important development because most of the brief caricatures of universalism found in the literature include the idea that remedial punishment in hell is an essential element of every universalist theology. Here

---

[2] The word "re-embodiment" was chosen in favor of "resurrected" because resurrection in the classic sense has to do with the reconstitution of a body that has died and been buried here on earth. Re-embodiment may include a form of resurrection or not. This leaves open the possibility that a new body may simply be provided by God for a person to use in the intermediate state as some of these theologians seem to imply in their discussions.

[3] Hick, *Death and Eternal Life*, 414–24, 456–58; Hick, *The Fifth Dimension*, 250–55.

[4] Hick, *The Fifth Dimension*, 251.

[5] Smart and Konstantine, *Christian Systematic Theology*, 295.

we see that seventy-five percent of contemporary universalists in our study have abandoned a doctrine that was once considered an irreplaceable essential of the Christian faith. That the "No Hell" option has become much more popular than the classic position verifies that the revolt against the doctrine of hell, which began to gain traction in the seventeenth century, has continued unabated into our own times and has gathered considerable momentum. Today a universalist is much more likely to reject the necessity of hell than not.

3. Conclusions

This study has sought to survey contemporary expressions of universalism against the backdrop of the historical development of the doctrine. When one considers recent universalist proposals within this context the first thing that stands out is how well they were anticipated in history. There is indeed a substantial continuity in approach that emerges between the historical and the contemporary.

Sometimes this continuity emerges as a result of a conscious endorsement of the past. This is seen in the frequent positive references made by contemporary universalists to Origen and his doctrine of apokatastasis. As was noted in our discussion of him, Origen has cast a long shadow over the field and his influence continues into our own times. He is indeed the true father of universalism in so far as his exposition of the doctrine continues to be a key driver in the contemporary debate.

Often the continuity between the historical and the contemporary occurs in a serendipitous fashion. A prime example of this phenomenon is to be found in the universalism of Thomas Talbott, which closely parallels that of Friedrich Schleiermacher (1768–1834). Although Talbott had never studied Schleiermacher[6] and Schleiermacher was writing some 170 years prior to Talbott, there is an almost point-by-point agreement between the two. Both men base their universalism upon the affirmation that all of God's attributes are merged together in a singular attribute of love. From this essential principle each of them proceed to lay out a system of universalism that has an amazing equivalence.

Other examples of serendipitous correspondence represent broad agreement on theoretical grounds as opposed to the precise details. Ninian Smart and Steven Konstantine put forward a vision of the Trinity that stresses the imminence of the Godhead to humanity. As we have noted, this approach was roughly anticipated in the work of both Marcellus of Ancyra (d. c. 374) and Amaury of Bène (d. c. 1207). The position taken Martin Zender regarding instant translation into heaven mirrors closely the "death and glory" soteriology of Hosea Ballou (1771–1852). The pantheistic outcome found in the eschatology of contemporary writers such as John Hick, Karl Rahner, and Hans Küng was broadly envisioned in the theologies of Johannes Scotus Eriugena (c. 810–c. 877) and the Free Spirit heretics (c. 1200).

We also see substantial continuity between historical and contemporary universalism in terms of the outcome that is anticipated. A chief example of this would be the continuity we find between the trajectory of Origen's doctrine

---

[6] Dr. Talbott affirmed this point in a personal conversation he had with me.

apokatastasis and the apokatastasis that we find in Jürgen Moltmann's theology. A central motivator for both men is the notion that in the end God must be "all in all." For each man mere universalism is not enough to satisfy such a lofty ideal and this tenet in turn drives a broad eschatological vision that results in all things returning to God and all things being restored through God.

The weight of all this evidence goes to show that there is much more continuity between contemporary and historical expressions of universalism than might be expected. However, this conclusion makes sense when one considers that historically universalist thinkers have had to address many of the same questions and issues that contemporary proponents still face today. The struggle to produce a coherent universalism has resulted in similar answers and proposals that span centuries and transcend cultural boundaries.

On the other hand, the study has also revealed that contemporary universalists have produced unique expressions that respond to the distinctive issues and circumstances that have emerged in our own times. In particular, the issue of pluralism has taken center stage and has driven universalists to contemplate entirely new ways of thinking and theologizing. The shrinking globe, the information explosion, instantaneous communications, and the focus on the watchwords of "diversity" and "multiculturalism" have all contributed to an atmosphere in which plurocentric universalism could be developed and given a level legitimacy that would have been unthinkable fifty years ago. Indeed, the speed with which plurocentric proposals have been cultivated and received serves to underscore the unique volatility of the times in which we live.

The ascendancy of pluralist thought in theological circles corresponds directly to the promotion and acceptance of relativism linked to pluralist ideas within post-modern western cultures. In the 1960s and the 1970s western confidence in the superiority of its traditions and way of life was aggressively challenged on many fronts by post-modern thinkers. For the sixties generation growing up in the United States and Europe, it seemed that virtually any and every foreign culture was to be preferred to its own. Thus, it is no coincidence that John Hick's ground-breaking book *God and the Universe of Faiths* was published in 1973, during the rapid expansion of the post-modern upheaval in the West.

Jean-François Lyotard defined post-modernism as extreme "incredulity toward metanarratives"[7]—a metanarrative being a sort of all-encompassing self-story that orders and explains a society's knowledge, values, and truths. The metanarrative of the West included the notion that it had possession of absolute truth. It was this claim in particular that was so vociferously attacked by post-modernism. Seen through this lens, Hick's attempt to administer the coup de grâce to Christian exclusivism is in keeping with the post-modern critique and its embrace of cultural relativism. From a post-modern perspective, absolute truth claims are viewed as the source of most conflicts and as such must be tenaciously eliminated. The plurocentric universalism of both Hans Küng and Paul Knitter also fit in well with this post-modern agenda in that they are in broad agreement with its relativism and its attack on absolutes. The

---

[7] Lyotard, *The Post-Modern Condition*, xxiv.

approaches of Küng and Knitter both identify exclusivism as the primary opponent toward which their eschatological schemas are aimed and they attempt to provide the means through which Christian exclusivism can be ultimately done away with.

Raimundo Panikkar, on the other hand, does not seem to have a post-modern axe to grind. His plurocentric universalism is unique in that it does not appear to be driven by Western cultural and philosophical developments. Instead, Panikkar's proposal seems to be genuinely motivated by his family background and his efforts to reconcile his father's Hinduism with his mother's Catholicism. Of course, this project rapidly expanded to embrace all religions, but, at its heart, we still perceive an intensely personal motivation. Although Panikkar was also interested in eliminating exclusivism, his approach is to propose an expansive harmonization between religions and religious concepts that is elastic enough to embrace all. Thus Panikkar's solution to the problem of exclusivism is a sort of conquest through modified adoption. In this regard he is not a relativist. Panikkar believes that his cosmotheandrism has captured the true panorama of reality.

The upshot of all this is that the development of plurocentric universalism reveals a theology that has been primarily influenced and molded by contemporary issues and circumstances. It is clear that this sort of theology did not develop in a vacuum, but rather that it is the product of many forces including socio-cultural factors and global realities as opposed to strictly theological considerations. It would seem that what we have then with plurocentric proposals is an example of socio/global dynamics driving theology rather than dogmatic issues and concerns. Plurocentric universalism emerges as a unique solution that is offered in response to a rapidly developing understanding of our contemporary state of affairs.

From the point of view of exegesis and biblical hermeneutics, the study has underscored the fact that serious problems remain for universalist proposals. If there is an Achilles' heel that affects the entire movement it is its fragile interpretation of Scripture. The critiques offered to the various approaches taken by contemporary universalists reveal that the New Testament's consistent affirmations of hell and eternal punishment remain remarkably resistant to all efforts to deconstruct them. In point of fact, it appears that the exegetical case has only increased in strength over the years as the fruits of the application of the historical critical method have added to our understanding of both context and meaning. On the other side of the ledger, the debate over those New Testament passages that seem to affirm universalism has been joined by competent scholars who offer viable non-universalist interpretations to the passages that are consistent with an affirmation of hell and eternal punishment. A critical weakness found in most universalist proposals is a failure to adequately engage the arguments made on the other side. It is interesting to note that even for plurocentric universalists that the key battle ground remains the Bible. All parties recognize that in order to win, the scriptural high-ground must be taken.

The study has also brought to light several structural issues that will likely remain the subject of further discussion and debate for some time. Chief among these is the very definition of Christianity itself. It is obvious from our discussion of Christocentric universalism that many of these proposals push the limits in terms of doctrinal boundaries. Plurocentric universalism, with its essential reduction of the role of Christ and its explicit embrace of other religions and salvific means, has also raised anew the issue of defining appropriate doctrinal fences. Surely there is a point that one crosses where doctrinal modification results in the formation of something other than Christianity. When is this point reached? What is the key doctrinal core that defines the Christian faith? What is it that makes a Christian a Christian? These are non-trivial questions that are raised by the many proposals we have explored and the various theologies that underlie them.

Related to this issue is the question of the viability of plurocentric universalism as a legitimate expression of Christian theology. Whereas Christocentric universalism has always gained its legitimacy through an embrace of Christ, plurocentric universalism has abandoned this fundamental feature and in so doing seems to have chosen to reside on the open ocean of non-commitment as opposed to dropping anchor in any one particular port. This approach would seem to have much more in common with the affirmations made by the Bahá'í Faith than those of Christianity. A cursory examination of the writings of Bahá'u'lláh (1817–1892), the founder of the Bahá'í Faith, reveals that they promote a very similar universalist vision, which includes the salvation of all people, an acceptance of the validity of other religions, and an acknowledgment that the founders and central figures of other religions represent unique manifestations of God.[8] The three essential unities of the Bahá'í Faith—the oneness of God, the oneness of religion, and the oneness of humanity—could well be embraced by several of the pluralists whom we have discussed. The Bahá'í approach has been recognized by scholars to be the establishment of an entirely new religion as opposed to an extension cobbled onto the back of Islam, which is the cultural milieu from which it emerged. In light of this determination, the question must be asked if the plurocentric universalists have not just recapitulated the role of Bahá'u'lláh in the creation of yet another new pluralistic religion.

4. Postscript

I wish they were wrong. I wish I could say that God is too loving, too kind, and too generous to condemn any soul to eternal punishment. I would like to believe that hell can only be the anteroom to heaven, a temporary and frightful discipline to bring the unregenerate to final moral perfection. . . . But all of this wishful speculation, if not quite beside the point, is surely not decisive. The structure of reality cannot be clawed out of the web of human wishes.[9]

Kenneth S. Kantzer

[8] A bibliography of key Bahá'í writings may be found in Robert H. Stockton and Jonah Winters, *A Resource Guide for the Study of the Bahá'í Faith* (Wilmette, Ill.: Research Office, Bahá'í National Center, 1997).
[9] Kenneth S. Kantzer, "Troublesome Questions," *CT* 31/5 (March 20, 1987): 45.

Ultimately, the universalist enterprise is the quest to find an innocuous eschatology; an eschatology that is harmless and inoffensive; an eschatology that has a happy ending. If the theologians we have studied share a common failing, it is their predisposition to reject any negative eschatological outcome. Armed with this mindset they come to the question of eternal destiny with the end already in sight. Is it any wonder then that when they look down into the deep well of biblical eschatology that they find reflected at the bottom an eschatology that is made in their own image?

This explains the inability of the movement as a whole to handle the Bible with a straightforward hermeneutic. With universalists we find that there must always be an exegesis of deconstruction. With universalists we find that there must always be an effort made to show that a simple reading of the text is wrong. With universalists we find that there must always be an oblique rationalization. The result is an interpretation of the text that is demonstrably strained, artificial, and unreal. It is an interpretation that also runs counter to the basic demand of faith in the here and now placed upon people by the New Testament: "Believe on the Lord Jesus Christ, and you will be saved." (Acts 16:31)

At the end of the day the fundamental debate over the eschatological disposition of human beings must come down to the Bible itself. It is the Bible that raises the specter of the Day of Judgment and a final separation. It is the Bible that raises the specter of the Lake of Fire. It is the Bible that raises the specter of eternal punishment. Universalism—the salvation of all—is an appealing idea, however, it still runs afoul of the scriptural warnings and injunctions. The weight of the biblical evidence against universalism remains too heavy to be overcome and it must be the Bible that is given the last word in this study.

It has been rightly said that goodness shines all the more against the backdrop of evil. The same thing is true of salvation in Christ as it is presented in the New Testament documents. The stark contrast drawn between the eternal fate of the saved and the lost in the New Testament serves to focus our attention all the more on the glory of the Savior. To be sure the Lord Jesus Christ spoke of hell fire and eternal punishment more than any other figure in the Bible. However, it is his words of life that stand out all the more against that backdrop:

"Come unto Me, all you who labor and are heavy laden," the Savior says, "and I will give you rest." (Matt. 11:26) And again He reminds us: "For even the Son of Man did not come to be served, but to serve, and to give His life a ransom for many." (Mk. 10:45)

Therefore let us take his vital warning to heart:

[13] "Enter by the narrow gate; for wide is the gate and broad is the way that leads to destruction, and there are many who go in by it. [14] Because narrow is the gate and difficult is the way which leads to life, and there are few who find it." (Matt. 7:13-14)

Universalism is a broad way that in the end must be rejected. Let us therefore put our feet on the narrow path that leads to the Savior and his Cross. We dare not trust any other.

BIBLIOGRAPHY

1. Books, Dissertations, and Theses

Adams, Marilyn McCord. *Christ and Horrors: The Coherence of Christology.* Cambridge: Cambridge University Press, 2006.

_____. *Horrendous Evils and the Goodness of God.* Ithaca, N.Y.: Cornell University Press, 1999.

Aland, Kurt and Eberhard Nestlé, et al., eds. *Novum Testamentum Graece.* Twenty-seventh edition. Stuttgart: Deutsche Bibelgesellschaft, 2001.

Alberigo, Giuseppe, Norman P. Tanner, et al., eds. *Decrees of the Ecumenical Councils.* 2 vols. London: Sheed and Ward; Washington D.C.: Georgetown University Press, 1990.

Altaner, Berthold. *Patrology.* Translated by Hilda C. Graef. Freiburg: Herder, 1960.

Anderson, Gerald H. and Thomas F. Stransky. *Christ's Lordship and Religious Pluralism.* Maryknoll, N.Y.: Orbis, 1981.

Ansell, Nicholas. *The Annihilation of Hell: Universal Salvation and the Redemption of Time in the Eschatology of Jürgen Moltmann.* Milton Keynes, U.K.: Paternoster Press, 2013.

Anz, Wilhelm. *Zur Frage nach dem Ursprung des Gnostizismus: ein religionsgeschichtlicher Versuch.* Leipzig: J.C. Hinrichs, 1897.

Aquinas, Thomas. *Summa Theologiae, vol. 32, Consequences of Faith.* Edited by Thomas Gilby. London: Blackfriars, Eyre & Spottiswoode, 1975.

Ayer, Joseph Cullen. *A Source Book for Ancient Church History: From the Apostolic Age to the Close of the Conciliar Period.* New York: Charles Scribner's Sons, 1952.

Bahmann, Manfred K. *A Preference for the Poor: Latin American Liberation Theology from a Protestant Perspective.* Lanham, Md.: University Press of America, 2005.

Ballou, Hosea. *The Ancient History of Universalism from the Time of the Apostles to its Condemnation in the Fifth General Council, A.D. 553 with an Appendix Tracing the Doctrine Down to The Reformation.* Providence, R.I.: Z. Baker, 1842.

Balthasar, Hans Urs von. *Epilog.* Einsiedeln-Trier: Johannes Verlag, 1987. English edition translated by Edward T. Oakes. *Epilogue.* San Francisco: Ignatius, 1992.

_____. *Herrlichkeit: Eine theologische Ästhetik.* 3 vols. Einsiedeln: Johannes Verlag, 1961–1984. English edition translated by Erasmo Leiva-Merikakis. *The Glory of the Lord: A Theological Aesthetics.* 7 vols. Edinburgh: T. & T. Clark, 1984–1991.

_____. *Kleiner Diskurs über die Hölle; Apokatastasis.* Einsiedeln: Johannes Verlag, 1999.

_____. *Theodramatik.* 4 vols. Einsiedeln: Johannes Verlag, 1973–1983. English edition translated by Graham Harrison. *Theo-Drama: Theological Dramatic Story.* 5 vols. San Francisco: Ignatius,1988–1998.

_____. *Theologik.* 3 vols. Einsiedeln: Johannes Verlag, 1985–1987. English edition translated by Adrian J. Walker. *Theo-Logic.* 3 vols. San Francisco: Ignatius, 2001–2005.

_____. *Was dürfen wir hoffen; und, Kleiner Diskurs über die Hölle.* Einsiedeln: Johannes Verlag, 1986. English edition translated by David Kipp and Lothar Krauth. *Dare We hope "That All Men Be Saved?" With a Short Discourse on Hell.* San Francisco: Ignatius, 1988.

Barna, George. *What Americans Believe: An Annual Survey of Values and Religious Views in the United States.* Ventura, Calif.: Regal Books, 1991.

Barth, Karl. *The Epistle to the Romans.* Sixth edition. Translated by Edwyn C. Hoskyns. Oxford: Oxford University Press, 1933.

_____. *Die kirchliche Dogmatik.* 13 vols. Zürich: Evangelischer Verlag, 1936–1977. English edition translated by G.W. Bromiley, et al. *Church Dogmatics.* 14 vols. Edinburgh: T. & T. Clark, 1936–1977.

_____. *Die protestantische Theologie im 19. Jahrhundert: Ihre Vorgeschichte und ihre Geschichte.* Zollikon, Zürich: Evangelischer Verlag, 1947. English edition. *Protestant Theology in the Nineteenth Century: Its Background and History.* Valley Forge, Pa.: Judson Press, 1973.

Bauckham, Richard J., ed. *God Will Be All In All: The Eschatology of Jürgen Moltmann.* Edinburgh: T. & T. Clark, 1999.

_____. *Moltmann: Messianic Theology in the Making.* Basingstoke, Hants, U.K.: Marshall Pickering, 1987.

_____. *The Theology of Jürgen Moltmann.* Edinburgh: T. & T. Clark, 1995.

Bauckham, Richard J. and Trevor Hart. *Hope Against Hope—Christian Eschatology in Contemporary Context.* Edinburgh: T. & T. Clark, 1999.

Bauer, Walter. *A Greek English Lexicon of the New Testament and Other Early Christian Literature.* Third edition. Revised by F. W. Danker, W. F. Arndt, and F. W. Gingrich. Chicago: University of Chicago Press, 2000.

Baur, F. C. *Die Christliche Gnosis oder die christliche Religions-Philosophie in ihrer geschichtlichen Entwicklung.* Tübingen: C. F. Osiander, 1835.

Baxter, S. Edward, Jr. "A Historical Study of the Doctrine of 'Apokatastasis' (Universalism)." Th.D. dissertation. Mid-America Baptist Seminary, 1988.

Beasley-Murray, George R. *John.* Word Biblical Commentary. Vol. 36. Waco, Tex.: Word, 1987.

Bell, Rob. *Love Wins: A Book About Heaven, Hell, and the Fate of Every Person Who Ever Lived.* New York: HarperOne, 2011.

Berdyaev, Nicholas. *The Destiny of Man.* English edition translated by Natalie Duddington. London: G. Bles, 1945.

_____. *Dream and Reality: An Essay in Autobiography.* London: G. Bles, 1950.

_____. *The Fate of Man in the Modern World.* London: S.C.M. Press, 1935.

Bettis, Joseph D. "The Good News and the Salvation of All Men: A Critique of the Doctrine of Universal Salvation." Ph.D. dissertation. Princeton University, 1964.

Bingaman, Brock. *All Things New: The Trinitarian Nature of the Human Calling in Maximus the Confessor and Jürgen Moltmann.* Eugene, Ore.: Pickwick Publications, 2014.

Blanchard, John. *Whatever Happened to Hell?* Durham, U.K.: Evangelical Press, 1993.

Boehme, Jakob. *Of Heaven and Hell: A Dialogue between a Student with his Master.* http://www.passtheword.org/DIALOGS-FROM-THE-PAST/heaven.htm.

_____. *Of Regeneration and the New Birth.* http://www.passtheword.org/DIALOGS-FROM-THE-PAST/jb-regen.htm.

_____. *Saemtliche Schriften.* 11 vols. Edited by August Faust and Will E. Peuckert. 1730. Reprint, Stuttgart: Frommanns, 1955–1960.

Borg, Marcus. *Jesus, A New Vision: Spirit, Culture, and the Life of Discipleship.* San Francisco: HarperSanFrancisco, 1987.

Borgen, Peder. *Logos Was the True Light, And Other Essays on the Gospel of John.* Trondheim, Norway: Tapir, 1983.

Bourke, F. R. "Universalism." Ph.D. dissertation. Trinity College, Dublin, 1961.

Bousset, Wilhelm. *Hauptprobleme der Gnosis.* Göttingen: Vandenhoeck und Ruprecht, 1907.

Bouwsma, William J. *The Career and Thought of Guillaume Postel (1510–1581).* Cambridge, Mass.: Harvard University Press, 1957.

Boyd, Gregory A. *Cynic, Sage, or Son of God: Recovering the Real Jesus in an Age of Revisionist Replies.* Wheaton, Ill.: BridgePoint/Victor Books, 1995.

Bressler, Ann Lee. *The Universalist Movement in America.* Oxford: Oxford University Press, 2001.

Brown, Colin. *Christianity and Western Thought: A History of Philosophers, Ideas, and Movements, From the Ancient World to the Age of the Enlightenment*, vol. 1. Downers Grove, Ill.: InterVarsity, 1990.

_____, ed. *The New International Dictionary of New Testament Theology.* 4 vols. Grand Rapids, Mich.: Zondervan, 1975–1986.

Brown, Raymond E. *Death of the Messiah.* 2 vols. New York: Doubleday, 1994.

Brunner, Heinrich Emil. *The Christian Doctrine of the Church, Faith, and the Consummation.* Translated by Olive Wyon. Philadelphia: Westminster Press, 1962.

_____. *Dogmatik: Bd. 1, Die christliche Lehre von Gott.* Zürich: Zwingli, 1946. Translated by Olive Wyon. *Dogmatics, vol. 1, The Christian Doctrine of God.* Philadelphia: Westminster, 1949.

Buchholz, Dennis D. *Your Eyes Will Be Opened: A Study of the Greek (Ethiopic) Apocalypse of Peter.* Atlanta, Ga.: Scholar's Press, 1988.

Bultmann, Rudolf. *Theology of the New Testament.* 2 vols. Translated by Kendrick Grobel. New York: Charles Scribner's Sons, 1951; 1955.

Byerly, Robert Allen. "A Biblical Critique of Universalism in Contemporary Theology." S.T.D. dissertation. Temple University, 1959.

Calvin, John. *Institutes of the Christian Religion.* Translated by Henry Beveridge. 1845. Reprint, Grand Rapids, Mich.: Eerdmans, 1995.

Cameron, Nigel M. de S., ed. *Universalism and the Doctrine of Hell: Papers Presented at the Fourth Edinburgh Conference in Christian Dogmatics, 1991.* Carlisle, U.K.: Paternoster, 1992.

Camporesi, Piero. *The Fear of Hell: Images of Damnation and Salvation in Early Modern Europe.* Translated by Lucinda Byatt. University Park, Pa.: Pennsylvania State University Press, 1990; 1991.

Carson, Donald A. *The Gagging of God: Christianity Confronts Pluralism.* Grand Rapids, Mich.: Zondervan, 1996.

Catholic Church. *Catechism of the Catholic Church: With Modifications from the Editio Typica.* New York: Image Books/Doubleday, 1995.

_____. *The Companion to The Catechism of the Catholic Church: A Compendium of Texts Referred to in The Catechism of the Catholic Church.* San Francisco: Ignatius, 1994.

Chardin, Pierre Teilhard de. *Le phénomène humain.* Paris: Du Seuil, 1955. English edition translated by Bernard Wall. *The Phenomenon of Man.* New York: Harper, 1959.

Charlesworth, James H., ed. *The Old Testament Pseudepigrapha, vol. 1, Apocalyptic Literature and Testaments.* Garden City, N.Y.: Doubleday, 1983–1985.

_____, ed. *The Old Testament Pseudepigrapha, vol. 2, Expansions of the "Old Testament" and Legends, Wisdom and Philosophical Literature, Prayers, Psalms, and Odes, Fragments of Lost Judeo-Hellenistic Works.* Garden City, N.Y.: Doubleday, 1985.

Cheetham, David. *John Hick: A Critical Introduction and Reflection.* Burlington, Vt.: Ashgate, 2003.

Christians, Clifford G. and Jay M. Van Hook, eds. *Jacques Ellul: Interpretive Essays.* Chicago: University of Illinois Press, 1981.

Church of England. The Doctrine Commission. *The Mystery of Salvation: The Story of God's Gift—A Report.* Harrisburg, Pa.: Morehouse Publishing, 1995.

Clark, Elizabeth A. *The Origenist Controversy: The Cultural Construction of an Early Christian Debate.* Princeton, N.J.: Princeton University Press, 1992.

Cohn, Norman. *The Pursuit of the Millennium.* London: Secker & Warburg, 1957.

Collins, Paul, ed. *From Inquisition to Freedom: Seven Prominent Catholics and Their Struggle with the Vatican.* London; New York: Continuum, 2001.

Colpe, Carsten. *Die Religionsgeschichtliche Schule; Darstellung and Kritik ihres Bildes vom gnostischen Erlösermythus.* Göttingen: Vandenhoeck & Ruprecht, 1961.

Colwell, John E. *Actuality and Provisionality: Eternity and Election in the Theology of Karl Barth.* Edinburgh: Rutherford House, 1989.

Conway, Anne. *The Principles of the Most Ancient and Modern Philosophy.* Amsterdam; London: M. Brown, 1692.

Conzelmann, Hans. *1 Corinthians: A Commentary on the First Epistle to the Corinthians.* Edited by George W. MacRae. Translated by James W. Leitch. Philadelphia: Fortress, 1975.

Costen, Michael. *The Cathars and the Albigensian Crusade.* Manchester: Manchester University Press, 1997.

Couliano, Ioan P. *The Tree of Gnosis.* San Francisco: Harper & Row, 1990.

Cox, Samuel. *Salvator Mundi or Is Christ the Savior of All Men?* London: Henry S. King & Co., 1877.

Craig, William Lane. *The Only Wise God: The Compatibility of Divine Foreknowledge and Human Freedom.* Grand Rapids, Mich.: Baker, 1987.

Crockett, William V., ed. *Four Views on Hell.* Grand Rapids, Mich.: Zondervan, 1996.

_____. "Universalism and the Theology of Paul." Ph.D. dissertation. University of Glasgow, 1986.

Cross Frank L. and Elizabeth A. Livingstone. *The Oxford Dictionary of the Christian Church.* Third edition. New York: Oxford University Press, 1997.

Crossan, John Dominic. *The Cross that Spoke.* San Francisco: Harper and Row, 1988.

_____. *The Historical Jesus: The Life of a Mediterranean Jewish Peasant.* San Francisco: HarperSanFrancisco, 1991.

Crouzel, Henri. *Origen: The Life and Thought of the First Great Theologian.* San Francisco: Harper and Row, 1989.

_____ and Manlio Simonetti, eds. *Origène: Traité des Principes.* 5 vols. Sources Chrétiennes edition. Paris: Éditions du Cerf, 1978–1984.

Daley, Brian. *The Hope of the Early Church: A Handbook of Patristic Eschatology.* Cambridge: Cambridge University Press, 1991.

Dalton, William J. *Christ's Proclamation to the Spirits: A Study of 1 Peter 3:18–4:6.* Second revised edition. Rome: Editrice Pontificio Instituto Biblico, 1989.

D'Costa, Gavin, ed. *John Hick's Theology of Religions: A Critical Evaluation.* Lanham, Md.: University Press of America, 1987.

_____, *Theology of Religious Pluralism: The Challenge of Other Religions.* Oxford: Basil Blackwell, 1986.

Deák, Esteban, "Apokatastasis: The Problem of Universal Salvation in Twentieth Century Theology." Ph.D. dissertation. University of St. Michael's College, 1977.

Deuser, Hermann, Gerhard Marcel Martin, Konrad Stock, and Michael Welker, eds. *Gottes Zukunft—Zukunft der Welt. Festschrift für Jürgen Moltmann zum 60 Geburstag.* Munich: Christian Kaiser, 1986.

Does, Marthe van der. *Antoinette Bourignon: sa vie (1616–1680), son oeuvre.* Groningen: Druk, Verenigde Reproduktie Bedrijven, 1974.

Downing, Kenneth, Jacob A. McDonough, and Hadwiga Höner, eds. *Gregorii Nysseni: Opera Dogmatica Minora.* Vol. 3, pt. 2. Leiden: Brill, 1987.

Dunn, James D. G. *Jesus Remembered, Christianity in the Making, vol. 1.* Grand Rapids, Mich.: Eerdmans, 2003.

Dupuis, Jacques. *Toward a Christian Theology of Religious Pluralism.* Maryknoll, N.Y.: Orbis, 1997; 2002.

Dych, William V. *Karl Rahner.* Collegeville, Minn.: Liturgical Press, 1992.

Eckhart, Meister Johannes. *Meister Eckhart's Sermons: First Time Translated into English.* Translated by Claud Field. London: H.R. Allenson, 1900–1910.

Eddy, Paul Rhodes. *John Hick's Pluralist Philosophy of World Religions.* Burlington, Vt.: Ashgate, 2002.

Eddy, Richard. *Universalism in America: A History.* 2 vols. Boston: Universalist Publishing House, 1884.

272	*Will All Be Saved?*

Ellis, Ieuan. *Seven against Christ: A Study of 'Essays and Reviews.'* Studies in the History of Christian Thought 23. Leiden: Brill, 1980.
Ellul, Jacques. *L'Apocalypse: architecture en mouvement.* Paris: Desclée, 1975. English edition translated by George W. Schreiner. *Apocalypse: The Book of Revelation.* New York: Seabury Press, 1977.
_____. *Ce que je crois.* Paris: Grasset & Fasquelle, 1987. English edition translated by Geoffrey W. Bromiley. *What I Believe.* Grand Rapids, Mich.: Eerdmans, 1989.
_____. *Éthique de la liberté.* Geneva: Labor et Fides, 1976. English edition translated by Geoffrey W. Bromiley. *The Ethics of Freedom.* Grand Rapids, Mich.: Eerdmans, 1976.
_____. *La technique; ou, L'en jeu du siècle.* Paris: Armand Colin, 1954. English edition translated by John Wilkinson. *The Technological Society.* New York: Knopf, 1964.
_____. *Perspectives on Our Age: Jacques Ellul Speaks on His Life and Work.* Edited by Joachim Neugroschel. Translated by William H. Vandenburg. New York: Seabury Press, 1981.
_____. *Présence au monde moderne: Problèmes de la civilisation post-chrétienne.* Geneva: Roulet, 1948. English edition translated by Olive Wyon. *The Presence of the Kingdom.* Philadelphia: Westminster, 1951.
Erickson, Millard J. *How shall they be saved? The Destiny of Those Who Do Not Hear of Jesus.* Grand Rapids, Mich.: Baker, 1996.
Eusebius Pamphilus. *Ecclesiastical History.* Translated by Christian F. Cruse. 1850. Reprint, Grand Rapids, Mich.: Baker, 1993.
Faber, Geoffrey. *Jowett: Portrait with a Background.* Cambridge, Mass.: Harvard University Press, 1957.
Farmer, Herbert H. *God and Men.* Nashville, Tenn.: Abingdon—Cokesbury Press, 1947.
Farrar, Fredric W. *Eternal Hope: Five Sermons Preached in Westminster Abbey, November and December 1877.* London: Macmillan, 1878.
_____. *Mercy and Judgment: A Few Last Words on Christian Eschatology with Reference to Dr. Pusey's 'What is of faith?'* London: Macmillan, 1881.
Fasching, Darrell J. *The Thought of Jacques Ellul: A Systematic Exposition.* New York: Edwin Mellen Press, 1981.
Fellows, Ward J. "The Dilemma of Universalism and Particularism in Four Christian Theological Views of the Relation of Christianity to Other Religions (Tillich, Rahner, Smith, Hick)." Ph.D. dissertation. Union Theological Seminary, 1988.
Ferm, Deane. *Third World Liberation Theologies: An Introductory Survey.* Maryknoll, N.Y.: Orbis, 1986.
Fernando, Ajith. *A Universal Homecoming? An Examination of the Case for Universalism.* Madras, India: Evangelical Literature Service, 1983.
Ferré, Nels F. S. *The Christian Understanding of God.* New York: Harper & Bros, 1951.
Flannery, Austin. *Vatican Council II: The Basic Sixteen Documents.* Northport, N.Y.: Costello Publishing Co., 1995.
Geivett, R. Douglas. *Evil and the Evidence for God: The Challenge of John Hick's Theodicy.* Philadelphia: Temple University Press, 1993.
Gergen, Kenneth. *The Saturated Self: Dilemmas of Identity in Contemporary Life.* New York: Basic Books, 1991.
Gibellini, Rosino. *The Liberation Theology Debate.* Maryknoll, N.Y.: Orbis, 1987.
Gillis, Chester. *A Question of Final Belief: John Hick's Pluralistic Theory of Salvation.* New York: St. Martin's Press, 1989.
Gould, Stephen Jay. *Wonderful Life: The Burgess Shale and the Nature of History.* New York: W.W. Norton & Co., 1989.
Gray, Tony J. "Hell: An Analysis of Some Major Twentieth-Century Attempts to Defend the Doctrine of Hell." D.Phil. dissertation. Oxford University, 1996.

Gulley, Philip and James Mulholland. *If God Is Love: Rediscovering Grace in an Ungracious World*. San Francisco: HarperSanFrancisco, 2004.

_____. *If Grace Is True: Why God Will Save Every Person*. San Francisco: HarperSanFrancisco, 2003.

Gutiérrez, Gustavo. *Gustavo Gutiérrez: Essential Writings*. Edited by James B. Nickoloff. Minneapolis, Minn.: Fortress, 1996.

_____. *On Job: God-Talk and the Suffering of the Innocent*. Maryknoll, N.Y.: Orbis, 1987.

_____. *The Power of the Poor in History*. Maryknoll, N.Y.: Orbis, 1983.

_____. *A Theology of Liberation*. Fifteenth anniversary edition. Maryknoll, N.Y.: Orbis, 1973; 1988.

_____. *The Truth Shall Make You Free*. Maryknoll, N.Y.: Orbis, 1990.

_____. *We Drink From Our Own Wells: The Spiritual Journey of a People*. Maryknoll, N.Y.: Orbis, 1984.

Hagner, Donald A. *Matthew 14–28*. Word Biblical Commentary. Vol. 33b. Dallas: Word, 1995.

Hall, Lindsey. *Swinburne's Hell and Hick's Universalism: Are We Free to Reject God?* Burlington, Vt.: Ashgate, 2003.

Hamnett, Ian, ed. *Religious Pluralism and Unbelief: Studies Critical and Comparative*. London: Routledge, 1990.

Hanson, J. W. *Universalism: The Prevailing Doctrine of the Christian Church During Its First Five-Hundred Years*. Boston: Unversalist Publishing House, 1899.

Harmon, Kendall S. "Finally Excluded by God? Some Twentieth-Century Theological Explorations of the Problems of Hell and Universalism with Reference to the Historical Development of These Doctrines." D.Phil. dissertation. Oxford University, 1993.

Harmon, Steven R. "Apokatastasis and Exegesis: A Comparative Analysis of the Use of Scripture in the Eschatological Universalism of Clement of Alexandria, Origen, and Gregory of Nyssa." Ph.D. dissertation. Southwestern Baptist Theological Seminary, 1997.

Hebblethwaite, Peter. *The New Inquisition: The Case of Edward Schillebeeckx and Hans Küng*. San Francisco: Harper & Row, 1980.

Heim, S. Mark. *Salvations: Truth and Difference in Religion*. Maryknoll, N.Y.: Orbis, 1995.

Hengel, Martin. *The Son of God: The Origin of Christology and the History of Jewish-Hellenistic Religion*. Philadelphia: Fortress, 1976.

Hennelly, Alfred T. *Liberation Theology: A Documentary History*. Maryknoll, N.Y.: Orbis, 1990.

Herzog, J. J., Philip Schaff, et al., eds. *The New Schaff-Herzog Encyclopedia of Religious Knowledge*. 13 vols. New York: Funk and Wagnalls Co., 1908–1914.

Herzog, Markwart. *Descensus ad Inferos*. Frankfurt: Josef Knecht, 1997.

Hewitt, Harold, ed. *Problems in the Philosophy of Religion: Critical Studies of the Work of John Hick*. New York: St. Martin's Press, 1991.

Hick, John. *Between Faith and Doubt: Dialogues on Religion and Reason*. New York: Palgrave McMillian, 2010.

_____. *Death and Eternal Life*. New York: Harper and Row, 1994; 1976.

_____. *Disputed Questions in Philosophy of Religions*. New York: Palgrave, 2001.

_____. *Evil and the God of Love*. Revised Edition. San Francisco: Harper and Row, 1978; 1966.

_____. *The Fifth Dimension: An Exploration of the Spiritual Realm*. Oxford: Oneworld Publications, 2004; 1999.

_____. *God and the Universe of Faiths: Essays in the Philosophy of Religion*. New York: St. Martins Press, 1973.

_____. *God Has Many Names*. Philadelphia: Westminster, 1982.

_____. *An Interpretation of Religion: Human Responses to the Transcendent.* Second edition. New Haven, Conn.: Yale University Press, 1989; 2004.
_____. *John Hick: An Autobiography.* Oxford: Oneworld, 2002.
_____. *The Metaphor of God Incarnate: Christology in a Pluralistic Age.* Louisville, Ky.: Westminster/John Knox, 1993.
_____, ed. *The Myth of God Incarnate.* Philadelphia: SCM Press, 1977.
_____. *Problems of Religious Pluralism.* New York: St. Martin's Press, 1985.
Hillert, Sven. "Limited and Universal Salvation: A Text Oriented and Hermeneutical Study of Two Perspectives in Paul." Ph.D. dissertation. Uppsala University, 1999.
Jefferson, Thomas. *The Life and Morals of Jesus of Nazareth.* 1803. Reprint edition. Boston: Beacon Press, 1989.
Jukes, Andrew J. *The Second Death and the Restitution of All Things: With Some Preliminary Remarks on the Nature and Inspiration of Holy Scripture; A Letter to a Friend.* London: Longmans, Green, 1867.
Kant, Immanuel. *Foundations of Metaphysics and What is Enlightenment?* Translated by Lewis White Beck. Indianapolis, Ind.: Bobbs-Merrill, 1959.
_____. *Religion within the Boundaries of Mere Reason: And Other Writings.* Edited by Allen W. Wood and George Di Giovani. Cambridge: Cambridge University Press, 1998.
Kärkkäinen, Veli-Matti. *An Introduction to the Theology of Religions: Biblical, Historical, and Contemporary Perspectives.* Downers Grove, Ill.: InterVarsity, 2003.
Kasser, Rodolphe, Marvin W. Meyer and Gregor Wurst, eds. *The Gospel of Judas: From Codex Tchacos.* Washington D.C.: National Geographic, 2006.
Keizer, Heleen M. *Life Time Entirety: A Study of AIΩN in Greek Literature and Philosophy, the Septuagint and Philo.* The Hague: n.p., 1999; 2010.
Kim, Van Nam. *A Church of Hope: A Study of the Eschatological Ecclesiology of Jürgen Moltmann.* Lanham, Md.: University Press of America, 2005.
Kinsella, Kate et al. *Prentice Hall Literature: Timeless Voices, Timeless Themes—The American Experience.* Upper Saddle River, N.J.: Prentice Hall, 2002.
Kirk, J. Andrew. *Liberation Theology: An Evangelical View from the Third World.* Atlanta: John Knox, 1979.
Kittel, Gerhard, ed. *Theological Dictionary of the New Testament.* 10 vols. Edited and translated by Gerhard Friedrich and Geoffrey W. Bromiley. Grand Rapids, Mich.: Eerdmans, 1964–1976.
Kiwiet, John. *Hans Küng.* Waco, Tex.: Word, 1985.
Knitter, Paul F. *Introducing Theologies of Religions.* Maryknoll, N.Y.: Orbis, 2002.
_____. *Jesus and the Other Names: Christian and Global Missionary Responsibility.* Maryknoll, N.Y.: Orbis, 1996.
_____. *No Other Name? A Critical Survey of Christian Attitudes Towards the World Religions.* Maryknoll, N.Y.: Orbis, 1985.
_____. *One Earth, Many Religions: Multifaith Dialog and Global Responsibility.* Maryknoll, N.Y.: Orbis, 1995.
_____, ed. *Pluralism and Oppression: Theology in World Perspective.* Lanham, Md.: University Press of America, 1991.
_____. *Without Buddha I Could not be a Christian.* Oxford: Oneworld Publications, 2009.
Knoch, Adolph Ernst. *All in All: The Goal of the Universe.* Canyon Country, Calif.: Concordant Publishing Concern, 1978. Original date of publication not available.
_____. *Concordant Commentary on the New Testament.* Canyon Country, Calif.: Concordant Publishing Concern, n.d.
_____. *Concordant Literal New Testament.* Canyon Country, Calif.: Concordant Publishing Concern, 1983. Original date of publication not available.
_____. *Salvation of the Unbeliever.* Canyon Country, Calif.: Concordant Publishing Concern, n.d.

_____. *Two Studies on Heaven and Hell*. Canyon Country, Calif.: Concordant Publishing Concern, n.d.

_____. *The Unveiling of Jesus Christ*. Canyon Country, Calif.: Concordant Publishing Concern, 1935.

Komulainen, Jyri. *An Emerging Cosmotheandric Religion? Raimon Panikkar's Pluralistic Theology of Religions.* Leiden: Brill, 2005.

Kroll, Joseph. *Gott und Hölle: Der Mythos vom Descensuskampfe*. Darmstadt: Wissenshaftliche Buchgesellshaft, 1963.

Kronen, John and Eric Reitan. *God's Final Victory: A Comparative Philosophical Case for Universalism.* New York; London: Bloomsbury Academic, 2011; 2013.

Küng, Hans. *Christ Sein*. Munich: R. Piper, 1974. English edition translated by Edward Quinn. *On Being a Christian*. Garden City, N.Y.: Doubleday, 1976.

_____. *Erkämpfte Freiheit. Erinnerungen.* Munich: Piper Verlag, 2002. English edition translated by John Bowden. *My Struggle for Freedom: Memoirs.* Grand Rapids, Mich.: Eerdmans, 2003.

_____. *Ewiges Leben?* Munich: R. Piper, 1982. English edition translated by Edward Quinn. *Eternal Life? Life After Death as a Medical, Philosophical, and Theological Problem.* Garden City, N.Y.: Doubleday, 1984.

_____. *Justification: The Doctrine of Karl Barth and a Catholic Reflection.* London: Burns & Oates, 1965.

_____. *Umstrittene Wahrheit: Erinnerungen.* Munich: Piper Verlag, 2007. English edition translated by John Bowden. *Disputed Truth: Memoirs II.* London; New York: Continuum International Publishing Group, 2008.

_____. *Unfehlbar? eine Anfrage.* Zürich: Benziger, 1970. English edition translated by Edward Quinn. *Infallible? An Inquiry.* Garden City, N.Y.: Doubleday, 1971.

_____, Josef von Ess, Heinrich von Stietencron, and Heinz Bechert. *Christianity and World Religions: Paths to Dialogue.* Maryknoll, N.Y.: Orbis, 1986; 1993.

Kuntz, Marion L. *Guillaume Postel: Prophet of the Restitution of All Things—His Life and Thought.* The Hague: Martinus Nijhoff, 1981.

Lambert, Malcolm D. *Medieval Heresy: Popular Movements from Bogomil to Hus.* London: Edward Arnold, 1977.

Lampe, W. H. *A Patristic Greek Lexicon.* Oxford: Clarendon Press, 1961.

Law, William. *The Spirit of Love, vol. 2.* London: M. Richardson, 1754. http://www.passtheword.org/DIALOGS-FROM-THE-PAST/love2.htm.

_____. *The Spirit of Prayer or The Soul Rising out of the Vanity of Time into the Riches of Eternity, vol. 2.* Third edition. London: J. Richardson, 1750. http://www.passtheword.org/DIALOGS-FROM-THE-PAST/prayer3.htm.

Layton, Bentley. *The Gnostic Scriptures.* Garden City, N.J.: Doubleday, 1987.

Lead, Jane. *The Enochian Walks With God: Found Out by a Spiritual-Traveller whofe Face Towards Mount-Sion Above Was Set.* London: D. Edwards, 1694.

Learner, Robert. *The Heresy of the Free Spirit in the Later Middle Ages.* Berkeley, Calif.: University of California Press, 1972.

Leff, Gordon. *Heresy in the Later Middle Ages: The Relation of Heterodoxy to Dissent c. 1250–1450.* Manchester: Manchester University Press; New York: Barnes and Noble, 1967.

Lipsius, Richard A. and Maximilian Bonnet, eds. *Acta Apostolorum Apocrypha.* Leipzig: Hermann Mendelssohn, 1891–1903. Reprint, Darmstadt: Wissenschaftliche Buchgesellschaft, 1959.

Loudy, Adlai. *God's Eonian Purpose.* Los Angeles: Concordant Publishing Concern, 1929.

Lovekin, David. *Technique, Discourse, and Consciousness: An Introduction to the Philosophy of Jacques Ellul.* Bethlehem, Pa.: Lehigh University Press, 1991.

Ludlow, Morwenna. "Restoration and Consummation: The Interpretation of Universalistic Eschatology by Gregory of Nyssa and Karl Rahner." D.Phil. dissertation. Oxford University, 1996.

_____. *Universal Salvation: Eschatology in the Thought of Gregory of Nyssa and Karl Rahner.* Oxford: Oxford University Press, 2000.

Lyotard, Jean-François. *The Postmodern Condition: A Report on Knowledge.* English edition translated by Geoff Bennington and Brian Massumi. Minneapolis, Minn.: University of Minnesota Press, 1984.

MacCulloch, J. A. *The Harrowing of Hell.* Edinburgh: T. & T. Clark, 1930.

MacDonald, Gregory [Robin Parry], ed. *"All Shall Be Well": Explorations in Universal Salvation and Christian Theology from Origen to Moltmann.* Eugene, Ore.: Cascade Books, 2012.

_____. *The Evangelical Universalist,* 2nd ed. Eugene, Ore.: Cascade Books, 2008; 2012.

MacFadden, Bruce J. *Fossil Horses: Systematics, Paleobiology, and Evolution of the Family Equidae.* Cambridge: Cambridge University Press, 1992.

Macquarrie, John. *Christian Hope.* New York: Seabury, 1978.

Marmion, Declan and Mary E. Hines. *The Cambridge Companion to Karl Rahner.* Cambridge: Cambridge University Press, 2005.

Marshall, I. Howard. *I Believe in the Historical Jesus.* Grand Rapids, Mich.: Eerdmans, 1977.

Mathis, Terry R. *Against John Hick.* Lanham, Md.: University Press of America, 1985.

Maurice, Frederick D. *Theological Essays.* 1853. Introduction by Edward F. Carpenter. London: J. Clark, 1957.

Maurice, John F. *The Life of Frederick Denison Maurice, Chiefly Told in His Own Letters.* Fourth edition. 2 Vols. New York: Charles Scribner's Sons, 1884.

Mayr, Ernst. *What Evolution Is.* New York: Basic Books, 2001.

McGovern, Arthur F. *Liberation Theology and Its Critics.* Maryknoll, N.Y.: Orbis, 1989.

McGregor, Geddes. *Reincarnation in Christianity.* Wheaton, Ill.: Theosophical Publishing House, 1978.

Meeks, M. Douglas. *Origins of the Theology of Hope.* Philadelphia: Fortress, 1974; 1996.

Mesle, C. Robert. *John Hick's Theodicy: A Process Humanist Critique.* New York: St. Martin's Press, 1991.

Michaels, J. Ramsay. *1 Peter.* Word Biblical Commentary. Vol. 49. Waco, Tex.: Word, 1988.

Miller, Russell E. *The Larger Hope: The First Century of the Universalist Church in America 1770–1870.* Boston: Unitarian Universalist Association, 1979.

Moltmann, Jürgen. *Ethik der Hoffnung.* Gütersloh: Gütersloher Verlagshaus, 2010. English edition translated by Margaret Kohl. *Ethics of Hope.* Minneapolis, Minn.: Fortress, 2012.

_____. *Der gekreuzigte Gott; Das Kreuz Christi als Grund und Kritik christlicher Theologie.* Munich: Christian Kaiser Verlag, 1972. English edition translated by R.A. Wilson and John Bowden. *The Crucified God: The Cross of Christ as the Foundation and Criticism of Christian Theology.* Minneapolis, Minn.: Fortress, 1974; 1993.

_____. *Gott in der Schöpfung: Ökologische Schöpfungslehre.* Munich: Christian Kaiser, 1985. English edition translated by Margaret Kohl. *God in Creation: A New Theology of Creation and the Spirit of God.* The Gifford Lectures 1984–1985. Minneapolis, Minn.: Fortress Press, 1985; 1993.

_____. *Im Ende, der Anfang: eine kleine Hoffnungslehre.* Gütersloh: Christian Kaiser, Gütersloher Verlagshaus, 2003. English edition translated by Margaret Kohl. *In The End—The Beginning: The Life of Hope.* Minneapolis, Minn.: Fortress, 2004.

_____. *Das Kommen Gottes: Christliche Escatologie.* Gütersloh: Christian Kaiser, Gütersloher Verlagshaus, 1995. English edition translated by Margaret Kohl. *The Coming of God: Christian Eschatology.* Minneapolis, Minn.: Fortress, 1996.

_____. *Perspektiven der Theologie: Gesammelte Aufsätze.* Munich: Christian Kaiser, 1969. English edition translated by Margaret Clarkson. *Hope and Planning.* New York: Harper & Row, 1971.

_____. *Sein Name is Gerechtigkeit: Neue Beiträge zur christlichen Gotteslehre.* Gütersloh: Gütersloher Verlagshaus, 2009. English edition translated by Margaret Kohl. *Sun of God Arise! God's Future for Humanity and the Earth.* Minneapolis, Minn.: Fortress, 2010.

_____. *Theologie der Hoffnung: Untersuchungen zur Begründung und zu den Konsequenzes einer christlichen Eschatology.* Munich: Christian Kaiser, 1964. English edition translated by James W. Leitch. *Theology of Hope: On the Ground and Implications of a Christian Eschatology.* New York: Harper and Row, 1967.

_____. *Trinität und Reich Gottes: Zur Gotteslehre.* Munich: Christian Kaiser, 1980. English edition translated by Margaret Kohl. *The Trinity and the Kingdom: The Doctrine of God.* San Francisco: Harper & Row, 1981.

_____. *Der Weg Jesu Christi: Christologie in messianischen Dimensionen.* Munich: Christian Kaiser Verlag, 1989. English edition translated by Margaret Kohl. *The Way of Jesus Christ: Christology in Messianic Dimensions.* London: S.C.M. Press; San Francisco: HarperSanFrancisco, 1990.

_____. *Weiter raum: Eine Lebensgeschichte.* Gütersloh: Gütersloher Verlagshaus, 2006. English edition trans. Margaret Kohl. *A Broad Place: An Autobiography.* Minneapolis, Minn.: Fortress Press, 2008.

_____, ed. *Wir ich mich geändert habe.* Gütersloh: Christian Kaiser, 1997. English edition translated by John Bowden. *How I Have Changed: Reflections on Thirty Years of Theology.* Harrisburg, Pa.: Trinity Press Int., 1997.

_____. *Zukunft der Schöpfung: Gesammelte Aufsätze.* Munich: Christian Kaiser, 1977. English edition translated by Margaret Kohl. *The Future of Creation: Collected Essays.* Philadelphia: Fortress, 1979.

Moreland, J. P. and William Lane Craig. *Philosophical Foundations for a Christian Worldview.* Downers Grove, Ill.: InterVarsity, 2003.

Morris, Ian. *Death-Ritual and Social Structure in Classical Antiquity.* Cambridge: Cambridge University Press, 1992.

Morse, Christopher. *Origins of the Logic of Promise in Moltmann's Theology.* Philadelphia: Fortress, 1979.

Moule, C. F. D. *The Meaning of Hope: A Biblical Exposition with Concordance.* Philadelphia: Fortress, 1953; 1963.

Mülenberg, Ekkehard, ed. *Gregorii Nysseni Oratio Catechetica: Opera Dogmatica Minora.* Vol. 3, pt. 4. Leiden: Brill, 1996.

Musurillo, Herbert, translator. *The Acts of the Christian Martyrs.* Oxford: Clarendon Press, 1972.

Nah, David S. "A Critical Evaluation of John Hick's Theology of Religious Pluralism." Ph.D. dissertation. Claremont Graduate University, 2005.

Nash, Ronald H. *Is Jesus the Only Savior?* Grand Rapids, Mich.: Zondervan, 1994.

Nelli, Renè. *Spiritualitè De L'Hèrèsie: Le Catharisme.* Paris: Presses Universitaires de France, 1953.

Nengean, Isaiah. *The Imago Dei As the Imago Trinitatis: Jürgen Moltmann's Doctrine of the Image of God.* New York: Peter Lang Publishing, Inc., 2013.

The New American Standard Bible. La Habra, Calif.: The Lockman Foundation, 1977.

Nicholas of Cusa. *On Interreligious Harmony: Text, Concordance, and Translation of De pace fidei.* James E. Biechler and H. Lawrence Bond, eds. Lewiston, N.Y.: Edwin Mellen Press, 1991.

Nichols, Aidan. *No Bloodless Myth: A Guide Through Balthasar's Dramatics.* Edinburgh: T. & T. Clark, 2000.

Okholm, Dennis L. and Timothy R. Phillips, eds. *Four Views on Salvation in a Pluralistic World.* Grand Rapids, Mich.: Zondervan, 1995.

Origen. *On First Principles.* English translation by G. W. Butterworth. New York: Harper & Row, 1966.

Orr, James, ed. *New Testament Apocryphal Writings.* London: J. M. Dent & Co., 1903.

Paine, Thomas. *The Complete Writings of Thomas Paine.* 2 vols. Edited by Philip S. Foner. New York: Citadel, 1947.

Panikkar, Raimundo. *The Cosmotheandric Experience: Emerging Religious Consciousness.* Maryknoll, N.Y.: Orbis, 1993.

_____. *The Intrareligious Dialogue.* Bangalore: Asian Trading Corp., 1984.

_____. *Salvation in Christ: Concreteness and Universality, The Supername.* Santa Barbara: privately published, 1972.

_____. *The Trinity and the Religious Experience of Man; Icon—Person—Mystery.* Maryknoll, N.Y.: Orbis, 1973.

_____. *The Trinity and the World Religions: Icon—Person—Mystery.* Madras: The Christian Literature Society, 1970.

_____. *The Unknown Christ of Hinduism.* London: Darton, Longman & Todd, 1964.

_____. *The Unknown Christ of Hinduism.* Revised and enlarged edition. Maryknoll, N.Y.: Orbis, 1981.

Parkhurst, John. *A Greek and English Lexicon to the New Testament.* London: William Baynes & Son, 1822.

Parry, Robin. *Worshipping Trinity: Coming Back to the Heart of Worship.* Carlisle, U.K.: Paternoster, 2005.

_____ and Chris Partridge, eds. *Universal Salvation? The Current Debate.* Carlisle, U.K.: Paternoster, 2003.

Patrologia graeca. Edited by J.-P. Migne. 162 vols. Paris, 1857–1886.

Patrologia latina. Edited by J.-P. Migne. 217 vols. Paris, 1844–1864.

Pedersen, Nils Arne. *Demonstrative Proof in Defense of God: A Study of Titus of Bostra's Contra Manichaeos—The Work's Sources, Aims and Relation to its Contemporary Theology.* Leiden: Brill, 2004.

Pegler, Stephen T. "The Nature of Paul's Universal Language of Salvation in Romans." Ph.D. dissertation. Trinity Evangelical Divinity School, 2002.

Peters, Edward. *Heresy and Authority in Medieval Europe: Documents in Translation.* Philadelphia: University of Pennsylvania Press, 1980.

Petersen, Johann Wilhelm. *Mysterion apokatastaseos panton, das ist, Das Geheimniss der Wiederbringung aller Dinge durch Jesum Christum.* 3 vols. n.p. 1700; 1703; 1710.

Peterson, Robert A. *Hell on Trial: The Case for Eternal Punishment.* Phillipsburg, New Jersey: Presbyterian and Reformed, 1995.

Pinnock, Clark. *A Wideness in God's Mercy: The Finality of Jesus Christ in a World Full of Religions.* Grand Rapids, Mich.: Zondervan, 1992.

Postel, Guillaume. *De orbis terrae concordia.* Basel: Oporinus, 1544.

Prabhu, Joseph, ed. *The Intercultural Challenge of Raimon Panikkar.* Maryknoll, N.Y.: Orbis, 1996.

Preuschen, Erwin. *Vollstäandiges Griechisch-Deutsches Handwöterbuch Schriften des Neuen Testaments und der übrigen urchristlichen Lituratur.* Giessen: Alfred Töpelmann, 1910.

Proctor, Evert. *Christian Controversy in Alexandria: Clement's Polemic Against the Basilideans and the Valentinians.* New York: Peter Lang, 1995.

Pusey, E. B. *What is of Faith as to Everlasting Punishment? In Reply to Dr. Farrar's Challenge in His 'Eternal hope,' 1879.* Oxford: James Parker and Co., 1880.

Race, Alan. *Christians and Religious Pluralism.* Maryknoll, N.Y.: Orbis, 1982.

Rahner, Karl. *Geist in Welt: zur Metaphysik der endlichen Erkenntnis bei Thomas von Aquin.* Innsbruck: F. Rauch, 1939. English edition translated by William Dych. *The Spirit in the World.* Second edition. New York: Herder & Herder, 1957; 1968.

——. *Grundkurs des Glaubens: Einführung in den Begriff des Christentums.* Breisgau: Herder, 1976. English edition translated by William V. Dych. *Foundations of Christian Faith: An Introduction into the Idea of Christianity.* New York: Crossroad, 1978; 2000.

——. *Karl Rahner in Dialogue: Conversations and Interviews, 1965–1982.* Edited by Paul Imhof and Hubert Biallowons. Translated by John J. O'Neill. New York: Crossroad, 1986.

——. *Schriften zur Theologie.* 16 vols. Einsiedeln: Benziger & Co., 1954–1972. English edition translated by Boniface Kruger, et al. *Theological Investigations.* 23 vols. Baltimore, Md.: Helicon Press, 1961–1979.

Raj, Anthony Savari. *A New Hermeneutic of Reality: Raimon Panikkar's Cosmotheandric Vision.* New York: Peter Lang, 1998.

Ramelli, Ilaria L. E. *The Christian Doctrine of Apokatastasis: A Critical Assessment from the New Testament to Eriugena.* Leiden/Boston: Brill, 2013.

——— and David Konstan. *Terms for Eternity: Aiônios and Aïdios in Classical and Christian Texts.* Piscataway, N.J.: Gorgias Press, 2007; 2013.

Ramsey, Arthur M. *F. D. Maurice and the Conflicts of Modern Theology.* Cambridge: Cambridge University Press, 1951.

Reitzenstein, Richard. *Poimandres: Studien zur griechisch-ägyptischen und frühchristlichen Literatur.* Leipzig: Teubner, 1904.

Relly, James. *Union: Or a Treatise of Consanguinity and Affinity Between Christ and his Church.* London: n.p., 1759.

Reusch, Franz Heinrich, ed. *Die Indices liborum prohibitorum des sechzehnten Jahrhunderts.* Tübingen: Litterarischer Verein in Stuttgart, 1886.

Richardson Alan, and John Stephen Bowden, eds. *The Westminster Dictionary of Christian Theology.* Philadelphia: Westminster Press, 1983.

Ridderbos, Herman. *The Gospel According to John: A Theological Commentary.* Grand Rapids, Mich.: Eerdmans, 1997.

Ritschl, Albrecht. *Die christliche Lehre von der Rechtfertigung und Versöhnung.* 3 vols. Bonn: A. Markus, 1870–74. English edition translated by H.R. Mackintosh and A.B. Macaulay. *The Christian Doctrine of Justification and Reconciliation, vol. 3, The Positive Development of the Doctrine.* Edinburgh: T. & T. Clark, 1902.

Robinson, J. Armitage. *Texts and Studies: Contributions to Biblical and Patristic Literature.* vol. 1. Cambridge: Cambridge University Press, 1891.

Robinson, James M., ed. *The Nag Hammadi Library in English.* Third revised edition. San Francisco: HarperSanFrancisco, 1978; 1988.

Robinson, John A. T. *In The End God.* New York: Harper and Row, 1968.

——. *Truth is Two-Eyed.* Philadelphia: Westminster, 1979.

Röper, Anita. *De anonieme Christen.* Hilversum: Brand, 1964. English edition translated by Joseph Donceel. *The Anonymous Christian.* New York: Sheed & Ward, 1966.

Rose, Kenneth. *Knowing the Real: John Hick on the Cognitivity of Religions and Religious Pluralism.* Toronto Studies in Religion. Vol. 20. New York: Peter Lang, 1997.

Rowell, Geoffrey. *Hell and the Victorians.* Oxford: Clarendon Press, 1973.

Rudolph, Erwin Paul. *William Law.* Boston: Twayne Pub., 1980.

Ruokanen, Miikka. *The Catholic Doctrine of Non-Christian Religions According to the Second Vatican Council.* Leiden: Brill, 1992.

Rupp, Gordon. *Patterns of Reformation.* Philadelphia: Fortress, 1969.

Rust, George. *A Letter Concerning Origen and the Chief of His Opinions.* 1661. Reprint, New York: Facsimile Text Society / Columbia University Press, 1933.

Ruysbroeck, John von. *The Adornment of Christian Marriage; The Sparkling Stone; The Book of Supreme Truth*. Edited by Evelyn Underhill. Translated by C.A. Wynschenk. Grand Rapids, Mich.: Christian Classic Ethereal Library, 2002.

Salisbury, Joyce E. *Perpetua's Passion: The Death and Memory of a Young Roman Woman*. New York: Routledge, 1997.

Sanders, E. P. *Paul and Palestinian Judaism: A Comparison of Patterns of Religion*. Philadelphia, Fortress, 1977.

Sanders, John. *No Other Name: An Investigation into the Destiny of the Unevangelized*. Grand Rapids, Mich.: Eerdmans, 1992.

Saucy, Mark. *The Kingdom of God in the Teaching of Jesus in 20th Century Theology*. Dallas, Tex.: Word, 1997.

Schaff, Philip, ed. *Nicene and Post-Nicene Fathers*. First Series. 1886. 14 vols. Reprint, Peabody, Mass.: Hendrickson, 1994.

_____ and Henry Wace, eds. *Nicene and Post-Nicene Fathers*. Second Series. 1890. 14 vols. Reprint, Peabody, Mass.: Hendrickson, 1994.

Schleiermacher, Friedrich D.E. *Der christliche Glaube*. Berlin: G. Reimer, 1821–22. English edition edited by H.R. Mackintosh and J. S. Stewart. *The Christian Faith*. Translation of the Second German Edition. Edinburgh: T. & T. Clark, 1928; 1989.

Schneemelcher, Wilhelm, ed. *New Testament Apocrypha*, 2 vols. Philadelphia: Westminster, 1964.

Schneider, Ulrich. *Theologie als christliche Philosophie: zur Bedeutung der biblischen Botschaft im Denken des Clemens von Alexandria*. Berlin: W. de Gruyter, 1999.

Scholer: David M. *Nag Hammadi Bibliography: 1948–1969*. Leiden: Brill, 1971.

_____. *Nag Hammadi Bibliography: 1970–1994*. Leiden: Brill, 1997.

Schweitzer, Albert. *Von Reimarus zu Wrede: eine Geschichte der Leben-Jesu-Forschung*. Tübingen: J.C.B. Mohr [Paul Siebeck], 1906. English edition translated by W. Montgomery. With a new introduction by James M. Robinson. *The Quest of the Historical Jesus: A Critical Study of Its Progress from Reimarus to Wrede*. New York: Macmillan, 1968.

Shea, Victor and William Whitla, eds. *Essays and Reviews: The 1860 Text and its Reading*. Charlottesville, Va.: University Press of Virginia, 2000.

Shewring, Walter. *The Passion of SS. Perpetua and Felicity, MM: A New Edition and Translation of the Latin Text, Together with the Sermons of St. Augustine upon These Saints, Now First Translated into English*. London: Sheed & Ward, 1931.

Simpson, John, ed. *The Oxford English Dictionary Online*. Oxford: Oxford University Press, 2004. http://www.oed.com.

Smart, Ninian and Steven Konstantine. *Christian Systematic Theology in a World Context*. Minneapolis, Minn.: Fortress, 1991.

Smith, John Clark. *The Ancient Wisdom of Origen*. Cranbury, N.J.: Associated University Presses, 1992.

Smith, Wilfred Cantwell. *The Meaning and End of Religion*. Minneapolis, Minn.: Fortress, 1961. Reprint, New York: Harper and Row, 1991.

Sophocles, Evangelinus A. *Greek Lexicon of the Roman and Byzantine Periods (From B.C. 146 to A.D. 1100), vol. I*. 1870. Reprint, New York: F. Unger, 1957.

Sproul, R.C. *Reason to Believe*. Grand Rapids, Mich.: Zondervan, 1978.

Stählin, Otto, Ludwig Früchtel, and Ursula Treu, eds. *Clemens Alexandrinus, vol. 2, Stromata Buch I–VI*. Fourth edition. Die griechischen Schriftsteller der ersten drei Jahrhunderte. Vol. 52, pt. 15. Berlin: Akademie-Verlag, 1985.

_____. *Clemens Alexandrinus, vol. 3, Stromata Buch VII und VIII, Excerpta ex Theodoto, Eclogae propheticae, Quis dives salvetur, Fragmente*. Die griechischen Schriftsteller der ersten drei Jahrhunderte. Vol. 17, pt. 2. Leipzig: J.C. Hinrichs, 1909.

Stauffer, Ethelbert. *Die Theologie des Neuen Testaments.* Stuttgart: W. Kohlhammer, 1948. English edition translated by John Marsh. *New Testament Theology.* London: S.C.M. Press, 1955.

Stetson, Brad. *Pluralism and Particularity in Religious Belief.* Westport, Conn.: Praeger Publishers, 1994.

Stockton Robert H. and Jonah Winters. *A Resource Guide for the Study of the Bahá'í Faith.* Wilmette, Ill.: Research Office, Bahá'í National Center, 1997.

Stoeffler, F. Ernest. *Mysticism in the German Devotional Literature of Colonial Pennsylvania.* Allentown, Pa.: Pennsylvania Folklore Society, 1950.

Stout, Harry S., Nathan O. Hatch, and Kyle P. Farley, eds. *The Works of Jonathan Edwards, Volume 22: Sermons and Discourses, 1739–1742.* New Haven, Conn.: Yale University Press, 2003.

Strange, Daniel. *The Possibility of Salvation Among the Unevangelized: An analysis of Inclusivism in Recent Evangelical Theology.* Carlisle, U.K.: Paternoster, 2001.

Sullivan, Francis A. *Salvation Outside the Church: Tracing the History of the Catholic Response.* New York: Paulist, 1992.

Supplementum Epigraphicum Graecum. Amsterdam: J.C. Gieben, 1923.

Surin, Kenneth. *Theology and the Problem of Hell.* London: Blackwell, 1986.

Suso, Henry and Walter Hilton. *A Little Book of Eternal Wisdom to Which is Added the Parable of the Pilgrim by Walter Hilton.* London: Burns, Oates, & Washbourne, 1910.

Swindler, Leonard, ed. *Küng in Conflict.* Garden City, N.Y.: Doubleday, 1981.

Talbot, Thomas. *The Inescapable Love of God.* U.S.A.: Universal Publishers / uPUBLISH.com, 1999.

Terry, Milton S. *The Sibylline Oracles Translated from the Greek into English Blank Verse.* New York: Hunt & Eaton, 1890.

Thiselton, Anthony C. *The First Epistle to the Corinthians: A Commentary on the Greek Text, The New International Greek Testament Commentary.* Grand Rapids, Mich.: Eerdmans, 2000.

_____. *Interpreting God and the Postmodern Self: On Meaning, Manipulation, and Promise.* Grand Rapids, Mich.: Eerdmans, 1995.

Toynbee, Arnold. *An Historian's Approach to Religion.* New York: Oxford University Press, 1956.

Toynbee, Joycelyn C. M. and John Ward Perkins. *Death and Burial in the Roman World.* Baltimore, Md.: Johns Hopkins University Press, 1996.

Trigg, Joseph W. *Origen: The Bible and Philosophy in the Third-Century Church.* Atlanta, Ga.: John Knox, 1983.

Troeltsch, Ernst. *Die Absolutheit des Christentums und die religionsgeschichte. Vortrag gehalten auf der Christlichen welt zu Mühlacker am 3. oktober 1901. Erweitert und mit einem vorwort versehen.* Third edition. Tübingen: J.C.B. Mohr [Paul Siebeck], 1902; 1929. English edition translated by David Reid. *The Absoluteness of Christianity and the History of Religions.* Richmond, Va.: John Knox, 1971.

Trumbower, Jeffrey A. *Rescue for the Dead: The Posthumous Salvation of Non-Christians in Early Christianity.* Oxford: Oxford University Press, 2001.

The United States Catholic Conference. *The Küng Dialogue.* Washington, D.C.: United States Catholic Conference, 1980.

Vidler, Alec. *F. D. Maurice and Company: Nineteenth Century Studies.* London: S.C.M. Press, 1966.

Vogels, Heinz-Juergen. *Christi Abstieg ins Totenreich und das Laeuterungsgericht an den Toten.* Frieburg: Herder, 1976.

Vorgrimler, Herbert. *Understanding Karl Rahner.* London: SCM Press, 1986.

Wakefield, James L. *Jürgen Moltmann: A Research Bibliography.* Lanham, Md.: Scarecrow Press, 2002.

Wakefield, Walter L. and Austin P. Evans. *Heresies of the High Middle Ages: Selected Sources Translated and Annotated.* New York: Columbia University Press, 1969.

Walker, A. Keith. *William Law: His Life and His Thought.* London: S.P.C.K., 1973.

Walker, D. P. *The Decline of Hell: Seventeenth-Century Discussions of Eternal Torment.* Chicago: University of Chicago Press, 1964.

Ward, Keith. *Ethics and Christianity.* London: George Allen & Unwin, 1970.

_____. *God, Faith & The New Millennium: Christian Belief in an Age of Science.* Oxford: Oneworld Publications, 1998.

_____. *Morality, Autonomy, and God.* London: One World Publications, 2013.

_____. *Religion and Creation.* Oxford: Clarendon Press, 1996.

_____. *Religion and Human Nature.* Oxford: Clarendon Press, 1998.

_____. *A Vision to Pursue: Beyond the Crisis in Christianity.* London: SCM Press, 1991.

Watson, David Lowes. *God Does Not Foreclose: The Universal Promise of Salvation.* Nashville, Tenn.: Abingdon, 1990.

Weatherhead, Leslie D. *The Christian Agnostic.* London: Hodder and Stoughton, 1965.

Wenham, David. *Paul: Follower of Jesus or Founder of Christianity?* Grand Rapids, Mich.: Eerdmans, 1995.

White, Jeremiah. *The Restoration of All Things, or, A Vindication of the Goodness and Grace of God to be Manifested at Last in the Recovery of His Whole Creation out of Their Fall.* London: N. Cliff & D. Jackson, 1712.

Whittemore, Thomas. *The History of Modern Universalism from the Era of The Reformation to the Present Time.* Boston: Power Press, 1830.

Williams, George H. *The Radical Reformation.* Third edition. Kirksville, Mo.: Sixteenth Century Journal Publishers, Inc., 1962; 1992.

Williams, Michael Allen. *Rethinking "Gnosticism": An Argument for Dismantling a Dubious Category.* Princeton, N.J.: Princeton University Press, 1996.

Wilson, A. N. *Paul: The Mind of the Apostle.* New York: W.W. Norton & Co., 1997.

Wilson, Robert Mcl. *Gnosis and the New Testament.* Oxford: Blackwell, 1968.

Wollaston, William. *Religion of Nature Delineated.* Sixth edition. London: John and Paul Knapton, 1722; 1738.

Wrede, William. *Das Messiasgeheimnis in den Evangelien: Zugleich ein Beitrag zum Verständnis des Markusevangeliums.* Göttingen: Vandenhoeck & Ruprecht, 1901. English edition translated by J. C. G. Greig. *The Messianic Secret.* Cambridge: J. Clark, 1971.

Wright, N. T. *The Climax of the Covenant: Christ and the Law in Pauline Theology.* Minneapolis: Fortress, 1991.

_____. *Jesus and the Victory of God.* Minneapolis: Fortress, 1996.

_____. *The New Testament and the People of God.* Minneapolis: Fortress, 1992.

_____. *The Resurrection of the Son of God.* Minneapolis: Fortress, 2003.

_____. *What Saint Paul Really Said: Was Paul of Tarsus the Real Founder of Christianity?* Grand Rapids, Mich.: Eerdmans, 1997.

Yamauchi, Edwin M. *Pre-Christian Gnosticism: A Survey of Proposed Evidences.* Second edition. Eugene, Or.: Wipf and Stock, 1983.

Zagorin, Perez. *How the Idea of Religious Toleration Came to the West.* Princeton, N.J.: Princeton University Press, 2003.

Zender, Martin. *How to Quit Church without Quitting God: 7 Good Reasons to Escape the Box.* Canton, Ohio: Starke & Hartmann, 2002.

_____. *Martin Zender Goes to Hell.* Canton, Ohio: Starke & Hartmann, 2004.

2. Articles

Adams, Marilyn McCord. "Divine Justice, Divine Love, and the Life to Come." *Crux* 13 (1996–1997): 12–28.

_____. "Hell and the God of Justice." *Religious Studies* 11 (December 1975): 433–47.

_____. "The Problem of Hell: A Problem of Evil for Christians." In Eleonore Stump ed., *A Reasoned Faith*. Ithaca, N.Y.: Cornell University Press, 1993, 301–327.

_____. "Universal Salvation: A Reply to Mr. Bettis." *Religious Studies* 7 (September 1971): 245–249.

Aland, Barbara. "Gnosis und Christentum." In Bentley Layton, ed., *The Rediscovery of Gnosticism, vol. 1, The School of Valentius*. Leiden: Brill, 1980, 319–50.

Ansell, Nicholas. "The Annihilation of Hell and the Perfection of Freedom: Universal Salvation and the Theology of Jürgen Moltmann." In Gregory MacDonald, ed., *"All Shall Be Well: Explorations in Universal Salvation and Christian Theology from Origen to Moltmann*. Eugene, Ore.: Cascade Books, 2011, 417–39.

Balthasar, Hans Urs von. "A Résumé of My Thought." *Communio* 15 (Winter 1988): 468–473.

Barth, Karl. "Evangelical Theology in the Nineteenth Century." In Karl Barth, *The Humanity of God*. Translated by Thomas Weiser. Atlanta, Ga.: John Knox, 1960; 1978, 11–33.

Bauckham, Richard J. "Descent to the Underworld." In David Noel Freeman, et al., eds., *The Anchor Bible Dictionary*. 6 vols. New York: Doubleday, 1992, 2:145–59.

_____. "Jews and Jewish Christians in the Land of Israel at the Time of the Bar Kochba War, with Special Reference to the *Apocalypse of Peter*." In Graham N. Stanton and G.G. Stroumsa, eds., *Tolerance and Intolerance in Early Judaism and Christianity*. Cambridge: Cambridge University Press, 1998, 228–38.

_____. "Jürgen Moltmann." In David F. Ford and Rachel Muers, eds., *The Modern Theologians: An Introduction to Christian Theology Since 1918*. Third edition. Oxford: Blackwell, 2005, 147–62.

_____. "Universalism: A Historical Survey." *Themelios* 4/2 (January 1979): 48–53.

Benedict XVI. "Address of His Holiness Benedict XVI to the Roman Curia Offering Them His Christmas Greetings, Thursday, 22 December 2005." The Vatican. http://www.vatican.va/holy_father/benedict_xvi/speeches/2005/december/ documents/hf_ben_xvi_spe_20051222_roman-curia_en.html. Accessed on July 2, 2014.

_____. "Message of His Holiness Benedict XVI for The Centenary of the Birth of Fr. Hans Urs Von Balthasar (October, 6, 2005)." The Vatican. http://www.vatican/ va/holy_father/benedict_xvi/messages/pont-messages/2005/documents/ hf_ben-xvi_mes_20051006_von-balthasar_en.html. Accessed on June 1, 2014.

Beougher, Timothy K. "Are All Doomed to be Saved? The Rise of Modern Universalism." *The Southern Baptist Journal of Theology* 2/2 (Summer 1998): 6–24.

Bettis, Joseph D. "A Critique of the Doctrine of Universal Salvation." *Religious Studies* 6 (December 1970): 329–344.

_____. "Is Karl Barth a Universalist?" *Scottish Journal of Theology* 20 (December 1967): 423–36.

Borgen, Peder. "Observations on the Targumic Character of the Prologue of John." *New Testament Studies* 16 (1970): 288–95.

Boring, M.E. "The Language of Universal Salvation in Paul." *Journal of Biblical Literature* 105 (1986): 269–292.

Bultmann, Rudolf. "Die Bedeutung der neuerschlossenen mandäischen und manichäischen Quellen für das Verständnis des Johannesevangeliums," *Zeitschrift für die neutestamentliche Wissenschaft* 24 (1925): 100–146.

Cameron, Nigel M. de S. "Universalism and the Logic of Revelation." *Evangelical Review of Theology* 11 (October 1987): 321–35.

Colón-Emeric, Edgardo Antonio. "Symphonic Truth: Von Balthasar and Christian Humanism." *The Christian Century* 122/11 (May 31, 2005): 30–34.

Colwell, John E. "The Contemporaneity of the Divine Decision: Reflections on Barth's Denial of 'Universalism.'" In Nigel M. de S. Cameron, ed., *Universalism and the Doctrine of Hell*. Carlisle, U.K.: Paternoster, 1992, 139–160.

_____. "Proclamation As Event: Barth's Supposed 'Universalism' in the Context of His View of Mission." In Paul Beasley-Murray, ed., *Mission to the World: Essays to Celebrate the 50th Anniversary of the Ordination of George Raymond Beasley-Murray to the Christian Ministry*. Didcot, U.K.: Baptist Historical Society, 1991, 42–46.

Craig, William Lane. "No Other Name: A Middle Knowledge Perspective on the Exclusivity of Salvation Through Christ." *Faith and Philosophy* 6/2 (April 1989): 172–88.

Crockett, William V. "Will God Save Everyone in the End?" In William V. Crockett and James G. Sigountos, eds., *Through No Fault of Their Own? The Fate of Those Who Have Never Heard*. Grand Rapids, Mich.: Baker, 1991, 159–166.

_____. "Wrath that Endures Forever." *Journal of the Evangelical Theological Society* 34 (1991): 195–202.

Crouzel, Henri. "Fonte prenicene della dottrina di Ambrogio sulla risurrezione dei morti." *La Scuola Cattolica* 102/4 (1974): 374–88.

D'Costa, Gavin. "'Extra ecclesiam nulla salus' revisited." In Ian Hamnett, ed., *Religious Pluralism and Unbelief: Studies Critical and Comparative*. London: Routledge, 1990, 130–47.

DiNoia, Joseph A. "Christian Universalism: The Nonexclusive Particularity of Salvation in Christ." In Carl E. Braaten and Robert W. Jensen, eds., *Either/or: The Gospel or Neopaganism*. Grand Rapids, Mich.: Eerdmans, 1995, 37–48.

_____. "Varieties of Religious Aims: Beyond Exclusivism, Inclusivism, and Pluralism." In Bruce D. Marshall, ed., *Theology and Dialogue: Essays in Conversation with George Lindbeck*. Notre Dame, Ind.: University of Notre Dame Press, 1990, 249–74.

Dockrill, David W. "The Heritage of Patristic Platonism in Seventeenth-Century English Philosophical Theology." In Graham A. J. Rogers, Jean M. Vienne, and Yves C. Zarka, eds., *The Cambridge Platonists in Philosophical Context: Politics, Metaphysics and Religion*. Dordrecht, Netherlands: Kluwer Academic Pub., 1997, 55–77.

Duthie, C.S. "Ultimate Triumph." *Scottish Journal of Theology* 14/2 (June 1961): 156–171.

Emmet, C. W. "The Bible and Hell." In Burnett H. Streeter, A. Clutton-Brock, C. W. Emmet, and J. A. Hadfield, eds., *Immortality: An Essay in Discovery Co-ordinating Scientific, Psychical, and Biblical Research*. London: Macmillan, 1917, 167–217.

Fairhurst, Alan M. "Death and Destiny." *Churchman* 95/4 (1981): 313–325.

Falkenroth, U. ἐκδίκησις. In Colin Brown, ed., *The New International Dictionary of New Testament Theology*. 4 vols. Grand Rapids, Mich.: Zondervan, 1975–1986, 3:92–93.

Fiering, Norman. "Irresistible Compassion: An Aspect of Eighteenth-Century Sympathy and Humanitarianism." *Journal of the History of Ideas*, 37/2 (April–June, 1976): 195–218.

Geismar, Eduard. "Das ethische Stadium bei Søren Kierkegaard," *Zeitschrift für systematische Theologie* 1 (1923): 227–300.

George, Timothy, Carl F.H. Henry, D.A. Carson, Scott Hafemann, and C. Ben Mitchell. "The *SBJT* Forum: Responses to the Inclusivist Challenge." *The Southern Baptist Journal of Theology* 2/2 (Summer 1998): 50–60.

Green, J.B. "The Gospel of Peter: Source for a Pre-Canonical Passion Narrative?" *Zeitschrift für die neutestamentliche Wissenschaft* (1987): 293–301.

Hall, Gerhard. "Multi-Faith Dialogue in Conversation with Raimon Panikkar." Australian Association for the Study of Religions. Annual Conference, 4th–6th July 2003. Multi-Faith Centre, Griffith University. Nathan Campus, Nathan, Qld, Australia. http://dlibrary.acu.edu.au/staffhome/gehall/Hall_Panikkar.htm.

Hamnett, Ian. "Religious Pluralism." In Ian Hamnett, ed., *Religious Pluralism & Unbelief: Studies Critical and Comparative.* London: Routledge, 1990, 3–12.

Hertzberg, Hendrik. "'Father, the Atheists?' Even the Atheists." *The New Yorker*, June 2, 2013. 2014. http://www.newyorker.com/news/hendrik-hertzberg/father-the-atheists-even-the-atheists. Accessed on December 10, 2014.

Hick, John. "Is there only One Way to God?" *Theology* 85/703 (January 1982): 4–7.

_____. "The Non-Absoluteness of Christianity." In John Hick and Paul F. Knitter, eds., *The Myth of Christian Uniqueness: Towards a Pluralistic Theology of Religions.* Maryknoll, N.Y.: Orbis, 1987, 16–36.

_____, "A Pluralist View." In Dennis L. Okholm and Timothy R. Phillips, eds., *Four Views on Salvation in a Pluralistic World.* Grand Rapids, Mich.: Zondervan, 1995, 27–59.

_____. "Response to R. Douglas Geivett and W. Gary Phillips." In Dennis L. Okholm and Timothy R. Phillips, eds., *Four Views on Salvation in a Pluralistic World.* Grand Rapids, Mich.: Zondervan, 1995, 246–50.

Hilborn, David and Don Horrocks. "Universalistic Trends in the Evangelical tradition: An Historical Perspective." In Robin Parry and Chris Partridge, eds., *Universal Salvation? The Current Debate.* Carlisle, U.K.: Paternoster, 2003, 219–244.

Hoehler, Harry H. "Syncretistic Universalism: A Critique." *American Journal of Theology and Philosophy* 6/2–3 (May–September 1985): 159–171.

The Huffington Post. "Pope Francis Say Atheists Who Do Good Are Redeemed, Not Just Catholics," May 23, 2013. http://www.huffingtonpost.com/2013/05/22/pope-francis-good-theists_n_3320757.html?view=print&comm_ref=false. Accessed on November 24, 2014.

James, M.R. "New Text of the Apocalypse." *Journal of Theological Studies* 12 (1910): 36–54.

Jefford, Clayton N. "Pilate, Acts of." In David Noel Freeman, et al., eds., *The Anchor Bible Dictionary.* 6 vols. New York: Doubleday, 1992, 5:371–72.

Jensen, Paul T. "Intolerable but Moral? Thinking About Hell." *Faith & Philosophy* 10/2 (April 1993): 235–241.

John Paul II, *"Redemptoris missio."* The Vatican. http://www.vatican.va/edocs/ENG0219/__P3.HTM.

Kant, Immanuel. "What is Enlightenment?" In Immanuel Kant, *Foundations of Metaphysics and What is Enlightenment?* Trans. Lewis White Beck. Indianapolis, Ind.: Bobbs-Merrill, 1959, 3–10.

Kantzer, Kenneth S. "Troublesome Questions." *Christianity Today* 31/5 (March 20, 1987): 45.

Knitter, Paul F. "My Dialogical Odyssey." In Paul F. Knitter, *One Earth Many Religions: Multifaith Dialogue and Global Responsibility.* Maryknoll, N.Y.: Orbis, 1995, 1–20.

_____. "Roman Catholic Approaches to other Religions: Developments and Tensions." *International Bulletin of Missionary Research* 8 (April 1984): 50–54.

_____. "Toward a Liberation Theology of Religions." In John Hick and Paul F. Knitter, eds., *The Myth of Christian Uniqueness: Towards a Pluralistic Theology of Religions.* Maryknoll, N.Y.: Orbis, 1987, 178–200.

_____. "The Vocation of an Interreligious Theologian: My Retrospective on Forty Years in Dialogue." *Horizons* 31/1 (Spring 2004): 135–49.

Küng, Hans. "Is There One True Religion? An Essay in Establishing Ecumenical Criteria." In John Hick and Brian Hebblethwaite, eds., *Christianity and Other Religions: Selected Readings*. Revised edition. Oxford: Oneworld Publications, 2001, 118–145.

_____. "Towards an Ecumenical Theology of Religions: Some Theses for Clarification." In Hans Küng and Jürgen Moltman, eds., *Concilium: Christianity Among World Religions*. Edinburgh: T. & T. Clark: 1986, 119–125.

_____. "What is the True Religion? Toward an Ecumenical Criteriology." *Journal of Theology for Southern Africa* 56 (September 1986): 4–23.

Lacy, Larry. "Talbott on Paul as a Universalist." *Christian Scholar's Review* 21/4 (1992): 395–407.

Link, Hans-Georg. ἀποκάταστασις. In Colin Brown, ed., *The New International Dictionary of New Testament Theology*. Grand Rapids, Mich.: Zondervan, 1978–1986, 146–48.

Longenecker, Dwight. "Did Pope Francis Preach Salvation by Works??" *Patheos.com* (May 23, 2013). http://www.patheos.com/blogs/. Accessed on December 10, 2014. standingonmyhead/2013/05/did-pope-francis-preach-salvation-by-works.html.

Ludlow, Morwenna. "Universalism in the History of Christianity." In Robin Parry and Chris Partridge, eds., *Universal Salvation? The Current Debate*. Carlisle, U.K.: Paternoster, 2003, 191–218.

Luther, Martin. "Letter to Hans von Rechenberg." In Helmut T. Lehmann and Gustav K. Wiencke, eds., *Luther's Works, vol. 43, Devotional Writings II*. Philadelphia: Fortress, 1968, 51–55.

Marshall, I. Howard. "Does the New Testament Teach Universal Salvation?" In Trevor A. Hart and Daniel P. Thimell, eds., *Christ in our Place: The Humanity of God in Christ for the Reconciliation of the World: Essays Presented to Professor James Torrance*. Exeter, U.K.: Paternoster; Allison Park, Pa.: Pickwick Publications, 1989, 313–329.

_____. "The New Testament does *not* Teach Universal Salvation." In Robin Parry and Chris Partridge, eds., *Universal Salvation? The Current Debate*. Carlisle, U.K.: Paternoster, 2003, 55–76.

Maurice, F. D. "On Eternal Life and Eternal Death." In F. D. Maurice, *Theological Essays*. New Edition with Introduction by Edward F. Carpenter. London: James Clark, 1957, 302–32.

McCant, J. W. "The Gospel of Peter: Docetism Reconsidered." *New Testament Studies* 40 (1994): 572–95.

Medawar, Peter B. "The Phenomenon of Man." In Peter B. Medawar, *The Strange Case of the Spotted Mice and Other Classic Essays on Science*. Oxford: Oxford University Press, 1996, 1–11.

Menninger, David C. "Marx in the Social Thought of Jacques Ellul." In Clifford G. Christians and Jay M. Van Hook, eds., *Jacques Ellul: Interpretive Essays*. Chicago: University of Illinois Press, 1981, 17–31.

Milikowsky, Chaim. "Which Gehenna? Retribution and Eschatology in the Synoptic Gospels and in Early Jewish Texts." *New Testament Studies* 34/2 (1988): 238–49.

Mirecki, Paul Allan. "Basilides," In David Noel Freeman, et al., eds., *The Anchor Bible Dictionary*. 6 vols. New York: Doubleday, 1992, 1:624–25.

Moltmann, Jürgen. "Is there Life after Death?" In John Polkinghorne and Michael Welker, eds., *The End of the World and the Ends of God: Science and Theology on Eschatology*. Harrisburg, Pa.: Trinity Press Int., 2000, 238–55.

_____. "The Logic of Hell." In Richard Bauckham ed., *God Will Be All in All: The Eschatology of Jürgen Moltmann*. Edinburgh: T. & T. Clark, 1999, 43–47.

_____. "The World in God or God in the World." In Richard J. Bauckham, ed., *God Will Be All In All: The Eschatology of Jürgen Moltmann*. Edinburgh: T. & T. Clark, 1999, 35–41.

Moo, Douglas J. "Paul on Hell." In Christopher W. Morgan and Robert A. Peterson, eds., *Hell Under Fire: Modern Scholarship Reinvents Eternal Punishment*. Grand Rapids, Mich.: Zondervan, 2004, 91–109.

Morris, Kenneth R. "Puritan Roots of American Universalism." *Scottish Journal of Theology* 44/4 (1991): 457–487.

Müller, Gotthold. "Die Idee einer Apokatastasis ton panton in der europaïschen Theologie von Schleiermacher bis Barth." *Zeitschrift für Religions und Geistesgeschichte* 16/1 (1964): 1–22.

Murray, Michael J. "Three Versions of Universalism." *Faith and Philosophy* 16/1 (January 1999): 56–68.

The National Archives. "The Declaration of Independence: A Transcription." *National Archives*. http://www.archives.gov/national-archives-experience/charters/declaration_transcript.html. Accessed on October 31, 2014.

O'Connor, James T. "Von Balthasar and Salvation." *Homiletic and Pastoral Review* (July 1989): 10–21.

Oepke, Albrecht. ἀποκάταστασις. In Gerhard Kittel, ed., *Theological Dictionary of the New Testament*. 10 vols. Translated and edited by Gerhard Friedrich and Geoffrey W. Bromiley. Grand Rapids, Mich.: Eerdmans, 1964–1976, 1:387–393.

Paine, Thomas. "The Age of Reason." In Thomas Paine, *The Complete Writings of Thomas Paine*, 2 vols., ed. Philip S. Foner. New York: Citadel Press, 1947, 1:523–668.

Panikkar, Raimundo. "A Christophany for Our Times." *Theology Digest* 39/1 (Spring 1992): 3–21.

_____. "Ecology from an Eastern Philosophical Perspective." *Monchanin* 50 (June–December 1975): 23–28.

_____. "Philosophy as Life-Style." In A. Mercier and M. Svilar, eds., *Philosophers On Their Own Work, vol. IV*. Berne: Herbert Lang, 1978, 193–228.

Powys, David J. "The Nineteenth and Twentieth Century Debates About Hell and Universalism." In Nigel M. de S. Cameron, ed., *Universalism and the Doctrine of Hell*. Carlisle, U.K.: Paternoster, 1992, 93–138.

Rahner, Karl. "Anonymous and Explicit Faith." In Karl Rahner, *Theological Investigations*. 23 vols. Baltimore, Md.: Helicon Press, 1961–1979, 16:52–59.

_____. "Anonymous Christianity and the Missionary Task of the Church." In Karl Rahner, *Theological Investigations*. 23 vols. Baltimore, Md.: Helicon Press, 1961–1979, 12:390–98.

_____. "Anonymous Christians." In Karl Rahner, *Theological Investigations*. 23 vols. Baltimore, Md.: Helicon Press, 1961–1979, 6:390–398.

_____. "Christian Dying." In Karl Rahner, *Theological Investigations*. 23 vols. Baltimore, Md.: Helicon Press, 1961–1979, 8:236, 241.

_____. "Church, Churches, and Religions." In Karl Rahner, *Theological Investigations*. 23 vols. Baltimore, Md.: Helicon Press, 1961–1979, 10:33–34.

_____. "Hell." In Karl Rahner, et al., eds. *Sacramentum Mundi: An Encyclopedia of Theology*. 6 vols. English translation by W. J. O'Hara, et al. New York: Herder and Herder, 1968–1970, 3:7–9.

_____. "The Hermeneutics of Eschatological Assertions." In Karl Rahner, *Theological Investigations*. 23 vols. Baltimore, Md.: Helicon Press, 1961–1979, 4:338–39.

_____. "Observations on the Problem of Anonymous Christians." In Karl Rahner, *Theological Investigations*. 23 vols. Baltimore, Md.: Helicon Press, 1961–1979, 14:280–94.

_____. "The One Christ and the Universality of Salvation." In Karl Rahner, *Theological Investigations*. 23 vols. Baltimore, Md.: Helicon Press, 1961–1979, 16:199–224.

_____. "Purgatory." In Karl Rahner, *Theological Investigations*. 23 vols. Baltimore, Md.: Helicon Press, 1961–1979, 9:184–85.

Ratzinger, Joseph Cardinal. "Declaration '*Dominus Iesus*' On the Unicity and Salvific Universality of Jesus Christ and the Church." Aug. 6, 2000. *The Congregation for the Doctrine of the Faith*. http://www.vatican.va/roman_curia/congregations/cfaith/documents/rc_con_cfaith_doc_20000806_dominus-iesus_en.html.

_____. "Relativism: The Central Problem for Faith Today." *Origins* 26/20 (October 1996): 309–16. This article may also be found online at: Eternal Word Television Network. http://www.ewtn.com/library/CURIA/RATZRELA.HTM.

Richard, Pierre. "Enfer." In A. Vacant and E. Mangenot, eds., *Dictionnaire de Théologie Catholique*. 15 vols. Paris: Letouzey et Ané, 1924, 5:82–83.

Robinson, James M. "Nag Hammadi: The First Fifty Years." In John D. Turner and Anne McGuire, eds., *The Nag Hammadi Library After Fifty Years: Proceedings of the 1995 Society of Biblical Literature Commemoration*. Leiden: Brill, 1997, 3–33.

Rosica, Thomas. "Explanatory Note on the Meaning of 'Salvation' in Francis' Daily Homily of May 22." *Zenit.org* (May 23, 2013). http://www.zenit.org/en/articles/explanatory-note-on-the-meaning-of-salvation-in-francis-daily-homily-of-may-22. Accessed on December 10, 2014.

Rosscup, James E. "Paul's Concept of Eternal Punishment." *The Master's Seminary Journal* 9/2 (Fall 1998): 169–192.

Rowell, Geoffrey. "The Origins and History of Universalist Societies in Britain 1750–1850." *Journal of Ecclesiastical History* 22/1 (January 1971): 35–56.

Rudolf, Kurt. "Gnosticism," In David Noel Freeman, et al., eds., *The Anchor Bible Dictionary*. 6 vols. New York: Doubleday, 1992, 2:1033–40.

Russell, Jeffrey B. "The Brethren of the Free Spirit." In Jefferey B. Russell, ed., *Religious Dissent in the Middle Ages*. New York: John Wiley & Sons, 1971, 86–91.

Sanneh, Kelefa. "The Hell-Raiser: A megachurch pastor's search for a more forgiving faith." *The New Yorker* (November 26, 2012): 56–60.

Schmidt-Leukel, Perry. "Exclusivism, Inclusivism, Pluralism: The Tripolar Typology Clarified and Reaffirmed." In Paul F. Knitter, ed., *The Myth of Religious Superiority: Multifaith Explorations of Religious Pluralism*. Maryknoll, N.Y.: Orbis, 2005, 13–27.

Scott, Jr. J. Julius. "Restoration of Israel." In Gerald F. Hawthorne, Ralph P. Martin, and Daniel G. Reid, eds., *Dictionary of Paul and His Letters*. Downers Grove, Ill.: InterVarsity Press, 796–805.

Seaburg, Alan. "Recent Scholarship in American Universalism: A Bibliographical Essay." *Church History* 41 (December 1972): 513–523.

Smith, Wilfred Cantwell. "An Attempt at Summation." In G. H. Stransky and T. F. Stransky, eds., *Christ's Lordship and Religious Pluralism*. Maryknoll, N.Y.: Orbis, 1981, 196–204.

Stegner, William R. "Diaspora." In Gerald F. Hawthorne, Ralph P. Martin, and Daniel G. Reid, eds., *Dictionary of Paul and His Letters*. Downers Grove, Ill.: InterVarsity Press, 211–13.

Talbott, Thomas B. "A Case for Christian Universalism." In Robin A. Parry and Christopher H. Partridge, eds., *Universal Salvation? The Current Debate*. Carlisle, U.K.: Paternoster, 2003, 3–52.

_____. "Craig on the Possibility of Eternal Damnation." *Religious Studies* 28 (1992): 495–510.

_____. "The Doctrine of Everlasting Punishment." *Faith and Philosophy* 7 (1990): 19–42.

_____. "Freedom, Damnation, and the Power to Sin with Impunity." *Religious Studies* 37 (2001): 417–434.

_____. "The Love of God and the Heresy of Exclusivism." *Christian Scholar's Review* XXVII/1 (1999): 99–112.

_____. "Misery and Freedom: A Reply to Walls." *Religious Studies* 40 (2005): 217–224. Available online at: http://www.willamette.edu/~ttalbott/Reply-Walls2.pdf. Accessed on July 10, 2014.

_____. "The New Testament and Universal Reconciliation." *Christian Scholar's Review* 21/4 (1992): 376–394.

_____. "Punishment, Forgiveness, and Divine Justice." *Religious Studies* 29 (1993): 151–168.

_____. "Three Pictures of God in Western Theology." *Faith and Philosophy* 12 (1995): 79–94.

_____. "Universal Reconciliation and the Inclusive Nature of Election." In Chad Owen Brand. *Perspectives on Election: Five Views.* Nashville: Broadman and Holman Publishers, 2006, 206–261.

_____. "Universalism." In Jerry L. Walls, ed., *The Oxford Handbook of Eschatology* New York; Oxford: Oxford University Press, 2007, 446–461.

Tauler, Johann. "Sermon for the Second Sunday in Lent—Matt. 15:21–28." In Susannah Winkworth, ed., *The History and Life of The Reverend Doctor John Tauler with Twenty-Five of His Sermons Translated from The German, with Additional Notices of Tauler's Life and Times.* London: Allenson & Co., 1905, 302–316.

Taylor, Kathryn. "Respect for other Religions: A Christian Antidote to Colonialist Discourse." *Modern Theology* 9 (1993): 1–18.

Tennyson, Alfred. "In Memoriam A.H.H." The Literature Network. http://www.online-literature.com/tennyson/718.

_____. "To the Rev. F. D. Maurice" (1854). The Literature Network. http://www.online-literature.com/tennyson/731.

Tetz, Martin. "Die Theologie des Markell von Ankyra III: Die pseudo-athanasianische Epistula ad Liberium, ein Markellisches Bekenntnis." *Zeitschrift für Kirchengeschichte* 83 (1972): 145–94.

Treitler, Wolfgang. "True Foundations of Authentic Theology." In David L. Schindler, ed., *Hans Urs von Balthasar: His Life and Work.* San Francisco: Ignatius, 1991, 169–82.

Trigg, Joseph W. "Origen." In David Noel Freeman, et al., eds., *The Anchor Bible Dictionary.* 6 vols. New York: Doubleday, 1992, 5:42–48.

Troeltsch, Ernst. "The Place of Christianity among the World Religions." In John Hick and Brian Hebblethwaite, eds., *Christianity and Other Religions.* Philadelphia: Fortress, 1980, 11–31.

Watson, Duane F. "Gehenna." In David Noel Freeman, et al., eds., *The Anchor Bible Dictionary.* 6 vols. New York: Doubleday, 1992, 2:926–928.

Weber, Katherine. "Rob Bell Tells How 'Love Wins' Led to Mars Hill Departure." *Christian Post* (12/3/12). http://www.christianpost.com/news/rob-bell-tells-how-love-wins-led-to-mars-hill-departure-85995/#oFZ3ZEYqYJehcLaq.99. Accessed on December 27, 2014.

Williams, D. J. "Judas Iscariot." In Joel B. Green, Scot McKnight, and I. Howard Marshall, eds., *Dictionary of Jesus and the Gospels.* Downer's Grove, Ill.: InterVarsity, 1992, 406–408.

Wilson, H.B. "Séances Historiques de Genève—the National Church." In Victor Shea and William Whitla, eds., *Essays and Reviews: The 1860 Text and its Reading.* Charlottesville, Va.: University Press of Virginia, 2000, 275–344.

Wilson, Robert McL. "Gnosis at Corinth." In Morna D. Hooker and S. G. Wilson, eds., *Paul and Paulinism: Essays in Honor of C.K. Barrett.* London: S.P.C.K., 1982, 102–114.

SCRIPTURE INDEX

GENERAL INDEX

ND - #0070 - 270225 - C0 - 229/152/17 - PB - 9781842278048 - Gloss Lamination